The Disclosure Ref

The Disclosure Referencer

Caroline Bradley
Barrister, 23 Essex Street Chambers

Alastair Munt
Barrister, KCH Garden Square Chambers

Bloomsbury Professional

Bloomsbury Professional Limited, Maxwelton House, 41–43 Boltro Road, Haywards Heath, West Sussex, RH16 1BJ

© Bloomsbury Professional Limited 2013
Bloomsbury Professional is an imprint of Bloomsbury Publishing Plc

A CIP Catalogue record for this book is available from the British Library.

ISBN   978 1 84766 943 8

Printed and bound by CPI Group (UK) Ltd, Croydon, CR0 4YY

Foreword

Issues involving disclosure arise in many criminal trials. They can be very difficult indeed. Given the extensive work that has been done in this area over recent years, a publication that brings together all the relevant material is to be welcomed. It will undoubtedly assist everyone involved in the process of criminal justice to navigate through the complex issues that arise; something which is essential to ensure a correct and just outcome in every case.

The correct approach to disclosure is crucial for a fair trial. However, the process must be managed intelligently if it is not to overwhelm the system. It is essential that everyone clearly understands the principles and applies them appropriately. As Lord Justice Gross stated in his 2011 Disclosure Review:

> 'Improvements in disclosure must be prosecution led or driven, in such a manner as to require the defence to engage – and to permit the defence to do so with confidence. The entire process must be robustly case managed by the judiciary. The tools are available; they need to be used.'

The available tools are of course the Criminal Procedure Rules (the application of which it is worth underlining is mandatory), the Code of Practice issued under Part II of the CPIA, the Attorney General's Guidelines (2005 and 2011) and the Judicial Protocol. They need both to be understood and used by practitioners. This book draws them together and underlines the important direction that they set down.

In short, full compliance with the duties of disclosure must be seen as fundamental for investigators, prosecution and defence lawyers and advocates. Each person engaged in the process has an individual responsibility. It will not always be easy. There is no 'quick fix'. Judges will provide the necessary leadership as is appropriate. The days of the 'ambush defence' are over. There should be no place for late or uninformative defence case statements.

I therefore welcome this comprehensive review of the relevant law and practice of disclosure. It has been prepared by two practitioners who, between them, have a wealth of experience and expertise. They have set out in a comprehensive and clear manner, both the broad principles and the details of the disclosure regime.

This will be an invaluable guide for all criminal practitioners in this difficult and challenging area.

Rt Hon Lord Justice Goldring QC
Senior Presiding Judge

Preface

The inspiration for the Disclosure Referencer dates back to 20 February 2006 and the judicial publication of a protocol for the disclosure of unused material in the crown court. The protocol was designed to establish firm principles for the management of disclosure, whether by the prosecution or the defence, in order to improve the efficient delivery of justice and thereby enhance public confidence in the criminal justice system. The introduction to the protocol states:

> 'Disclosure is one of the most important – as well as one of the most abused – of the procedures relating to criminal trials. There needs to be a sea-change in the approach of both judges and the parties to all aspects of the handling of the material which the prosecution do not intend to use in support of their case.'

The introduction goes on to highlight how, for too long, misunderstandings and misconceptions as to the nature of disclosure have proved 'extremely and unnecessarily costly' and have 'hampered justice'.

Since the introduction of the protocol, more duties have been placed upon the defence and the Criminal Procedure Rules have continued to promote a cultural change in the way that criminal litigation is conducted. It is no longer acceptable to use the 'ambush' tactics which have previously been deployed by the defence to obtain a technical advantage. The obligations set out under the Criminal Procedure Rules mean that parties have to be pro-active rather than re-active to disclosure issues. The defence must now identify what issues they have with the prosecution's case and address these openly at an early stage or face ever more severe penalties.[1]

A major difficulty is that the legal sources dealing with disclosure are scattered far and wide. There is little agreement between prosecution and defence as to what material is relevant and what is not. Some argue that the prosecution see disclosure as a battle to be fought and won with non-disclosure being the prize, irrespective of where the interests of justice may lie; others argue that the defence, without foundation, make unwarranted requests for disclosure which delay proceedings and further add demands on legal aid resources. Disclosure is still so fraught with 'misunderstandings' and 'misconceptions' that no party has confidence in the other.

---

1 Lord Justice Gross and Mr Justice Treacy are currently heading a review of sanctions for disclosure failures in criminal cases and considering whether there are options for strengthening them.

Were disclosure to be carried out by those having a complete knowledge and understanding of the relevant legal sources, then greater efficiency and confidence in the system would be achieved.

The aim of the Disclosure Referencer is to provide a practical guide to the complex area of disclosure in criminal proceedings. It has been designed as a resource book for judges, legal practitioners, investigators and any party involved in the disclosure process. In writing the book, our aim has been to present all the information clearly and consistently so as to allow the reader to navigate through what is often a complex and fast moving area of the criminal law. The many disparate sources[2] of rules and guidance in this area are therefore available in a single text and in an updated and accessible form.

The Disclosure Referencer, although principally aimed for use in crown court cases, has a chapter that covers the basics of disclosure in the adult magistrates' court to cater for practitioners with a dual practice.

The Disclosure Referencer is set out chronologically (as best we can) to enable the reader to see practically how the disclosure process unfolds by tracing disclosure from its commencement with a criminal investigation through to the conclusion of a case. We have also put tables at the front of the book that identify the duties and responsibilities (together with their source) of participants who are key to the disclosure process. This allows the reader to see 'at a glance' whether there has been compliance with their disclosure obligations.

The experience of the authors has shown that, all too frequently, errors do occur in the disclosure process, which practitioners, if armed with the necessary knowledge of the relevant rules and laws, could identify to the court and each other at an early stage. Such actions will doubtless help to prevent adjournments of a case which are not only prohibitive in their cost and wastefulness, but also normally avoidable.

The authors have, for reasons of conciseness only, used the male gender to include the female gender. Also, although the words 'accused' and 'defendant' are interchangeable, for reasons of consistency we have sought to use the word 'accused' wherever possible.

We are grateful for the input of the judiciary, in particular to His Honour Judge Stokes QC, Recorder of Nottingham, the CPS, the police, in particular Lincolnshire Police, and our fellow practitioners who have assisted us by indicating the areas which have caused them most concern. Special thanks are due to Robert Glansfield, Chris Evans and Robert Bashforth.

---

2 As identified in the 'Disclosure in Criminal Proceedings' Review conducted by Gross LJ (September 2011).

We are indebted to the patience of our respective clerks, particularly Anthony Krogulec, and to Bloomsbury Professional who have guided us through the process of publication with a great deal of understanding. We would like to mention Kiran Goss, Rebecca Cupit and Jenny Burdett. And, of course, thanks also go to our respective families for their tolerance and support.

Finally, we cannot end without mentioning William Coker QC.[3] In our view, he is undoubtedly the leading expert in the area of disclosure. He has guided us through the writing process, given us access to his materials and provided the inspiration for the tables that are a 'must have' for any criminal practitioner.

Regular updates will be provided by us at our website, www.the disclosurereferencer.co.uk. We invite anyone with any interesting rulings on disclosure to contact us at carolinebradley@thedisclosurereferencer.co.uk or alastairmunt@thedisclosurereferencer.co.uk.

The authors believe that, at the time of going to press, the law is accurately stated.

Caroline Bradley
Alastair Munt
November 2012

---

3   For a recent ruling on disclosure in which Coker QC was involved in highlighting prosecution disclosure failures, see http://www.judiciary.gov.uk/resources/JCO/documents/judgments/r-v-mouncher-ruling.pdf.

Contents

Contents

Contents

APPENDICES

Contents

Table of statutes

All references are to paragraph number.

Table of statutory instruments

All references are to paragraph number.

Table of cases

Table of non-statutory sources of law

All references are to paragraph number.

Attorney General's Guidelines

Tables of duties and obligations

The following tables are intended to act as an 'at a glance' guide to identify many of the duties and obligations of the main participants in the disclosure process as set out in the Criminal Procedure and Investigations Act 1996, the Code, AG Guidelines 2005/2011 and the Disclosure Protocol.

We have also made reference to the CPS Disclosure Manual but these references are incomplete and by no means exhaustive. The Manual should be further consulted.

Key

CPIA	Criminal Procedure and Investigations Act 1996
CPIA Code	Criminal Procedure and Investigations Act 1996: Code of Practice
AG 2005	Attorney General's Guidelines on Disclosure (2005)
AG 2011	Supplementary Attorney General's Guidelines on Disclosure – Digitally Stored Material (2011)
Protocol	Disclosure: A Protocol for the Control and Management of Unused Material in the Crown Court
DM	Crown Prosecution Service Disclosure Manual

DISCLOSURE OFFICER

Duties/obligations	CPIA	CPIA Code	AG 2005	AG 2011	Protocol	DM
To reveal to the prosecutor any material that is relevant to sentence.						2.9
To be fair and objective and work together with the prosecutor to ensure that disclosure obligations are met.			23			
To have the requisite experience, skills, competence and resources to undertake their role and perform tasks thoroughly, scrupulously and fairly.			24		13–14	

continued overleaf

xxxiii

Tables of duties and obligations

Duties/obligations	CPIA	CPIA Code	AG 2005	AG 2011	Protocol	DM
To act promptly to make sure that justice is not delayed, denied or frustrated.					16	
To be fully familiar with the facts and background of the case to perform their duties correctly.						3.10
To consult with the prosecutor.			30			3.9, 6.2, 8.6, 10.5
To consult closely with the OIC and the investigator where the roles of the OIC, the disclosure officer and the investigator are undertaken by more than one person.		3.1				3.3, 3.4,
To inform persons of the investigation and to invite them to retain material.		3.6				
To take reasonable steps to identify and consider material held by government departments or other crown agencies which appears to be relevant. To consider what further steps are needed if access is denied.			47–50		53	Ch 4
To take appropriate steps to obtain material held by a third party where grounds exist for believing that such material might be relevant and satisfies the prosecution disclosure test.			51–54		54	Ch 4
To have regard to whether relevant material may exist in relation to other linked investigations. Reasonable enquiries must be carried out.						4.4
Where there is more than one disclosure officer, the lead disclosure officer shall be the focus of enquiries and ensure that an investigator's disclosure obligations are complied with.			26			3.5

continued overleaf

Duties/obligations	CPIA	CPIA Code	AG 2005	AG 2011	Protocol	DM
To personally examine, inspect, view or listen to all relevant material that has been retained by the investigator – generally this must be done in detail.			26–27			3.9, 5.14, 30.3, 30.7
To seek advice from the prosecutor about whether material may be relevant.		6.1				
To list and number retained material on the MG6C and MG6D. The MG6D must be submitted even if there is no sensitive material.		6.2–6.4	29	50	14	3.9, Chs 6, 7, 8
To describe items in MG6C in detail, clearly and accurately, to enable the prosecutor to make an informed decision on disclosure. To describe items on the MG6D with sufficient information to enable the prosecutor to make an informed decision as to whether or not the material itself should be viewed without compromising the confidentiality of the information.		6.9– 6.10, 6.12	29	50, 51		3.9, Chs 6, 7, 8
Where the nature of the material and its form prevents its detailed examination (e.g. digitally stored material) the extent and manner of its examination must be described together with justification for such action.			27	43–49		
To indicate on MG6C which items satisfy the prosecution disclosure test where items are described generically.				51		7.5
To keep a copy of the schedules sent to prosecutor.						7.6
To edit out issues of sensitivity from the non-sensitive material (MG6C).						7.8

continued overleaf

Duties/obligations	*CPIA*	*CPIA Code*	*AG 2005*	*AG 2011*	*Protocol*	*DM*
To provide detailed reasons dealing with issues such as why material is sensitive, why its disclosure will create a real risk of serious prejudice and the consequences of its revelation.						Ch 8
To submit the schedules, signed and dated, to the prosecutor. Wherever practicable, this should be done promptly at the same time as the file is given to the prosecutor containing the material for the prosecution case.		7.1			14	3.9, 6.1, 10.7, 8.3.
To provide the prosecutor with copies of any material which falls into the following categories: –Information provided by an accused which indicates an explanation for the offence. –Material casting doubt about the reliability of a confession. –Material casting doubt about a prosecution witness. –Material which the investigator believes may satisfy the prosecution disclosure test. –Crime report, log of messages (CAD) or incident log.		7.3				3.9, 10.7, 10.8
To draw the attention of the prosecutor to any material that may satisfy the prosecution disclosure test (including material regarded as too sensitive to be entered on the sensitive schedule) and to explain why.		7.2				3.9, 10.1, 10.2, 10.7
To draw the prosecutor's attention to material where any doubt exists whether it satisfies the prosecution disclosure test.			30			10.5

continued overleaf

Duties/obligations	CPIA	CPIA Code	AG 2005	AG 2011	Protocol	DM
To put any comments regarding the contents of the schedules on MG6.						6.6
To take care that copies of sensitive material sent to the prosecutor are handled with commensurate security.						11.11
To allow or make arrangements for the prosecutor to inspect any retained material.						3.9, 10.7, 8.7, 15.24
To keep schedules accurate and up-to-date, effect any amendments promptly and provide any further reports (as appropriate).		8.1–8.2				3.9, 10.22–10.26, 14.5, 15.21–15.24
To look again at sensitive and non-sensitive material upon receipt of the defence statement. To draw the attention of the prosecutor which satisfies the prosecution disclosure test.		8.3				15.20
To notify the prosecutor of enquiries made in response to the defence statement.						10.26, 15.21–15.24
To certify that all retained material made available to him has been revealed to the prosecutor: –when the material was first submitted to prosecutor, –when the material was reconsidered upon receipt of the defence statement, –whenever a schedule is otherwise given or a schedule is otherwise revealed to the prosecutor.		9.1	26			3.9
To disclose material to the accused which has not been copied to the prosecutor and the prosecutor requests its disclosure or the court orders its disclosure.		10.1				
						continued overleaf

Duties/obligations	CPIA	CPIA Code	AG 2005	AG 2011	Protocol	DM
To disclose material to the accused which has been copied to the prosecutor.		10.2				12.22, 12.23
To certify that any transcribed material is a true record.		10.4				12.25
To notify the prosecutor whenever a disclosable item is provided to the defence and, if necessary, supply a copy to the prosecutor.						12.24
To make arrangements for the defence to inspect material and provide adequate facilities and supervision. To comply with defence requests for copies of any material unless it is neither practicable nor desirable to do so. If a copy is made for the accused, a copy should be also sent to the prosecutor.		10.3				3.9, 12.43, 12.44, 30.11, 30.12
To keep a careful record of what items are copied to or inspected by the accused.						12.24
To attend any PII hearing where the officer has provided schedules listing the items under consideration. To make the arrangements where the judge requests sight of the material in advance of the hearing.						13.21, 13.22

THE INVESTIGATOR

An investigator is any police officer or police support employee involved in the conduct of the criminal investigation.

Duties/obligations

Duties/obligations	*CPIA*	*CPIA Code*	*AG 2005*	*AG 2011*	*Protocol*	*DM*
To be alive to the potential need to reveal to the prosecutor material in the interests of justice and fairness before their duties under CPIA 1996 apply, e.g. for a bail application.			55		19	
To reveal to the prosecutor any material that is relevant to sentence.						2.9
To be fair and objective and work together with the prosecutor to ensure that disclosure obligations are met.			23			
To carry out the duties imposed under the CPIA Code.		2.1				3.6
To gather, inspect, retain and record relevant unused material thoroughly, scrupulously and fairly.					13	
To consult closely with the OIC and the disclosure officer where the roles of the OIC, the disclosure officer and the investigator are undertaken by more than one person.		3.1				3.3, 3.4
To record any information (including negative information) at the time obtained or as soon as practicable.		2.1, 4.3, 4.4				3.1
To notify the disclosure officer of the existence and whereabouts of material that has been retained.						3.7
						continued overleaf

Duties/obligations	*CPIA*	*CPIA Code*	*AG 2005*	*AG 2011*	*Protocol*	*DM*
To retain material/information obtained in a criminal investigation, created or discovered, which may be relevant to the investigation. The material may be photographed.		2.1, 5.1	28			3.1, 3.6
To err on the side of recording and retaining material where there is any doubt as to whether it may be relevant.			24, 28			5.8
To retain material where it may be relevant including: –crime reports, –custody records, –tapes of telephone messages, –final and draft versions of witness statements, –interview records with actual/ potential witnesses or suspects, –communications between police and experts, –first descriptions of suspects.		5.4				
To retain material which satisfies the prosecution disclosure test such as: –an explanation by the accused for the offence charged, –any material which casts doubt on the reliability of a confession, –any material which casts doubt on the reliability of a prosecution witness.		5.5				
To retain material until: –a decision is taken whether to institute proceedings, –the accused is acquitted or the case is discontinued, –six months from the date of conviction or release from prison/discharge hospital (whichever is longer), –the conclusion of appeal or referral to the CCRC.		5.1, 5.7– 5.10				

continued overleaf

Duties/obligations	CPIA	CPIA Code	AG 2005	AG 2011	Protocol	DM
To pursue all reasonable lines of enquiry, whether these point towards or away from the suspect.		3.5		41	16	4.2
To have regard to whether relevant material may exist in relation to other linked investigations. Reasonable enquiries must be carried out.						4.4
To act promptly to make sure justice is not delayed, denied or frustrated.					16	
To be aware of strong legal constraints that apply to legally professionally privileged material.				9, 13		
Not to take action which changes the data held on computer.				8		
To seek advice from the prosecutor about whether material may be relevant.		6.1				
To reveal material directly to the prosecutor where material is too sensitive to be listed on MG6D. To allow the prosecutor to inspect the material in order to assess whether it is disclosable and/or needs a PII hearing.		6.13, 6.14				
To take reasonable steps to identify and consider material held by government departments or other crown agencies which appears to be relevant. To consider what further steps are needed if access is denied.			47–50		53	Ch 4
To take appropriate steps to obtain material held by a third party where grounds exist for believing that such material might be relevant and satisfies the prosecution disclosure test.			51–54		54	Ch 4

continued overleaf

Duties/obligations	CPIA	CPIA Code	AG 2005	AG 2011	Protocol	DM
To ensure the prosecution advocate is aware of any disclosure problems.					22	

OFFICER IN CHARGE (OIC)

Duties/obligations

Duties/obligations/ responsibilities	CPIA	CPIA Code	AG 2005	AG 2011	Protocol	DM
To direct the investigation.		2.1				3.5
To ensure that all duties under the CPIA Code are carried out by those involved in the investigation.						3.1
To ensure that all reasonable lines of enquiry are pursued.						3.1, 3.5
To ensure that proper procedures exist to record and retain information (in a durable and retrievable form) and other material.		2.1, 4.1				3.5, 5.10, 5.18
To identify information and ensure its transfer to a durable form where the initial record forms part of a larger record which will be destroyed, e.g. CCTV, custody tapes, 999 calls.		4.2				5.18
To consult closely with the disclosure officer and the investigator where the roles of the OIC, the disclosure officer and the investigator are undertaken by more than one person to ensure effective performance of duties.		3.1				3.3, 3.4
To be responsible for delegating tasks to others and ensure such tasks are carried out.		3.4				3.1, 3.5

continued overleaf

Duties/obligations/ responsibilities	CPIA	CPIA Code	AG 2005	AG 2011	Protocol	DM
To appoint the disclosure officer and ensure there is no conflict of interest. To appoint a lead disclosure officer if required.						3.5
To account for any general policies followed in the investigation.		3.4				3.5
To ensure all relevant material is retained and made available to the disclosure officer or, exceptionally, revealed directly to the prosecutor.		3.4				3.5, 10.12
To ask the disclosure officer to inform third parties of the existence of the investigation if it is believed they may hold relevant material.		3.6				4.7
To take all practicable steps to recover material that was inspected but not retained which may have become relevant due to developments.		5.3				3.5, 5.25
To seek advice from the prosecutor about whether the material may be relevant to the investigation.		6.1				

THE PROSECUTOR (SEE ALSO PROSECUTING ADVOCATE)

Duties/obligations

Duties/obligations/ responsibilities	CPIA	CPIA Code	AG 2005	AG 2011	Protocol	DM
To do all he can to facilitate proper disclosure, as part of his general and personal professional responsibility to act fairly and impartially, in the interests of justice and in accordance with the law.			32			11.1
To be fair and objective and work together with the investigators and disclosure officers to ensure disclosure obligations are met.			23			
To be alert to the need to provide advice to, and where necessary probe actions taken by, disclosure officers to ensure that disclosure obligations are met.			32			11.1
To be alive to the potential need to disclose material in the interests of justice and fairness before their duties under CPIA 1996 apply, e.g. for a bail application.			55		19	2.7–2.8
To give advice to the OIC if there is any doubt whether a conflict of interest precludes an individual acting as a disclosure officer.						3.5
To have regard to whether relevant material may exist in relation to other linked investigations. Reasonable enquiries must be carried out.						4.4
To review the schedules prepared by disclosure officers thoroughly. To log date of receipt.			33			11.7, 11.9

continued overleaf

Duties/obligations/ responsibilities	CPIA	CPIA Code	AG 2005	AG 2011	Protocol	DM
To be alert to the possibility that relevant material may exist which has not been revealed to him or material included in the schedules which should not have been.			33			
To take action at once to obtain properly completed schedules where: –no schedules have been provided, –there are apparent omissions, –documents or other items are inadequately described or are unclear, –irrelevant items are included.			33			11.8
To raise the matter with a senior investigator if dissatisfaction remains with the quality or content of schedules.			33			11.8
To raise the matter with the disclosure officer at once if concerned that he has not inspected, viewed or listened to the relevant material and request that it be done.			34			
To always inspect, view or listen to the material (sensitive or non-sensitive) where he believes it satisfies the prosecution disclosure test and satisfy himself that the prosecution can properly be continued.			35			11.13
To consider whether the sensitive material satisfies the disclosure test and if so, whether or not there is a 'real' risk of 'serious' prejudice by disclosing the material to the defence.						8.12, 8.17, 8.19.

continued overleaf

Duties/obligations/ responsibilities	CPIA	CPIA Code	AG 2005	AG 2011	Protocol	DM
To disclose to the accused any prosecution material which satisfies the prosecution disclosure test or provide a statement that there is no such material (subject to PII and RIPA) as soon as reasonably practicable upon receipt of the prosecution file.	3					11.3, 12.18, 12.20
To contact the defence if the defence statement is not served or is inadequate.			18			15.11, 15.12
To be open, alert and promptly responsive to requests for the disclosure of material supported by a comprehensive defence statement.			18			15.10
To consider schedules afresh and be pro-active in identifying disclosable material upon receipt of the defence statement. To inspect, view or listen to any material that he considers satisfies the disclosure test.	7A		36			Ch 15
To copy the defence statement to the disclosure officer and the investigator as soon as reasonably practicable. To draw the disclosure officer's attention to any key issues.			36			15.14
To advise the investigator if any reasonable and relevant lines of further enquiry should be pursued.			36	45		15.15
To answer requests for disclosure if in accordance with and relevant to the defence statement (once initial disclosure is completed and the defence statement is served).			38			

continued overleaf

Duties/obligations/ responsibilities	CPIA	CPIA Code	AG 2005	AG 2011	Protocol	DM
To keep under review at all times whether the material satisfies the prosecution disclosure test which has not previously been disclosed (particularly after receipt of the defence statement). Such material must be disclosed to the accused as soon as is reasonably practicable.	7A	8.2	17			14.1– 14.4
To consider afresh material upon receipt of a section 8, CPIA application.						16.1, 16.2
To record in writing all actions and decisions made in discharging his disclosure responsibilities. To make this information available to the prosecuting advocate if requested or if it is relevant to the issue.			39			2.11, 11.9, 11.15, 12.24, 15.4, 16.8
To ensure that any new material generated is properly scheduled and the schedules are endorsed and dated with any new disclosure decisions.						14.5
To forward to the police the details of any witness notice as soon as possible so that a decision can be made whether to interview a witness.						15.34
To take reasonable steps to identify and consider material held by government departments or other crown agencies which appears to be relevant. To consider what further steps are needed if access is denied.			47–50		53	Ch 4
To take appropriate steps to obtain material held by a third party where grounds exist for believing such material might be relevant and satisfies the prosecution disclosure test.			51–54		54	Ch 4

continued overleaf

Duties/obligations/ responsibilities	CPIA	CPIA Code	AG 2005	AG 2011	Protocol	DM
To record in a durable form relevant information arising as a result of liaison with third parties.			53			4.9
To disclose as much material as possible in edited form before making a public interest immunity application to the court to withhold sensitive material.			20			
To examine all sensitive material prior to a public interest immunity hearing, make any enquiries of the investigator and rigorously apply *R v H & C*, para 36, per Lord Bingham.			21, 22			
To seek a judicial ruling on the disclosability of material only in truly borderline cases.			40			
To discontinue a case where material which satisfies the prosecution disclosure test cannot be disclosed and this cannot be remedied.			41			1.11
To consider disclosing material in the interests of justice which is relevant to sentence.			58			2.9
To take all practicable steps to recover material that was inspected but not retained which may have become relevant due to developments.						3.5, 5.25
To consider disclosing material after the conclusion of proceedings in the interests of justice that might cast doubt upon the safety of the conviction.			59, 60			2.10, 2.13

PROSECUTING ADVOCATE

Duties/obligations

Duties/obligations/ responsibilities	CPIA	CPIA Code	AG 2005	AG 2011	Protocol	DM
To consider as a priority all the information regarding disclosure of material upon receipt of instructions.			43			
To consider in every case whether he is in possession of all relevant documentation and has been instructed fully regarding disclosure matters.			43			
To ensure that all material that ought to be disclosed under CPIA 1996 is disclosed. To be fully informed, as far as is possible, to enable him to make decisions on disclosure.			42			
To review decisions already made regarding disclosure and advise in writing if further information or action is required.			43			
To advise on disclosure in accordance with CPIA 1996 and, if necessary, to hold a conference.			43			
To keep disclosure under review until the conclusion of the trial.	7A		44			
To specifically consider whether it is necessary to inspect further material or to reconsider material already inspected to discharge his duty of continuing review.			44			
To disclose only material that satisfies the prosecution disclosure test and not to abrogate his disclosure responsibilities.			44			12.7, 12.8
						continued overleaf

Tables of duties and obligations

Duties/obligations/responsibilities	CPIA	CPIA Code	AG 2005	AG 2011	Protocol	DM
To make disclosure decisions in consultation with those instructing and the disclosure officer prior to the start of the trial.			45			
It is desirable to be able to consult on disclosure issues with those instructing and the disclosure officer during the trial if it can be achieved without unduly affecting the trial.			45			
To examine all material relevant to the application before a public interest immunity hearing and make any necessary enquiries of the investigator.			21			
To draw the judge's attention to any foreseeable disclosure difficulties at the preliminary hearing.					23	12.1–12.4
To be fully instructed about any disclosure difficulties at the PCMH. To able to put forward realistic timetables to comply with disclosure.					26, 27	

Chapter 1

The criminal investigation

INTRODUCTION

1.01   The Criminal Procedure and Investigations Act 1996 (CPIA 1996) was enacted to 'make provision about criminal procedure and criminal investigations':[1] Part I provides for disclosure and Part II is concerned with criminal investigations. The CPIA 1996 applies to all investigations that were commenced on or after 1 April 1997 but was amended by the Criminal Justice Act 2003. The CPIA 1996, as amended, applies to investigations commenced on or after 4 April 2005.[2] Under the provisions of the CPIA 1996 the accused is entitled, subject to some exceptions,[3] to all material and information that does not form part of the prosecution case against him and which satisfies the prosecution disclosure test. Material satisfies the prosecution disclosure test if it might reasonably be considered capable of undermining the case for the prosecution against the accused or assisting the case for the accused.[4] A number of roles and duties are imposed by the CPIA 1996 upon relevant participants which are designed to ensure that all information or material which may be relevant, whether obtained or generated, is properly recorded and retained. The procedure whereby unused material passes to the defence begins with the criminal investigation.

1.02   This chapter deals with:

• the criminal investigation	**1.03–1.06**
• specific roles	**1.07–1.08**
• specific duties	
– to pursue all reasonable lines of enquiry	**1.09–1.19**
– relevance of material	**1.20–1.26**
– to record information that may be relevant	**1.27–1.33**
– to retain material that may be relevant	**1.34–1.41**

---

1   Preamble to CPIA 1996.
2   This book is concerned only with investigations commenced on or after 4 April 2005.
3   See Regulation of Investigatory Powers Act 2000, s 17 and public interest immunity.
4   CPIA 1996, s 3(1).

1

THE CRIMINAL INVESTIGATION

1.03   A criminal investigation, as defined by section 22(1), CPIA 1996 is:

'... an investigation conducted by police officers[5] with a view to it being ascertained –

(a)   whether a person should be charged with an offence, or

(b)   whether a person charged with an offence is guilty of it.'[6]

1.04   A code of practice (the CPIA Code) has been issued under section 23, Part II, CPIA 1996 that sets out 'the manner in which police officers are to record, retain and reveal to the prosecutor material obtained in a criminal investigation and which may be relevant to the investigation, and related matters'.[7] Paragraph 2.1, CPIA Code provides that a criminal investigation will include:

'–   investigations into crimes that have been committed;

–   investigations whose purpose is to ascertain whether a crime has been committed, with a view to the possible institution of criminal proceedings; and

–   investigations which begin in the belief that a crime may be committed, for example when the police keep premises or individuals under observation for a period of time, with a view to the possible institution of criminal proceedings.'

1.05   The CPIA Code is mandatory in relation to police officers. The CPIA 1996 also states that 'persons other than police officers' who are charged with the duty of conducting an investigation shall have regard to any relevant provision of a Code which would apply if the investigation were conducted by police officers.[8] 'Persons other than police officers' will include those working in agencies such as the Health and Safety Executive, the Serious Fraud Office, the Financial Services Authority and the Royal Society for Protection of Animals.

1.06   In the early stages of an investigation there is often little or no prosecution supervision and no judicial oversight. Defence input is routinely limited to the accused's answers in interview. The police are entrusted with the responsibilities

---

5   *DPP v Metten* (unreported, 22 January 1999), per Buxton LJ – the instantaneous reaction of police officers to an incident that takes place in their presence is not part of an investigation of the type envisaged by CPIA 1996.

6   CPIA 1996, Part I, s 1(4) has an identical definition.

7   See the preamble to the CPIA Code.

8   CPIA 1996, s 26.

of gathering and preserving material that may point towards the innocence of the accused. It is imperative that this work is carried out with complete integrity.

SPECIFIC ROLES

1.07   The CPIA Code defines three distinct roles in the investigation:[9]

1   An investigator: An investigator is any police officer involved in the conduct of a criminal investigation. All investigators have a responsibility for carrying out the duties imposed on them under the CPIA Code including recording information and retaining records of information and other material.

2   The officer in charge of an investigation (often referred to as the OIC): The officer in charge is responsible for directing the criminal investigation and ensuring that proper procedures are in place for recording information and retaining records of information together with other material in the investigation.

3   The disclosure officer: The disclosure officer is responsible for examining the material and revealing it to the prosecutor. He must certify that certain functions have been carried out and disclose material to the accused at the request of the prosecutor.

1.08   Although specific duties attach to each role, these roles are often performed by one and the same officer.

SPECIFIC DUTIES

To pursue all reasonable lines of enquiry

1.09   One of the statutory objectives of the CPIA Code is to ensure that where a criminal investigation is conducted all reasonable lines of enquiry are pursued. Paragraph 3.5 of the CPIA Code provides:

'In conducting an investigation, the investigator should pursue all reasonable lines of enquiry, whether these point towards or away from the suspect. What is reasonable in each case will depend on the particular circumstances. For example, where material is held on computer, it is a matter for the investigator

---

9   CPIA Code, para 2.1.

to decide which material on the computer it is reasonable to inquire into, and in what manner.'

1.10   The duty to pursue all reasonable lines of enquiry arises as soon as an investigation starts and continues until it has been ascertained whether the accused is guilty.[10] This duty cannot be avoided. In *R v Adam Joof*[11] Hooper LJ stated:

> 'The responsibilities imposed by the Criminal Procedure and Investigations Act and by the Attorney General's Guidelines cannot be sidestepped by not making an enquiry. A police officer who believes that a person may have information which might undermine the case for the prosecution or assist the case for the suspect or defendant cannot decline to make enquiries of that person in order to avoid the need to disclose what the person might say.'

1.11   The lines of enquiry must be reasonable as opposed to speculative. What would be a reasonable enquiry will depend on the circumstances of each case and, in particular, the information available at any particular time. In cases involving digital material it is not the duty of the prosecution to comb through all the material in its possession – e.g. every word or byte of computer material – for anything which might conceivably or speculatively assist the defence. In some cases a sift could be made by the disclosure officer manually assessing a computer or other digital material from its directory to determine which files may be relevant; in other cases, it would be proper to use search tools to identify relevant passages.[12]

1.12   The need to pursue reasonable lines of enquiry may arise at the scene. It may be necessary, inter alia, to make enquiries of potential eyewitnesses, seize CCTV footage or seek alternative suspects. Equally, what an accused said in interview may give rise to further reasonable lines of enquiry.

1.13   Before the accused is charged with an offence a prosecutor is required, when assessing the reliability of the evidence, to consider the accuracy, reliability and credibility of the witnesses and whether further enquiries should be pursued which may support or undermine the account of a witness.[13]

1.14   Following service of the defence statement, prosecutors are under a specific duty to copy the defence statement to the disclosure officer and

---

10 CPIA 1996, s 22(1).
11 *R v Adam Joof* [2012] EWCA Crim 1475, per Hooper LJ, para 17.
12 Supplementary Attorney General's Guidelines on Disclosure – Digitally Stored Material (2011), paras 40–43.
13 Code for Crown Prosecutors (February 2010), para 4.7(g), (h).

investigator as soon as practicable and advise the investigator if, in their view, reasonable and relevant lines of further enquiry should be pursued.[14] This should also apply upon the service or giving of an updated defence statement.[15]

1.15   An investigator should not show the defence statement to a non-expert witness. The extent to which the detail of a defence statement is made known to a witness will depend upon the extent to which it is necessary to clarify the issues disputed by the defence or assist the prosecutor in identifying further disclosable material or reasonable lines of enquiry. The investigator should seek guidance from the prosecutor if there is any doubt as to how the defence statement should be used in conducting further enquiries.[16]

1.16   Prosecution advocates should ensure that all material that ought to be disclosed under the CPIA 1996 is disclosed to the defence. They cannot, however, be expected to disclose material if they are not aware of its existence. As far as is possible, prosecution advocates must place themselves in a fully informed position to enable them to make decisions on disclosure.[17] Upon receipt of instructions, they should consider whether they can be satisfied that they are in possession of all relevant documentation and that they have been instructed fully regarding disclosure matters.[18]

1.17   Decisions already made regarding disclosure should be reviewed. If as a result, the advocate considers that further information or action is required, written advice should be promptly provided setting out the aspects that need clarification or action.[19] There is, by implication, a duty on the advocate to advise upon any further reasonable lines of enquiry whether they point towards or away from the accused.

1.18   The duty of fairness to the accused, of which the duty to pursue all reasonable lines of enquiry forms a part, is contained in the Criminal Procedure Rules 2012 (CPR 2012). The police, the prosecutor and prosecution advocates are all participants[20] in the conduct of a criminal case and subject to a duty to prepare and conduct the case in accordance with the overriding objective.[21] The

---

14 Attorney General's Guidelines on Disclosure (2005), paras 36–37.
15 CPIA 1996, s 6B which deals with updated defence statements is not yet in force.
16 CPS Disclosure Manual, para 15.19.
17 Attorney General's Guidelines on Disclosure (2005), para 42.
18 Attorney General's Guidelines on Disclosure (2005), para 43.
19 Attorney General's Guidelines on Disclosure (2005), para 43.
20 CPR 2012, r 1.2(2): 'Anyone involved in any way with a criminal case is a participant in its conduct for the purposes of this rule.'
21 CPR 2012, r 1.2.

overriding objective '.... is that criminal cases be dealt with justly'.[22] Dealing with a criminal case justly includes:

(a)   acquitting the innocent and convicting the guilty;

(b)   dealing with the prosecution and the defence fairly;

(c)   recognising the rights of an accused, particularly those under Article 6 of the European Convention on Human Rights.[23]

1.19   A serious and significant failure to pursue a reasonable line of enquiry which points away from the guilt of the accused or to take reasonable steps to secure material which satisfies the prosecution disclosure test[24] may breach the duty to assist the court in achieving the overriding objective.

Relevance of material

1.20   There is a duty on an investigator to record information which may be relevant[25] and a duty to retain material which may be relevant.[26] Paragraph 2.1 of the CPIA Code provides:

> 'material is material of any kind, including information and objects, which is obtained in the course of a criminal investigation and which may be relevant to the investigation. This includes not only material coming into the possession of the investigator (such as documents seized in the course of searching premises) but also material generated by him (such as interview records)'.[27]

1.21   The terms 'information' and 'material' are intended to be all embracing to cover anything such as words, documents, objects and electronic records, whether obtained or seized during the investigation or generated by it.

1.22   The duties to record and retain material do not require that the material is relevant or that it passes the prosecution disclosure test.[28] It is sufficient that it

---

22   CPR 2012, r 1.1(1).
23   CPR 2012, r 1.1(2).
24   i.e. any prosecution material which might reasonably be considered capable of undermining the case for the prosecution against the accused or of assisting the case for the accused.
25   CPIA Code, para 4.
26   CPIA Code, para 5. See Attorney General's Guidelines on Disclosure (2005), para 28.
27   CPIA Code, para 2.1. Under CPIA 1996, s 22(2), references to material means material of all kinds, and in particular references to information and objects of all descriptions.
28   i.e. any prosecution material which might reasonably be considered capable of undermining the case for the prosecution against the the accused or of assisting the case for the accused.

'may be relevant' and this is a widely defined concept. Paragraph 2.1 of the CPIA Code provides:

> 'material may be *relevant to an investigation* if it appears to an investigator, or to the officer in charge of an investigation, or to the disclosure officer, that it has some bearing on any offence under investigation or any person being investigated, or on the surrounding circumstances of the case, unless it is incapable of having any impact on the case'.

1.23 Investigating officers, in determining whether material 'may be relevant' should consider:

- whether the information adds to the total knowledge of how the offence was committed, who may have committed it, and why;

- whether the information could support an alternative explanation, given the current understanding of events surrounding the offence; and

- what the potential consequences will be if the material is not preserved.[29]

1.24 It may not be possible to make a considered decision on the relevance of an item until later in the case when the facts are clearer.[30] Once an item is retained, the officer in charge, the disclosure officer or the investigator may seek the prosecutor's advice about whether a particular item 'may be relevant'.[31]

1.25 Investigators should always err on the side of recording and retaining information where there is any doubt whether the material may be relevant.[32] This inclusive approach should reduce the risk of disclosable material failing to be recorded and retained and, if it is non-sensitive, will ensure the defence are aware of its existence by its appearance on the non-sensitive material schedule.[33]

1.26 As a general rule, pure opinion or speculation, e.g. police officers' theories about who committed the crime, is not unused material. If the opinion or speculation is based on some other information or fact, not otherwise notified or apparent to the prosecutor, that information or fact might well be relevant to the investigation.[34] Likewise reports, advices and other communications between the

---

29 CPS Disclosure Manual, para 5.15.
30 CPS Disclosure Manual, para 5.11.
31 CPIA Code, para 6.1.
32 Attorney General's Guidelines on Disclosure (2005), para 24; CPS Disclosure Manual, para 5.8.
33 Review of Disclosure in Criminal Proceedings, The Rt Hon Lord Justice Gross (September 2011), Executive summary, para 8(v) considered but decided against narrowing the relevance test.
34 CPS Disclosure Manual, para 5.12.

CPS and police will usually be of an administrative nature or contain professional opinion based on evidential material or material already subject to revelation. They will usually have no bearing on the case and thus will not be relevant.[35]

To record information that may be relevant

1.27 The duty to record information that may be relevant to the investigation in a durable or retrievable format is mandatory. Paragraph 4.1 of the CPIA Code provides:

> 'If material which may be relevant to the investigation consists of information which is not recorded in any form, the officer in charge of an investigation must ensure that it is recorded in a durable or retrievable form (whether in writing, on video or audio tape, or on computer disk).'[36]

1.28 Information will often consist of words spoken with a police officer, be they words at the scene of a crime, during a telephone conversation, before or after a witness makes a witness statement, or between a witness and a family liaison officer. Information may be within messages such as running commentaries and the details of a pursuit. Conversations with experts and other investigators, where the information discussed is likely to be relevant to the case and is not recorded elsewhere, should be recorded.[37]

1.29 Where it is not practicable to retain the initial record of information because it forms part of a larger record which is to be destroyed, its contents should be transferred as a true record to a durable and more easily-stored form before that happens.[38] Such a larger record could include control room audio, custody suite tapes, traffic car videos of speeding offences or other similar recordings.[39] The officer in charge of the investigation should identify information that should be retained and ensure that it is transferred accurately to a durable and retrievable form before the tapes are destroyed.[40]

1.30 The impact of negative information can be significant and, where it may be relevant, must be recorded. Negative information may include:[41]

---

35 CPS Disclosure Manual, para 5.15. Note: If the content of any such document is relevant and not recorded elsewhere then the material should be described on the appropriate schedule.
36 See also CPIA 1996, s 22(3).
37 CPS Disclosure Manual, para 5.19.
38 CPIA Code, para 4.2.
39 CPS Disclosure Manual, para 5.18.
40 CPS Disclosure Manual, para 5.18.
41 CPIA Code, para 4.3; CPS Disclosure Manual, para 5.16.

- information that a number of people present at the scene of an alleged offence state they saw nothing unusual;

- CCTV footage inconsistent with the prosecution case;

- the presence of fingerprints at a crime scene which cannot be identified as belonging to the accused; and

- crime scene samples that do not match those of the accused.

1.31   Where information which may be relevant is obtained, it must be recorded at the time it is obtained or as soon as practicable thereafter. This would include information obtained in house-to-house enquiries. The requirement to record information promptly does not require an investigator to take a statement from a potential witness where it would not otherwise be taken.[42]

1.32   Operations for intelligence purposes may, subject to public interest immunity considerations, become disclosable. Any officers involved in intelligence operations should regularly and actively consider whether information they possess has a bearing on any live investigations or prosecutions. If this is the case, the officer should act quickly to see that it is brought to the attention of the disclosure officer or prosecutor.[43]

1.33   Any information, once recorded in compliance with paragraph 4 of the CPIA Code, becomes material to which the duty to retain under paragraph 5 of the CPIA Code applies.

To retain material that may be relevant

1.34   The duty to retain material that may be relevant is mandatory. Paragraph 5.1 of the CPIA Code provides:

> 'The investigator must retain material obtained in a criminal investigation which may be relevant to the investigation. Material may be photographed, video-recorded, captured digitally or otherwise retained in the form of a copy rather than the original at any time, if the original is perishable; the original was supplied to the investigator rather than generated by him and is to be returned to its owner; or the retention of a copy rather than the original is reasonable in all the circumstances.'

---

42 CPIA Code, para 4.4.
43 See *R v Barkshire* [2011] EWCA Crim 1885 for the consequences of failing to disclose information received by an undercover officer.

1.35   The duty to retain material is subject to section 22, Police and Criminal Evidence Act 1984 which details how anything seized under section 19 (general power of seizure) and section 20 (powers of seizure for computerized information) may be retained:

- for use as evidence at a trial;

- for forensic examination and for investigation in connection with an offence; and

- to establish its lawful owner.[44]

1.36   Previously examined material which was not retained, as it was not thought to be relevant, may become relevant as the case develops and issues are clarified. In such circumstances the officer in charge should take steps, wherever practicable, to obtain the material or ensure that it is retained for further inspection or for production in court if required.[45]

1.37   If the officer in charge believes that other persons may be in possession of material that may be relevant to the investigation which has not been obtained, he should ask the disclosure officer (if he is a different person) to invite those persons to retain the material in case it becomes relevant.[46]

1.38   The developments in a case, triggering the responsibilities of the officer in charge to obtain and retain, may often derive from information provided by the accused in his interview or in his defence statement.

1.39   Some categories of material are specifically identified by the CPIA Code as material that should be retained where it 'may be relevant'.[47] These categories are:

- '–   crime reports (including crime report forms, relevant parts of incident report books or police officer's notebooks);

- –   custody records;

- –   records which are derived from tapes of telephone messages (for example, 999 calls) containing descriptions of an alleged offence or offender;

- –   final versions of witness statements (and draft versions where their content differs from the final version), including any exhibits

---

44   Police and Criminal Evidence Act 1984, s 22(2).
45   CPIA Code, para 5.3.
46   CPIA Code, para 3.6.
47   CPIA Code, para 5.4.

mentioned (unless these have been returned to their owner on the understanding that they will be produced in court if required);

– interview records (written records or audio or video tapes, of interviews with actual or potential witnesses or suspects);

– communications between the police and experts such as forensic scientists, reports of work carried out by experts, and schedules of scientific material prepared by the expert for the investigator, for the purpose of criminal proceedings;

– records of the first description of a suspect by each potential witness who purports to identify or describe the suspect, whether or not the description differs from that of subsequent descriptions by that or other witnesses;

– any material casting doubt on the reliability of a witness.'[48]

1.40   The duty to retain material where it 'may be relevant' to the investigation specifically includes material which may satisfy the prosecution disclosure test.[49] This would include:

'– information provided by an accused which indicates an explanation for the offence with which he has been charged;

– any material casting doubt on the reliability of a confession;

– any material casting doubt upon the reliability of a prosecution witness.'[50]

1.41   Material which may be relevant to the investigation must be retained until a decision is taken whether to institute proceedings against a person for an offence.[51] If proceedings are instituted, the material must be retained at least until the accused is acquitted, convicted or the prosecutor decides not to proceed with the case.[52] If the accused is convicted, the material must be retained at least until six months from the date of conviction or upon his release from prison or discharge from hospital if the period is longer than six months. In the event of an appeal against conviction (or referral to the Criminal Cases Review Commission) the material must be retained until the appeal or referral has concluded.[53]

---

48   CPIA Code, para 5.4.
49   i.e. any prosecution material which might reasonably be considered capable of undermining the case for the prosecution against the accused or of assisting the case for the accused.
50   CPIA Code, para 5.5.
51   CPIA Code, para 5.7.
52   CPIA Code, para 5.8.
53   CPIA Code, paras 5.9–5.10.

Chapter 2

The role of the disclosure officer

INTRODUCTION

2.01 The skill, competence and diligence of the disclosure officer are central to the operation of the disclosure process. He is responsible, inter alia, for examining material and generating proper, accurate and transparent schedules of unused material that are integral to determining what is ultimately disclosed to the defence.

2.02 This chapter deals with:

• the disclosure officer	**2.03–2.11**
• examination of material	**2.12–2.19**
• scheduling	
– timing	**2.20–2.24**
– contents and format	**2.25–2.29**
– non-sensitive material (MG6C)[1]	**2.30–2.31**
– sensitive material (MG6D)[2]	**2.32–2.38**
– block scheduling	**2.39–2.40**
• revelation to the prosecutor	
– schedules	**2.41**
– the disclosure officer's report (MG6E)[3]	**2.42–2.49**
– other police forms	**2.50–2.51**
• continuing disclosure	**2.52–2.54**
• amending and updating	**2.55–2.57**
• certifications by the disclosure officer	**2.58–2.60**
• disclosure to the defence	**2.61–2.65**

---

1 For a copy of an MG6C see **Appendix 8**.
2 For a copy of an MG6D see **Appendix 8**.
3 For a copy of an MG6E see **Appendix 8**.

THE DISCLOSURE OFFICER

2.03   The disclosure officer must:

- examine all relevant material that has been retained by the investigator and that does not form part of the prosecution case;

- create schedules that fully describe the material and detail its precise location;

- reveal this material to the prosecutor;

- continually review the schedules and retained material, particularly after service of the defence statement;

- certify that certain disclosure steps have been complied with; and

- disclose material to the defence as requested by the prosecutor.[4]

2.04   The disclosure officer should, in addition:

- alert third parties to the need to preserve material that may be relevant to the investigation and give consideration to obtaining it;[5] and

- consider whether relevant material may exist in relation to other linked investigations or prosecutions.[6]

2.05   The disclosure officer must discharge his responsibilities promptly and properly in order to ensure that justice is not delayed, denied or frustrated.[7]

2.06   The Chief Officer of Police for each police force is responsible for ensuring that disclosure officers and their deputies have sufficient skills and authority, commensurate with the complexity of the investigation, to discharge their functions effectively.[8] It is crucial that the police (and indeed all investigative bodies) implement appropriate training regimes and appoint competent disclosure officers, who have sufficient knowledge of the issues in the case.[9] For instance, where a case involves the inspection of digital material, the disclosure officer will

---

4   CPS Disclosure Manual, para 3.9. See also disclosure officer's duties under the schedule of responsibilities.
5   Attorney General's Guidelines on Disclosure (2005), paras 47–54. This responsibility is shared with investigators and the prosecutor.
6   CPS Disclosure Manual, paras 4.4–4.5. This responsibility is shared with investigators and the prosecutor.
7   Disclosure: A Protocol for the Control and Management of Unused Material in the Crown Court ('Disclosure Protocol'), para 16.
8   CPIA Code, para 3.3.
9   Disclosure Protocol, para 14.

need to have the necessary skills to liaise with any computer forensic experts.[10] Likewise, in an enquiry using the Holmes2 system,[11] the disclosure officer must have completed training in the specific Holmes2 disclosure facility.[12]

2.07 The Chief Officer of Police is responsible for putting in place arrangements to ensure that in every investigation the appointment of the officer in charge and the disclosure officer is recorded. Any replacement must also be recorded.[13]

2.08 Practitioners commonly find that the officer in the case is also the disclosure officer. Whether the role of disclosure officer is performed by the officer in the case or by another officer depends on the complexity of the case and the administrative arrangements within each police force.[14] Where more than one person undertakes these roles, close consultation between them is essential to the effective performance of the duties imposed by the CPIA Code.[15]

2.09 A person must not be appointed as disclosure officer or continue to act in that role if it is likely to result in a conflict of interest.[16] The advice of a more senior officer must always be sought about any potential conflict, as should the advice of a prosecutor where necessary.[17]

2.10 The officer in charge may delegate tasks to another investigator.[18] The CPS Disclosure Manual fixes the officer in charge with the responsibility of appointing the disclosure officer and, in particular, where there is more than one disclosure officer, for ensuring that there is a lead disclosure office who is the focus for enquiries and responsible for ensuring that an investigator's disclosure obligations are complied with.[19] Whether the officer in charge appoints a disclosure officer at the outset or later will depend on the seriousness, complexity

---

10 CPS Disclosure Manual, para 30.4.
11 Home Office Large Major Enquiry System 2 – a computer database for large-scale investigations.
12 CPS Disclosure Manual, para 31.8.
13 CPIA Code, paras 3.3, 3.7.
14 CPIA Code, para 3.1.
15 CPIA Code, para 3.1.
16 CPIA Code, para 3.3; see *R v Adam Joof* [2012] EWCA Crim 1475.
17 Attorney General's Guidelines on Disclosure (2005), para 25.
18 CPIA Code, para 3.4.
19 CPS Disclosure Manual, para 3.5; Attorney General's Guidelines on Disclosure (2005), para 26.

and scale of the case.[20] A disclosure officer should be appointed at the beginning of an enquiry involving the Holmes2 system.[21]

2.11   The appointment must be in sufficient time to enable the disclosure officer, with the assistance of the officer in charge and investigators, to become fully familiar with the facts and background to the case and to prepare the unused schedules.

EXAMINATION OF MATERIAL

2.12   Disclosure officers, or deputy disclosure officers, must inspect, view or listen to all relevant material that has been retained by the investigator and the disclosure officer must provide a personal declaration to the effect that this task has been undertaken.[22] If the disclosure officer is uncertain whether all relevant material has been revealed to him, enquiries should be made of the officer in charge to resolve the matter.[23] It is the responsibility of the lead disclosure officer to ensure that an investigator's disclosure obligations are complied with.[24]

2.13   Generally, the disclosure officer will be required to examine in detail all relevant material retained by an investigator, however, the extent and manner of the examination will depend on the nature of the material and its form. With technological advances and the explosion of electronic materials the physical examination of every document in paper or electronic format, particularly but not exclusively in fraud cases, will be virtually impossible.[25] This will place unrealistic or disproportionate demands on the investigator and prosecutor.

2.14   To satisfy the prosecution disclosure test it may be reasonable to examine digital material using software search tools or to establish the contents of large volumes of material by dip sampling.[26]

2.15   Where cases involve large quantities of data the officer in charge will develop a strategy setting out how the material should be examined to identify

---

20 CPS Disclosure Manual, para 3.11. The CPIA Code makes no provision as to when the disclosure officer must be appointed.
21 CPS Disclosure Manual, para 31.9.
22 Attorney General's Guidelines on Disclosure (2005), para 24; CPIA Code, para 2.1.
23 CPS Disclosure Manual, para 10.13.
24 Attorney General's Guidelines on Disclosure (2005), para 26.
25 Review of Disclosure in Criminal Proceedings, The Rt Hon Lord Justice Gross (September 2011), Executive summary, para 8.
26 Attorney General's Guidelines on Disclosure (2005), paras 26–27.

certain categories of data.[27] If search tools are used to examine digital material it will usually be appropriate to provide the accused with a copy of the reasonable search terms used, or to be used, and invite defence input of search terms to ensure that reasonable and proportionate searches are carried out.[28] The service of a defence statement is not a pre-condition to this defence input.

2.16   With vast quantities of electronic material, it is important that parties cooperate responsibly to see that the case is dealt with efficiently and expeditiously. As part of its case management function, the court should give a firm and clear steer as to what is required and short shrift to any party not engaging appropriately.[29]

2.17   If such material is not examined in detail, it must still be described on the disclosure schedules accurately and as clearly as possible. The extent and manner of the examination of the material must also be described together with justification for such action.[30]

2.18   The prosecutor is required to take action where he believes the disclosure officer has not examined all relevant material retained by the investigator and request that it be done.[31]

2.19   A disclosure officer's examination of material retained by an investigator must be at least sufficient for him to:

- decide whether the material may be relevant;

- describe the material that may be relevant adequately on the appropriate schedule;

- decide whether the material satisfies the prosecution test for disclosure; and

- decide whether the material is non-sensitive or sensitive (in whole or in part) and, if it is sensitive, to explain why.

---

27 Supplementary Attorney General's Guidelines on Disclosure – Digitally Stored Material (2011), para 44; CPS Disclosure Manual, Chs 29–31.
28 Supplementary Attorney General's Guidelines on Disclosure – Digitally Stored Material (2011), para 44.
29 Review of Disclosure in Criminal Proceedings, The Rt Hon Lord Justice Gross (September 2011), Executive summary, para 8(xxvii); CPR 2012, r 3.2.
30 Attorney General's Guidelines on Disclosure (2005), para 27.
31 Attorney General's Guidelines on Disclosure (2005), para 34.

SCHEDULING

Timing

2.20   The disclosure officer is responsible for preparing the schedules and he must give them, signed and dated, to the prosecutor. He must ensure that a schedule is prepared where:

'–   the accused is charged with an offence which is triable only on indictment;

–   the accused is charged with an offence which is triable either way, and it is considered either that the case is likely to be tried on indictment or that he is likely to plead not guilty at a summary trial;

–   the accused is charged with a summary offence, and it is considered that he is likely to plead not guilty.'[32]

2.21   In respect of either way and summary offences, a schedule may not be needed if a person has admitted the offence or if a police officer witnessed the offence and that person has not denied it.[33] Where it is believed that the accused is likely to plead guilty at summary trial, it is not necessary to prepare a schedule in advance.[34] If the accused subsequently pleads not guilty or the matter is to be tried on indictment, the disclosure officer must ensure that a schedule is prepared as soon as is reasonably practicable thereafter.[35]

2.22   The duty to prepare a schedule does not arise under the CPIA Code until the accused has been charged. This duty is not inflexible and the officer in charge should be mindful that there may be advantages to the early preparation of schedules and early appointment of a disclosure officer.[36]

2.23   The submission of the schedules by the disclosure officer should be at the same time,[37] wherever practicable,[38] as he gives the prosecutor the full file containing the material for the prosecution case.[39]

---

32 CPIA Code, para 6.6.
33 CPIA Code, para 6.7.
34 CPIA Code, para 6.8.
35 CPIA Code, para 6.8.
36 CPS Disclosure Manual, para 6.3.
37 Or as soon as reasonably practicable after the decision on mode of trial or the plea, in cases to which CPIA Code, para 6.8 applies.
38 Disclosure Protocol, para 14 says 'wherever possible' the schedules should be sent to the prosecutor at the same time as the file; CPS Disclosure Manual, paras 3.11, 6.1 anticipate that the schedules will be included with the full file.
39 CPIA Code, para 7.1; CPS Disclosure Manual, para 6.1.

2.24   Discussions between the police and prosecution before the schedules are prepared may help greatly in large or complicated cases and the disclosure officer or officer in charge should not hesitate to contact the prosecution for early advice.[40]

Contents and format

2.25   Material must be listed on a schedule if:

- it may be relevant and has been retained in accordance with the CPIA Code; and

- the disclosure officer believes that it will not form part of the prosecution case.[41]

2.26   Material may be relevant if it appears to an investigator, the officer in charge or the disclosure officer that it has some bearing on any offence under investigation or any person being investigated, or on the surrounding circumstances of the case, unless it is incapable of having any impact on the case.[42]

2.27   The officer in charge, disclosure officer or an investigator may seek advice from the prosecutor about whether any particular item of material may be relevant to the investigation[43] and this should take place as soon as practicable.[44]

2.28   It is essential that the disclosure officer ensures that individual items, subject to the exception of block scheduling (see **2.39**), are listed separately on the schedule and are numbered consecutively. It is crucial that descriptions by disclosure officers in non-sensitive schedules are detailed, clear and accurate. The descriptions may require a summary of the contents of the retained material to assist the prosecutor to make an informed decision on disclosure.[45] Where continuation sheets are used or additional schedules sent in later submissions, the numbering of items must be consecutive to the numbering on the earlier schedules.[46]

---

40 CPS Disclosure Manual, para 10.11.
41 CPIA Code, para 6.2.
42 As defined in CPIA Code, para 2.1.
43 CPIA Code, para 6.1.
44 CPS Disclosure Manual, para 6.2.
45 Attorney General's Guidelines on Disclosure (2005), para 29. See CPIA Code, para 6.9; Supplementary Attorney General's Guidelines on Disclosure – Digitally Stored Material (2011), para 50; Disclosure Protocol, para 14; CPS Disclosure Manual, paras 7.2–7.3.
46 CPS Disclosure Manual, para 7.2.

2.29   Sensitive schedules must contain sufficient information to enable the prosecutor to make an informed decision as to whether or not the material itself should be viewed, to the extent possible without compromising the confidentiality of the information.[47]

Non-sensitive material (MG6C)[48]

2.30   Material which the disclosure officer does not believe to be sensitive must be listed on a schedule of non-sensitive material (MG6C). The schedule must contain a statement that the disclosure officer does not believe the material to be sensitive.[49] Material which contains some sensitive information (such as personal contact details) but is otherwise non-sensitive should be edited and the edited material scheduled on the MG6C. The unedited version can be scheduled on the MG6D.[50]

2.31   In practice, the non-sensitive schedules are valuable to the defence in that they allow the defence to request hitherto undisclosed material which might satisfy the prosecution disclosure test[51] as well as to point out inadequately described items.

Sensitive material (MG6D)[52]

2.32   Sensitive material is material the disclosure of which the disclosure officer believes would give rise to a real risk of serious prejudice to an important public interest.[53]

2.33   Any material believed to be sensitive must be listed either on a schedule of sensitive material or, in exceptional circumstances, revealed to the prosecutor separately. Where there is no sensitive material, the disclosure officer must record this fact on a schedule of sensitive material.[54] The schedule must include a

---

47   Attorney General's Guidelines on Disclosure (2005), para 29.
48   For a copy of an MG6C form see **Appendix 8**.
49   CPIA Code, para 6.3.
50   CPS Disclosure Manual, para 8.21.
51   i.e. any prosecution material which might reasonably be considered capable of undermining the case for the prosecution against the accused or of assisting the case for the accused.
52   For a copy of an MG6C form see **Appendix 8**.
53   CPIA Code, para 2.1.
54   CPIA Code, para 6.4.

statement that the disclosure officer believes the material to be sensitive and the reason for that belief.[55]

2.34   Paragraph 6.12, CPIA Code provides a list[56] of examples of material which might be sensitive:

'–   material relating to national security;

–   material received from the intelligence and security agencies;

–   material relating to intelligence from foreign sources which reveals sensitive intelligence gathering methods;

–   material given in confidence;[57]

–   material relating to the identity or activities of informants, or undercover police officers, or witnesses, or other persons supplying information to the police who may be in danger if their identities are revealed;

–   material revealing the location of any premises or other places used for police surveillance, or the identity of any person allowing a police officer to use them for surveillance;

–   material revealing, either directly or indirectly, techniques and methods relied upon by a police officer in the course of a criminal investigation, for example covert surveillance techniques, or other methods of detecting crime;

–   material whose disclosure might facilitate the commission of other offences or hinder the prevention and detection of crime;

–   material upon the strength of which search warrants were obtained;

–   material containing details of persons taking part in identification parades;

–   material supplied to an investigator during a criminal investigation which has been generated by an official of a body concerned with the regulation or supervision of bodies corporate or of persons engaged in financial activities, or which has been generated by a person retained by such a body;

---

55   CPIA Code, para 6.12.

56   This list is not determinative and each item must be considered independently before it is included in the sensitive schedule.

57   Any doubts as to whether the information was given in confidence should be clarified with the provider of the information: see CPS Disclosure Manual, para 8.8.

– material supplied to an investigator during a criminal investigation which relates to a child or young person and which has been generated by a local authority social services department, an Area Child Protection Committee or other party contacted by an investigator during the investigation;

– material relating to the private life of a witness.'

2.35 To assist the prosecutor in deciding how to deal with sensitive material that satisfies the prosecution disclosure test,[58] paragraph 8.13, CPS Disclosure Manual advises that the investigator and disclosure officer should provide detailed information of:

'• the reasons why the material is said to be sensitive

• the degree of sensitivity said to attach to the material, in other words, why it is considered that disclosure will create a real risk of serious prejudice to an important public interest

• the consequences of revealing to the defence

  • the material itself

  • the category of the material

  • the fact that an application may be made

• the apparent significance of the material to the issues in the trial

• the involvement of any third parties in bringing the material to the attention of the police

• where the material is likely to be the subject of an order for disclosure, what the police view is regarding continuance of the prosecution

• whether it is possible to disclose the material without compromising its sensitivity.'

2.36 There is no requirement to include material on the sensitive schedule where the investigator considers the material so sensitive that it would be inappropriate to record it. This exception will only apply where compromising the material would be likely to lead directly to the loss of life, or directly threaten national security.[59]

---

58 i.e. any prosecution material which might reasonably be considered capable of undermining the case for the prosecution against the accused or of assisting the case for the accused.

59 CPIA Code, para 6.13.

2.37   The investigator who knows the details of the 'highly' sensitive material should inform the prosecutor as soon as is reasonably practicable after the file containing the material for the prosecution case is sent to the prosecutor. Such material should be listed and described on a separate 'highly sensitive' MG6D. It must be ensured that the prosecutor is able to inspect the material to assess its disclosability.[60]

2.38   Where there is no sensitive material the disclosure officer should still submit the MG6D endorsed and signed to that effect.[61]

Block scheduling

2.39   It may not be practicable to list each item of material separately when there are many items of a similar or repetitive nature. These items may be listed in a block and described by a quantity and generic title.[62] Block scheduling[63] is subject to the caveat that the disclosure officer must ensure that any items among the material that is listed in a block which might satisfy the prosecution disclosure test[64] are listed and described individually.[65]

2.40   The inappropriate use of generic listing by the disclosure officer is likely to lead to requests from the prosecutor and the defence to see the items which may lead to wasted resources and unnecessary delay.[66]

REVELATION TO THE PROSECUTOR

Schedules

2.41   The disclosure officer must give the schedules to the prosecutor. Wherever practicable this should be done at the same time as he gives him the file containing the material for the prosecution case.[67]

---

60 CPIA Code, para 6.14.
61 CPS Disclosure Manual, para 8.3.
62 CPIA Code, para 6.10.
63 Review of Disclosure in Criminal Proceedings, The Rt Hon Lord Justice Gross (September 2011), paras 8(vi), 57–58, 120 called for the greater use of block listing.
64 i.e. any prosecution material which might reasonably be considered capable of undermining the case for the prosecution against the accused or of assisting the case for the accused.
65 CPIA Code, para 6.11; see Supplementary Attorney General's Guidelines on Disclosure – Digitally Stored Material (2011), para 51; CPS Disclosure Manual, paras 7.5, 31.42.
66 CPS Disclosure Manual, para 7.4.
67 CPIA Code, para 7.1.

Disclosure officer's report (MG6E)[68]

2.42   The disclosure officer is required to submit the disclosure officer's report (MG6E) detailing any material an investigator has retained, including sensitive material not listed on the MG6D,[69] which may satisfy the prosecution disclosure test.[70] He should also explain on the MG6E, with reference to the relevant item number, why he has come to that view.[71] Copies of the material that the disclosure officer believes satisfies the prosecution disclosure test should accompany the MG6E.

2.43   Material that can satisfy the prosecution disclosure test will include anything that tends to show a fact inconsistent with the elements of the case that must be proved by the prosecution.[72] This can be through its use in cross-examination or by its capacity to support a legal argument or suggest an explanation for the accused's actions.[73]

2.44   Unless this material has already been supplied in the prosecution file, certain categories of material are so self-evidently capable of satisfying the prosecution disclosure test that paragraph 7.3, CPIA Code expressly stipulates that it must be given to the prosecutor, namely:

'–   information provided by an accused person which indicates an explanation for the offence with which he has been charged;

–   any material casting doubt on the reliability of a confession;[74]

–   any material casting doubt on the reliability of a prosecution witness;

–   any other material which the investigator believes may satisfy the test for prosecution disclosure in the Act.'

2.45   Other examples of material that would satisfy the prosecution disclosure test are:

---

68   For a copy of an MG6E form see **Appendix 8**.
69   CPIA Code, para 7.2. Note this is in contrast to CPIA Code, para 6.13 which states that the responsibility for informing the prosecutor of material too sensitive to be entered on the sensitive schedule lies with the investigator. See also **fn 54**.
70   i.e. any prosecution material which might reasonably be considered capable of undermining the case for prosecution against the accused or of assisting the case for the accused.
71   CPIA Code, para 7.2; CPS Disclosure Manual, para 10.7.
72   Attorney General's Guidelines on Disclosure (2005), para 10; CPS Disclosure Manual, para 10.3.
73   Attorney General's Guidelines on Disclosure (2005), para 10.3.
74   This may include the accused's mental or physical health, his intellectual capacity or any alleged ill-treatment in custody; see CPS Disclosure Manual, para 10.1.

- material which may point to another person, whether charged or not (including a co-accused) having involvement in the commission of the offence;[75]

- material that might support a defence that is either raised by the defence or apparent from the prosecution papers;[76]

- material which may have a bearing on the admissibility of any prosecution evidence;[77]

- any previous convictions and cautions for prosecution witnesses;[78]

- any motives for making false allegations by prosecution witnesses;[79] and

- whether the witness has sought, been offered or received a reward.[80]

2.46   To assist prosecutors to review the case, copies of the crime report and the log of messages (edited if necessary) should routinely be copied to the prosecutor in every case in which a full file is provided.[81] If sensitive material cannot be edited the material should be listed on the MG6D.[82] Local arrangements between the police and CPS may provide for other types of material to be routinely disclosed.

2.47   The disclosure officer should use a wide interpretation when identifying material that might satisfy the prosecution disclosure test.[83] He should consult with the prosecutor where necessary to help identify material that may require disclosure.[84] While items of material when viewed in isolation may not satisfy the prosecution disclosure test they may do so when viewed together.[85]

2.48   If the prosecutor asks to inspect material which has not already been copied to him, the disclosure officer must allow him to inspect it. If the prosecutor asks for a copy of material (which has not already been copied to him) he must be given a copy unless the disclosure officer believes, having consulted with the officer in charge, that the material is too sensitive to be copied and can only be inspected.[86]

---

75 Attorney General's Guidelines on Disclosure (2005), para 12.2.
76 Attorney General's Guidelines on Disclosure (2005), para 12.5.
77 Attorney General's Guidelines on Disclosure (2005), para 12.6.
78 CPS Disclosure Manual, para 10.1.
79 CPS Disclosure Manual, para 10.1.
80 CPS Disclosure Manual, para 10.1.
81 CPS Disclosure Manual, para 10.8–10.9.
82 CPS Disclosure Manual, paras 10.9–10.10.
83 CPS Disclosure Manual, para 10.5.
84 CPS Disclosure Manual, para 10.5.
85 Attorney General's Guidelines on Disclosure (2005), para 13.
86 CPIA Code, para 7.4.

2.49   Where material consists of information, which is recorded other than in writing, it is for the disclosure officer and prosecutor to agree whether the information should be given in its original form or in relevant extracts in the same form or in a transcript.[87]

Other police forms

2.50   The disclosure officer should submit an MG6 in the prosecution file. The MG6 contains any observations or explanations regarding the contents of the schedules and indicates whether the investigation commenced on or before 4 April 2005.[88] Where a relevant officer has misconduct or disciplinary findings against him these should be recorded on the MG6B.[89] The disclosure officer should inform the prosecutor of any additional enquiries that have been carried out in response to the defence statement and any results. This should be done on the MG20.[90]

2.51   The schedules and accompanying material should be brought to the attention of the prosecutor 'as soon as possible'.[91] There is no other time stipulation in either the CPIA Code or CPS Disclosure Manual.

CONTINUING DISCLOSURE

2.52   Section 7A, CPIA 1996 imposes a continuing duty on the prosecutor, for the duration of criminal proceedings against the accused, to disclose material which satisfies the prosecution disclosure test (subject to public interest immunity and section 17, Regulation of Investigatory Powers Act 2000). To enable the prosecutor to discharge this continuing duty of disclosure, any new material coming to light after the initial investigations should be treated in the same way as the earlier material.[92]

2.53   New material, which may be relevant to the investigation but which does not form part of the prosecution case, must be described on a further MG6C, MG6D or a continuation sheet and signed and dated before being submitted to

---

87 CPIA Code, para 7.5
88 Prior to 4 April 2005, different disclosure provisions apply. See CPS Disclosure Manual, paras 6.6–6.7.
89 CPS Disclosure Manual, para 11.6 and Ch 18 generally.
90 CPS Disclosure Manual, para 15.21. For a copy of an MG20 form see **Appendix 8**.
91 CPS Disclosure Manual, para 11.7.
92 CPIA Code, para 8.2.

the prosecutor. A further MG6E[93] should be submitted even if none of the new material satisfies the prosecution disclosure test.[94]

2.54   After a defence statement has been served, the CPIA Code places a specific duty on the disclosure officer to look again at the material (sensitive and non-sensitive) that has been retained and draw the attention of the prosecutor to any material which satisfies the prosecution disclosure test.[95]

Amending and updating

2.55   The disclosure officer is responsible for keeping the schedules accurate and up-to-date. As the investigation progresses schedules may need to be amended and any such amendments should be done promptly and returned to the prosecutor as soon as possible.[96] If the disclosure officer is required by the prosecutor to remedy defects in the schedules, he must immediately take all necessary remedial action to furnish the prosecutor with properly completed schedules.[97]

2.56   When the schedules are first submitted to the prosecutor, the disclosure officer may not know exactly what material will form the case against the accused and the prosecutor may not have given advice about the likely relevance of particular items. Once these matters have been determined, paragraph 8.1, CPIA Code provides that:

'the disclosure officer must be given to the prosecutor, where necessary, any amended schedule listing any additional material:

–   which may be relevant to the investigation,

–   which does not form part of the case against the accused,

–   which is not already listed on the schedule, and

–   which he believes is not sensitive,

unless he is informed in writing by the prosecutor that the prosecutor intends to disclose the material to the defence.'

---

93   Disclosure officer's report.
94   CPS Disclosure Manual, para 10.25–10.26.
95   i.e. any prosecution material which might reasonably be considered capable of undermining the case for prosecution against the the accused or of assisting the case for the accused. CPIA Code, para 8.3; CPS Disclosure Manual, para 15.20.
96   CPIA Code, para 10.24.
97   CPS Disclosure Manual, para 10.22.

2.57   If the prosecutor creates unused material by extracting statements or documents from the evidence bundle in the prosecution file and disclosing it straight to the defence, he can do so without waiting for the disclosure officer to amend the schedules but should advise the disclosure officer accordingly.[98]

CERTIFICATIONS BY DISCLOSURE OFFICER

2.58   The purpose of certification is to provide an assurance to the prosecutor that all relevant material that has been retained and made available to the disclosure officer has been identified, considered and revealed to the prosecutor.[99]

2.59   Certifications are required to show:

(i)   that the disclosure officer has revealed to the prosecutor all relevant retained material. He should certify on the MG6E –

'To the best of my knowledge and belief, all relevant material which has been retained and made available to me has been inspected, viewed or listened to and revealed to the prosecutor in accordance with the Criminal Procedure and Investigations Act 1996 as amended, the Code of Practice and the Attorney General's Guidelines.'[100]

(ii)   that the disclosure officer believes that there is no material that satisfies the disclosure test. He should certify on the MG6E –

'I have reviewed all the relevant material which has been retained and made available to me and there is nothing to the best of my knowledge and belief that might reasonably be considered capable of undermining the prosecution case against the accused or assisting the case for the accused.'[101]

(iii)   that the disclosure officer believes that there is no material that satisfies the disclosure test following receipt of the defence statement. He should certify on a further MG6E –

'I have considered the defence statement and further reviewed all the retained relevant material made available to me and there is nothing to the best of my knowledge and belief which might reasonably

---

98   CPS Disclosure Manual, para 10.21.
99   CPIA Code, para 9.1; CPS Disclosure Manual, para 10.16.
100   CPS Disclosure Manual, para 10.16.
101   CPS Disclosure Manual, para 10.17.

be considered capable of undermining the case for the prosecution against the accused or of assisting the case for the accused.'[102]

2.60   The disclosure officer must sign and date each certification. Further certifications are necessary when any later schedule or material is revealed to the prosecutor and must also be signed and dated.[103] The case against each accused must be considered and certified separately.[104]

DISCLOSURE TO THE DEFENCE

2.61   The prosecutor is responsible for ensuring the disclosure of material under the CPIA 1996.[105] The disclosure officer, however, must disclose it to the accused[106] where the material has not already been copied to the prosecutor and the prosecutor requests its disclosure on the grounds that:

(i)   the material satisfies the prosecution disclosure test;[107] or

(ii)   the court has ordered disclosure after considering an application from the accused.

2.62   If material has been copied to the prosecutor and it is to be disclosed, whether the prosecutor or disclosure officer discloses it is a matter of agreement between the two of them.[108]

2.63   The disclosure officer must disclose material to the accused either by giving him a copy or by allowing him to inspect it. Where the accused asks for a copy of any material which he has been allowed to inspect, the disclosure officer must give it to him, unless in the opinion of the disclosure officer that is not practicable (e.g. the material consists of an object which cannot be copied or the volume of material is too great) or it is not desirable (e.g. a statement of a child witness in relation to a sexual offence).[109]

---

102   CPS Disclosure Manual, paras 10.14, 15.22.
103   CPIA Code, para 9.1.
104   CPS Disclosure Manual, para 10.15.
105   CPIA 1996, s 3.
106   CPIA Code, para 10.1.
107   i.e. any prosecution material which might reasonably be considered capable of undermining the case for the prosecution against the accused or of assisting the case for the accused.
108   CPIA Code, para 10.2.
109   CPIA Code, para 10.3.

2.64   Where the accused has been allowed to inspect material consisting of information which is recorded other than in writing, whether it should be given to the accused in its original form or in the form of a transcript is a matter for the discretion of the disclosure officer. If the material is transcribed, the disclosure officer must ensure that the transcript is certified to the accused as a true record of the material which has been transcribed.[110]

2.65   Where a court concludes that a sensitive document must be disclosed to the defence, it will be necessary to disclose this material if the case is to proceed. The document need not be disclosed in its original form. The court may agree that sensitive details still requiring protection should be blocked out or the contents of the documents summarised or that the prosecutor makes an admission[111] about the substance of the material.[112]

---

110 CPIA Code, para 10.4.
111 Pursuant to Criminal Justice Act 1967, s 10.
112 CPIA Code, para 10.5.

Chapter 3

Receipt and review by the prosecutor

INTRODUCTION

3.01 When the prosecutor receives the prosecution file from the police he has a number of functions to perform to ensure that the disclosure process runs smoothly.

3.02 This chapter deals with:

ROLE OF THE PROSECUTOR

3.03 The prosecutor must do all that he can to facilitate proper disclosure as part of his general and personal professional responsibility to act fairly and impartially, in the interests of justice and in accordance with the law.[1]

3.04 The prosecutor must also be alert to the need to provide advice to, and where necessary probe the actions of, the disclosure officers to ensure that their disclosure obligations are met.[2]

3.05 The (lead) disclosure officer is the first point of contact for all enquiries regarding the contents of the schedules and access to material which has not been

---

1 Attorney General's Guidelines on Disclosure (2005), para 32.
2 Attorney General's Guidelines on Disclosure (2005), para 32.

copied. The prosecutor should liaise closely with him and consult him regularly during the disclosure process.[3] Where the prosecutor has reason to believe that the disclosure officer has not inspected, viewed or listened to material, he should raise the matter immediately with the disclosure officer and request him to do so.[4]

OBLIGATIONS OF THE PROSECUTOR

3.06   Upon receiving the full prosecution file from the disclosure officer, the file should contain:

- an MG6[5] which contains any comments, observations or explanations of the schedules;

- an MG6B which details any criminal conviction, caution or relevant misconduct of police officers;

- copies of all material that satisfies the prosecution disclosure test and a brief explanation for that belief on form MG6E (disclosure officer's report);

- an MG6C[6] (schedule of non-sensitive material);

- an MG6D[7] (schedule of sensitive material or declaration that there is no sensitive material);

- copies of disclosable sensitive material (where appropriate);

- copies of the crime report and log of messages (edited where appropriate); and

- certifications of compliance by the disclosure officer on the MG6E (disclosure officer's report).[8]

3.07   Upon receipt of the prosecution file, the prosecutor's specific obligations under paragraph 33, Attorney General's Guidelines on Disclosure (2005) are to:

- review the schedules thoroughly;

---

3 Attorney General's Guidelines on Disclosure (2005), para 26; CPS Disclosure Manual, para 11.5.
4 Attorney General's Guidelines on Disclosure (2005), para 34; CPS Disclosure Manual, para 12.2.
5 The MG forms are found in the CPS/ACPO Manual of Guidance. See **Appendix 8**.
6 For a copy of an MG6C form see **Appendix 8**.
7 For a copy of an MG6D form see **Appendix 8**.
8 CPS Disclosure Manual, paras 6.6–6.7, 11.6; see CPS Disclosure Manual, Ch 18.

- be alert to the possibility that relevant material may exist which has not been revealed to him or material included which should not have been;

- take action at once to obtain properly completed schedules if no schedules have been provided or there are apparent omissions[9] from the schedules;

- take action at once if documents or other items are inadequately described or are unclear;

- return schedules for amendment if irrelevant items are included; and

- raise the matter with a senior investigator if the prosecutor remains dissatisfied with the quality or content of the schedules.

3.08   In addition to the above obligations, the prosecutor should check for items which ought to be listed on the MG6C[10] but have been wrongly included on the MG6D[11] and vice versa.[12] As the MG6D is not served on the defence, it is important that items erroneously appearing on the MG6D are identified as otherwise the defence may not be aware of their existence.

3.09   The prosecutor must always inspect, view or listen to any material, whether sensitive or non-sensitive, which he believes might reasonably be considered capable of undermining the prosecution case against the accused or assisting the case for the accused.[13] He should not simply rely on its description in the schedule. He should also satisfy himself that the prosecution can properly be continued having regard to the disclosability of the material reviewed.[14] The judgment as to what other material to inspect, view or listen to will depend on the circumstances of each case.[15]

3.10   The prosecutor should always inspect any material, whether sensitive or non-sensitive, where:

- the description (or the reasons given as to its sensitivity) remains inadequate despite requests for clarification;

- he is unsure of whether the material satisfies the prosecution disclosure test.[16]

---

9   CPS Disclosure Manual, para 11.8 – omissions should not delay disclosure as a continuation schedule can be provided.
10   Schedule of non-sensitive material.
11   Schedule of sensitive material.
12   CPS Disclosure Manual, paras 10.22, 11.12.
13   i.e. the prosecution disclosure test.
14   Attorney General's Guidelines on Disclosure (2005), para 35; CPS Disclosure Manual, para 12.1.
15   Attorney General's Guidelines on Disclosure (2005), para 35.
16   CPS Disclosure Manual, paras 11.13, 12.1.

3.11   For most crown court cases, the review and preparation of unused material for disclosure to the defence will normally start at the same time as the preparation of the papers for sending the accused to the crown court.[17]

3.12   Care must be taken to ensure that sensitive material is handled with the commensurate level of security.[18]

CONTINUING DUTY TO DISCLOSE

3.13   Section 7A, CPIA 1996 imposes a continuing duty on the prosecutor to keep the issue of disclosure under constant review until the accused is convicted or acquitted, or the case is discontinued. If at any given time there is prosecution material which satisfies the prosecution disclosure test[19] and it has not been disclosed to the accused, the prosecutor must disclose it as soon as is reasonably practicable.[20]

3.14   Any new material coming to light after the initial prosecution file has been compiled should be treated in the same way as material received earlier. It must be described on a further MG6C, MG6D or a continuation sheet and submitted to the prosecutor together with a further MG6E.[21] Numbering of items submitted at a later stage should be consecutive to those on the previously submitted schedules.

3.15   Section 7A, CPIA 1996 places particular significance upon the need to review disclosure after service of a defence statement.[22] Once the prosecutor is in receipt of a defence statement, a copy of it should be sent immediately to the lead disclosure officer. At the same time the prosecutor should draw the attention of the disclosure officer to any key issues raised by the defence statement and, where appropriate, give advice to the disclosure officer in writing as to the type of material to look for.[23]

---

17 CPS Disclosure Manual, para 11.16. At the time of going to press (November 2012), committals are in the process of being abolished.
18 CPS Disclosure Manual, paras 11.10–11.11, 11.17–11.28.
19 i.e. any prosecution material which might reasonably be considered capable of undermining the prosecution case against the accused or of assisting the case for the accused.
20 CPIA 1996, s 7A(2), (3).
21 CPS Disclosure Manual, paras 10.25–10.26.
22 CPIA 1996, s 7A (2), (5).
23 CPS Disclosure Manual, para 15.14.

3.16   Advice to the disclosure officer may include:

*   guidance on what material might have to be disclosed;

*   advice on whether any further lines of enquiry need to be followed, e.g. where an alibi has been given;

*   suggestions on what to look for when reviewing the unused material;

*   suggestions on whether an alibi witness be interviewed; and

*   the appropriate use of a defence statement in conducting further enquiries, particularly when it is necessary to speak again to prosecution witnesses.[24] The defence statement should not be shown to a non-expert witness.[25]

3.17   Upon receipt of the defence statement, the CPIA Code places a specific duty on the disclosure officer to re-visit the unused material (sensitive and non-sensitive) that has been retained and draw the attention of the prosecutor to any material which satisfies the prosecution disclosure test.[26] The disclosure officer should inform the prosecutor of any additional enquiries that have been carried out in response to the defence statement and any results. This should be done on form MG20. If no further enquiries are made the disclosure officer should explain why.[27]

3.18   Where the accused has reasonable cause to believe that there is prosecution material which is required by section 7A, CPIA 1996 to be disclosed to him and has not been, he may apply to the court for an order requiring the prosecutor to disclose it under section 8, CPIA 1996 (section 8 application). Applications for further disclosure should not be made as ad hoc applications but dealt with under the proper procedures.[28] (See **Chapter 6** for section 8 applications.)

ENDORSEMENTS TO THE SCHEDULES[29]

3.19   When considering his duty to disclose, the prosecutor should record all decisions on the MG6C, giving brief reasons for each decision in the 'comment' column where:

---

24 CPS Disclosure Manual, para 15.15.
25 CPS Disclosure Manual, para 15.19.
26 i.e. any prosecution material which might reasonably be considered capable of undermining the prosecution case against the accused or of assisting the case for the accused. CPIA Code, para 8.3; CPS Disclosure Manual, para 15.20.
27 CPS Disclosure Manual, para 15.21.
28 Attorney General's Guidelines on Disclosure (2005), para 19.
29 For the format of MG schedules see **Appendix 8**.

- the disclosability or otherwise of an item may not be apparent from its description;

- the prosecutor has decided to disclose material not identified as disclosable by the disclosure officer; or

- reasons might otherwise be helpful.[30]

3.20 Where an item is to be 'disclosed' the prosecutor should mark it with a 'D' and indicate whether a copy is attached. If the prosecutor considers that disclosure by 'inspection' is more appropriate the item should be marked with an 'I'.[31] The MG6C should be signed and dated by the prosecutor upon completion.[32]

3.21 Items that are 'clearly not disclosable' should be marked 'CND'.[33] Where the schedule description of an item is inadequate and there is insufficient time for the schedule to be amended, the item should be viewed and, if the material does not satisfy the prosecution disclosure test, be marked 'ND'.[34] The prosecutor must note that the disclosure test has been applied and that the item neither undermines the prosecution case nor assists the case for the defence.[35]

3.22 Where the defence are entitled to an item under the Police and Criminal Evidence Act 1984, e.g. a tape of the police interview or the custody record, yet the item does not satisfy the prosecution disclosure test, the prosecutor is instructed to mark it as 'CND' or 'ND' to ensure that there is no confusion between automatic entitlement and disclosure under the CPIA 1996.[36] In practice, the prosecutor will usually make a note that the item is available under the Police and Criminal Evidence Act 1984.

3.23 The decision of a prosecutor that an item is 'clearly not disclosable' (CND) should be based upon the disclosure officer's description of the item in the schedule. This applies both to sensitive and non-sensitive schedules. In practice, and in breach of the CPS Disclosure Manual, it is not uncommon to see items, whose descriptions are plainly inadequate for any proper assessment to be made upon disclosure, to be marked 'CND'.

---

30 CPS Disclosure Manual, para 12.27.
31 CPS Disclosure Manual, para 12.29.
32 CPS Disclosure Manual, para 12.28.
33 CPS Disclosure Manual, para 12.30.
34 CPS Disclosure Manual, para 12.31.
35 CPS Disclosure Manual, para 12.31.
36 CPS Disclosure Manual, para 12.32.

DISCLOSURE RECORD SHEET

3.24   A single disclosure record sheet should be completed in respect of all unused material, whether sensitive or non-sensitive.[37] The disclosure record sheet should record all decisions, enquiries or requests and the date upon which they are made relating to:

- the disclosure of material to the defence;

- the withholding of material from the defence;

- the inspection of material; and

- the transcribing or recording of information into a suitable form.[38]

3.25   The disclosure record sheet should also record all actions and events that occur in the discharge of prosecution disclosure responsibilities.[39]

3.26   For sensitive material, paragraph 11.26, CPS Disclosure Manual provides that:

'the disclosure record sheet is used to record all events and actions, which will include the following:

- receipt of the MG6D

- that a disclosure review has taken place (the outcome of such reviews will be recorded on the schedule itself)

- the receipt and review of any addenda to the MG6D

- contact with the disclosure officer or investigating officer in relation to sensitive unused material

- receipt of defence statements and further reviews

- any consultation with the prosecution advocate

- any discussions with any other parties regarding sensitive unused material such as the court, the defence advocate or third parties

- receipt of the prosecution advocate's advice in relation to sensitive unused material

- details of any informal disclosure, should it occur

- the fact of any PII applications.'

---

37   CPS Disclosure Manual, para 11.15.
38   CPS Disclosure Manual, para 11.14.
39   CPS Disclosure Manual, para 11.14.

3.27   Unlike the non-sensitive material schedule, the disclosure record sheet entries should not contain sensitive information and will only record the fact that an event occurred as opposed to detailing the reasons. The reasons and decisions should be detailed on the MG6D and cross-referenced to the disclosure record sheet.[40]

3.28   The disclosure record sheet is an important document in any disclosure challenge as it provides a chronological paper trail of the disclosure process from start to finish.

---

40   CPS Disclosure Manual, para 11.25.

Chapter 4

Defence statements

INTRODUCTION

4.01   Trial by ambush is no longer an acceptable defence trial tactic.[1] The defence need to adopt a proactive 'cards on the table approach'. The defence statement,[2] which is mandatory in the crown court, is a formal document that sets out the accused's defence and the issues with the prosecution case. It can also be used to identify areas of disclosure or reasonable lines of enquiry for the prosecution to consider.

4.02   This chapter deals with:

---

1   *R v Penner* [2010] EWCA Crim 1155, per Thomas LJ, para 19; *R (on application of DPP) v Chorley Justices.*
2   Often erroneously referred to as the defence case statement; *R v Rochford* [2010] EWCA Crim 1928, per Hughes LJ, para 1.
3   For a copy of a defence statement form for use with CPR 2012, Pt 22 (listed in Consolidated Criminal Practice Direction, Annex D) see **Appendix 9**.

COMPULSORY DISCLOSURE OF DEFENCE STATEMENT

4.03   Under sections 1(2) and 5(1), CPIA 1996, an accused in a trial on indictment in the crown court must give a defence statement to the court and prosecutor where:

1   the provisions of Part 1, CPIA 1996 apply; *and*

2   the prosecutor complies or purports to comply with his initial duty of disclosure under section 3(1), CPIA 1996.

4.04   Section 1, CPIA 1996[4] provides that Part 1 applies where:

- a person pleads not guilty in the magistrates' court or the youth court;

- a person is charged with an offence for which he is sent for trial;[5]

- a count charging a person with a summary offence is included in an indictment;[6] and

- a bill of indictment charging a person with an indictable offence is preferred.[7]

4.05   Where a person is charged with an offence for which he is sent to trial, the accused is not required to serve a defence statement unless:

- copies of the documents containing the evidence have been served on him;[8] and

- a notice pursuant to section 51D, Crime and Disorder Act 1998 has been served on him.[9]

4.06   To comply with, or purport to comply[10] with, his initial duty of disclosure under section 3(1), CPIA 1996 the prosecutor must:

---

4   This section, as amended by Criminal Justice Act 2003, s 41 and Sch 3, came into force on 18 June 2012 (see SI 2012/1320) and abolishes committal proceedings which used to trigger CPIA 1996, Part 1. All relevant cases are now sent to the crown court under the Crime and Disorder Act 1998. At the time of going to press (November 2012), this section had not been fully implemented in all local justice areas.

5   Crime and Disorder Act 1998, s 51.

6   Criminal Justice Act 1988, s 40.

7   Administration of Justice (Miscellaneous Provisions) Act 1933, s 2(2)(b) or Prosecution of Offences Act 1985, s 22B(3)(a).

8   CPIA 1996, s 5(3A)(a) and Crime and Disorder Act 1998, Sch 3, para 1.

9   CPIA 1996, s 5(3A)(b). The notice details the offences for which the accused is sent for trial and the place where he is to be tried.

10   CPIA 1996, s 5(1)(b).

'(a) disclose to the accused any prosecution material which has not previously been disclosed to the accused and which might reasonably be considered capable of undermining the case for the prosecution against the accused or of assisting the case for the accused,[11] or

(b) give to the accused a written statement that there is no material of a description mentioned in paragraph (a).'

If either of the above conditions is not satisfied the defence are not required to serve a defence statement.

4.07   The defence cannot ignore any failure by the prosecution to provide initial disclosure. Under the CPR 2012, each party must actively assist the court in fulfilling its case management duties[12] in furtherance of the overriding objective.[13] The defence must immediately notify the court and all parties where there is a 'significant' failure in the disclosure process and, if necessary, apply for a direction for disclosure. A failure is 'significant' where it might hinder the court in furthering the overriding objective.[14]

4.08   There is a statutory duty on the prosecutor to serve the non-sensitive schedule (MG6C) in order to comply with his duties of initial disclosure if it is in his possession at the time.[15] A failure by the prosecutor to serve the MG6C will not prevent time beginning to run for the service of the defence statement as the 'schedule is not itself a necessary component of nor the mark of primary [*initial*] disclosure'.[16] The CPS Disclosure Manual envisages that the MG6C will be served at the time of initial disclosure.[17]

4.09   When the prosecutor complies or purports to comply with his duty of initial disclosure by either disclosing material to the defence or serving a written statement that there is no such material, he must at the same time inform the court officer.[18]

---

11   i.e. prosecution disclosure test.
12   See CPR 2012, rr 1.2(1)(c), 3.2–3.3.
13   Which includes dealing with cases 'efficiently and expeditiously; CPR 2012, r 1.1(2)(e).
14   CPR 2012, r 1.2(1)(c).
15   CPIA 1996, ss 4(1), (2) and 24.
16   *DPP v Wood and McGillicuddy* [2006] EWHC 32 (Admin), per Mr Justice Ouseley, para 23.
17   CPS Disclosure Manual, paras 12.35–12.36.
18   CPR 2012, r 22.2.

CONTENTS OF DEFENCE STATEMENT[19]

4.10   Section 6A(1)(a)–(d), CPIA 1996[20] provides:

'... a defence statement is a written statement –

(a)   setting out the nature of the accused's defence, including any particular defences on which he intends to rely,

(b)   indicating the matters of fact on which he takes issue with the prosecution,

(c)   setting out, in the case of each such matter, why he takes issue with the prosecution,

(ca)[21] setting out the particulars of the matters of fact on which he intends to rely for the purposes of his defence, and

(d)   indicating any point of law (including any point as to admissibility or an abuse of process) which he wishes to take, and any authority on which he intends to rely for that purpose.'

4.11   Where a defence statement is served, details of an alibi must also be provided. Section 6A(2), CPIA 1996 provides:

'A defence statement that discloses an alibi must give particulars of it, including –

(a)   the name, address and date of birth of any witness the accused believes is able to give evidence in support of his alibi, or as many of those details as are known to the accused when the defence statement is given;

(b)   any information in the accused's possession which might be of material assistance in identifying or finding any such witness in whose case any of the details mentioned in paragraph (a) are not known to the accused when the statement is given.'

4.12   Evidence in support of an alibi is evidence tending to show that by reason of the presence of the accused at a particular place or in a particular area at a particular time he was not, or was unlikely to have been, at the place where the offence is to have been committed at the time of its alleged commission.[22]

---

19 For a copy of a defence statement form for use with CPR 2012, Pt 22 (listed in Consolidated Criminal Practice Direction, Annex D) see **Appendix 9**.

20 As inserted by Criminal Justice Act, s 33.

21 As inserted by Criminal Justice and Immigration Act 2008, s 60.

22 CPIA 1996, s 6A(3).

DEFENCE OBLIGATIONS

Generally

4.13   What the accused is required to disclose by section 6A, CPIA 1996 is what is going to happen at the trial.[23] Where the accused advances a positive case there must be compliance with the statutory obligations, clearly set out in section 6A, or the accused is at risk of the sanctions available under section 11, CPIA 1996.[24]

4.14   The accused is not required to disclose confidential discussions with his advocate nor is he obliged to incriminate himself if he does not want to. The fundamental rights of legal professional privilege and the accused's privilege against self-incrimination have not been taken away by section 6A, CPIA 1996.[25]

4.15   The accused is under a statutory obligation to serve a defence statement and his lawyers must not advise him against doing so. In *R v Rochford*[26] Hughes LJ stated:

> 'Can the lawyer properly advise an accused not to file a defence statement? The answer to that is "No". The obligation to file a defence statement is a statutory obligation on the accused. It is not open to a lawyer to advise his client to disobey the client's statutory obligation. It is as simple as that.' (para 22)

4.16   The accused equally cannot be advised to omit something from the defence statement which section 6A, CPIA 1996 requires. In *R v Rochford*[27] Hughes LJ stated:

> '... the lawyer's duty is first of all never to advise either the absence of a defence statement or the omission from it of something which section 6A requires to be there because of the way the trial is going to be conducted. The lawyer's duty is not to give the accused advice on what to do. The lawyer's duty is to explain the statutory obligation that he has and to explain the consequences which follow from disobedience of it.' (para 25)

---

23 *R v Rochford* [2010] EWCA Crim 1928, per Hughes LJ, para 21.
24 *R v Patrick Malcolm* [2011] EWCA Crim 2069; *R v Rochford* [2010] EWCA Crim1928, per Hughes LJ, paras 16, 24.
25 *R v Rochford* [2010] EWCA Crim 1928, per Hughes LJ, para 21; see the reasoning in the context of the Criminal Procedure Rules in *R (Kelly) v Warley Magistrates Court* [2007] EWHC 1836 (Admin).
26 [2010] EWCA Crim 1928.
27 [2010] EWCA Crim 1928. See also *R v Essa* [2009] EWCA Crim 43, para 18.

4.17   Where the accused admits guilt to his lawyer within the cloak of legal privilege but refuses to plead guilty he cannot be prevented from this course of action. He is entitled to sit through the trial to see whether the prosecution can prove the case or not. He is not under an obligation to declare an admission of guilt in his defence statement.[28] Likewise, an accused who refuses to give instructions either at all or on specific points is not obliged to declare his refusal to answer questions in his defence statement.[29]

4.18   In *R v Rochford*[30] Hughes LJ laid down general guidance where the accused advances no positive case:

'The defence statement must say that the defendant does not admit the offence or the relevant part of it as the case may be, and calls for the Crown to prove it. But it must also say that he advances no positive case because if he is going to advance a positive case that must appear in the defence statement and notice of it must be given. Unless the requirement is that the statement is made but no positive case is advanced it would be open to defendants simply to ignore sections 5(5) and 6A.' (para 24)

4.19   The CPR 2012 require 'a cards on the table' approach and a rigorous examination of each case is required at a plea and case management hearing (PCMH) in which there is a not guilty plea.[31] It is therefore necessary that:

'A typed defence statement must be served before the PCMH. If there is no defence statement by the time of the PCMH, then a judge will usually require the trial advocate to see that such a statement is provided and not proceed with the PCMH until that is done. In the ordinary case the trial advocate will be required to do that at court and the PCMH resumed later in the day to avoid delay and further costs to the public purse.'[32] (para 34)

4.20   Where an accused's solicitor purports to give a defence statement on behalf of the accused the defence statement shall, unless the contrary is proven, be deemed to be given with the authority of the accused.[33] Although it is good practice for the defence statement to be signed by the accused,[34] a court has

---

28   *R v Rochford* [2010] EWCA Crim 1928, per Hughes LJ, para 24.
29   *R v Rochford* [2010] EWCA Crim 1928, per Hughes LJ, para 24.
30   *R v Rochford* [2010] EWCA Crim 1928. See *R v Wayne Patrick Malcolm* [2011] EWCA Crim 2069.
31   *R v Alan Newell* [2012] EWCA Crim 650, per Sir John Thomas P, para 32.
32   *R v Alan Newell* [2012] EWCA Crim 650, per Sir John Thomas P.
33   CPIA 1996, s 6E(1); Attorney General's Guidelines on Disclosure (2005), para 16.
34   *R v Wheeler* [2001] 1 Cr App R 10, per Potter LJ, paras 52–53.

no power to order that a defence statement be signed.[35] A judge can require an accused where a statement is unsigned to satisfy him that the document really is his statement.[36]

Privilege against self-incrimination

4.21   The privilege against self-incrimination cannot be used to justify non-compliance with the disclosure requirements under the CPIA 1996. In *R v Rochford*[37] Hughes LJ, in considering the disclosure that an accused is required to give in a defence statement, said:

> 'Do legal professional privilege and the defendant's privilege against self-incrimination survive section 6A?[38] The answer to that is "Yes". What the defendant is required to disclose by section 6A is what is going to happen at the trial. He is not required to disclose his confidential discussions with his advocate, although of course they may bear on what is going to happen at the trial. Nor is he obliged to incriminate himself if he does not want to. Those are fundamental rights and they have certainly not been taken away by section 6A ...'

4.22   A deficiency in the prosecution case that could give the accused an advantage must be identified in the defence statement even though it gives the prosecution the opportunity to rectify it. As Stanley Burton LJ stated in *Malcolm v DPP*:[39]

> 'Criminal trials are no longer to be treated as a game, in which each move is final and any omission by the prosecution leads to its failure. It is the duty of the defence to make its defence and the issues it raises clear to the prosecution and to the court at an early stage. That duty is implicit in rule 3.3 of the Criminal Procedure Rules ...' (para 31)

4.23   His Lordship further stated:

> 'A criminal trial is not a game under which a guilty defendant should be provided with a sporting chance. It is a search for truth in accordance with the twin principles that the prosecution must prove its case and that a defendant

---

35   *R (on the application of Sullivan) v Maidstone Crown Court* [2002] EWHC 967, Kennedy LJ, para 17.

36   *R v Alan Newell* [2012] EWCA Crim 650, per Sir John Thomas P, para 32.

37   [2010] EWCA Crim 1928, para 21.

38   CPIA 1996 (contents required to be included in a defence statement).

39   [2007] EWHC 363 (Admin).

is not obliged to inculpate himself, the object being to convict the guilty and acquit the innocent.' (para 34)

4.24 Where the accused has a defence but he refuses to allow his legal representative to disclose it, there is a positive duty under rule 1.2(1)(c), CPR 2012 to notify the court. It is then for the court to decide how to proceed. The legal representative must not make himself complicit in a manipulation of the court process.[40] The Law Society Practice Note states:[41]

'It is essential to appreciate that the purpose of Rule 1.2(1)(c) is to enable the court to control the preparation process and avoid ineffective and wasted hearings.

When something goes wrong because of a failure of a defendant to co-operate with you the court should be made aware of this and if you fail to keep the court informed, you risk breaching your duty to the court under the provisions of the Rules.'

4.25 Where issues are not raised at an early stage and unnecessary costs are incurred as a result, the court can impose a costs order[42] (see **Chapter 11**).

Putting the prosecution to proof

4.26 Where an accused has no positive case to assert he is entitled to require the prosecution to prove its case but he must make his position clear to the court (see **4.18**). It is no longer sufficient to simply record on the defence statement that the prosecution are put to 'strict proof'.[43] The accused must state that he does not intend to assert a positive case. If he subsequently asserts a positive case at trial, it is likely that sanction will follow. A judge cannot require counsel to reveal his instructions if no positive case is going to be made. In *R v Rochford*[44] Hughes LJ stated:

'The judge was entitled to ask, and indeed to ask insistently and trenchantly. He was not, however, entitled to require counsel to reveal his instructions if no positive case was going to be made in any of the ways which we have

---

40 See *R v SVS Solicitors* [2012] EWCA Crim 319.
41 Law Society Practice Note, Criminal Procedure Rules 2011 (5 April 2012), para 5.4.
42 Costs in Criminal Cases (General) Regulations 1986 and Prosecution of Offences Act 1985, ss 19 and 19A.
43 In *Balogun v DPP* [2010] EWHC 799 (Admin), Leveson LJ, para 16 stated: 'For my part ... I do not accept that the spirit or letter of the Criminal Procedure Rules is complied with by asserting that the Crown is put to "strict proof"...'.
44 [2010] EWCA Crim 1928. See also *R v Essa* [2009] EWCA Crim 43, para 18.

identified or any other. From a position of ignorance the judge was not in a position to know, any more than we are at this stage, whether there had been a breach of section 6A or not. Only time will tell as the trial, which has not yet begun, proceeds.' (para 17)

4.27   Where the prosecution is simply being put to proof by the accused and no positive case is asserted, the accused may lose his right to determine which witnesses will be called. The 'Stop Delaying Justice' initiative[45] states that in those circumstances the choice of witness:

'... would remain an issue for the CPS. They would be charged with deciding what evidence they wish to call and how. They may ... decide not to call a witness where the defence will not accept them section 9, if they feel they can conduct the trial without them.'

4.28   If the evidence of a particular witness is not in dispute, it may more readily be admitted into evidence under the hearsay provisions of section 114, Criminal Justice Act 2003. In *R v Ishmael Adams*,[46] where a witness could not be located on the day of trial and his statement could not be read under the provisions of section 116, Criminal Justice Act 2003 (witness unavailable)[47] it was admitted under section 114. Hughes LJ, in giving judgment, stated:[48]

'... the true issue in the case was not possession but intent to supply [*drugs*] ... it was plainly in the interests of justice for the uncontentious matter of possession to be proved by the Crown by the admission of the edited witness statement ... To hold otherwise would not be to do justice; it would rather be to afford a defendant an escape on purely technical grounds ... There is no question of relieving the Crown of the duty of proving the essential elements of the case. The question is not whether it is for the Crown to prove it, but how the Crown shall be permitted to prove it. If parts of the Crown's evidence are in dispute, it is quite likely that it will not be in the interests of justice to permit those parts to be proved by the reading of a hearsay statement when the witness cannot be cross-examined and properly challenged. But if parts of the Crown's case are not in dispute then it is plainly in the interests of justice that those parts shall be permitted to be proved by them by means of the hearsay statement as in this case.' (para 19)

---

45   'Stop Delaying Justice', p 11. This initiative was implemented in magistrates' courts with the support of the Senior Presiding Judge (Goldring LJ).
46   [2007] EWCA Crim 3025.
47   As such steps as were reasonably practicable had not been taken to locate him.
48   *R v Adams* [2007] EWCA Crim 3025.

4.29   It is unclear whether the provisions of section 114, Criminal Justice Act 2003 may be deployed to prevent witnesses being called simply to see if they turn up.[49]

4.30   If it becomes clear that there is a positive case to assert, not previously identified to the court, an adjournment may be necessary. If costs are incurred as a result, the court may impose a costs order[50] (see **Chapter 11**).

TIME LIMITS

4.31   The accused must give a defence statement within 28 days for trials in the crown court from when the prosecutor complies or purports to comply with his initial duty to disclose.[51] The 28-day period applies to investigations commencing on or after 28 February 2011. In cases of any complexity, this time limit will often be too short, as it does not afford the defence sufficient time to assimilate the material and take an adequate proof of evidence from the accused.

4.32   The accused can apply for an extension of days in which to serve the defence statement. The court will only make an order if it is satisfied that it would be unreasonable to require the defence to comply within the specified time period.[52] The application must be made by the accused before the expiry of the time limit, specify the grounds and state the number of days of extension required.[53] There is no limit to the number of applications that can be made.[54]

UPDATED DEFENCE STATEMENT

4.33   Section 6B,[55] CPIA 1996 is not yet in force and, until implemented, the court has no power to order the service of an updated defence statement.

---

49   'Stop Delaying Justice', p 13.
50   Costs in Criminal Cases (General) Regulations 1986 and Prosecution of Offences Act 1985, ss 19 and 19A.
51   CPIA 1996, s 3(3) and Criminal Procedure and Investigations Act 1996 (Defence Disclosure Time Limits) Regulations 2011.
52   Criminal Procedure and Investigations Act 1996 (Defence Disclosure Time Limits) Regulations 2011, r 3(2).
53   Criminal Procedure and Investigations Act 1996 (Defence Disclosure Time Limits) Regulations 2011, r 3(2) and (3).
54   Criminal Procedure and Investigations Act 1996 (Defence Disclosure Time Limits) Regulations 2011, r 3(4).
55   As inserted by Criminal Justice Act 2003, s 33.

4.34   *Defence statements*

When in force, section 6B(1), CPIA 1996 will impose a duty upon the defence to update the prosecution as to the defence case either by the service of an 'updated defence statement' or by the provision of a written statement to the effect that there are no changes to be made to the defence statement as initially served.

4.34   An updated defence statement must comply with the requirements imposed by section 6A, CPIA 1996 by reference to the state of affairs at the time when the statement is given.[56] Section 6B(5) and (6), CPIA 1996 allows the court to order the service of the updated defence statement on other co-accused either of its own motion or on the application of any party.

4.35   Additional prosecution evidence and unused material, which has significance to an accused's case, is regularly served after his initial defence statement. Section 6B, CPIA 1996 will give the defence an opportunity to update their defence or provide further information that will allow the prosecutor to make informed decisions on disclosure or advise on further lines of enquiry.

SANCTIONS FOR FAULTS IN DEFENCE STATEMENT

4.36   Section 11, CPIA 1996 provides the sanctions for failing to comply with the statutory duty to (i) file a defence statement, and (ii) include those things which are required by section 6A, CPIA 1996. It is not open to the court to add an additional extra-statutory sanction of punishment for contempt of court.[57] The fact that a defence statement is served late does not prevent sanctions applying pursuant to section 11, CPIA 1996.[58]

4.37   Section 11(2), CPIA 1996 identifies nine triggers which will put the accused at risk of the sanction.[59] These are:

(a)   the accused fails to give an initial defence statement;

(b)   the accused is late in giving an initial defence statement;

(c)   not applicable (section 6B updated defence statements is not yet in force);

(d)   not applicable (section 6B updated defence statements is not yet in force);

(e)   the accused sets out inconsistent defences in his defence statement; or

---

56   CPIA 1996, s 6B(3).
57   *R v Rochford* [2010] EWCA Crim 1928, per Hughes LJ, para 18.
58   *DPP v Wood; DPP v McGillicuddy* [2006] EWHC 32 (Admin).
59   Seven triggers currently apply as s 6B is not yet in force.

(f)   at his trial the accused –

   (i)   puts forward a defence which was not mentioned in his defence statement or was different from any defence set out in that statement,

   (ii)   relies on a matter which, in breach of the requirements imposed by or under section 6A,[60] was not mentioned in the defence statement,

   (iii)   adduces evidence in support of an alibi without having given particulars of the alibi in his defence statement, or

   (iv)   calls a witness to give evidence in support of an alibi without having complied with section 6A(2)(a) or (b)[61] as regards the witness in his defence statement.

4.38   The consequence of any of the above faults is that, unless the fault involves failing to mention a point of law, the court or any party (i.e. prosecution or co-accused) may make such comment as appears appropriate and the court or jury may draw such inferences as appear proper in deciding whether the accused is guilty of the offence concerned.[62]

4.39   Where the accused puts forward a defence which is different from any defence set out in his defence statement, before deciding or in deciding to do anything the court shall have regard to (a) the extent of the differences in the defence, and (b) whether there is any justification for it.[63]

4.40   If the fault involves reliance on a point of law (including any point on admissibility of evidence or abuse of process), which was not mentioned in the defence statement, leave of the court is required before another party can make comment.[64]

4.41   Where no defence statement has been served or the defence statement is lacking specificity or otherwise does not meet the requirements of section 6A, CPIA 1996, the prosecutor should send a letter to the defence pointing this out. If the position is not resolved satisfactorily, the prosecutor should consider raising the issue at a hearing for directions to enable the court to give a warning or appropriate directions.[65] Section 6E, CPIA 1996 states that the judge, at a pre-trial hearing, shall warn an accused if it appears to him that the accused has not

---

60 For the text of s 6A see **Appendix 1**.
61 For the text of s 6A(2)(a)(b) see **Appendix 1**.
62 CPIA 1996, s 11(5).
63 CPIA 1996, s 11(8).
64 CPIA 1996, s 11(6).
65 Attorney General's Guidelines on Disclosure (2005), para 18.

fully complied with the statutory requirements relating to a defence statement so that there is a possibility of comment being made or inferences drawn.[66]

4.42   Leave is not required for a party to cross-examine an accused on the differences between his defence and defence statement.[67]

ADMINISTRATIVE SANCTIONS

4.43   Rule 3.5(6), CPR 2012 provides that if a party fails to comply with a rule or a direction:

'the court may –

(a)   fix, postpone, bring forward, extend, cancel or adjourn a hearing;

(b)   exercise its power to make a costs order; and

(c)   impose such other sanctions as may be appropriate.'

4.44   The danger of breaching the Criminal Procedure Rules and the inherent conflict between the client/solicitor privilege and a solicitor's duty to the court is illustrated in *R v SVS Solicitors*.[68] In this case the solicitors objected to the admission of hearsay evidence but failed to comply with the Criminal Procedure Rules[69] in that they did not give their reasons for the objection or disclose their defence case.[70] A prosecution witness (Mr Amoako) was flown from Australia for the trial but ultimately not called to give evidence. The Court of Appeal upheld a wasted costs order against the solicitors. Field J in giving judgment stated:

'24. ... No application setting out the grounds of objection to the admission of Mr Amoako's statement was served within the stipulated time or at all. This in our judgment, as the judge found, was a clear breach of CPR 34.3(2)(d). The judge was entitled to conclude that a cross-application setting out that part of Nseki's case [*defendant*] that he had to put to Mr Amoako should have been served or, if the client refused to sanction this step, the appellant firm should have ceased to act for him. The appellant's failure to take either of these steps was not a mere error of judgment. The defendant Nseki was manifestly seeking to manipulate the court's process. By insisting on the appearance of Mr Amoako without disclosing the defence case that was to be put to the

---

66   As inserted by Criminal Justice Act 2003, s 36; see also Disclosure Protocol, para 39.

67   *R v Tibbs* [2000] 2 Cr App R 309, per Beldam LJ, para 34.

68   [2012] EWCA Crim 319.

69   CPR 2010 applied at the relevant time.

70   As required by CPR 2010, r 34.3 (now incorporated into CPR 2012).

witness, the appellant firm made itself complicit in the manipulation being practised by their client. The judge was entitled to hold that the failure to comply with the rule was deliberate and that it was a serious breach. He was also entitled to find that the appellant's conduct was improper, unreasonable and negligent, for the reasons he gave.'

4.45   The impact of *R v SVS*[71] is significant. The Law Society have issued an updated practice note advising solicitors to inform the court if their clients prevent them complying with their obligations under the Criminal Procedure Rules:

'… a failure to do so, could be interpreted by the court as a manipulation of its process, and as improper, unreasonable or negligent conduct, could give rise to a Wasted Costs Order being made against the solicitor.'[72]

4.46   It must be borne in mind that the primary object of a wasted costs order is not to punish but to compensate. As the costs order can be regarded as having a penal element when it is ordered against a non-party, a mere mistake by a legal representative (or his employee) is not sufficient to justify an order; there must be a more serious error.[73]

4.47   For a wasted costs order to be made, the normal civil standard of proof applies but if the allegation is one of serious misconduct or crime, clear evidence will be required to meet the standard.[74] The procedure to be used is set out in rule 76.9, CPR 2012.

4.48   In relation to sanctions other than costs, where a party seeks to call an alibi witness not previously identified in the defence statement, a refusal to allow that witness to be called is likely to be regarded as a step too far and one that would require primary legislative sanction.[75] Different considerations apply to expert evidence: Part 34, CPR 2012 applies.[76]

---

71   [2012] EWCA Crim 319.

72   Law Society of England and Wales Practice Note, Criminal Procedure Rules 2011 (5 April 2012).

73   Practice Direction (Costs in Criminal Proceedings) [2011] 1 Cr App R 13, para 4.2.5(i), (iv), issued by Judge LCJ (30 July 2010).

74   Practice Direction (Costs in Criminal Proceedings) [2011] 1 Cr App R 13, para 4.2.5(vi).

75   *R (on the application of Tinnion) v Reading Crown Court* [2009] EWHC 2930 (Admin), per Mitting J, para 37; *R v Ullah* [2011] EWCA Crim 3275, per Moses LJ, para 13. Both cases were before the introduction of CPR 2011, r 3.5(6).

76   *R v Ensor* [2009] EWCA Crim 2519.

SHOPPING LISTS

4.49   Instructions permitting, the defence statement should be detailed, comprehensive and tailored to the issues in the case. The use of formulaic generalized 'shopping lists' is to be deprecated. Under the guidance available[77] there is scope for focused and reasoned defence requests for disclosure linked to a comprehensive defence statement to which the prosecution must respond.

4.50   The trial process is not well served if the defence make general and unspecified allegations and then seek far-reaching disclosure in the hope that material may turn up. The more detail a defence statement contains the more likely it is that the prosecutor will make an informed decision about disclosure and whether to advise the investigator to undertake further lines of enquiry.[78] The prosecution can identify further material under their continuing duty to disclose under section 7A, CPIA 1996 and the need for an application under section 8, CPIA 1996 (a section 8 application) may be eliminated, or at least, the areas of dispute narrowed.

4.51   A detailed defence statement assists not only the court in the management of the trial by focusing on the issues in dispute but also adds weight to defence submissions of prosecution failings in the disclosure process. In practice the defence frequently serve requests for disclosure upon the prosecution within the body of the defence statement. It is submitted that such requests are compliant with a party's duties under Parts 1 and 3, CPR 2012.

EXAMPLES OF DISCLOSURE REQUESTS

4.52   Listed below are examples of defence disclosure requests. Requests for disclosure must not be used indiscriminately and must be relevant and tailored to the issues in the case.

- Please provide the defence with copies of unused items (*insert numbers*) from the MG6C (*give date and reference number*).

- Has the complainant made previous false allegations against any other person? If so, please disclose copies of the relevant documentation.

---

77 Attorney General's Guidelines on Disclosure (2005), para 18; Disclosure Protocol, paras 43–44; CPS Disclosure Manual, para 15.10.
78 Attorney General's Guidelines on Disclosure (2005), para 15. The essential need for a full and careful defence statement is spelt out in Disclosure Protocol, paras 32–40; see *R v H & C* [2004] Cr App R 10, per Lord Bingham CJ, para 35.

- Please disclose the date, time, circumstances and any contemporaneous notes or record of every occasion when the complainant has given an account of the allegation.

- Has the complainant made any application to the CICA[79] or to any other agency for compensation? If so, please disclose details of the application including any account given of the alleged facts. Does the complainant intend to make any such application? Has the complainant received any advice from the police as to when and in what circumstances they might make such claims?

- Has the complainant received any counselling for the effects of the alleged offence? If so, provide details of when and by whom. Please supply all relevant documentation.

- Please provide copies of all notes and records of any contact the police have had with any civilian prosecution witnesses.

- Please confirm that all relevant entries in police notebooks have been read for disclosure purposes and are accurately and sufficiently described on the MG6C.

- Please give details of any investigations regarding contamination or collusion between the complainants.

- Has a major incident police book or equivalent record of actions or decisions been maintained and, if so, has it been reviewed for disclosure purposes?

- As far as the officer in the case, investigators or disclosure officers are aware, has there been any failure to record relevant material, such as a first complaint of witnesses, or has any relevant material been lost?

- Please confirm that the reviewing lawyer and/or prosecuting advocate has read the MG6D and the material described therein and satisfied himself that such material is properly categorized as sensitive as opposed to non-sensitive.

- Was any decision made as to what complainants should be told of the complaints of others? If so, please disclose full details.

- Please identify the disclosure officer and the date of his appointment.

- Please confirm that the disclosure officer has been trained under an 'appropriate training regime' in accordance with paragraph 14, Disclosure Protocol and, if so, when?

---

79   Criminal Injuries Compensation Authority (also sometimes referred to as the CICB).

- Please disclose copies of all police press releases and police copies of media broadcasts.

CROSS SERVICE OF DEFENCE STATEMENTS

4.53 The CPIA 1996 requires the accused to serve his defence statement on the court and the prosecutor,[80] not upon a co-accused. It is for the prosecutor to decide, and keep under review, whether the defence statement of one co-accused satisfies the test for disclosure to another, subject to issues of public interest immunity.[81]

4.54 Good practice would be for the prosecution to give the accused notice of any intention to disclose his defence statement to a co-accused, so that any issues of privilege, sensitivity, relevance and editing can be raised.

4.55 If the judge is of the opinion that seeing a copy of a defence statement would help the jury to understand the case or to resolve any issue in the case,[82] he may direct that the jury be given a copy of any defence statement, edited if necessary, to exclude inadmissible evidence.[83] The defence statement itself is not evidence, all it can ever do is to refer to matters which may become the subject of evidence.[84] It is sensible to take any defence statement(s) from the jury when they retire to deliberate.[85]

4.56 The direction to provide the jury with a copy of the defence statement may be made on the judge's own motion or on the application of any party.[86] In order to challenge on appeal a judge's decision to put a defence statement before the jury, the appellant would need to show that the judge's opinion was an unreasonable one that no judge could properly have reached.[87]

---

80 CPIA 1996, s 5(5).
81 *R v Cairns* [2002] EWCA Crim 2838, per Keene LJ, para 78; CPIA 1996, s 11(5). See also CPS Disclosure Manual, para 15.29.
82 CPIA 1996, s 6E(5)(b).
83 CPIA 1996, s 6E(4).
84 *R v Sanghera* [2012] EWCA Crim 16, per Aikens LJ, para 51.
85 *R v Sanghera* [2012] EWCA Crim 16, per Aikens LJ, para 80.
86 CPIA 1996, s 6E(5)(a).
87 *R v Sanghera* [2012] EWCA Crim 16, per Aikens LJ, para 49.

DRAFTING THE DEFENCE STATEMENT

4.57   The Bar Standards Committee (BSC) warns counsel that there is no halfway house when accepting instructions to draft a defence statement and that the professional obligations are considerable. Where counsel accepts the brief for trial, his legal aid fee will be deemed to include all necessary preparation including the settling of a defence statement.[88]

4.58   In their guidance[89] the BSC advises that when settling a defence statement counsel should recognize the crucial importance of obtaining all prosecution statements and documentary exhibits, a signed proof of evidence from the lay client (of sufficient detail to address properly the necessary issues) and statements from other material witnesses.

4.59   Counsel should ensure that the lay client realises the importance of the defence statement and the potential adverse consequences of an inaccurate or inadequate statement. There should be a proper informed approval of the draft by the lay client given the risks of professional embarrassment (should the lay client seek to disown the statement during cross examination).

4.60   Counsel ought to insist upon a written acknowledgement from the lay client that:

- he understands the importance of the accuracy of the defence statement; and

- he has had an opportunity of considering the contents of the defence statement carefully and approves it.

4.61   A conference may be necessary to ensure compliance with these fundamentals or, depending on the case, a written advice accompanying the defence statement may suffice.

---

88 Bar Standards Board Code of Conduct, r 604(b).
89 'The Preparation of Defence Statements', Bar Standards Committee (9 March 2011).

Chapter 5

Witness notices

INTRODUCTION

5.01   The accused is required to give to the prosecutor a witness notice that indicates which witnesses he intends to call at trial and to provide their details. The requirement to give a witness notice is compulsory regardless of whether the case is in the magistrates' court or the crown court and is a further indication of the change of culture effected through the provisions of the CPIA 1996 and CPR 2012 designed to abolish trial by ambush.[1] Before its introduction the only obligation on the accused to give notice of a witness that he intended to call at trial related to alibi witnesses.

5.02   This chapter deals with:

• the contents of a witness notice[2]	**5.03–5.06**
• the duty to amend	**5.07**
• the intention to call a witness	**5.08–5.10**
• time limits	**5.11–5.13**
• sanctions for faults in the witness notice	**5.14–5.18**
• administrative sanctions	**5.19–5.21**
• interviews of witnesses notified by the accused[3]	**5.22–5.34**
• interviewing witnesses for the other side	**5.35–5.38**
• expert witnesses	**5.39–5.40**

---

1 *R v Rochford* [2010] EWCA Crim 1928, per Hughes LJ, para 10.
2 For a copy of a defence witness notice for use with CPR 2012, Part 22 (listed in Consolidated Criminal Practice Direction, Annex D) see **Appendix 10**.
3 For a copy of the Code of Practice for arranging and conducting interviews of witnesses notified by the accused see **Appendix 11**.

CONTENTS OF A WITNESS NOTICE[4]

5.03   A witness notice requires the accused to provide to the prosecutor and the court the identity and particulars of any witness whom he intends to call. The notice applies to witnesses of fact and character. Section 6C, CPIA 1996[5] states:

'(1)   The accused must give to the court and the prosecutor a notice indicating whether he intends to call any persons (other than himself) as witnesses at his trial and, if so –

    (a)   giving the name, address and date of birth of each such proposed witness, or as many of those details as are known to the accused when the notice is given;

    (b)   providing any information in the accused's possession which might be of material assistance in identifying or finding any such proposed witness in whose case any of the details mentioned in paragraph (a) are not known to the accused when the notice is given.'

5.04   The requirement is only to provide the particulars of the witness. There is no requirement to disclose the substance of the evidence a witness is expected to give or identify the issue(s) to which his evidence relates. Additional provisions apply to expert witnesses (see **5.39**).

5.05   Details of alibi witnesses do not have to be given to the extent that they have already been given in the defence statement in accordance with section 6A(2), CPIA 1996.

5.06   The requirement for an accused to give a witness notice is compulsory. It applies in all cases in which either the accused pleaded not guilty in the magistrates' court or was sent or committed to the crown court on or after 1 May 2010.[6]

DUTY TO AMEND

5.07   The provision of a witness notice is a continuing duty and an amended notice must be given if there are any changes to the witnesses it is intended to call. Section 6C(4), CPIA 1996 states:

---

4   For a copy of a defence witness notice for use with CPR 2012, Part 22 (listed in Consolidated Criminal Practice Direction, Annex D) see **Appendix 10**.

5   As inserted by Criminal Justice Act 2003, s 34.

6   At the time of going to press (November 2012), committals are in the process of being abolished.

'If, following the giving of a notice under this section, the accused –

(a)   decides to call a person (other than himself) who is not included in the notice as a proposed witness, or decides not to call a person who is so included, or

(b)   discovers any information which, under subsection (1), he would have had to include in the notice if he had been aware of it when giving the notice,

he must give an appropriately amended notice to the court and the prosecutor.'

INTENTION TO CALL A WITNESS

5.08   There is no authority as to what 'intends' means in the context of section 6C, CPIA 1996. Assistance may be obtained from *R v Ensor*,[7] in which Aikens LJ, in considering the late service of a defence expert's report under CPR 2005, Part 24,[8] stated:

'In our view the effect of CPR Parts 1.2 and 3.3[9] together is that it is incumbent upon both the prosecution and defence ... to alert the court and the other side at the earliest practicable moment if they are intending or may be intending to adduce expert evidence. That should be done if possible at a PCMH. If it cannot be done then it must be done as soon as the possibility [of calling expert evidence] becomes live.' (para 30)

5.09   In light of *Ensor*, the most likely interpretation of 'intends' would be that an accused intends to call a witness when he has decided that he might call the witness. If a witness notice was required only after a final and settled intention had been reached, it would defeat the purpose of section 6C, CPIA 1996 to abolish ambush defences and may result in costly adjournments in order for the prosecution to interview the defence witness or investigate any potential bad character issues.[10]

---

7   [2010] 1 Cr App R 18.

8   CPR 2005, r 24.1 states: '... if any party to the proceedings who proposes to adduce expert evidence in the proceedings ... he shall as soon as practicable ... (i) furnish the other party or parties with a statement in writing of any finding or opinion which he proposes to adduce by way of such evidence ...'

9   The wording of CPR 2005, rr 1.2 (duty of participants in a criminal case) and 3.3 (the duty of parties) is identical in CPR 2012.

10   See **5.22** 'Interviews of witnesses notified by the accused' below.

5.10   Good practice dictates that a statement should be obtained from any potential defence witness before deciding whether it is intended to call him. To do otherwise is to risk giving the prosecutor details of a prospective witness who may support the prosecution case.

TIME LIMITS

5.11   The accused must give a witness notice within 28 days[11] for trials in the crown court from when the prosecutor complies or purports to comply with his initial duty to disclose.[12] The 28-day period applies to investigations commencing on or after 28 February 2011.[13] In cases of any complexity, this time limit will often be too short, as it does not afford the defence sufficient time to assimilate the material, take an adequate proof of evidence from the accused or obtain the contact details of potential eyewitnesses. Even when the solicitors or enquiry agents establish contact with potential defence witnesses, all too often the witnesses fail to maintain that contact or attend appointments.

5.12   The accused can apply for an extension of days in which to serve the witness notice. The court will only make an order if it is satisfied that it would be unreasonable to require the defence to comply within the specified time period.[14] The application must be made by the accused before the expiry of the time limit, specify the grounds and state the number of days of extension required.[15] There is no limit to the number of applications that can be made.[16]

5.13   As the filing of a witness notice is a compulsory statutory obligation it is not open to an accused's lawyers to advise him to disobey it.[17]

---

11   CPIA 1996, s 6C(3) – previously the time limit was 14 days.
12   CPIA 1996, s 3(3) and Criminal Procedure and Investigations Act 1996 (Defence Disclosure Time Limits) Regulations 2011.
13   Previously the time limit was 14 days.
14   Criminal Procedure and Investigations Act 1996 (Defence Disclosure Time Limits) Regulations 2011, r 3(2).
15   Criminal Procedure and Investigations Act 1996 (Defence Disclosure Time Limits) Regulations 2011, r 3(2) and (3).
16   Criminal Procedure and Investigations Act 1996 (Defence Disclosure Time Limits) Regulations 2011, r 3(4).
17   *R v Rochford* [2010] EWCA Crim 1928, per Hughes LJ.

SANCTIONS FOR FAULTS IN WITNESS NOTICE

5.14   Section 11(4), CPIA 1996 identifies two triggers which put the accused at risk of sanctions. These are where the accused:

(a)   is late in giving the witness notice; and

(b)   at his trial calls a witness (other than himself) not included, or not adequately identified, in a witness notice.

5.15   The consequence of either of the above faults is that the court or any party (i.e. prosecution or co-accused) may make such comment as appears appropriate but the prosecution or co-accused may only do so with leave of the court.[18] The court may also draw such inferences as appear proper in deciding whether the accused is guilty of the offence concerned.[19]

5.16   Where the accused calls a witness whom he has failed to include, or to identify adequately in a witness notice, the court must have regard as to whether there is any justification for the failure before it allows any comment to be made or adverse inference to be drawn.[20]

5.17   An accused need not call a witness indicated in the witness notice and no sanction attaches under section 11, CPIA 1996 or the CPIA Code for this failure. Having regard to the burden of proof, we suggest that it would be inappropriate for either the judge or prosecution to comment upon this failure save, if necessary, for the standard jury direction not to speculate about what a witness might have said.[21]

5.18   The judge, at a pre-trial hearing, shall warn an accused if it appears to him that the accused has not fully complied with the statutory requirements relating to a witness notice so that there is a possibility of comment being made or inferences drawn.[22]

---

18   CPIA 1996, s 11(7).
19   CPIA 1996, s 11(5).
20   CPIA 1996, s 11(9).
21   *R v Paul Wheeler* (1968) 52 Cr App R 28, per Winn LJ; *R v Shani Wright* 1999 WL 1457234, per Kennedy LJ, para 14, Criminal Law Review 2010, p 690.
22   CPIA 1996, s 6E(2); Disclosure Protocol, para 39.

ADMINISTRATIVE SANCTIONS

5.19   Rule 3.5(6), CPR 2012 provides that if a party fails to comply with a rule or a direction:

'the court may –

(a)   fix, postpone, bring forward, extend, cancel or adjourn a hearing;

(b)   exercise its power to make a costs order; and

(c)   impose such other sanctions as may be appropriate.'

5.20   Where a party seeks to call a witness not previously identified in the witness notice, a refusal to allow that witness to be called is likely to be regarded as a step too far and one which would require primary legislative sanction.[23]

5.21   A party who does not call a witness indicated in a witness notice may be at risk of costs if there has been a clear wastage of police resources as a result of not amending the notice.

INTERVIEWS OF WITNESSES NOTIFIED BY THE ACCUSED

5.22   The Code of Practice[24] for arranging and conducting interviews of witnesses notified by the accused (the Interview Code) came into force on 1 May 2010.[25] Any police officer or other person charged with the duty of investigating offences who arranges or conducts an interview of a person notified by the accused either as an alibi witness[26] or as a witness identified in the witness notice[27] must have regard to the Interview Code.[28] The main provisions of the Interview Code, often drafted in mandatory terms, are summarized below.

---

23 *R (on the application of Tinnion) v Reading Crown Court* [2009] EWHC 2930 (Admin), per Mitting J, para 37; *R v Ullah* [2011] EWCA Crim 3275, per Moses LJ, para 13. Both cases were before the introduction of CPR 2012, r 3.5(6).

24 For the text of the Code see **Appendix 11**.

25 The Criminal Procedure and Investigations Act 1996 (Code of Practice for Interviews of Witnesses Notified by Accused) Order 2010, pursuant to Criminal Procedure and Investigations Act 1996, s 21A.

26 CPIA 1996, s 6A(2).

27 CPIA 1996, s 6C.

28 CPIA 1996, s 21A(3).

5.23 *Witness notices*

5.23   Paragraph 3.1 requires that before any interview may take place a witness must be:

- asked whether he consents to being interviewed;

- informed why the interview is being requested;

- informed that he is not obliged to attend the proposed interview;

- informed that he is entitled to be accompanied by a solicitor;[29] and

- informed that a record will be made and he will be sent a copy.

5.24   Paragraph 3.2 requires that if the witness consents to being interviewed he must be asked:

- whether he wishes to have a solicitor present at the interview;

- whether he consents to a solicitor attending on behalf of the accused as an observer; and

- whether he consents to a copy of the record being sent to the accused and informed that it may nevertheless be required to be disclosed to the accused or any co-accused.

5.25   Paragraph 4 requires that before any interview takes place the accused or, if he is legally represented, his legal representative must be notified:

- that the interview has been requested;

- whether the witness consented to the interview; and

- whether he consented to a solicitor attending on behalf of the accused as an observer.

5.26   Paragraphs 5 and 6 deal with notification to the witness of the date, time and venue of the interview. There is no requirement to notify the accused's solicitor unless the witness has consented to his presence as an observer. Where the witness has consented to his presence, the accused's solicitor must be given reasonable notice of the proposed interview.

5.27   Paragraph 7 requires that:

- the identity of the investigator is recorded;

- the investigator has sufficient skills and authority to discharge his functions effectively; and

---

29   There is no extra legal aid funding for this role.

- the investigator must not conduct the interview if it is likely to lead to conflict of interest.

5.28   Paragraph 8 provides:

- the accused's solicitor may only attend if the witness has consented;

- the interview may proceed in the absence of the accused's solicitor provided he was given reasonable notice of the interview;

- if the witness withdraws his consent to the presence of the accused's solicitor the interview may continue in his absence; and

- the accused's solicitor may only attend as an observer.

5.29   Paragraph 9 requires that where a witness has indicated that he wishes to appoint a solicitor to be present that solicitor must be permitted to attend.

5.30   Paragraph 10 requires that a witness under the age of 18 or a witness who is mentally disordered or otherwise mentally vulnerable must be interviewed in the presence of an appropriate person.

5.31   Paragraph 11 requires an accurate record to be made of the interview whether it takes place at a police station or elsewhere. The record must be made, where practicable, by audio or visual recording with sound, or otherwise in writing. A copy of the record must be given to the witness within a reasonable time and, if the witness consents, to the accused.

5.32   Where the accused's solicitor is present as an observer in the interview of a potential defence witness, he has no right to intervene with the questioning as there is no solicitor/client relationship with the witness.[30] Provided there is no conflict of interest and the accused consents, the accused's solicitor can represent the witness if asked to do so and he can then intervene to protect the interests of the witness. The solicitor must withdraw if a conflict of interest arises between the witness and the accused.

5.33   The Interview Code does not contain any provision for warning witnesses of the consequences of withholding consent. Should any witness refuse their consent to be interviewed, it would be open to the prosecution or a co-accused to seek to cross-examine him on his reasons for the refusal to be interviewed. Further, any exchanges between the investigator and witness,

---

30   Law Society of England and Wales Practice Note, Defence Witness Notices (6 October 2011) sets out the obligations and ethical considerations that apply (see http://www.lawsociety.org. uk).

particularly under paragraph 3 above, may be material which may be relevant to the investigation[31] and must be recorded by the investigator.

5.34   The accused may be unaware of what a potential defence witness has said in interview because the witnesses account does not satisfy the prosecution disclosure test[32] and the witness has refused to allow the accused's legal representative to attend the interview or has refused to allow a copy to be sent to the accused. To persist in calling the witness in such circumstances creates an obvious danger to the accused that the witness will be cross-examined by the prosecution or a co-accused on an undisclosed account adverse to his case.

INTERVIEWING WITNESSES FOR THE OTHER SIDE

5.35   There is no property in a witness[33] and it is permitted for either the prosecution or defence to take a statement from a witness for the other side who has given evidence or, it is known, will be giving evidence. Where it is intended to take this course of action, it is wise to give notice to the other side stating –

*   that an interview is required;

*   the reasons for the interview; and

*   that a representative from the other side be present.[34]

5.36   The presence of a representative from the other side will help to avoid any suggestion of any attempt to change the account of a witness.[35]

5.37   A witness can refuse his consent to be interviewed. CPS guidance[36] suggests that where a witness agrees only to be interviewed at a police station, this facility should be made available. Where the defence seek to interview a police officer who is a prosecution witness, a senior police officer may be present,

---

31   CPIA Code, paras 2.1 and 4.1.
32   i.e. any prosecution material which might reasonably be considered capable of undermining the case for the prosecution against the accused or of assisting the case for the accused. Where the interview satisfies the prosecution disclosure test in respect of a co-accused it will be disclosed to that co-accused.
33   *Connolly v Dale* [1996] QB 120, per Balcombe LJ.
34   CPS Legal Guidance, Interviewing Witnesses for the Other Side.
35   Bar Standards Board Code of Conduct, Written Standards for the Conduct of Professional Work, para 6.2.7 states: '… a barrister should not discuss the substance of the case or any evidence with the other side's witnesses except in rare and exceptional circumstances and only then with the prior knowledge of his opponent.'
36   CPS Legal Guidance, Interviewing Witnesses for the Other Side.

who should preferably be unconnected with the proceedings in question.[37] If the defence wish to interview a police officer as a potential defence witness, CPS guidance suggests it is a matter for the Chief Constable or the CPS to determine the conditions for the interview, provided they are reasonable.

5.38 It may be a contempt of court for the prosecution to seek to prevent or discourage the defence from interviewing a prosecution witness or a potential prosecution witness.[38]

EXPERT WITNESSES

5.39 The advanced disclosure of expert evidence is governed by rule 33.4, CPR 2012 which requires a party who 'wants' to introduce expert evidence to serve the expert's report on the court officer and each other party as soon as practicable. A party may not adduce evidence if he has not complied with rule 33.4 unless every party agrees or the court gives permission.[39] This is in contrast to other defence witnesses where the substance of their evidence need not be disclosed to the prosecution (see **5.04** above).

5.40 Section 6D,[40] CPIA 1996, which is not yet in force, will impose an obligation on the defence to notify the court of an expert's name and address if he 'instructs a person with a view to his providing any expert opinion for possible use as evidence at the trial'. This is different from section 6C, CPIA 1996 (defence witness notices) in that it does not require any intention on the part of the defence to call the expert.

---

37 CPS Legal Guidance, Interviewing Witnesses for the Other Side.
38 *Connolly v Dale* [1996] QB 120, per Balcombe LJ.
39 *R v Ensor* [2010] 1 Cr App R 18.
40 As inserted by Criminal Justice Act 2003, s 35.

Chapter 6

Application for prosecution disclosure (section 8 application)[1]

INTRODUCTION

6.01   Once the defence statement has been served, the defence have the opportunity to apply formally to the court for further disclosure where they believe that the prosecution have not fully complied with their obligations under the CPIA 1996. This chapter deals with the application and procedure.

APPLICATION

6.02   Although the prosecution's continuing duty of disclosure under section 7A, CPIA 1996 exists until the conclusion of the trial, where the accused believes there is material that should still be disclosed he should make an application under section 8, CPIA 1996 (a section 8 application). Section 8(2)[2] provides:

'If the accused has at any time reasonable cause to believe that there is prosecution material which is required by section 7A[3] to be disclosed to him and has not been, he may apply to the court for an order requiring the prosecutor to disclose it to him.'

6.03   The section 8 application for disclosure can be made *only after* the accused has given a defence statement and the prosecutor has complied with, purported to comply with, or failed to comply with his duty to make disclosure as a result of the defence statement.[4]

---

1   For a copy of an application for prosecution disclosure form for use with CPR 2012, Pt 22 (listed in Consolidated Criminal Practice Direction, Annex D) see **Appendix 12**.
2   As amended by Criminal Justice Act 2003, s 38.
3   Continuing duty to disclose.
4   CPIA 1996, s 8(1); see CPIA 1996, s 7A(5).

6.04   Prosecution material[5] includes material which:

• is in the prosecutor's possession and came into his possession in connection with the case for the prosecution against the accused;

• in pursuance of a code operative under Part II, CPIA 1996, he has inspected in connection with the prosecution case against the accused; or

• in pursuance of a code operative under Part II, CPIA 1996, the prosecutor must, if he asked for the material, be given a copy of, or be allowed to inspect, in connection with the case against the accused.

6.05   Before making a section 8 application the accused should have considered an informal approach to the prosecution for disclosure of the material sought. The CPS Disclosure Manual advises that the prosecutor should consider each approach on its merits and, wherever possible, the disclosure issues should be resolved without the need for a court hearing.[6] Any informal disclosure should be recorded on the disclosure record sheet.

6.06   Section 8 applications should be limited to material which is referable to an issue in the case as identified by the defence statement. The use of generalized and non-tailored 'shopping lists' is wholly improper.[7]

PROCEDURE

6.07   In order to make a section 8 application, rule 22.5, CPR 2012 provides:

'(2)   The defendant must serve an application on –

    (a)   the court officer; and

    (b)   the prosecutor.

(3)   The application must –

    (a)   describe the material that the defendant wants the prosecutor to disclose;

    (b)   explain why the defendant thinks there is reasonable cause to believe that –

        (i)   the prosecutor has that material, and

---

5   CPIA 1996, s 8(3) and (4).

6   CPS Disclosure Manual, para 16.8.

7   Disclosure Protocol, para 45.

(ii)   it is material that the Criminal Procedure and Investigations Act 1996 requires the prosecutor to disclose; and

(c)   ask for a hearing, if the defendant wants one, and explain why it is needed.

(4)   The court may determine an application under this rule –

(a)   at a hearing, in public or in private; or

(b)   without a hearing.

(5)   The court must not require the prosecutor to disclose material unless the prosecutor –

(a)   is present; or

(b)   has had at least 14 days in which to make representations.'

6.08   A copy of the defence statement and copies of any correspondence with the prosecutor about disclosure should be attached to the section 8 application.

6.09   The wording of rule 22.5(5), CPR 2012 allows the accused to make a section 8 application and for the court to seek an immediate determination provided the prosecutor is present. In such circumstances, the CPS Disclosure Manual advises that the prosecution advocates should be robust in obtaining the necessary time to consider the matter properly and not allow the court to expedite timescales without good reason.[8]

6.10   Upon receipt of a section 8 application the prosecutor should consider afresh the items requested by the defence in consultation with the disclosure officer and, if necessary, ask for copies of the items or inspect the material as appropriate.[9] If he concludes that all or part of the requested material should be disclosed, that decision should be communicated to the defence without delay.[10]

6.11   Material must not be disclosed as a result of a section 8 application to the extent that the court, on an application by the prosecutor, concludes that it is not in the public interest to disclose it and orders accordingly.[11] If the material has already been the subject of a public interest immunity ruling, the prosecutor should remind the defence to use the procedures that are available to review the

---

8   CPS Disclosure Manual, para 16.8B.
9   CPS Disclosure Manual, para 16.2.
10   CPS Disclosure Manual, para 16.3.
11   CPIA 1996, s 8(5).

public interest ruling[12] to avoid the risk of jeopardizing the confidentiality of the material.[13]

6.12   Material must not be disclosed under a section 8 application to the extent that it is material the disclosure of which is prohibited by section 17, Regulation of Investigatory Powers Act 2000.[14]

6.13   If at the hearing of a section 8 application agreement is reached between the advocates in respect of the material to be disclosed, the agreement should be incorporated into a formal consent order to prevent any misunderstanding by the parties as to what has been agreed.[15]

6.14   The defence can only seek disclosure of material of which they are aware. Often this knowledge will be predicated upon the material detailed in the non-sensitive schedule of unused material (MG6C). A failure by the prosecution to prepare the MG6C properly in accordance with its disclosure obligations may adversely affect the disclosure obtained by the defence.

---

12   CPIA 1996, ss 14–15; CPR 2012, r 22.6.
13   CPS Disclosure Manual, para 16.7.
14   CPIA 1996, s 8(6).
15   *R v O* [2007] EWCA Crim 3483.

Chapter 7

Prosecution disclosure to the defence

INTRODUCTION

7.01   The prosecutor must disclose material to the defence where it satisfies the prosecution disclosure test[1] under the CPIA 1996 and he must be alive to the possibility that disclosure may be required under common law before the statutory duty to disclose is triggered. In addition, a suspect has certain entitlements to disclosure upon arrest and at the police station before charge.

7.02   This chapter deals with:

• pre-charge disclosure	**7.03–7.14**
• pre-caution disclosure (non statutory disposal)	**7.15–7.17**
• common law disclosure	**7.18–7.23**
• statutory disclosure	
– initial disclosure	**7.24–7.36**
– continuing disclosure	**7.37–7.41**
– time of service	**7.42–7.44**

PRE-CHARGE DISCLOSURE

7.03   Although there is no legal obligation under the CPIA 1996 or the CPIA Code to disclose material to the suspect prior to charge,[2] certain disclosure

---

1   i.e. any prosecution material which might reasonably be considered capable of undermining the case for the prosecution against the accused or of assisting the case for the accused, subject to considerations of public interest immunity and Regulation of Investigatory Powers Act 2000, s 17.

2   *R v Ara* [2001] EWHC Admin 493, per Rose LJ, para 25.

must be provided following the arrest of a suspect under the Police and Criminal Evidence Act 1984 (PACE) Codes of Practice, namely:

- A person who is arrested, or further arrested, must be informed at the time, or as soon as practicable thereafter, that they are under arrest and the grounds for their arrest.[3]

- An arrested person must be given sufficient information to enable them to understand that they have been deprived of their liberty and the reason they have been arrested, e.g. when a person is arrested on suspicion of committing an offence they must be informed of the nature of the suspected offence, when it was committed and where. The suspect must also be informed of the reason or reasons why the arrest is considered necessary. Vague or technical language should be avoided.[4]

- The legal representative or the appropriate adult must be permitted to consult a detainee's custody record[5] as soon as practicable after their arrival at the station and at any other time whilst the person is detained. Arrangements for this access must be agreed with the custody officer and may not reasonably interfere with the custody officer's duties.[6]

7.04   The legal adviser's right to view the custody record should never be overlooked as matters may be contained therein over and above any disclosure provided by an interviewing officer.

7.05   Sufficient disclosure should be provided to a suspect before his police interview to enable a solicitor to properly advise him.[7] A lack of police disclosure at a suspect's interview is particularly significant as it may prevent an adverse inference being drawn under section 34, Criminal Justice and Public Order Act 1994 where the accused has failed to mention in his interview a fact which he later relies on in court. In *R v Nottle*[8] Simon J stated:

---

3 PACE 1984 Code C, para 10.3 – where the issue is identification this may include the first description of the suspect.

4 PACE 1984 Code C, note 10B.

5 At the police station the custody officer shall record on the custody record the offences and the reasons that the detainee has been arrested, note any comment the detainee makes in relation to the arresting officer's account and, if the custody officer authorizes a person's detention, the detainee must be informed of the grounds as soon as practicable and before he is questioned about any offence.

6 PACE 1984 Code C, para 2.4.

7 *R v Argent* [1997] 2 Cr App R 27, per Lord Bingham CJ.

8 [2004] EWCA Crim 599.

'The purpose of the pre-interview disclosure[9] derives from the realisation by the police that, without proper disclosure, solicitors cannot properly advise their clients. They [*the police*] voluntarily provide disclosure in order to counter an argument at trial that no adverse inferences should be drawn under section 34 of the Criminal Justice and Public Order Act 1994 from the suspect's failure to answer questions ... The quality and quantity of disclosure will depend on the case. The officer must assess the risk of giving inadequate disclosure, namely that no adverse inferences will be drawn.'(para 14)

7.06   The Court of Appeal in *R v Argent*[10] rejected the argument that insufficient disclosure by the police prior to interview should render evidence of the accused's silence inadmissible.

7.07   The term 'sufficient disclosure' does not require the police to disclose the case against the suspect before interview[11] or to give his legal representative a full briefing.[12] The police must not actively mislead the suspect,[13] but they do not need to present him with all the evidence they have to prevent him from lying to them.[14]

7.08   There is no rule of law that requires the police to a reveal to a suspect the questions that they may wish to put to him in interview nor are they required to reveal in advance the topics that they wish to cover, even in the most general terms.[15] In some cases providing those details in advance of an interview will prejudice the police enquiries, but this is a judgment that must be left to the police.[16] Interviews must be conducted fairly but advance notice is not regarded as a pre-requisite to fairness.[17]

7.09   The CPS legal guidance on pre-interview disclosure[18] advises that if an investigator feels that it is necessary to withhold information from the legal representative during a pre-interview briefing, he should be able to explain clearly the reasons supporting this approach in any further proceedings.

---

9   See also *R v Hoare and Pierce* [2004] EWCA Crim 784, per Auld LJ, para 53 for the rationale behind Criminal Justice and Public Order Act 1994, s 34.
10   *R v Argent* [1997] 2 Cr App R 27, per Lord Bingham CJ.
11   *R v Ara* [2001] EWHC Admin 493, per Rose LJ, para 25.
12   *R v Imran and Hussain* [1997] EWCA Crim 1401, per Rougier J.
13   *R v Imran and Hussain* [1997] EWCA Crim 1401.
14   *R v Imran and Hussain* [1997] EWCA Crim 1401; see *R v Farrell* [2004] EWCA Crim 597.
15   *Ward v Police Service of Northern Ireland* [2007] UKHL 50, per Appellate Committee, para 22.
16   *Ward v Police Service of Northern Ireland* [2007] UKHL 50.
17   *Ward v Police Service of Northern Ireland* [2007] UKHL 50.
18   See CPS Legal Guidance, Adverse Inferences.

7.10   There may be good reason to prevent an adverse inference being drawn where a solicitor cannot 'usefully advise' his client because the interviewing officer has disclosed little or nothing of the nature of the case against his client[19] or where the suspect is unable to sensibly respond to the questions as a result of the complexity of the case,[20] the lapse of time,[21] the suspect's condition (ill-health, mental disability, confusion, intoxication, shock, etc.)[22] or his inability genuinely to recollect events without reference to documents which are not to hand or communication with other persons who may be able to assist his recollection.[23]

7.11   In complex or heavy fraud cases, the Protocol for the control and management of heavy fraud and complex criminal cases[24] recognizes the need to provide disclosure before the interview and to properly structure the interview to bring about some reduction in the length of trials. The protocol is primarily aimed at jury trials likely to last eight or more weeks but should also be followed in all cases estimated to last longer than four weeks. Paragraph 1(ii), Protocol states:

'(ii) Interviews

a)   At present many interviews are too long and too unstructured. This has a knock-on effect on the length of trials. Interviews should provide an opportunity for suspects to respond to the allegations against them. They should not be an occasion to discuss every document in the case. It should become clear from judicial rulings that interviews of this kind are a waste of resources.

b)   The suspect must be given sufficient information before or at the interview to enable them to meet the questions fairly and answer them honestly; the information is not provided to give the suspect the opportunity to manufacture a false story which fits undisputable facts.

c)   It is often helpful if the principal documents are provided either in advance of the interview or shown as the interview progresses; asking detailed questions about events a considerable period in the past without reference to the documents is often not very helpful.'

---

19   *R v Roble* (1997) CLR 449, per Rose LJ. The words 'usefully advise' are not defined.

20   *R v Roble* (1997) CLR 449, per Rose LJ.

21   *R v Roble* (1997) CLR 449, per Rose LJ.

22   *R v Howell* [2003] EWCA Crim 1, per Laws LJ, para 24.

23   *R v Howell* [2003] EWCA Crim 1, per Laws LJ, para 24.

24   Issued by the Lord Chief Justice (22 March 2005): 'The Protocol supplements the Criminal Procedure Rules and summarises good practice which experience has shown may assist in bringing about some reduction in the length of trials of fraud and other crimes that result in complex trials.' (Introduction to the Protocol)

7.12   The less complex the case, the more prepared the court will be to permit the drawing of adverse inferences where minimal disclosure has been made pre-interview.[25]

7.13   Laws LJ in *R v Howell*[26] observed that legal advisers should always bear in mind that there must be soundly-based objective reasons for silence, such as the accused's infirmness, his age or the complexity of the case which are sufficiently cogent and telling to weigh in the balance against the clear public interest in an account being given to the police. This observation must be considered in light of note 6D, PACE 1984 Code C, which stipulates that the solicitor's only role in the police station is to protect and advance the legal rights of his client. This may require the solicitor to give advice which has the effect of the client avoiding giving evidence which strengthens the prosecution case.

7.14   Paragraph 11.4A, PACE 1984 Code C provides that at the beginning of an interview the interviewer, after cautioning the suspect, shall put to him any significant statement or silence[27] which occurred in the presence or hearing of a police officer or other police staff before the start of the interview and which has not been put to the suspect in a previous interview. The interviewer shall ask the suspect whether he confirms or denies that earlier statement or silence and if he wants to add anything. This does not prevent the interviewer from putting significant statements and silences to a suspect again at a later stage or in further interviews.[28]

PRE-CAUTION DISCLOSURE

7.15   A caution is a non-statutory disposal that, though not classified as a conviction, may cause significant adverse consequences to the accused in that it may be used in subsequent court proceedings, place the accused on the sex offender's register or handicap his employment prospects on the job market.[29]

---

25 See *R v Argent* [1997] 2 Cr App R 27 and *R v Farrell* (2004) EWCA Crim 597.

26 *R v Howell* [2003] EWCA Crim 1, per Laws LJ, para 24.

27 A significant statement is one which appears capable of being used in evidence against the suspect, in particular a direct admission of guilt. A significant silence is a failure or refusal to answer a question or answer satisfactorily when under caution, which might give rise to an inference under the Criminal Justice and Public Order Act 1994, Part III.

28 PACE 1984 Code C, para 11.4, note 11A.

29 Home Office Circular 30/2005, Cautioning of Adult Offenders, paras 27–29. A conditional caution is available for youths aged 16–17.

7.16   For the police to be in a position to give a caution, there must be a clear and reliable admission of the offence, the accused must understand the significance of the caution and give an informed consent to being cautioned.[30]

7.17   Although there is no general obligation on the police to disclose material prior to charge,[31] the question of whether or not an accused should accept a caution is inextricably linked to his entitlement to informed legal advice. In *R v Ara*[32] the Divisional Court held that the justices were correct to have stayed proceedings for abuse of process where the police refused to supply a copy of the accused's interview to his legal adviser. In order for informed legal advice to be given, a legal adviser needs to know accurately the terms of the interview which form the basis of the caution. Without such disclosure, informed advice from a legal adviser is not possible and an informed consent from the accused cannot follow.

COMMON LAW DISCLOSURE

7.18   Common law disclosure occurs before initial statutory disclosure is triggered. Initial statutory disclosure by the prosecutor under the CPIA 1996 is triggered where[33] –

- a person pleads not guilty in the magistrates court or the youth court;

- a person is charged with an offence for which he is sent for trial;[34]

- a count charging a person with a summary offence is included in an indictment;[35] and

- a bill of indictment charging a person with an indictable offence is preferred.[36]

---

30   Home Office Circular 30/2005, Cautioning of Adult Offenders, paras 7, 18, 19, 27, 34.
31   *R v Ara* [2001] EWHC Admin 493 , per Rose LJ, para 25.
32   *R v Ara* [2001] EWHC Admin 493, per Rose LJ, para 25.
33   CPIA 1996, s 1. This section is amended by Criminal Justice Act 2003, s 41 and Sch 3 which came into force on 18 June 2012 (see SI 2012/1320). This amendment only applies to certain local justice areas; other areas are due to follow. Where it applies, committal to the crown court is abolished and all relevant cases will be sent to the crown court under the Crime and Disorder Act 1998, as amended.
34   Crime and Disorder Act 1998, s 51.
35   Criminal Justice Act 1988, s 40.
36   Administration of Justice (Miscellaneous Provisions) Act 1933, s 2(2) or Prosecution of Offences Act 1985, s 22B(3)(a).

7.19   The wording of section 3(1), CPIA 1996 that the prosecutor 'must (a) disclose to the accused any prosecution material which has not previously been disclosed to the accused' clearly envisages the possibility that some disclosure (common law disclosure) may have already occurred.

7.20   Kennedy LJ in *R v DPP ex parte Lee*[37] reviewed the common law of disclosure and the following propositions emerged. (Note: These propositions must now be considered in light of the abolition of committals. It will no longer be possible for a case to be discontinued or withdrawn at a committal hearing. Statutory disclosure is now triggered, in most cases, by a person being sent for trial.)

'(1)   The 1996 Act considerably reduced the ability of the defence to take an active part in committal proceedings, so the need for disclosure prior to committal was also reduced.

(2)   Part I of the 1996 Act introduced a completely new regime in relation to disclosure. It replaces most if not all of the provisions of the common law from the moment of committal with a two stage process set out in sections 3 and 7 of the Act. The second stage only occurs in response to a defence statement.

(3)   The disclosure required by the Act is and is intended to be less extensive than would have been required prior to the Act at common law.

(4)   Although some disclosure may be required prior to committal (and thus prior to the period to which the Act applies) it would undermine the statutory provisions if the pre-committal discovery were to exceed the discovery obtainable after committal pursuant to the statute.

(5)   The 1996 Act does not specifically address the period between arrest and committal, and whereas in most cases prosecution disclosure can wait until after committal without jeopardising the defendant's right to a fair trial the prosecutor must always be alive to the need to make advance disclosure of material of which he is aware (either from his own consideration of the papers or because his attention has been drawn to it by the defence) and which he, as a responsible prosecutor, recognises should be disclosed at an earlier stage. Examples[38] canvassed before us were –

---

37   [1999] 1 WLR 1950, section 9 'Conclusion'.
38   See Disclosure Protocol, para 19.

(a)   Previous convictions of a complainant or deceased if that information could reasonably be expected to assist the defence when applying for bail;

(b)   Material which might enable a defendant to make a pre-committal application to stay the proceedings as an abuse of process;

(c)   Material which might enable a defendant to submit that he should only be committed for trial on a lesser charge, or perhaps that he should not be committed for trial at all;

(d)   Material which will enable the defendant and his legal advisors to make preparations for trial which may be significantly less effective if disclosure is delayed (e.g. names of eye witnesses who the prosecution do not intend to use).

(6)   Clearly any disclosure by the prosecution prior to committal cannot normally exceed the primary disclosure which after committal would be required by section 3 of the 1996 Act (i.e. disclosure of material which in the prosecutor's opinion might undermine the case for the prosecution). However, to the extent that a defendant or his solicitor chooses to reveal what he would normally only disclose in his defence statement the prosecutor may in advance if justice requires give the secondary disclosure which such a revelation would trigger, so whereas no difficulty would arise in relation to disclosing material of the type referred to in sub-paragraph 5(a)(b) and (c) above, and I accept that such material should be disclosed, the disclosure of material of the type referred to in sub-paragraph 5(d) would depend very much on what the defendant chose to reveal about his case.

(7)   No doubt additions can be made to the list of material which in a particular case ought to be disclosed at an early stage, but what is not required of the prosecutor in any case is to give what might be described as full blown common law discovery at the pre-committal stage. Although the 1996 Act has not abolished pre-committal discovery the provisions of the Act taken as whole are such as to require that the common law obligations in relation to the pre-committal period be radically recast in the way that I have indicated.

(8)   Within framework which I have attempted to outline I would accept Mr Turner's submission that even before committal a responsible prosecutor should be asking himself what if any immediate disclosure justice and fairness requires him to make in the particular circumstances of the case. Very often the answer will be none, and rarely if at all should the prosecutor's answer to that continuing piece of self examination be the subject matter of dispute in this court. If the

matter does have to be ventilated it should, save in a very exceptional case, be before the trial judge.'[39]

7.21   To suggest that matters of early disclosure be ventilated before the trial judge 'save in a very exceptional case' (in proposition 8 above) will, in practice, be difficult to implement as trial judges are rarely identified until after the plea and case management hearing.

7.22   The CPR 2012 impose an obligation to deal with a case efficiently and expeditiously[40] and parties must actively assist the court in the early identification of the real issues.[41] Notwithstanding the absence of any established procedure to trigger common law disclosure, an early identification of issues by the defence should allow relevant material or information to be obtained and disclosed sooner rather than later.[42]

7.23   The defence should be mindful that to reveal the accused's defence to the prosecution at an early stage in a disclosure letter may carry a risk of sanctions being applied should a different defence be put forward either in a defence statement or at trial. As the disclosure letter should be based on the accused's instructions, the prosecution, though unable to rely on section 11, CPIA 1996 (defence sanctions), may seek to adduce it as an inconsistent or a hearsay statement. Although the chances of a prosecution application succeeding are remote, good practice dictates that such disclosure letters must be carefully worded and submitted only after their potential significance has been explained to the accused and a signed endorsement obtained.[43]

STATUTORY DISCLOSURE

Initial disclosure

7.24   Once initial statutory disclosure is triggered under section 3(1), CPIA 1996 the prosecution must –

---

39 These examples, in large measure, have been incorporated in the Attorney General's Guidelines on Disclosure (2005), paras 55–56. See also CPS Disclosure Manual, Ch 2.

40 CPR 2012, r 1.1(2)(e).

41 CPR 2012, rr 1.2(1), 3.2, 3.3, 3.10(a).

42 See Attorney General's Guidelines on Disclosure (2005), para 56.

43 See *R v Newell* [2012] EWCA Crim 650, per Sir John Thomas P, para 36: 'provided the case is conducted in accordance with the letter and spirit of the Criminal Procedure Rules … information or a statement written on a PCMH form should in the exercise of the Court's discretion under s 78 [Police and Criminal Evidence Act 1984] not be admitted in evidence as a statement that can be used against the defendant.'

'(a)   disclose to the accused any prosecution material which has not previously been disclosed to the accused and which might reasonably be considered capable of undermining the case for the prosecution against the accused or assisting the case for the accused, or

(b)   give to the accused a written statement that there is no material of a description mentioned in paragraph (a).'

7.25   While the CPS Disclosure Manual advises service of the non-sensitive schedule (MG6C) upon the defence,[44] a failure to serve the MG6C will not be regarded as a failure on the part of the prosecution to provide initial statutory disclosure.[45]

7.26   In determining what material must be disclosed to the defence, paragraph 12.4, CPS Disclosure Manual states that it will always be necessary to consider:

'•   the nature and strength of the case against the accused

•   the essential elements of the offence alleged

•   the evidence upon which the prosecution relies

•   any explanation offered by the accused, whether in formal interview or otherwise

•   what material or information has already been disclosed.'

7.27   Under paragraph 10, Attorney General's Guidelines on Disclosure (2005):

'Material can fulfil the prosecution disclosure test:

(a)   by the use to be made of it in cross-examination;

(b)   by its capacity to support submissions that could lead to:

   (i)   the exclusion of evidence; or

   (ii)   a stay of proceedings; or

   (iii) a court or tribunal finding that any public authority had acted incompatibly with the accused's rights under the ECHR;[46] or

(c)   by its capacity to suggest an explanation or partial explanation of the accused's actions.

---

44   CPS Disclosure Manual, paras 12.35–12.36.

45   *DPP v Wood, DPP v McGillicuddy* [2006] EWHC 32 (Admin), per Ouseley J, paras 23, 66.

46   European Convention of Human Rights.

7.28 *Prosecution disclosure to the defence*

7.28 It is not intended that material be disclosed which simply encourages speculative arguments or the manufacture of defences.[47]

7.29 Examples of material that might reasonably be considered capable of undermining the case for the prosecution against the accused or assisting the case for the accused[48] are:

- any material casting doubt upon the accuracy of any prosecution evidence;

- any material which may point to another person, whether charged or not, (including a co-accused) having involvement in the commission of the offence;

- any material which may cast doubt upon the reliability of a confession;

- any material that might go to the credibility of a prosecution witness;

- any material that might support a defence that is either raised by the defence or apparent from the prosecution papers;

- any material which may have a bearing on the admissibility of any prosecution evidence;

- any material that might assist the accused to cross-examine prosecution witnesses as to credit and/or substance;

- any material that might enable the accused to call evidence or advance a line of enquiry or argument; and

- any material that might explain or mitigate the accused's actions.[49]

7.30 The CPS Disclosure Manual[50] instructs disclosure officers and prosecutors to give careful consideration to:

- recorded scientific or scenes of crime findings retained by the investigator;

- where identification is or may be in issue, all previous descriptions of suspects, however recorded, together with all records of identification procedures in respect of the offence(s) and photographs of the accused taken at the time of arrest;

- information that any prosecution witness has received, been promised or requested any payment or reward in connection with the case;

---

47 Attorney General's Guidelines on Disclosure (2005), para 11.
48 i.e. the prosecution disclosure test.
49 Attorney General's Guidelines on Disclosure (2005), para 12; CPS Disclosure Manual, para 12.11.
50 Para 12.14.

- plans of crime scenes or videos made by investigators of crime scenes;

- names, within the knowledge of the investigators, of individuals who may have relevant information and whom the investigators do not intend to interview; and

- records, which the investigator has made, of information provided by any individual which may be relevant. This will include records of conversations with individuals such as expert witnesses.

7.31   Where material satisfies the prosecution disclosure test, it should be disclosed even if it suggests a defence inconsistent with or alternative to one already advanced by the accused.[51] It should be borne in mind that while items of material viewed in isolation may not satisfy the prosecution disclosure test, several items when taken together could have that effect.[52]

7.32   Material relating to the accused's mental or physical health or intellectual capacity, or to any ill treatment that the accused may have suffered when in the investigator's custody, is likely to fall within the prosecution disclosure test.[53]

7.33   In *R v Olu, Wilson and Brooks*[54] the Court of Appeal was severely critical of a disclosure exercise in so far as it related to material generated by the investigation (e.g. the taking of eyewitness statements) as opposed to pre-existing material. The court held that the defence should be provided with all notes, records and statements in relation to the evidence of eyewitnesses irrespective of whether or not the prosecution deemed them disclosable under the provisions of the CPIA 1996. Thomas LJ stated:

> '45.   ... what a witness says when first seen, even informally, in a case which depends on eyewitness evidence, is often the most reliable. Thus it was important that all of these notes and statements were obtained (where available) and scheduled at the outset. .... Once scheduled, it would have been a pointless exercise and a waste of police resources to go through each note of contact with the eyewitnesses (as opposed to the other witnesses) to decide whether it did or did not undermine the prosecution case or whether it assisted or did not assist the defence. All the statements in relation to the eyewitnesses should have been obtained, scheduled and disclosed as unused material so that the defence could determine whether such notes, records or statements assisted or did not assist ...

---

51   CPS Disclosure Manual, para 12.11.
52   Attorney General's Guidelines on Disclosure (2005), para 13.
53   Attorney General's Guidelines on Disclosure (2005), para 14.
54   [2010] EWCA Crim 2975.

46.   We also recognise that a failure to disclose the material documentation prior to a trial has two adverse consequences for the defence. Without proper disclosure a defence advocate cannot plan how the trial is to be conducted and what to put to the witnesses called by the Crown. Secondly, disclosure during the trial distracts a defence advocate from the proper and expeditious conduct of a trial. Experience shows it inevitable that there may be some late disclosure, but late disclosure on the scale that occurred in this case is unacceptable.'

7.34   In light of *R v Olu*[55] the defence can expect that all notes, records and statements of eyewitnesses that do not form part of the case against the accused will be served as part of initial disclosure.

7.35   When deciding what material is to be disclosed, prosecutors should resolve any doubts in favour of disclosure 'unless the material is sensitive and to be placed before the court in a PII application'.[56]

7.36   If material substantially undermines the prosecution case, assists the accused or raises a fundamental question about the prosecution, the prosecutor will need to re-assess the case in accordance with the Code for Crown Prosecutors and decide, after consultation with the police, whether the case should continue.[57]

Continuing disclosure

7.37   Once the prosecutor has complied or purported to comply with initial disclosure, section 7A, CPIA 1996[58] requires him to keep disclosure under review at all times applying the same prosecution disclosure test as that applied to initial disclosure.[59] The duty of continuing disclosure exists until the accused is acquitted or convicted or the case is discontinued.[60]

7.38   If material which has not previously been disclosed to the accused is identified as satisfying the prosecution disclosure test, the prosecutor must, unless disclosure is prohibited under section 17, Regulation of Investigatory Powers Act

---

55   [2010] EWCA Crim 2975.
56   CPS Disclosure Manual, para 12.18.
57   CPS Disclosure Manual, para 12.19.
58   Inserted by Criminal Justice Act 2003, s 37.
59   i.e. any prosecution material which might reasonably be considered capable of undermining the case for prosecution against the accused or of assisting the case for the accused.
60   CPIA 1996, s 7A(1)(b).

2000[61] or subject to public interest immunity considerations,[62]disclose it to the accused as soon as is reasonably practicable.[63]

7.39   Prosecutors should be alert to the possibility that further unused material may be generated or come to light after initial statutory disclosure as a result of investigations being conducted following advice from the prosecutor or, for example, upon the receipt of fingerprint and scientific evidence.[64]

7.40   The duty to keep disclosure under review is a continuing one, but it is particularly important after the service of a defence statement[65] as it may identify issues not apparent at the outset of the disclosure procedure. Prosecutors should be 'open, alert and promptly responsive to requests for disclosure of material supported by a comprehensive defence statement'[66] (see **Chapters 2** and **3**).

7.41   Where the accused has reasonable cause to believe that there is prosecution material that should be disclosed to him pursuant to section 7A, CPIA 1996 which has not been disclosed, he may apply to the court for an order requiring the prosecutor to disclose it under section 8, CPIA 1996 (a section 8 application). Section 8 applications for further disclosure should not be made ad hoc but should be dealt with under the proper procedures[67] (see **Chapter 6**).

Time of service

7.42   Although there is provision[68] for the Secretary of State to make regulations to prescribe time limits for the service of initial disclosure, as none are in force, the default position is that the prosecutor must act 'as soon as is reasonably practicable'.[69]

7.43   The CPS Disclosure Manual envisages that initial disclosure will be served by the prosecutor 'as soon as possible' after a not guilty plea in the

---

61 CPIA 1996, s 7A(9).
62 CPIA 1996, s 7A(8).
63 CPIA 1996, s 7A(3).
64 CPS Disclosure Manual, para 14.3.
65 CPIA 1996, s 7A(2).
66 Attorney General's Guidelines on Disclosure (2005), para 18.
67 Attorney General's Guidelines on Disclosure (2005), para 19.
68 CPIA 1996, s 12.
69 CPIA 1996, ss 3(8), 13.

magistrates' court or immediately after the sending[70] of the prosecution case to the crown court.[71] This initial disclosure will consist of[72] –

- the endorsed schedule of non-sensitive material (MG6C); and

- copies of any documents which satisfy the prosecution disclosure test.[73]

7.44 Where cases are sent to the crown court, paragraph 21, Disclosure Protocol provides:

> 'the court will need to consider at the Magistrates' Court or preliminary hearing whether … it is practicable for the prosecution to comply with its duty of initial disclosure at the same time as service of the case papers, or whether disclosure ought to take place after a certain interval, but before the matter is listed for a PCMH.'[74]

---

70 At the time of going to press (November 2012), committals are in the process of being abolished.
71 CPS Disclosure Manual, para 12.36.
72 CPS Disclosure Manual, para 12.35.
73 i.e. any prosecution material which has not previously been disclosed to the accused and which might reasonably be considered capable of undermining the case for the prosecution against the accused or of assisting the case for the accused.
74 See also CPR 2012, r 3.2 (duty of court to actively manage the case).

Chapter 8

Public interest immunity (sensitive material)

INTRODUCTION

8.01   Sensitive material is material that, if disclosed, would give rise to a real risk of serious prejudice to an important public interest.[1] The golden rule of full disclosure,[2] namely, that the prosecution must disclose to the accused any prosecution material which satisfies the prosecution disclosure test[3] is subject to two exceptions:

- 'Material must not be disclosed under this section to the extent that the court, on an application by the prosecutor, concludes it is not in the public interest to disclose it and orders accordingly';[4] and

- 'Material must not be disclosed under this section to the extent that it is material the disclosure of which is prohibited by section 17 of the Regulation of Investigatory Powers Act 2000'.[5]

8.02   This chapter deals with the following areas:

---

1 CPIA Code, para 2.1.
2 *R v H & C* [2004] UKHL 3, per Lord Bingham CJ, paras 14, 18, 36.
3 i.e. any prosecution material which might reasonably be considered capable of undermining the case for prosecution against the accused or of assisting the case for the accused.
4 CPIA 1996, ss 3(6), 7A(8), 8(5).
5 CPIA 1996, ss 3(7), 7A(9), 8(6).

RELEVANCE

8.03   The first step is to determine whether the material may be relevant to the investigation. Paragraph 2.1, CPIA Code provides:

> 'Material may be relevant if it appears to the investigator, to the officer in charge of an investigation, or the disclosure officer, that it has some bearing on any offence under investigation or any person being investigated, or on the surrounding circumstances of the case, unless it is incapable of having any impact on the case.'

8.04   Material which 'may not be relevant' must not be scheduled or disclosed, regardless of its sensitivity. The officer in charge, disclosure officer or investigator may seek advice from the prosecutor about whether material may be relevant.[6]

WHAT IS SENSITIVE MATERIAL?

8.05   Material is only sensitive (i.e. subject to public interest immunity) where the disclosure officer believes its disclosure would give rise to a 'real risk of serious prejudice to an important public interest'.[7]

8.06   A non-exhaustive list of examples of material that may be sensitive are set out in paragraph 6.12, CPIA Code, namely:

---

6   CPIA Code, para 6.1.
7   CPIA Code, para 2.1.

'•   Material relating to national security;

•   Material received from the intelligence and security agencies;

•   Material relating to intelligence from foreign sources which reveals sensitive intelligence gathering methods;

•   Material given in confidence;

•   Material relating to the identity or activities of informants, or undercover police officers, or witnesses, or other persons supplying information to the police who may be in danger if their identities are revealed;

•   Material revealing the location of any premises or other place used for police surveillance, or the identity of any person allowing a police officer to use them for surveillance;

•   Material revealing, either directly or indirectly, techniques and methods relied upon by a police officer in the course of a criminal investigation, for example covert surveillance techniques, or other methods of detecting crime;

•   Material whose disclosure might facilitate the commission of other offences or hinder the prevention and detection of crime;

•   Material upon the strength of which search warrants were obtained;

•   Material containing details of persons taking part in identification parades;

•   Material supplied to an investigator during a criminal investigation which has been generated by an official of a body concerned with the regulation or supervision of bodies corporate or of persons engaged in financial activities, or which has been generated by a person retained by such a body;

•   Material supplied to an investigator during a criminal trial which relates to a child or young person and which has been generated by a local authority social services department, an Area Child Protection Committee or other party contacted by an investigator during the investigation;

•   Material relating to the private life of a witness.'

TREATMENT OF SENSITIVE MATERIAL

8.07 The disclosure officer, subject to one exception (see **8.09**), must list the sensitive material on the schedule of sensitive material (MG6D).[8] He must state in the MG6D that he believes the material to be sensitive and the reason for that belief.[9] If there is no sensitive material, the disclosure officer must record this fact on the sensitive schedule.[10]

8.08 The MG6D must be provided to the prosecutor[11] and will not be served on the defence.[12]

8.09 The exception to listing sensitive material on the MG6D applies 'where compromising the material would be likely to lead directly to the loss of life, or directly threaten national security'.[13] In such circumstances the sensitivity of the material makes its recording on the MG6D inappropriate and its existence must be revealed to the prosecutor separately. The investigator who knows the detail of the sensitive material should not only inform the prosecutor as soon as is reasonably practicable after the file is sent to the prosecutor, he must also ensure that the prosecutor is able to inspect the material so that he can properly assess whether it is disclosable.[14]

8.10 Material that falls within the examples listed in paragraph 6.12, CPIA Code or which is potentially sensitive for other reasons will not qualify for inclusion in the MG6D unless it is believed that its disclosure would give rise to 'a real risk of serious prejudice to an important public interest'. If not, the material must be listed on the non-sensitive material schedule (MG6C).

8.11 To assist the prosecutor in deciding how to deal with disclosable sensitive material, paragraph 8.13, CPS Disclosure Manual states that the investigator and disclosure officer(s) should provide:

'• the reasons why the material is believed to be sensitive

• the degree of sensitivity said to attach to the material, in other words, why it is considered that disclosure will create a real risk of serious prejudice to an important public interest

---

8   CPIA Code, para 6.4.
9   CPIA Code, para 6.12.
10   CPIA Code, para 6.4.
11   CPIA Code, para 7.1.
12   CPS Disclosure Manual, para 8.2.
13   CPIA Code, para 6.13.
14   CPIA Code, para 6.14. Such material should be included on a highly sensitive schedule and dealt with in accordance with the guidance in CPS Disclosure Manual, Ch 9.

- the consequences of revealing to the defence:

  - the material itself

  - the category of the material

  - the fact that an application may be made

- the apparent significance of the material to the issues at trial

- the involvement of any third parties in the bringing of the material to the attention of the police

- where the material is likely to be the subject of an order for disclosure, what the police view is regarding continuance of the prosecution

- whether it is possible to disclose the material without compromising its sensitivity.'

8.12   To further ascertain the degree of sensitivity, consideration should be given as to whether the public interest may be prejudiced not only directly but also indirectly through incremental or cumulative harm.[15]

8.13   Paragraph 8.15, CPS Disclosure Manual lists examples of direct harm:

- '• exposure of secret information to enemies of the state

- death or injury to an intelligence source through reprisals

- revelation of a surveillance post and consequent damage to the property or harm to the occupier

- exposure of a secret investigative technique.'

8.14   Paragraph 8.16, CPS Disclosure Manual provides examples of incremental or cumulative harm:

- '• exposure of an intelligence source that … discourages others from giving information in the future because they lose faith in the system

- revelation of a surveillance post leading to reluctance amongst others to allow their premises to be used

- exposure of investigative technique that makes the criminal community more aware and therefore better able to avoid detection

- exposure of material given in confidence … that may make the source of the material, or others, reluctant to cooperate in the future …'[16]

---

15   CPS Disclosure Manual, para 8.14.
16   The CPS should neither confirm nor deny the use of a source.

ROLE OF THE PROSECUTOR

8.15   The prosecutor must consider, firstly, whether the material satisfies the prosecution disclosure test[17] and, secondly, whether the material is sensitive (i.e. subject to public interest immunity). If the material does not satisfy the prosecution disclosure test, there is no requirement to disclose it.

8.16   In assessing whether the material is sensitive, the 'risk' of prejudice to an important public interest must be real, as opposed to fanciful,[18] and the 'prejudice' must be serious, as opposed to trivial.[19] Such assessments are made on a document-by-document basis.

8.17   Neutral material or material damaging to the accused need not be disclosed and, unless the issue of disclosability is 'truly borderline', should not be brought to the court's attention.[20]

8.18   The prosecutor will need to consult with the police, normally at a senior level, and consideration be given as to whether material which passes the prosecution disclosure test[21] can be disclosed in an edited, summarised or formally admitted way. For the consultation with the police to be effective the prosecutor will need to be provided with the necessary information to make a proper decision.[22]

8.19   Where material is disclosed, having been edited, the original must not be marked and the defence should be informed of the fact that editing has taken place. An application to the court will be required to withhold the remainder of the material if it is disclosable under the CPIA 1996.[23] It may be possible to separate non-sensitive and sensitive parts of a document and schedule them accordingly.[24]

8.20   Under paragraph 8.22, CPS Disclosure Manual:

'Where the prosecutor decides:

---

17 i.e. any prosecution material which might reasonably be considered capable of undermining the case for the prosecution against the accused or of assisting the case for the accused.
18 CPS Disclosure Manual, paras 8.17–8.18.
19 CPS Disclosure Manual, para 8.19.
20 *R v H & C* [2004] UKHL 3, per Lord Bingham CJ, para 35; Attorney General's Guidelines on Disclosure (2005), para 20; CPS Disclosure Manual, para 23.
21 i.e. any prosecution material which might reasonably be considered capable of undermining the case for the prosecution against the accused or of assisting the case for the accused.
22 CPS Disclosure Manual, paras 8.24–8.26.
23 CPS Disclosure Manual, para 8.20.
24 CPS Disclosure Manual, para 8.21.

- that sensitive material requires disclosure to the accused because it satisfies the disclosure test, and

- in consultation with the police, that it is not possible to disclose in a way that does not compromise the public interest in question, and

- that disclosure should be withheld on public interest grounds,

the ruling of the court must be sought or the case abandoned.'[25]

VOLUNTARY DISCLOSURE[26]

8.21   There is no provision[27] for material which truly attracts public interest immunity to be disclosed to the defence without the approval of the court. This is clear from the wording of sections 3(6), 7A(8) and 8(5), CPIA 1996[28] which state:

'Material must not be disclosed under this section to the extent that the court, on an application by the prosecutor, concludes that it is not in the public interest to disclose it and orders accordingly'.

8.22   Voluntary disclosure, if permitted, would deny a person claiming to have an interest in material subject to a public interest immunity application to be heard.[29]

PROCEDURE FOR APPLICATIONS TO THE COURT

8.23   Under rule 22.3(2), CPR 2012, the prosecutor's application to the court must be in writing and served on –

- the court officer;

---

25 CPS Disclosure Manual, para 8.22.

26 For a copy of the model protocol between the Crown Prosecution Service, police and local authorities in the exchange of information in the investigation and prosecution of child abuse cases see **Appendix 13**.

27 Under CPIA 1996, CPIA Code, Attorney General's Guidelines on Disclosure (2005/2011) or Disclosure Protocol.

28 These sections concern the initial duty of the prosecutor to disclose, the continuing duty of the prosecutor to disclose and the application by the accused for disclosure respectively.

29 CPIA 1996, s 16 specifically allows for a person claiming to have an interest in such material to be heard. See also CPR 2012, r 22.3(2)(b).

- any person who the prosecutor thinks would be directly affected by disclosure of the material; and

- the defendant.[30]

8.24   Rule 22.3(3), CPR 2012 requires that the application must describe the material and explain why the prosecutor thinks that:

- it is material that the prosecutor would have to disclose;

- it would not be in the public interest to disclose that material; and

- no measure such as the prosecutor's admission of any fact, or disclosure by summary, extract or edited copy would adequately protect both the public interest and the accused's right to a fair trial.[31]

8.25   The extent to which the accused can, if at all, be made aware of the nature and content of the material was recognised in *R v Davis, Johnson and Rowe*.[32] Three types of application were identified:

- Type 1: This application is served on the appropriate officer of the crown court and on the accused. It specifies the nature of the material to which the application relates.

- Type 2: The prosecutor believes that revealing to the accused the nature of the application to which the material relates would in effect disclose the information which the prosecutor contends should not, in the public interest, be disclosed. This application is served on the appropriate officer of the crown court and on the accused. The nature of the material is not specified.

- Type 3: The prosecutor believes that revealing to the accused the existence of an application would in effect disclose the information that the prosecutor contends should not be disclosed. The application is served on the appropriate officer of the crown court but not the accused.

8.26   The prosecutor decides the nature and extent of what material is served on the accused. He must omit from any part of the application that is served on the accused any reference that would disclose what the prosecutor thinks ought not to be disclosed. The application to the court should clearly identify any part

---

30 But only to the extent that serving it on the defendant would not disclose what the prosecutor thinks ought not to be disclosed.

31 For the importance of the accuracy of the information provided to the court, see *R v Jackson* [2000] Crim LR 377 and *R v Early* [2002] EWCA Crim 1904.

32 [1993] 97 Cr App R 110.

that has not been served on the accused with an explanation as to why it was withheld.[33]

8.27   Unless already done, the court may direct the prosecutor to serve an application on the accused and/or any person who the court considers would be directly affected by the disclosure of the material.[34]

8.28   The public interest immunity hearing will be in private unless the court otherwise directs and, if the court so directs, the hearing may take place wholly or in part in the accused's absence.[35]

LEGAL PRINCIPLES TO BE APPLIED

8.29   The principles to be applied have been set out by Lord Bingham CJ in *R v H & C*[36] in a series of questions. These principles should be rigorously applied firstly by the prosecutor and then by the court to ensure that the procedure for examination of material in the absence of the accused is compliant with Article 6, ECHR.[37] The series of questions in *R v H & C* are:

'When any issue of derogation from the golden rule of full disclosure comes before it the court must address a series of points:

(1)   What is the material which the Crown seek to withhold? This must be considered by the court in detail.

(2)   Is the material such as may weaken the prosecution case or strengthen that of the defence? If No, disclosure should not be ordered. If Yes, full disclosure should (subject to (3), (4) and (5) below) be ordered.

(3)   Is there a real risk of serious prejudice to an important public interest (and, if so what) if full disclosure of the material is ordered? If No, full disclosure should be ordered.

(4)   If the answer to (2) and (3) is Yes, can the defendant's interest be protected without disclosure or disclosure be ordered to an extent or in a way which will give adequate protection to the public interest in question and also afford adequate protection to the interests of the defence?

---

33   CPR 2012, r 22.3(3), (4).
34   CPR 2012, r 22.3(5).
35   CPR 2012, r 22.3(6).
36   [2004] UKHL 3, per Lord Bingham CJ, para 36.
37   Attorney General's Guidelines on Disclosure (2005), para 22.

This question requires the court to consider, with specific reference to the material which the prosecution seek to withhold and the facts of the case and the defence as disclosed, whether the prosecution should formally admit what the defence seek to establish or whether disclosure short of full disclosure may be ordered. This may be done in appropriate cases by the preparation of summaries or extracts of evidence, or the provision of documents in an edited or anonymised form, provided the documents supplied are in each instance approved by the judge ...

(5) Do the measures proposed in answer to (4) represent the minimum derogation necessary to protect the public interest in question? If No, the court should order such greater disclosure as will represent the minimum derogation from the golden rule of full disclosure.

(6) If limited disclosure is ordered pursuant to (4) or (5), may the effect be to render the trial process, viewed as a whole, unfair to the defendant? If Yes, then fuller disclosure should be ordered even if that leads or may lead the prosecution to discontinue the proceedings so as to avoid having to make disclosure.

(7) If the answer to (6) when first given is No, does that remain the correct answer as the trial unfolds, evidence is adduced and the defence advanced?

It is important that the answer to (6) should not be treated as a final, once-and-for-all answer but as a provisional answer which the court must keep under review.' (para 36)

8.30   Before applying to the court to withhold sensitive material, the prosecutor should aim to disclose as much of the material as he properly can, for example, by giving the defence redacted or edited copies or summaries. Neutral material or material damaging to the accused need not be disclosed and must not be brought to the attention of the court. The prosecution should seek a ruling only in 'truly borderline' cases[38] as to whether material in its possession satisfies the prosecution disclosure test[39] (point (2) in *R v H & C*, para 36 above).

---

38 *R v H & C* [2004] UKHL 3, per Bingham CJ, para 35; Attorney General's Guidelines on Disclosure (2005), para 20. In *R v B* [2000] Crim LR 50 the court held that questions of disclosure had to be decided by the prosecution. The judge's assistance should only be sought if the questions could be properly decided by him, most obviously where questions of public interest immunity are involved.

39 i.e. any prosecution material which might reasonably be considered capable of undermining the case for prosecution against the accused or of assisting the case for the accused.

8.31   As material damaging to one accused may assist the case for a co-accused, the prosecutor must keep the issue of disclosure of such material under constant review.

PREPARATION OF PROSECUTION FOR THE HEARING

8.32   If the prosecution can give notice of the nature of or at least the fact of a public interest immunity application[40] the court can set a timetable for the service of material, submissions and a date for the application. To assist with timetabling the plea and case management hearing the 'Advocates Questionnaire'[41] asks whether any 'on notice' public interest immunity application is to be made.

8.33   Prior to the hearing the prosecutor and the prosecution advocate must examine all material which is the subject matter of the hearing and make any necessary enquiries of the investigator. The prosecutor (or representative) and/or the investigator should attend such applications.[42] What enquiries are necessary will depend on the facts of the case but will be of a similar nature to those addressed by the investigators and disclosure officer in **8.11** above.

8.34   Prior to or at the hearing, the court must be provided with full and accurate information to allow the court to satisfy the requirements of paragraph 36, *R v H & C*.[43]

8.35   Paragraph 13.14.1, CPS Disclosure Manual provides that the written submissions of the prosecution to the court should contain:

'•   a summary of the facts of the case. Where a case summary or prosecution opening note has been served and this is believed still to be accurate and adequate, the background submission should refer to this document which should be annexed to the submission

•   a list of trial issues which the prosecutor has been able to identify

---

40   See *R v Davis, Johnson and Rowe* [1993] 97 Cr App R 110.
41   Published in accordance with CPR 2012. For a copy of the Advocates Questionnaire for use with CPR 2012, Part 3 (listed in Consolidated Criminal Practice Direction, Annex E) see **Appendix 14**.
42   Attorney General's Guidelines on Disclosure (2005), para 21; CPS Disclosure Manual, paras 13.23–13.24 advise that the disclosure officer should attend.
43   Attorney General's Guidelines on Disclosure (2005), para 21; CPS Disclosure Manual, para 13.16.

- a summary of the defence case which has been advanced in a defence statement, section 8 application or correspondence

- in relation to Type Two and Three applications, reasons why it is considered inappropriate for there to be a Type One (or Type Two) application ...'

8.36   Paragraph 13.14.2, CPS Disclosure Manual provides that the written submissions should also contain:

'•   the number of the item as it appeared on form MG6D. Where more than one MG6D has been submitted, e.g. where the case has generated 'highly sensitive' material and involves more than one disclosure officer, each MG6D should be given its own reference

- a detailed description of the material

- in the case of lengthy items, a summary of their content

- an assessment giving reasons why it is considered that the material satisfies the disclosure test, or why the reviewing prosecutor is unable to determine whether or not the disclosure test is satisfied

- why it is considered that disclosure of the material will cause a real risk of serious prejudice to an important public interest and the degree of sensitivity that attaches to the material

- why it would not be appropriate to provide to the accused a formal admission, summary, extract or edited version of the material

- why the prosecutor contends that the public interest in withholding the material outweighs the public interest in disclosing it and

- where the material is the subject of a Type Two application, why it is considered inappropriate to inform the defence of the category of material into which the material falls

- where, exceptionally, the material is the subject of a Type Three application, why it is considered inappropriate to inform the defence at all.'[44]

8.37   In advance of the court hearing, the prosecution, where possible, ought to clarify with the court whether the hearing should be in open court, whether the hearing or any part of it should take place in the accused's absence[45] and, unless already done so, whether the court requires the prosecutor to serve an application

---

44   CPS Disclosure Manual, para 13.17 deals with the form of the submission. See *R v H & C* [2004] UKHL 3, per Bingham CJ, para 36.

45   CPR 2012, r 22.3(6)(a), (b) – the hearing will be in private unless otherwise directed.

on the accused and any other person whom the court considers would be directly affected by disclosure of the material.[46]

8.38   Once the submissions have been provided to the court, the prosecutor should ascertain whether the judge wishes to view the material in advance of the hearing and, if so, make the necessary arrangements.[47]

THE HEARING

8.39   The hearing should be before the trial judge. The court must address the questions set out in paragraph 36, *R v H & C*.[48] The application should be recorded and the judge should give a short statement of reasons, often on a document-by-document basis.[49]

8.40   The importance of involving the defence, where possible, was emphasised in *R v H & C*:[50]

'Throughout his or her consideration of any disclosure issue … the judge should involve the defence to the maximum extent possible without disclosing that which the general interest requires to be protected but taking full account of the specific defence which is relied on. There will be very few cases indeed in which some measure of disclosure to the defence will not be possible, even if this is confined to the fact that an ex parte application is to be made. If even that information is withheld and if the material to be withheld is of significant help to the defendant, there must be a very serious question whether the prosecution should proceed, since special counsel, even if appointed, cannot then receive any instructions from the defence at all.' (para 37)

8.41   Defence submissions that the accused can only have a fair trial if sensitive material is disclosed will be more credible if founded on a detailed defence statement supported by tailored and reasoned representations demonstrating, for example, why the location of the observation point or the existence of or identity of an informant would satisfy the prosecution disclosure test.[51] The defence run the risk, in the absence of such detail, of being suspected by the court of

---

46   CPR 2012, r 22.3(5)(a), (b).
47   CPS Disclosure Manual, paras 13.21–13.23.
48   See **8.29**; Attorney General's Guidelines on Disclosure (2005), para 22.
49   Disclosure Protocol, para 51(e).
50   [2004] UKHL 3, per Lord Bingham CJ.
51   i.e. any prosecution material which might reasonably be considered capable of undermining the case for prosecution against the accused or of assisting the case for the accused.

manoeuvring the prosecution into deciding between disclosure or offering no evidence on groundless tactical bases.

8.42   A ruling is needed before the hearing, or any part of it, can take place in the absence of the accused.[52] There must be a proper basis for any ex parte application.[53]

8.43   As a general rule when the accused is present, the court will hear firstly from the prosecutor and any other interested party served with the application; secondly, from the defence in the presence of the other parties; and thirdly, from the prosecutor and any such other person in the accused's absence.[54]

8.44   The court may only determine the application if satisfied that it has been able to take adequate account of such rights of confidentiality as apply to the material and the accused's rights to a fair trial.[55] Duties of confidentiality are placed on the court officer who must not give notice to anyone other than the prosecutor of the hearing of an application (unless the prosecutor has served the application on that person) or the courts decision, unless directed to do so by the court.[56]

REVIEW

8.45   Although the crown court of its own motion must keep its decision not to disclose material on the grounds of public interest under review,[57] the defence may apply to the court for a review.[58]

8.46   Under rule 22.6(2), CPR 2012, where the accused seeks a review he must serve an application on the prosecution and court officer describing:

•   the material he wants the prosecution to disclose; and

•   explain why it is no longer in the public interest for the prosecution not to disclose it.

---

52   CPR 2012, r 22.3(6)(b).
53   *R v Smith (David James)* [1998] 2 Cr App R 1.
54   CPR 2012, r 22.3(7)(a)(i), (ii).
55   CPR 2012, r 22.3(8).
56   CPR 2012, r 22.3(9).
57   CPIA 1996, s 15(3) – there is no such obligation in the magistrates' court.
58   CPIA 1996, s 15(4).

8.47   The prosecution must serve the application on any person who would be directly affected if the material were disclosed and as directed by the court.[59] The prosecutor and any person directly affected must serve any representations on the court officer, the accused (unless to do so would reveal something that ought not be disclosed) and as directed by the court.[60]

8.48   The court may only conclude a review if satisfied that it has been able to take adequate account of such rights of confidentiality as apply to the material and the accused's rights to a fair trial.[61]

CONSEQUENCES OF AN ORDER FOR DISCLOSURE

8.49   Where the court orders disclosure, it will be necessary for the prosecution to disclose the material in question if the case is to proceed. In appropriate cases disclosure may be by the preparation of summaries, extracts of evidence or the provision of documents in an edited or anonymised form, provided the documents supplied are approved by the judge. The prosecution may also formally admit what the defence seek to establish under section 10, Criminal Justice Act 1967.[62]

8.50   An order by the court that the prosecution disclose material may lead to discontinuance of the case to avoid having to make this disclosure.[63] This situation is anticipated by the Attorney General's Guidelines on Disclosure (2005) which state:

> 'If prosecutors are satisfied that a fair trial cannot take place where material which satisfies the disclosure test cannot be disclosed, and that this cannot or will not be remedied including by, for example, making formal admissions, amending the charges or presenting the case in a different way so as to ensure fairness or in other ways, they must not continue with the case.'[64] (para 41)

---

59   CPR 2012, r 22.6(3), (5)(a).
60   CPR 2012, r 22.6(4), (5)(b).
61   CPR 2012, r 22.3(8).
62   *R v H & C* [2004] UKHL 3, per Lord Bingham CJ, para 36; CPIA Code, para 10.5.
63   *R v H & C* [2004] UKHL 3, per Lord Bingham CJ, para 36, point (6).
64   CPS Disclosure Manual, para 31.1.

SPECIAL COUNSEL

8.51   The House of Lords in *R v H & C*[65] approved the use of special counsel in public interest immunity hearings in exceptional circumstances to protect the accused's right to a fair trial. Special counsel are appointed by the Attorney General on request from the trial judge. The Special Advocates Support Office has responsibility for providing formal instructions to special counsel in criminal cases on behalf of the Attorney General.[66]

8.52   Special counsel are designed to protect the interests of an accused against whom an adverse order may be made and who cannot (either personally or through his legal representative), for security reasons, be fully informed of all the material relied on against him.[67] As the accused's lawyers are unable to make informed submissions on his behalf, special counsel become necessary to ensure that the contentions of the prosecution are tested and the interests of the accused are protected.[68]

8.53   The judge has to be satisfied that no other course will adequately meet the overriding requirement of fairness to the accused.[69] The appointment of special counsel will always be exceptional and a matter of last, and never first, resort. There has to be something that a special advocate can do which cannot properly be done by the judge.[70]

8.54   Special counsel may be instructed only to deal with a single aspect of a case such as bail. The reasons may be more compelling for the appointment of special counsel where a decision has an immediate consequence upon the liberty of the accused.[71]

8.55   Special Counsel should always see the material which is the subject of the public interest immunity application. Where the public interest immunity application is on notice, special counsel may obtain information from the defence.

---

65   [2004] UKHL 3 para 22.
66   See *Special Advocates – A Guide to the Role of Special Advocates and the Special Advocates Support Office (SASO)*, (November 2006), p 20.
67   *R v H & C* [2004] UKHL 3, per Lord Bingham CJ, para 21.
68   *R v H & C* [2004] UKHL 3, per Lord Bingham CJ, para 36, point (4).
69   *R v H & C* [2004] UKHL 3, per Lord Bingham CJ, para 22.
70   *Chief Constable and AA v K* [2010] EWHC 2438 (Fam), per Sir Nicholas Wall P, para 92.
71   *R (on the application of S) v Northampton Crown Court* [2010] EWHC 723 (Admin), per Langstaff J, paras 23–25, 28.

Chapter 9

Third party material

INTRODUCTION

9.01   Third party material is material, within the UK or outside the UK, held by a person, organisation, government department or crown body other than the investigator and prosecutor.[1] Material that is in the possession of a third party falls outside the CPIA 1996.[2] Third parties are under no obligation to reveal material to the police or the prosecutor, nor need they retain material that may be relevant to a criminal investigation. The CPIA Code and the Attorney General's Guidelines do impose, however, obligations upon the investigator, disclosure officer and prosecutor to take appropriate steps to obtain material from third parties.

9.02   This chapter deals with:

• the duties of the police and the prosecution	**9.03–9.10**
• the methods of obtaining third party material	
– voluntary disclosure	**9.11–9.16**
– witness summons[3]	**9.17–9.27**
• the procedure for witness summons	**9.28–9.33**

---

1   Supplementary Attorney General's Guidelines on Disclosure – Digitally Stored Material (2011), para 54.
2   Attorney General's Guidelines on Disclosure (2005), para 48 – prosecutors are deemed not to be in constructive possession of material held by government departments or crown bodies.
3   For a copy of the witness summons form for use with CPR 2012, Part 28 (listed in Consolidated Criminal Practice Direction, Annex D) see **Appendix 16**.

DUTIES OF POLICE AND PROSECUTION

9.03   Paragraph 3.5, CPIA Code provides that an investigator should pursue all reasonable lines of enquiry, whether these point towards or away from the suspect. Reasonable lines of enquiry will include enquiries of third parties. What is reasonable will depend on the particular circumstances.[4]

9.04   Paragraph 3.6, CPIA Code requires that where:

'the officer in charge of an investigation believes that other persons may be in possession of material that may be relevant to the investigation, and if this has not been obtained under paragraph 3.5 above, he should ask the disclosure officer to inform them of the existence of the investigation and to invite them to retain the material in case they receive a request for its disclosure. The disclosure officer should inform the prosecutor that they may have such material ...'

9.05   The Attorney General's Guidelines on Disclosure (2005) place the burden upon the prosecutor, if necessary by a witness summons, to obtain material which satisfies the prosecution disclosure test.[5] The Guidelines state:

'51.   There may be cases where the investigator, disclosure officer or prosecutor believes that a third party (for example, a local authority, a social services department, a hospital, a doctor, a school, a provider of forensic services) has material or information which might be relevant to the prosecution case. In such cases, if the material or information might reasonably be considered capable of undermining the prosecution case or of assisting the case for the accused prosecutors should take what steps they regard as appropriate in the particular case to obtain it.'

9.06   A different approach is taken where government departments or other crown bodies hold material. For departments in England and Wales there should be established 'Enquiry Points' to deal with disclosure issues.[6] The investigator, disclosure officer and prosecutor should take reasonable steps to identify and consider material which may be relevant and inform the department or body of the case and the issues involved and ask whether it has such material.[7]

---

4   CPIA Code, para 3.5.
5   i.e. any prosecution material which might reasonably be considered capable of undermining the case for the prosecution against the accused or of assisting the case for the accused.
6   Attorney General's Guidelines on Disclosure (2005), para 49.
7   Attorney General's Guidelines on Disclosure (2005), para 47; Disclosure Protocol, para 53.

9.07   Where, after reasonable steps have been taken, access is still denied, consideration must be given as to what further steps might be taken to obtain the material or the defence should be informed.[8]

9.08   The obligation on the investigator and prosecutor to pursue all reasonable lines of enquiry applies to material held outside the United Kingdom.[9] Where it appears that there is relevant material held overseas, the prosecution must take reasonable steps to obtain it, either informally or under the Crime (International Co-operation) Act 2003 and any European Union/international conventions.[10]

9.09   There may be cases where a foreign state or court refuses to make the material available or, though willing for the material to be inspected, does not allow notes or copies to be made.[11] It is for these reasons that there is no absolute duty on the prosecutor to disclose material held by overseas entities not subject to the jurisdiction of courts in England and Wales.[12] There will be no breach by the prosecution of its duty of disclosure by its failure to obtain material overseas provided the police and prosecution have taken reasonable steps. It is for the court to judge in each case whether the prosecution have complied with its duty.[13]

9.10   The prosecutor enjoys a 'margin of consideration' as to what steps he regards appropriate in a particular case. He will only be in breach of his obligations in relation to obtaining third party material if it can be shown that he did not act within the permissible limits afforded by the Guidelines.[14]

---

8 Attorney General's Guidelines on Disclosure (2005), para 50.
9 Supplementary Attorney General's Guidelines on Disclosure – Digitally Stored Material (2011), para 58; *R v Flook* [2009] EWCA Crim 682, per Longmore LJ, para 35.
10 Supplementary Attorney General's Guidelines on Disclosure – Digitally Stored Material (2011), para 59.
11 Supplementary Attorney General's Guidelines on Disclosure – Digitally Stored Material (2011), para 60. See CPS Legal Guidance, International Enquiries.
12 Supplementary Attorney General's Guidelines on Disclosure – Digitally Stored Material (2011), para 62.
13 Supplementary Attorney General's Guidelines on Disclosure – Digitally Stored Material (2011), para 62; see *R v Flook* [2009] EWCA Crim 682, per Thomas LJ, para 37.
14 *R v Alibhai* [2004] EWCA Crim 681, per Longmore LJ, paras 62–63. But see *R v Flook* [2009] EWCA Crim 682, per Thomas LJ, para 37 where the court declined to decide whether the crown any longer has the margin of consideration referred to in *Alibhai*.

METHODS OF OBTAINING THIRD PARTY MATERIAL

Voluntary disclosure

9.11   Third parties may, in some circumstances, provide disclosure voluntarily. In cases involving child abuse there is a model protocol[15] endorsed by the Home Office that provides a framework within which the CPS, police and local authorities can co-operate voluntarily to share and exchange information. A disclosure officer will examine social services and education files to ascertain whether any material satisfies the prosecution disclosure test.[16] This process obviates the need for witness summonses. Once the disclosure officer has inspected material it is in the possession of the prosecution and should be dealt with according to the CPIA disclosure regime. Most areas have adopted the model protocol, tailored as necessary, to suit local needs. Other local protocols may exist in respect of third party material and practitioners need to have a working knowledge of them.

9.12   Paragraph 4.19, CPS Disclosure Manual suggests that it may be appropriate for the prosecution, in the absence of any relevant protocol, to make a disclosure request directly to the third party concerned. Any formal request for the voluntary disclosure by the third party should:

- set out the nature of the allegations against the accused and the issues in the case;

- list the reasons why access to the material is sought;

- list what material it is believed is held;

- ask whether the third party is prepared to release the material or allow its inspection;

- explain what will happen if the material is released;

- explain what will happen if the material is not released;

- ask whether the third party considers the material to be sensitive and, if so, why; and

- ask that the material is retained.[17]

---

15 For a copy of the model protocol between the Crown Prosecution Service, police and local authorities in the exchange of information in the investigation and prosecution of child abuse cases see **Appendix 13**.

16 i.e. any prosecution material which might reasonably be considered capable of undermining the case for prosecution against the accused or of assisting the case for the accused.

17 CPS Disclosure Manual, para 4.19; CPS Disclosure Manual, Annex B, Explanatory Note and 'Specimen letter B1 – Letter to third parties'.

The third party should also be asked to list any additional material held in relation to the case, whether inspection of that material is permitted (and if not, why) and to retain such material.[18]

9.13   Sufficient time should be given for a third party to respond to any request for disclosure before making an application for a witness summons.[19] If sufficient time is not allowed, the summons may be set aside and may attract a wasted costs order.

9.14   Relevant information which comes to the knowledge of investigators or prosecutors as a result of liaison with third parties, such as information conveyed verbally, should be recorded in a durable or retrievable form, e.g. relevant information revealed in discussions at a child protection conference attended by police officers.[20]

9.15   Where material is disclosed voluntarily to the prosecution, consultation with the third party should take place before disclosure is made as there may be public interest immunity issues that would require the issue of disclosure to be placed before the court.[21] Where a person claiming to have an interest in that material applies to be heard and shows that he was involved in bringing the material to the prosecutor's attention, the court must not make an order without giving him an opportunity to be heard.[22]

9.16   The Data Protection Act 1998 gives individuals the right, subject to exceptions, to access their own personal data. Generally, provided the persons who are the subject of the data concerned consent, information relating to them, such as their medical records, may be obtained by written request upon payment of the appropriate fee.[23]

---

18 CPS Disclosure Manual, Annex B, Explanatory Note and 'Specimen letter B1 – Letter to third parties'.
19 CPS Disclosure Manual, para 4.20.
20 Attorney General's Guidelines on Disclosure (2005), para 53; CPIA Code, para 4.1.
21 Attorney General's Guidelines on Disclosure (2005), para 54; Disclosure Protocol, para 54; CPS Disclosure Manual, para 4.9.
22 CPIA 1996, s 16.
23 Data Protection Act 1998 contains exceptions to this general principle.

Witness summons[24]

9.17   Although no specific procedure exists for the recovery of material from a third party, the witness summons is used to effect such disclosure. Paragraph 52, Attorney General's Guidelines on Disclosure (2005) provides:

> 'If the investigator, disclosure officer or prosecutor seeks access to the material or information but the third party declines or refuses to allow access to it, the matter should not be left. If despite any reasons offered by the third party it is still believed that it is reasonable to seek production of the material or information, and the requirements of section 2 of the Criminal Procedure (Attendance of Witnesses) Act 1965[25] ... are satisfied, then the prosecutor or investigator should apply for a witness summons causing a representative of the third party to produce the material to the Court.'

9.18   Where the third party declines to allow inspection of the material or requires the prosecution to obtain an order before handing over copies of the material, the prosecutor will need to consider whether it is appropriate to issue a witness summons.[26]

9.19   The issue of a witness summons is only appropriate where the statutory requirements are satisfied and where the prosecutor considers that the material may satisfy the prosecution disclosure test.[27]

9.20   Where the prosecution do not consider it appropriate to seek such a summons, the defence should consider doing so. The defence must not sit back and expect the prosecution to make the running.[28] To ensure that third party issues are identified at an early stage, the judge at the PCMH should specifically enquire whether enquiries with a third party are likely to be appropriate and, if so, identify who is going to make the request, what material is to be sought, from whom the material is to be sought and within what timescale the matter is to be resolved.[29] The 'Advocates Questionnaire' also requires the parties at the PCMH

---

24   For a copy of the witness summons form for use with CPR 2012, Part 28 (listed in Consolidated Criminal Practice Direction, Annex D) see **Appendix 16**.

25   Or Magistrates Courts Act 1980, s 97 if in the magistrates' court.

26   Disclosure Protocol, para 55.

27   Disclosure Protocol, para 55; i.e. any prosecution material which might reasonably be considered capable of undermining the case for the accused or of assisting the case for the accused.

28   Disclosure Protocol, para 58.

29   Disclosure Protocol, para 56; see CPR 2012, r 3.2 (the duty of the court to actively manage a case).

to complete a section asking what third party material is sought, from whom and why?[30]

9.21   Section 2(1), Criminal Procedure (Attendance of Witnesses) Act 1965 provides that a witness summons may be issued where the crown court is satisfied that:

'(a)   a person is likely to be able to give evidence likely to be material evidence, or produce any document or thing likely to be material evidence, for the purposes of any criminal proceedings before the Crown Court, and

(b)   it is in the interests of justice to issue a summons under this section to secure the attendance of that person to give evidence or to produce the document or thing.'[31]

9.22   Material evidence needs to be evidence that is admissible per se. Documents, such as social services[32] or medical records, may be material admissible per se if they can be said to be business records within section 117, Criminal Justice Act 2003.[33] Evidence that is merely likely to afford or assist a relevant line of enquiry or challenge or which may simply be useful in cross-examination is not admissible per se and cannot be extracted from third parties by the use of witness summonses.[34] In *R v Reading Justices ex p Berkshire County Council*[35] documentation that was requested merely for the purposes of cross-examination was held not to be material evidence.[36] Simon Brown LJ in giving judgment considered a number of authorities and stated:

'The central principles to be derived from these authorities are as follows:

i.   to be material evidence documents must be not only relevant to issues arising in the criminal proceedings, but also documents admissible as such in evidence;

---

30   For a copy of the Advocates Questionnaire for use with CPR 2012, Part 3 (listed in Consolidated Criminal Practice Direction, Annex E) see **Appendix 14**.

31   Similar provisions apply in the magistrates' court by virtue of Magistrates Court Act 1980, s 97.

32   *R v M* (unreported, 5 November 1999) (N 98/03990/Y4), per Rose LJ: 'Not only would the [social services records] have provided highly relevant and potentially damaging material for cross examination ... but the records would have been admissible under sections 23 and 24 Criminal Justice Act 1988.'

33   *R v Clowes* (1992) 95 Cr App R 440, per Phillips J; see *R v Humphris* [2005] EWCA Crim 2030, per Lord Woolf; *Wellington v DPP* 171 JP 497, QBD in relation to business records.

34   *R v H (L)* [1997] 1 Cr App R 176, per Sedley J.

35   (1996) 1 Cr App R 239.

36   See also *R v Azmy* (1996) 7 Med LR 415 – counselling records were for cross examination only and not admissible per se. Note: it is arguable that counselling records are business documents and not just an aide memoire.

ii.   documents which are desired merely for the purpose of possible cross-examination are not admissible in evidence and, thus, are not material for the purposes of s 97;

iii.   whoever seeks production of documents must satisfy the justices with some material that the documents are "likely to be material" in the sense indicated, likelihood for this purpose involving a real possibility, although not necessarily a probability;

iv.   it is not sufficient that the applicant merely wants to find out whether or not the third party has such material documents. This procedure must not be used as a disguised attempt to obtain discovery.'

9.23   A witness summons issued under section 2, Criminal Procedure (Attendance of Witnesses) Act 1965[37] requiring a person to produce a document or thing issued by the crown court may also require him to produce it for inspection before adducing it in evidence.[38] This gives the applicant the opportunity to decide not to adduce the material should it be unhelpful. In *R v Clowes*[39] Phillips J stated:

'It does not seem to me to offend against the letter or the spirit of section 2 of the 1965 Act to issue a witness summons for the production of documents which are admissible in evidence with the motive both of discovering the precise nature of the contents of the documents and, if these are helpful, adducing them in evidence.'

9.24   The crown court may issue a summons of its own motion requiring a person to give evidence or produce a thing or document.[40] A person who, without just excuse, disobeys a witness summons shall be in contempt of court.[41] Commercial confidentiality does not permit a third party to withhold material.[42]

9.25   'Fishing' exercises must not be embarked upon[43] and a speculative challenge to a refusal to disclose, in the hope that something might emerge 'might well amount to an "improper, unreasonable or negligent act" capable of attracting a wasted costs order'.[44] It is clear, however, that injustice may occur where third parties are in possession of material, unbeknown to the defence,

---

37   Magistrates' Court Act 1980, s 97 applies to the magistrates' court.

38   Criminal Procedure (Attendance of Witnesses) Act 1965, s 2A.

39   [1992] 95 Cr App R 440, p 448.

40   Criminal Procedure (Attendance of Witnesses) Act 1965, s 2D.

41   Criminal Procedure (Attendance of Witnesses) Act 1965, s 3.

42   *R v Alibhai* [2004] EWCA Crim 681, per Longmore LJ, para 107.

43   *R v Mildenhall Justices ex parte Graham* (unreported, 22 January 1987), QBD.

44   *R v H (L)* 1997 1 Cr App R, per Sedley J, p 176; Disclosure Protocol, para 59.

that is relevant and that the defence have no means of becoming aware of its existence.

9.26 The failure of the CPIA 1996 to directly address the disclosure of material in the hands of a third party is unsatisfactory.[45] A witness summons to produce a 'document or thing' will not elicit information[46] and cannot be issued to a person outside the jurisdiction. Further, the test to be applied for a witness summons, namely, that a person is likely to be able to give material evidence or produce any document or thing likely to be material evidence is different (and more onerous) to the prosecution disclosure test[47] under the CPIA 1996.

9.27 Ultimately, a court may not have the power to order the disclosure of material which would otherwise be disclosable if it were in the hands of the prosecution. This may occur where the criteria for issuing a witness summons are not satisfied[48] or an overseas third party refuses to make the material available.[49] In the absence of such material, the defence should consider making an abuse of process application (see **Chapter 11**).

PROCEDURE FOR WITNESS SUMMONS[50]

9.28 An application for a witness summons which requires the proposed witness to produce in evidence a document or thing or to give evidence about information apparently held in confidence must be in writing and in the required form[51] unless the court allows an oral application.[52] A party wishing to make an oral application must give as much notice as possible to those who would otherwise have received a written application and explain the reasons for wanting the court to consider the application orally.

9.29 A party seeking the witness summons must apply as soon as practicable after becoming aware of the grounds for doing so. He must identify the proposed witness, explain (i) what evidence the proposed witness can give or produce,

---

45 This was recognized by Auld LJ in *Review of the Criminal Courts in England and Wales* (2001).
46 *R v Alibhai* [2004] EWCA Crim 681, per Longmore LJ, para 34.
47 Disclosure Protocol, para 52.
48 Criminal Procedure (Attendance of Witnesses) Act 1965, s 2(3).
49 *R v Alibhai* [2004] EWCA Crim 681, per Longmore LJ, para 64; see Auld LJ, *Review of the Criminal Courts in England and Wales* (2001) who stated that statutory provisions disclosure of third party material were needed and the restrictions to third party material were inappropriate.
50 CPR 2012, Part 28 is set out in **Appendix 15**.
51 CPR 2012, r 28.5(1), (2).
52 CPR 2012, r 28.8(3).

(ii) why it is likely to be material evidence, and (iii) why it would be in the interests of justice to issue.[53]

9.30   Care must be taken to ensure that the witness summons is not defective either in form or content and that good grounds can be shown for its issue.[54] All persons to whom the application relates must have 14 days' notice in which to make representations before the court can issue a summons,[55] unless the court shortens or extends the time period allowed.[56] The hearing must be in private, unless the court otherwise directs.[57]

9.31   The party making the application must serve it on the proposed witness (unless the court otherwise directs) and the court may direct that it is also served on a person to whom the evidence relates and/or another party.[58] In *R (on the application of B) v Stafford Combined Court*[59] it was held that a patient should be given notice of an application for a witness summons to disclose his medical records and have the opportunity to make representations before any order is made.[60] Where confidential information is sought the court will usually direct that the application be served on the person to whom the information relates.[61]

9.32   Rule 28.7(1)(b), CPR 2012 provides that a witness or any person to whom the evidence relates can apply in writing for the summons to be withdrawn:

'on the grounds that –

(i)   he was not aware of any application for it, and

(ii)   he cannot give or produce evidence likely to be material evidence, or

(iii)   even if he can, his duties or rights, including rights of confidentiality, or those of any person to whom the evidence relates, outweigh the reasons for the issue of the summons ...'

9.33   The application to set the witness summons aside should be made as soon as practicable after becoming aware of the grounds for the application. The court may withdraw a witness summons if the party who applied for it no longer needs it.[62]

---

53   CPR 2012, r 28.3(1), (2).
54   Barristers (Wasted Costs Order: Criminal Proceedings) (No. 5 of 1997).
55   CPR 2012, r 28.5(4).
56   CPR 2012, r 28.8(1).
57   CPR 2012, r 28.2(2).
58   CPR 2012, r 28.5(3).
59   [2006] EWCA 1645 (Admin).
60   This is now reflected in CPR 2012, r 28.5(3)(b).
61   *R v Stafford Crown Court* (see above), per May LJ, paras 22–28.
62   CPR 2012, r 28.7(1)(a).

Chapter 10

Disclosure from family proceedings relating to children

INTRODUCTION

10.01   Cases involving the sexual and physical abuse of children may give rise to criminal and family proceedings. There is an overlap between the two jurisdictions as the same or similar factual issues, involving the same witnesses, are often before both courts. Any family proceedings in existence at the time of an associated criminal case can therefore provide an important source of material for the parties involved in criminal proceedings.

10.02   This chapter deals with:

• prohibition against publishing information	**10.03–10.06**
• permitted disclosure	**10.07–10.10**
• disclosure to investigation authorities	**10.11–10.15**
• disclosure to defence lawyers	**10.16–10.20**
• defence application for disclosure	**10.21–10.29**
• protection from self-incrimination	**10.30–10.32**

PROHIBITION AGAINST PUBLISHING INFORMATION

10.03   Family proceedings are held in private[1] and are therefore confidential. Section 12(1)(a), Administration of Justice Act 1960[2] provides that where proceedings relate wholly or mainly to the maintenance or upbringing of a minor it will be a contempt of court to publish 'information relating to the proceedings'

---

1   FPR 2010, r 27.10.
2   As amended.

except where it is disclosed in accordance with Part 12, Family Procedure Rules 2010 (FPR 2010) and its associated Practice Direction,[3] or with the permission of the family court.[4]

10.04　The prohibition applies to publishing 'information relating to the proceedings' which includes:

(a)　accounts of what has taken place in front of the judge sitting in private;

(b)　documents such as affidavits, witness statements, reports, position statements, skeleton arguments or other documents filed in the proceedings, transcripts or notes of evidence or submissions, and transcripts or notes of the judgment (this list is not necessarily exhaustive);

(c)　extracts or quotations from such documents;

(d)　summaries of such documents; and

(e)　information, even if not reduced into writing, which has emerged during the course of information gathering for the purpose of proceedings already commenced.[5]

10.05　The prohibition applies whether or not the information or the document being published has been anonymised.[6]

10.06　Disclosure of information not relating to proceedings is not prohibited but may still be subject to public interest immunity or other provisions.[7] The prohibition will not apply to documents (or the information contained in documents) not prepared for the purposes of the proceedings, even if the documents are lodged with the court or referred to in, or annexed to, a witness statement or report unless the document or information is published in such a way to link it with proceedings so that it can sensibly be said that what is published is 'information relating to [*the*] proceedings'.[8]

3　FPR 2010 Practice Direction 12G, Communication of Information.
4　FPR 2010, r 12.73.
5　*In the Matter of W* [2010] EWHC 16 (Fam), per Munby J, paras 76, 112.
6　*In the Matter of W* [2010] EWHC 16 (Fam), per Munby J, para 76.
7　See Children Act 1989, s 97(5) which prohibits the publication of material which is likely to identify a child involved in such proceedings, their home or school, to the public at large.
8　*In the Matter of W* [2010] EWHC 16 (Fam), per Munby J, para 112.

PERMITTED DISCLOSURE

10.07   Rule 12.73, FPR 2010 provides for information to be disclosed to certain prescribed persons. These include:

- the legal representative of the party;

- a professional legal advisor; and

- a professional acting in furtherance of the protection of children.

10.08   Practice Direction 12G permits disclosure by any party of:

- the text or summary of the whole or part of a judgment given in the proceedings to a police officer; and

- the text or summary of the whole or part of a judgment given in the proceedings to the crown prosecution service.

10.09   Disclosure of information to the public at large or any section of it is not permitted[9] nor is the disclosure of any unapproved judgment handed down by the court.[10]

10.10   An important distinction is made between the disclosure of information and the disclosure of documents. The FPR 2010 only allows for the disclosure of information. Once the information is disclosed in accordance with the FPR 2010 it can be used, but the documents from which the information comes cannot be used without the express permission of the court.[11]

DISCLOSURE TO INVESTIGATING AUTHORITIES

10.11   Where a police officer is a 'professional acting in furtherance of the protection of children',[12] information relating to the proceedings can be disclosed to him without the permission of the court. This information can thereafter be used for the investigation of criminal offences involving children.[13] A police officer is a 'professional acting in furtherance of the protection of children' where:

---

9   FPR 2010, r 12.73(2).

10   FPR 2010, r 12.73(3).

11   *Reading Borough Council v D (Angela)* [2006] EWHC 1465 (Fam), per Sumner J, para 70.

12   FPR 2010, r 12.73.

13   *Reading Borough Council v D (Angela)* [2006] EWHC 1465 (Fam), per Sumner J, para 73. For an alternative approach see *In A District Council v M* (2008) 2 FLR 390, per Baron J, para 21.

- he is exercising powers under the Children Act 1989, s 46 (removal and accommodation of children in cases of emergency); or

- he is serving in a child protection unit or paedophile unit of a police force.[14]

10.12   If a police officer does not meet the above criteria, no information can be disclosed to him, other than the court judgment, without permission of the court and he will need to make the necessary application.[15]

10.13   The distinction between information which may be disclosed and used without the permission of the court and documentation that requires the express permission of the court before it can be used creates difficulties because information is often disclosed in the form of documentation.[16] Once a document is disclosed into the possession of the prosecution, disclosure is governed by their obligations under the CPIA 1996. The documentation may still attract public interest immunity, but the issue of whether or not it should be disclosed to the defence will be a matter for the judge in the criminal proceedings and, to all intents and purposes, not under the control of the family court.

10.14   Although there are no guidelines on the distinction between using information and using a document, using a short quote from a document is unlikely to be regarded as using the document.[17]

10.15   Applications by the police to use documents, if unopposed, can be dealt with as a paper application or sought by the local authority on a directions hearing. The court can require an oral hearing if that appears advisable.[18] Practitioners must pay heed to the fact that many police authorities have developed their own protocols with their designated family judge which set out the procedures to be adopted when disclosure is sought and the information to be provided. There is also a national model protocol[19] between the Crown Prosecution Service, police and local authorities that concerns the exchange of information in the investigation and prosecution of child abuse cases.[20]

---

14 FPR 2010, r 2.3.

15 *Re B (A Child: Disclosure of Evidence in Care Proceedings)* [2012] 1 FLR 142.

16 *Reading Borough Council v D (Angela)* [2006] EWHC 1465 (Fam), per Sumner J, para 69 where this method of disclosure was considered to be perfectly proper.

17 *Reading Borough Council v D (Angela)* [2006] EWHC 1465 (Fam), per Sumner J, para 88.

18 *Reading Borough Council v D (Angela)* [2006] EWHC 1465 (Fam), per Sumner J, para 90.

19 For a copy of the model protocol see **Appendix 13**.

20 *Reading Borough Council v D (Angela)* [2006] EWHC 1465 (Fam), per Sumner J, paras 97–98.

DISCLOSURE TO CRIMINAL DEFENCE LAWYERS

10.16   This area of law is in a state of uncertainty. There is conflicting authority as to whether or not a criminal defence lawyer is a 'professional legal advisor' for the purposes of rule 12.73, FPR 2010. If he is, then information can be disclosed to him without the permission of the court.

10.17   A 'professional legal advisor' is defined as including a barrister or solicitor 'who is providing advice to a party but is not instructed to represent that party in the proceedings'.[21] In *Reading Borough Council v D*[22] Sumner J commented that the term 'professional legal advisor' did not cover a criminal defence lawyer because 'the language [*in the definition*] is not apt to cover advice to someone who is, or may become a defendant in criminal proceedings rather than a party'.[23] By contrast in *Re B (A Child: Disclosure of Evidence in Care Proceedings)*[24] Bodey J held that a defence solicitor was a 'professional legal advisor' for the purposes of the FPR 2010.[25]

10.18   Nothing in the FPR 2010 permits the disclosure of documents relating to the proceedings. Defence lawyers are best advised to seek the permission of the family court before receiving any disclosure, be it information or documentation, to ensure that they do not, albeit inadvertently, place themselves in contempt of court.

10.19   If, without the permission of the family court, a defence lawyer while in a conference with a criminal client receives information relating to family proceedings which assists his criminal case, he must apply to the family court before any document relating to the family proceedings is disclosed to him. The application to the family court must be made irrespective of whether the source of the document is the lay client or the solicitor.

10.20   If the defence lawyer intends to use the information (as opposed to the document) he has received without the permission of the family court in criminal proceedings, he should raise that matter with the prosecution and the trial judge, in chambers if necessary, so that any objections can be aired. The prosecution may want to seek their own disclosure from the family court to satisfy themselves that the information being put forward is accurate or to rebut it.

---

21   FPR 2010, r 2.3.
22   [2006] EWHC 1465 (Fam).
23   *Reading Borough Council v D (Angela)* [2006] EWHC 1465 (Fam), per Sumner J, paras 92–94. Although Sumner J was referring to the FLR 2005, the definition is identical for the FLR 2010.
24   [2012] 1 FLR 142.
25   *Reading Borough Council v D (Angela)* [2006] EWHC 1465 (Fam) was not cited before the court.

DEFENCE APPLICATION FOR DISCLOSURE

10.21   There is no prescribed form for making an application for disclosure from the family court. Having regard to the dicta in *Reading Borough Council v D*[26] it is suggested that the following approach is taken:

- any application should be in writing and served on all parties (including the guardian ad litem) in advance of any hearing at the court centre where the proceedings are listed;

- any application should identify the material being sought with an explanation as to why it is sought; and

- any application should be accompanied by the defence statement and any other material that would assist the court in determining whether or not disclosure should be ordered.

10.22   The family court has to carry out a balancing exercise when considering disclosure. In *Re L*[27] Sir Thomas Bingham MR stated:

'It is plain that the public interest in the fair administration of justice, and the right of a criminal defendant to defend himself, are accepted as potent reasons for disclosure. If, on the other hand, it could be shown that disclosure would, for some reason, be unfair or oppressive to a party, to the wardship or Children Act proceedings, that would weigh against an order for disclosure.'[28]

10.23   This statement was approved by Hale LJ in *Re R (Children)*.[29]

10.24   In *Re A (Criminal Proceedings: Disclosure)*[30] Butler-Sloss LJ, in considering the balancing exercise which the court had to perform, said that it was between:

'... the importance of maintaining confidentiality in family cases and the public interest in making available material for the purposes of a criminal trial. Factors to take into account include the purpose for which information was required, the weight and significance of the information, the importance of the witness and the gravity of the offence.'

---

26   [2006] EWHC 1465 (Fam), per Sumner J, paras 95–96.

27   [1996] 1 FCR 419.

28   See also *Reading Borough Council v D (Angela)* [2006] EWHC 1465 (Fam), *Re C (A Minor) (Care Proceedings: Disclosure)* [1997] 2 WLR 322 (ten factors to be taken into account when considering an order for disclosure) and *In the Matter of the X Children* [2008] EWHC 242.

29   [2003] 1 FCR 193.

30   [1996] 1 FLR 221.

10.25   Where an accused facing criminal charges has concurrent proceedings in the family jurisdiction, it is essential that there should be close liaison between the local social services authority and the Crown Prosecution Service.[31] Similarly, the judge in each jurisdiction must be fully informed.[32] Were the same judge to deal with both sets of proceedings, at least at the preliminary hearings, he would be able to keep abreast of disclosable family material. In *Re W*[33] Wall LJ said:

> '... there can be no excuse for either the profession or the judiciary not knowing about or following what is – or should be – a well established protocol particularly when, as here ... the Care Centre and the Crown Court are in the same building and there are many judges who have what has become known in the profession as both care and serious crime "tickets".'[34]

10.26   It is submitted that a judge would still be able to preside over the accused's criminal jury trial to its conclusion and thereafter properly conduct a 'finding of fact' hearing in family proceedings involving the same accused (but not vice versa).[35]

10.27   If the application for disclosure is unopposed, it can be considered as a paper application but the court will always reserve the right to hear argument from the defence lawyer.[36]

10.28   Alternatively, the authors submit that the defence can:

- draft a consent order;

- secure the written consent of all parties to the proceedings; and

- submit it to the court for approval.

---

31 *Re W (Children) (Care Order: Sexual Abuse)* [2009] EWCA Civ 644, per Wall LJ, para 73. Some areas, such as Greater London, have issued a Practice Statement setting out a scheme for the purpose of identifying cases where difficulties are likely to arise and providing for linked directions hearings to take place in the crown court to which the criminal case has been committed.

32 *Re W (Children) (Care Order: Sexual Abuse)* [2009] EWCA Civ 644, per Wall LJ, para 45.

33 *Re W (Children) (Care Order: Sexual Abuse)* [2009] EWCA Civ 644, per Wall LJ, para 45.

34 *Re W (Children) (Care Order: Sexual Abuse)* [2009] EWCA Civ 644, per Wall LJ, para 43.

35 In a jury trial it is the jury and not the judge who makes findings of fact and therefore no issue of bias arises. In *R v K* (unreported, 15–22 October 2012), Judge Lea (Nottingham Crown Court) simultaneously presided over a criminal jury trial and a fact-finding hearing in care proceedings in which the issues to be decided were the same, namely, had the accused sexually abused the complainant. Upon the conclusion of the criminal trial (conviction and sentence), the court constituted itself as a family court to hear submissions from the family lawyers, who had been present throughout the criminal trial as noting briefs, as to what (if any) fact-finding issues remained.

36 *Reading Borough Council v D (Angela)* [2006] EWHC 1465 (Fam), per Sumner J, para 96.

10.29   In the absence of approval, the court can hear argument.

PROTECTION FROM SELF-INCRIMINATION

10.30   Section 98, Children Act 1989,, which removes the privilege against self-incrimination in care, supervision and protection of children cases, provides:

‘(1)   In any proceedings in which a court is hearing an application for an order under Part IV or V,[37] no person shall be excused from –

(a)   giving evidence on any matter; or

(b)   answering any question put to him in the course of his giving evidence,

on the ground that doing so might incriminate him or his spouse of an offence.

(2)   A statement or admission made in such proceedings shall not be admissible in evidence against the person making it or his spouse in proceedings for an offence other than perjury.’

10.31   The prohibition, preventing a statement or admission being used against its maker in criminal proceedings, does not extend to a police investigation and makes no provision for the giving of a guarantee for all time as to confidentiality.[38]

10.32   The following legal principles can be identified:

•   A judge hearing civil proceedings can compel a party to explain the circumstances in which a child has been injured and, by virtue of section 98(1), Children Act 1989, that person cannot refuse to answer questions which might incriminate him.[39]

•   The proceedings under Parts IV and V, Children Act 1989[40] are confidential, but that is subject to the FPR 2010 and the power of the judge, in appropriate circumstances, to order disclosure. Nothing in section 98, Children Act 1989 detracts from that power and witnesses should be advised accordingly.[41]

---

37   Care and supervision, and protection of children.
38   *Re C (A Minor) (Care Proceedings: Disclosure)* (1997) 2 WLR 322, per Swinton Thomas LJ.
39   *Re Y and K (Split hearing: Evidence)* [2003] EWCA (Civ) 699.
40   Care and supervision, and protection of children.
41   *Re C (A Minor) (Care Proceedings: Disclosure)* (1997) 2 WLR 322, per Swinton Thomas LJ

- Questions involving disclosure to the police of information and documents connected with private family cases are of importance. Difficulties arise from the conflict between two principles, namely –

  (a)   the need for confidentiality in children cases, to protect the child and promote frankness; and

  (b)   the need to investigate and, where warranted, prosecute those criminally involved with children.[42]

- There is nothing to prevent a statement or admission being put to an accused during his police interview. It will be for the trial judge in the criminal proceedings to decide whether or not to admit into evidence any further admission made to the police in interview resulting from admissions made in care proceedings having regard to the provisions of section 98, Children Act 1989 and any warning given to the accused person during the care proceedings.[43]

- Putting inconsistent statements to a witness in order to challenge his evidence or attack his credibility does not amount to using those statements against him within the meaning of section 98(2), Children Act 1989[44] and the prosecution can use the material to challenge any account he seeks to put forward which is inconsistent with his evidence in the family proceedings.[45]

---

42   *Reading Borough Council v D (Angela)* [2006] EWHC 1465 (Fam), per Sumner J, paras 35–37.

43   *Re C (A Minor) (Care Proceedings: Disclosure)* (1997) 2 WLR 322, per Swinton Thomas LJ.

44   *Re L (Care: Confidentiality)* [1999] 1 FLR 165.

45   *In the matter of X* [2008] EWHC 242.

Chapter 11

Consequences of non-disclosure

INTRODUCTION

11.01   The disclosure regime set out in the CPIA 1996 and the CPIA Code must be scrupulously followed by the police and prosecutors.[1] Where disclosure fails to take place in accordance with those obligations, or as directed by the court, various consequences may follow.[2]

11.02   This chapter deals with:

• discontinuance	**11.03–11.04**
• staying the proceedings	**11.05–11.13**
• refusing to extend custody time limits	**11.14–11.21**
• orders for costs	**11.22–11.29**
• exclusion of evidence	**11.30–11.31**
• acquittal against the weight of the evidence	**11.32**

DISCONTINUANCE

11.03   There may be circumstances where it is not in the public interest to disclose material to the defence notwithstanding that the material satisfies the prosecution disclosure test.[3] The prosecution will have to decide whether to discontinue the case or make a public interest immunity application to withhold material from the defence. If they make an application and disclosure is ordered

---

1   Attorney General's Guidelines on Disclosure (2005), para 4; CPS Disclosure Manual, para 1.11.
2   CPR 2011, r 3.5(6) allows a court to, inter alia, cancel or adjourn a hearing, make a costs order or impose such other sanctions as 'may be appropriate'.
3   i.e. any prosecution material which might reasonably be considered capable of undermining the case for the prosecution against the accused or of assisting the case for the accused.

by the court, the prosecution will have to consider their position in the light of their obligations under paragraph 41, Attorney General's Guidelines on Disclosure (2005), which states:

'If prosecutors are satisfied that a fair trial cannot take place where material which satisfies the disclosure test cannot be disclosed, and that this cannot or will not be remedied including by, for example, making formal admissions, amending the charges or presenting the case in a different way so as to ensure fairness or in other ways, they must not continue with the case.'

11.04   The prosecution cannot disobey an order of the court.[4] If disclosure is ordered by the court, the prosecutor can disclose the material, discontinue the case or appeal against what is, in effect, a terminatory ruling. The prosecutor may not appeal against a terminatory ruling unless he agrees, in respect of each offence which is the subject of the appeal, that the accused should be acquitted if the appeal fails or is abandoned.[5]

STAYING THE PROCEEDINGS

11.05   Lack of disclosure can give rise to an abuse of process argument which may result in the proceedings being stayed. Two main strands of abuse were identified by Lord Dyson in *R v Maxwell*[6] at paragraph 13:

'It is well established that the court has the power to stay proceedings in two categories of case, namely (i) where it will be impossible to give the accused a fair trial, and (ii) where it offends the court's sense of justice and propriety to be asked to try the accused in the particular circumstances of the case. In the first category of case, if the court concludes that an accused cannot receive a fair trial, it will stay the proceedings without more. No question of the balancing of competing interests arises. In the second category of case, the court is concerned to protect the integrity of the criminal justice system. Here a stay will be granted where the court concludes that in all the circumstances a trial will "offend the court's sense of justice and propriety" (per *Lord Lowry in R v Horseferry Road Magistrates' Court, Ex p Bennett* [1994] 1 AC 42, 74G) or will "undermine public confidence in the criminal justice system and bring it into disrepute" (per Lord Steyn in *R v Latif and Shahzad* [1996] 1 WLR 104, 112F).'

---

4   *CPS v LR* [2010] EWCA Crim 924, per Judge LJ, para 16.

5   Criminal Justice Act 2003, s 58(8); see CPS Disclosure Manual, para 13.24.

6   [2010] UKSC 48.

11.06   In relation to the second category of case, Lord Dyson stated in *Curtis Francis Warren v Her Majesty's Attorney General of Jersey*[7] at paragraph 26:

'… the balance must always be struck between the public interest in ensuring that those who are accused of serious crimes should be tried and the competing public interest in ensuring that executive misconduct does not undermine public confidence in the criminal justice system and bring it into disrepute.'

11.07   A stay should only be imposed in exceptional circumstances.[8] In considering whether to allow an abuse argument for lack of disclosure,[9] the court should consider a series of steps identified in *R (on the application of Ebrahim) v Feltham Magistrates' Court:*[10]

1   Determine what the nature and extent of the duty of the investigating authority and the prosecutor was, if any, to obtain and/or retain the material in question having regard to the Code and Attorney General's Guidelines.[11]

2   If in all the circumstances there were no duties to obtain and/or retain the material before the defence first sought its retention, there can be no question of the subsequent trial being unfair on that ground.[12]

3   Where the material was not obtained and/or retained, in breach of the obligations set out in the CPIA Code and the Attorney General's Guidelines, the ultimate objective is to ensure that there should be a fair trial according to the law. That involves fairness to both the accused and the prosecution. The trial process itself is equipped to deal with the bulk of the complaints on which applications for a stay are founded.[13]

4   A stay will only be imposed, subject to point 6 below, if the defence can show, on a balance of probabilities, that owing to the failure of the police or the prosecution to obtain and/or retain the material the accused will suffer serious prejudice to the extent that no fair trial can be held, i.e. that the continuance of the prosecution would amount to a misuse of the powers of the court.[14]

---

7   [2011] UKPC 10.
8   Attorney General's Reference (No. 1 of 1990) [1992] 3 WLR 9.
9   Different considerations apply where material has been lost or destroyed.
10   [2001] EWHC Admin 130.
11   *R v Feltham Magistrates' Court* [2001] EWHC Admin 130, per Brooke LJ, para 16.
12   *R v Feltham Magistrates' Court* [2001] EWHC Admin 130, per Brooke LJ, para 16.
13   *R v Feltham Magistrates' Court* [2001] EWHC Admin 130, per Brooke LJ, para 25.
14   *R v Feltham Magistrates' Court* [2001] EWHC Admin 130, per Brooke LJ, para 16.

5   Where, apart from the missing evidence,[15] there is sufficient credible evidence, which, if believed, would justify a safe conviction, a trial should proceed.[16]

6   If point 4 above does not apply but the behaviour of the prosecution has been so very bad that it is not fair for the accused to be tried, the proceedings will be stayed on that ground. For a stay to be granted in such circumstances it is likely that there must be –

    (a)   an element of bad faith on the part of the police or the prosecution authorities; or

    (b)   at the very least some serious fault on their part.[17]

11.08   The reference to fairness in point 6 (above) must be read in conjunction with the judgment of Lord Kerr in *Curtis Francis Warren v Her Majesty's Attorney General of Jersey*[18] in which he stated at paragraph 84:

'For my part, I think that there is much to be said for discarding the notion of fairness when considering the second category of stay cases. Fairness to the accused, although not irrelevant in the assessment of whether it is fair to allow the trial to continue, is subsumed in the decision whether to grant a stay in second category cases based on the primary consideration of whether the stay is necessary to protect the integrity of the criminal justice system.'

11.09   The late disclosure of material is less likely to give rise to a stay of proceedings on the grounds of abuse than non-disclosure of material.[19]

11.10   On an application to stay proceedings, the trial judge should be invited to conduct a close analysis of the history of the case and should approach the issue of disclosure through the confines of the CPIA 1996.[20]

11.11   In order for an abuse of process argument to succeed, it is not always necessary to demonstrate that disclosure of material would have affected the outcome of the proceedings because, even with the benefit of hindsight, it will often be difficult to say whether or not an undisclosed item of evidence might

---

15   Such as fingerprint or scientific evidence.

16   *R v Feltham Magistrates' Court* [2001] EWHC Admin 130, per Brooke LJ, para 27; approved in *Ali, Altaf v CPS* [2007] EWCA Crim 691 by Moses LJ, para 30.

17   *R v Feltham Magistrates' Court* [2001] EWHC Admin 130, per Brooke LJ, paras 23, 74.

18   [2011] UKPC 10, para 84.

19   See *R v O* [2007] EWCA Crim 3483 and *R v MO* [2011] EWCA Crim 2845 for cases concerned with the staying of proceedings for late disclosure by the prosecution.

20   *R v O* [2007] EWCA Crim 3483, per Hooper LJ, para 42. This will normally require the defence to make an application for disclosure under CPIA 1996, s 8.

have shifted the balance or opened up a new line of defence.[21] In many cases, it would suffice for an accused to show a failure on the part of the prosecutor to meet disclosure obligations so that it is reasonable to suppose such failure might have affected the outcome of the trial.[22] Where there has been a failure on the part of the prosecution to make disclosure, the court will not regard a conviction as unsafe if the non-disclosure can properly be said to be of 'insignificance in regard to any real issue'.[23]

11.12   The procedure to apply to stay an indictment on the grounds of abuse of process application is set out in paragraph IV.36, Consolidated Criminal Practice Directions as follows:[24]

'IV.36.1   In all cases where a defendant in the Crown Court proposes to make an application to stay an indictment on the grounds of abuse of process, written notice of such application must be given to the prosecuting authority and to any co-defendant not later than 14 days before the date fixed or warned for trial ("the relevant date"). Such notice must:

(a)   give the name of the case and the indictment number;

(b)   state the fixed date or the warned date as appropriate;

(c)   specify the nature of the application;

(d)   set out in numbered sub-paragraphs the grounds upon which the application is to be made;

(e)   be copied to the chief listing officer at the court centre where the case is due to be heard.

IV.36.2   Any co-defendant who wishes to make a like application must give a like notice not later than seven days before the relevant date, setting out any additional grounds relied upon.

IV.36.3   In relation to such applications, the following automatic directions shall apply:

(a)   the advocate for the applicant(s) must lodge with the court and serve on all other parties a skeleton argument in support of the application, at least five clear working days before the relevant date. If reference is to be made to any

---

21   *R v Alibhai* [2004] EWCA Crim 681, per Longmore LJ, para 57; *R v Ward* [1993] 96 Cr App R 1, p 22.

22   *R v Alibhai* [2004] EWCA Crim 681, per Longmore LJ, para 57.

23   *R v Alibhai* [2004] EWCA Crim 681, per Longmore LJ, para 57; *R v Maguire* [1992] 94 Cr App R 133, p 148.

24   Supplementing CPR 2012.

document not in the existing trial documents, a paginated and indexed bundle of such documents is to be provided with the skeleton argument;

(b) the advocate for the prosecution must lodge with the court and serve on all other parties a responsive skeleton argument at least two clear working days before the relevant date, together with a supplementary bundle if appropriate.

IV.36.4 All skeleton arguments must specify any propositions of law to be advanced (together with the authorities relied upon in support, with page references to passages relied upon) and, where appropriate, include a chronology of events and a list of dramatis personae. In all instances where reference is made to a document, the reference in the trial documents or supplementary bundle is to be given.

IV.36.5 The above time limits are minimum time limits. In appropriate cases the court will order longer lead times. To this end in all cases where defence advocates are, at the time of the plea and directions hearing, considering the possibility of an abuse of process application, this must be raised with the judge dealing with the matter, who will order a different timetable if appropriate, and may wish, in any event, to give additional directions about the conduct of the application.'

11.13 The point at which an abuse of process application may be made has recently been clarified by Lord Judge CJ in *CPS v F*:[25]

'An application to stay for an abuse of process ought ordinarily to be heard and determined at the outset of the case, and before any evidence is heard, unless there is a specific reason to defer it because the question of prejudice and fair trial can be better determined at a later stage.' (para 48)

REFUSING TO EXTEND CUSTODY TIME LIMITS

11.14 A court may refuse to extend custody time limits where the prosecution has not complied with its disclosure obligations.

11.15 Where an application is made to extend the accused's custody time limits, it is for the prosecution to prove on a balance of probabilities that the two limbs of section 22(3), Prosecution of Offences Act 1985 are satisfied, namely:

---

25 *CPS v F* [2011] EWCA Crim 1844, per Lord Judge CJ.

'(a)   that the need for the extension is due to –

> (i)   the illness or absence of the accused, a necessary witness, a judge or a magistrate;

> (ii)   a postponement which is occasioned by the ordering by the court of separate trials in the case of two or more accused or two or more offences; or

> (iii) some other good and sufficient cause; and

(b)   that the prosecution has acted with all due diligence and expedition.'

11.16   If the court is not so satisfied, the custody time limits cannot be extended[26] and the accused is immediately entitled to bail subject to section 25(1), Criminal Justice and Public Order Act 1994.[27]

11.17   It will be open for the defence to argue that the late disclosure of the prosecution papers or the late/non-disclosure of material that satisfies the prosecution disclosure test[28] indicates that the prosecution have not acted with all due diligence and expedition.[29]

11.18   The prosecution are required to show such diligence and expedition as would be shown by a competent prosecutor, conscious of his duty to bring the case to trial as quickly, reasonably and fairly as possible.[30] They are not expected to be able to show that every action has been completed as quickly and efficiently as is humanly possible, nor should the history be approached on the unreal assumption that all involved on the prosecution side have been able to give the case their undivided attention.[31]

11.19   In a complex case the prosecutor cannot be expected to have detailed knowledge of every part of the investigation. Where the defence intend to criticize a particular part of the investigation in order to challenge an application to extend

---

26 *R v Manchester Crown Court ex parte McDonald* [1999] 1 Cr App R 409, per Lord Bingham CJ, p 413.

27 CJPO 1994, s 25 excludes the grant of bail to an accused charged with or convicted of homicide or rape with a previous conviction of such offences, save in exceptional circumstances. See *R (O) v Crown Court at Harrow* [2006] UKHL 42, per Lord Brown for the approach to be taken to this section.

28 i.e. any prosecution material which might reasonably be considered capable of undermining the case for the prosecution against the accused or of assisting the case for the accused.

29 Prosecution of Offences Act 1985, s 22(3)(b).

30 *R v Manchester Crown Court ex parte McDonald* [1999] 1 Cr App R 409, per Lord Bingham CJ, p 414.

31 *R v Manchester Crown Court ex parte McDonald* [1999] 1 Cr App R 409, per Lord Bingham CJ, p 414.

a custody time limit, reasonable notice should be given so that the prosecutor can respond appropriately.[32] In the absence of such notice, the court may decide that, at least for the time being, more general information from the prosecutor will suffice.[33]

11.20 While the prosecution cannot be responsible for the failures of third parties from whom they are seeking evidence, such as forensic science laboratories,[34] they do have an obligation to do all they can within their power to ensure that the evidence is available within the relevant custody time limit.[35] This would include notifying third parties of all the relevant dates and time limits, notifying them of the accused's remand status and maintaining good lines of communication.[36]

11.21 The CPS's Core Quality Standards sets out the levels of service to be expected from the CPS in the preparation of cases involving custody time limits. It is expected that the CPS, inter alia, will:

- announce in court the dates on which the relevant custody time limits expire;[37]

- note the expiry dates on the case file and in the custody time limit diary;[38]

- prioritise the preparation of custody cases;[39]

- review custody time limit diaries and the computerised case management system to check for approaching custody time limits;[40] and

- provide a chronology at any application to extend custody time limits.[41]

---

32 *R v Manchester Crown Court ex parte McDonald* [1999] 1 Cr App R 409, per Lord Bingham CJ, p 414.
33 *R v Woolwich Crown Court ex parte Smith* [2002] EWHC 995 (Admin).
34 Forensic Science laboratories do not form part of the prosecution for the purposes of Prosecution of Offences Act 1985, s 22.
35 *R v Central Criminal Court ex parte Johnson* [1999] 2 Cr App R 51, per Collins J.
36 In *R (Holland) v Leeds Crown Court* [2002] EWHC 1862 (Admin), per Bell J the extension of custody time limits, caused by the late service of prosecution expert scientific evidence, was refused as the prosecution had not acted with all due diligence.
37 CPS Core Quality Standards, Standard 5: Case preparation, para 5.27.
38 CPS Core Quality Standards, Standard 5: Case preparation, para 5.28.
39 CPS Core Quality Standards, Standard 5: Case preparation, para 5.29.
40 CPS Core Quality Standards, Standard 5: Case preparation, para 5.30.
41 CPS Core Quality Standards, Standard 5: Case preparation, para 5.30.

ORDERS FOR COSTS

11.22   Costs may be an effective remedy where a hearing is adjourned or cancelled or a trial is aborted because of the late or non-disclosure of material by either the defence or prosecution. Where an adjournment is applied for, there is a duty on the advocate to be frank with the court as to the reasons why.[42] The power of the court to make a costs order is specifically provided for in rule 3.5(6), CPR 2012 which states:

'If a party fails to comply with a rule or a direction, the court may –

(a)   fix, postpone, bring forward, extend, cancel or adjourn a hearing;

(b)   exercise its power to make a costs order; and

(c)   impose such other sanctions as may be appropriate.'

11.23   The court can order one party in criminal proceedings to pay the other party's costs where they have been incurred as a result of 'an unnecessary or improper act or omission'.[43] The CPS is a party to the proceedings for these purposes.

11.24   The procedure to be followed where one party may be liable to pay another party's costs is set out at rule 76.8, CPR 2012 and the Practice Direction (Costs in Criminal Proceedings) (July 2010).[44] The Practice Direction suggests that the courts may find it helpful to adopt a three-stage approach:

(a)   Has there been an unnecessary improper act or omission?

(b)   As a result, have any costs been incurred by another party?

(c)   If the answers to (a) and (b) are 'yes', should the court exercise its discretion to order the party responsible to meet the whole or any part of the relevant costs, and if so what specific sum is involved?

11.25   The power of the court to order one party to pay the other's costs is to be distinguished from a 'wasted costs' order against a legal representative. The court can order a legal representative (which includes the crown prosecutor and prosecution advocate) to pay such costs or prohibit the payment of costs to him where a party has incurred costs:

---

42   *R v McDonagh* [2011] EWCA Crim 3238, per Thomas LJ, para 25.
43   Prosecution of Offences Act 1985, s 19; Costs in Criminal Cases (General) Regulations 1986 (SI 1986/1335), reg 3(1).
44   [2010] 1 WLR 2351, per Lord Judge CJ, para 4.1.1.

- as a result of any improper, unreasonable or negligent act or omission by a legal or other representative (or employee); or

- which it has become unreasonable for that party to pay because of such an act or omission occurring after those costs were incurred.[45]

11.26   The procedure to be followed where a judge is considering 'wasted costs' is set out at rule 76.9, CPR 2012, and the Practice Direction (Costs in Criminal Proceedings) (July 2010).[46] The Practice Direction again recommends that the courts use a three-stage approach:

(a)   Has there been an unnecessary improper act or omission?

(b)   As a result, have any costs been incurred by another party?

(c)   If the answers to (a) and (b) are 'yes', should the court exercise its discretion to disallow or order the representative to meet the whole or any part of the relevant costs, and if so what specific sum is involved?

11.27   Costs payable under a costs order are limited to costs actually incurred under the graduated fee scheme, no matter how vital the work. The court has no power to make a costs order in respect of sums not claimable by the accused himself or those liable for his costs or the Legal Services Commission.[47]

11.28   Before any costs order is made in respect of either a party or legal representative, the court must hear from the parties and is entitled to take such an order into account when making any other costs order.

11.29   While the senior courts still have an inherent jurisdiction to make orders in respect of costs thrown away, given the present costs provisions the exercise of the inherent jurisdiction will occur only 'in the rarest of circumstances'.[48]

EXCLUSION OF EVIDENCE

11.30   The late or non-disclosure of material by the prosecution may lead to the exclusion of evidence. Section 78(1), Police and Criminal Evidence Act 1984 states:

---

45   Prosecution of Offences Act 1985, s 19A; Costs in Criminal Cases (General) Regulations 1986, reg 3B (SI 1986/1335); CPR 2012, r 76.9.

46   [2010] 1 WLR 2351, per Lord Judge CJ, para 4.2.4.

47   *R v Fitzgerald* [2012] 3 Costs LR 437, per His Honour Judge Gordon, para 17 (Central Criminal Court).

48   Practice Direction (Costs in Criminal Proceedings) [2010] 1 WLR 2351, per Lord Judge CJ, para 1.2.3.

'In any proceedings the court may refuse to allow evidence on which the prosecution proposes to rely to be given if it appears to the court that, having regard to all the circumstances, including the circumstances in which the evidence was obtained, the admission of the evidence would have such an adverse effect on the fairness of the proceedings that the court ought not to admit it.'

11.31   All cases are fact specific. Where the prosecution discloses material which satisfies the prosecution disclosure test[49] shortly before trial, there may be insufficient time for the defence to investigate the material properly. The prejudice caused to the defence may lead the trial judge to exclude the prosecution evidence to which the material relates. The judge is more likely to do this where there is no good reason for the late disclosure. Evidence, even of substantial probative value, may on rare occasions be excluded where section 78, Police and Criminal Evidence Act 1984 does not apply, but there has been a failure to comply with the Criminal Procedures Rules.[50]

ACQUITTAL AGAINST THE WEIGHT OF THE EVIDENCE[51]

11.32   Where the prosecution fail to comply with their disclosure obligations such failures may be highlighted in the closing speech of the defence advocate. These failures may include not pursuing a reasonable line of enquiry, not taking swabs or the lifts of fingerprints/footprints at the scene or, if taken, not sending them for scientific analysis. The defence may properly rely on these holes in the prosecution case to seek to persuade the jury[52] not to convict because evidence which might otherwise have been available was not before the court through no fault of the accused.[53] Where fairness to the accused demands it, an admission pursuant to section 10, Criminal Justice Act 1967 can be drafted to illustrate the prosecution failures.

---

49 i.e. any prosecution material which might reasonably be considered capable of undermining the case for the prosecution against the accused or of assisting the case for the accused.

50 *R v Musone* [2007] EWCA Crim 1237: An accused intentionally sought to ambush a co-accused in breach of the Criminal Procedure Rules. Moses LJ, para 56 stated '... the judge was entitled to exclude that evidence in circumstances where he concluded the appellant had deliberately manipulated the trial process so as to give his co-defendant no opportunity of dealing properly with the allegation.' Note: Police and Criminal Evidence Act 1984, s 78 did not apply because it was not evidence upon which the prosecution proposed to rely. There was also no express power to exclude the evidence under Criminal Justice Act 2003, s 101(e) (bad character relating to a co-accused).

51 Equally, an appeal against conviction may be successful as a result of the prosecution's failure to comply with the disclosure obligations.

52 Or Justices.

53 *R (on the application of Ebrahim) v Feltham Magistrates' Court* [2001] EWHC Admin 130 , per Brooke LJ, para 27.

Chapter 12

Post-conviction disclosure and review

INTRODUCTION

12.01   It is clear from section 7A, CPIA 1996 that the prosecution's statutory duty of continuing disclosure ceases upon conviction, acquittal or discontinuance of the case.[1] Duties of disclosure still remain in order to remedy miscarriages of justice.

12.02   The general duty of the police and CPS to investigate also ceases on conviction. 'A person convicted of a crime has no right to further disclosure to facilitate his re-investigation of the case, any more than the state is under a duty to re-investigate' his case.[2]

12.03   This chapter deals with:

• post-conviction disclosure	**12.04–12.10**
• post-conviction review	**12.11–12.13**
• the role of the courts	**12.14–12.15**

POST-CONVICTION DISCLOSURE

12.04   There is no statutory right to post-conviction disclosure and 'a person convicted of a crime has no right to further disclosure to facilitate his re-investigation of the case, any more than the state is under a duty to re-

---

1 *Nunn v Chief Constable of the Suffolk Constabulary* [2012] EWHC 1186 (Admin), per President QBD, paras 24, 32.
2 *Nunn v Chief Constable of the Suffolk Constabulary* [2012] EWHC 1186 (Admin), per President QBD, para 32.

investigate'.[3] Sir John Thomas stated in *Nunn v Chief Constable of the Suffolk Constabulary:*

> 'It is important to emphasise that the procedure leading to trial is specifically designed to give the defendant the fullest opportunity to receive disclosure of the information in the possession of the Crown and, with the benefit of that disclosure, to investigate the evidence and, in particular, the forensic evidence'.[4]

12.05   Any resulting conviction is also subject to review by the Court of Appeal Criminal Division.[5]

12.06   In *R v Makin,*[6] a case concerned with whether information could be withheld on the basis of public interest immunity, Hooper LJ stated: 'We add only this. The duty of disclosure continues as long as proceedings remain whether at first instance or on appeal'. In setting out what that duty is he said:

> '... there is an obligation to disclose material if it assists the defence by allowing the defendant to put forward a case in the best tenable light or if the material could assist the defence to make further enquiries and those enquiries might assist in showing the defendant's innocence or avoid a miscarriage of justice.'[7]

12.07   For the purposes of an appeal, that burden does not extend to facilitating a re-investigation by the appellant.

12.08   Where material comes to light post-conviction that may materially cast doubt upon the safety of a conviction, the prosecution has a duty to consider disclosure. This is embodied in the Attorney General's Guidelines on Disclosure (2005) which state:

'Post-conviction

59.   The interests of justice will also mean that where material comes to light after the conclusion of the proceedings, which might cast doubt upon the safety of the conviction, there is a duty to consider disclosure. Any such material should be brought immediately to the attention of line management.

---

3   [2012] EWHC 1186 (Admin), para 32.
4   [2012] EWHC 1186 (Admin), para 30.
5   The Criminal Cases Review Commission can also refer cases to the Court of Appeal.
6   [2004] EWCA Crim 1607, para 36.
7   [2004] EWCA Crim 1607, para 30. See *R v Puddick* [1865] 4 F&F 497; *R v Banks* [1916] 2 KB 621; *R v Agar* (1990) 90 Cr App R 318; *R v Hallett* [1986] Crim LR 462.

60.   Disclosure of any material that is made outside the ambit of Act will attract confidentiality by virtue of *Taylor v SFO* [1998].'[8]

12.09   The CPS Disclosure Manual advises that the disclosure test to be applied post-conviction is as set out in paragraph 59, Attorney General's Guidelines on Disclosure (2005) (see **12.08**). The defence case should be assessed as that advanced at trial or, if matters are raised on appeal which were not raised during the trial process, set out in the appellant's grounds of appeal.[9]

12.10   As a general rule, non-disclosure will not prevent an accused's guilty plea being regarded as safe. Where, however, the accused's decision to plead guilty is taken on the basis of information which was materially deficient due to the prosecution's failure to comply with its duty of disclosure, an appeal against conviction may succeed. In *R v Early*[10] B's conviction was quashed after he had pleaded guilty and the prosecution's failure to make proper disclosure had prevented him from pursuing an abuse of process argument. Rose LJ said:

'a defendant who pleads guilty at an early stage should not, if inadequate disclosure has not been made by then, be in any worse position than a defendant who, as the consequence of an argument to stay proceedings as an abuse, has the benefit of further disclosure which leads to the abandonment of the proceedings against him.'

POST-CONVICTION REVIEW

12.11   The CPS may be required to review the safety of convictions as a consequence of a trigger and conduct an assessment as to whether justice is served by allowing such convictions to stand.[11]

12.12   Triggers for potential CPS reviews of past convictions include:[12]

•   where the competence and/or credibility or methodology of an expert witness is in doubt;

•   where a police officer's evidence is discredited;

---

8   [1998] 4 All ER 801, per Kennedy LJ – disclosure by the prosecution of unused material created in the course of a criminal investigation is subject to an implied undertaking not to use the material for any collateral purpose.
9   CPS Disclosure Manual, paras 2.10, 2.13.
10   [2002] EWCA Crim 1904, para 74.
11   CPS Legal Guidance, Reviewing Previously Finalised Cases – CPS Policy.
12   CPS Legal Guidance, Reviewing Previously Finalised Cases – CPS Policy, para 6.

- new scientific breakthroughs;

- developments of the law which affect the offence/defence;

- where the CPS guidance relied upon is legally incorrect;

- systemic failings in the disclosure process; and

- where proceedings were based on a defective indictment.[13]

12.13   In order for the police and CPS to carry out a review, it will be necessary to show that something materially may cast doubt upon the safety of the conviction. This may arise, for example, where scientific advances enable tests unavailable at the time of trial to be carried out which might reasonably be anticipated to affect the safety of a conviction.[14]

ROLE OF THE COURTS

12.14   Where the claimant believes he has a proper case for further disclosure or the re-testing of items, he should write to the CPS setting out the grounds and reasons supporting his claim. The courts have the power to intervene following the refusal of the CPS or the police to disclose material. In *Kevin Nunn v Chief Constable of the Suffolk Constabulary* the President QBD stated:

> '…. observance of the duty of disclosure in a criminal cause or matter is ultimately a matter for the court. Where a proper case has been advanced for disclosure or retesting, it is for the court, in the event of refusal by the police or CPS to disclose, itself to determine whether there should be disclosure or re-testing.' (para 37)

12.15   The argument that post-conviction disclosure should only be ordered if the police or CPS have acted irrationally was expressly rejected[15] in favour of a more pro-active approach by the courts.

---

13   See CPS Legal Guidance, Reviewing Previously Finalised Cases – CPS Policy, paras A–E for potential actions available to the CPS.

14   *Nunn v Chief Constable of the Suffolk Constabulary* [2012] EWHC 1186 (Admin), per President QBD, para 32.

15   *Nunn v Chief Constable of the Suffolk Constabulary* [2012] EWHC 1186 (Admin), per President QBD, paras 36–37.

Chapter 13

Interception of communications

INTRODUCTION

13.01   The main purpose of the Regulation of Investigatory Powers Act 2000 (RIPA 2000) is to ensure that the relevant investigatory powers are used in accordance with a person's human rights.[1] As a result, the golden rule of full disclosure,[2] namely, that any material which satisfies the prosecution disclosure test[3] must be disclosed to the defence, is subject to the exception that the material must not be disclosed to the extent that its disclosure is prohibited by section 17, RIPA 2000,[4] (in addition to the public interest immunity exception).[5]

13.02   This chapter deals with:

• the types of intercept requiring a warrant	**13.03–13.08**
• protection for the accused	**13.09–13.21**
• the types of intercept not requiring a warrant	**13.22–13.28**
• private telecommunications	**13.29–13.31**

TYPES OF INTERCEPT REQUIRING A WARRANT

13.03   Section 1, RIPA 2000 provides that it is an offence for a person intentionally, and without lawful authority, to intercept any communication in the course of its transmission by means of:

---

1   See RIPA 2000, Explanatory Notes, para 3.
2   *R v H & C* [2004] UKHL 3, per Lord Bingham CJ, paras 14, 18, 36.
3   i.e. any prosecution material which might reasonably be considered capable of undermining the case for the prosecution against the accused or of assisting the case for the accused.
4   CPIA 1996, ss 3(7), 7A(9), 8(6) – these sections deal with the duties of initial disclosure, continuing disclosure and the application by the accused for disclosure respectively.
5   CPIA 1996, ss 3(6), 7A(8), 8(5) (see **fn 4** above).

(a)   a public postal service; or

(b)   a public telecommunications system.

13.04   This will include, inter alia:

*   any communications made via a public postal service;

*   telephone calls through a landline or mobile phone network;

*   text messages sent through a mobile phone network; and

*   e-mail communications via the internet.

13.05   The offences arise where the intercept is made in the 'course of its transmission' and will not apply to messages stored once the transmission has ceased, e.g. messages stored on answer machines.

13.06   An intercept is lawful where a warrant has been issued. Section 5(3), RIPA 2000 allows an interception warrant to be issued:

'if it is necessary –

(a)   in the interests of national security;

(b)   for the purpose of preventing or detecting serious crime;

(c)   for the purpose of safeguarding the economic well-being of the United Kingdom; or

(d)   for the purposes of ... any international mutual assistance agreement.'

13.07   Where a warrant is obtained for the intercept of a public postal or telecommunications system in the UK, all information relating to it is excluded from the public domain and cannot be disclosed to the defence or used in evidence. The rationale behind this practice is to protect the security of intercept usage and technology.

13.08   Section 17, RIPA 2000 sets out the prohibition against disclosing any information in relation to a warrant or the product of it. Subject to section 18, RIPA 2000 (see **13.11** onwards), evidence, questioning or asserting anything that is likely to reveal the existence or absence of a warrant is prohibited. The disclosure of any intercepted material, or associated communications data, and any suggestion that intercepted material has been unlawfully obtained is excluded.

PROTECTION FOR THE ACCUSED

13.09   Prosecutors may have intercepted evidence communicated to them which satisfies the prosecution disclosure test[6] but is not disclosed to the accused because of the prohibition imposed by section 17, RIPA 2000.

13.10   Some protection is afforded to the accused as the use of intercepted material is restricted to the minimum necessary for 'authorised' purposes[7] and must be destroyed as soon as it is not required for any 'authorised' purpose.[8] One of the authorised purposes is to 'ensure that a person conducting a criminal prosecution has the information he needs to determine what is required of him by his duty to secure the fairness of the prosecution'.[9]

13.11   The issuing of a warrant for the purpose of preventing or detecting serious crime[10] does not extend to gathering information for a prosecution and intercepted material may not survive to the prosecution stage.[11] If intercepted material is in existence after the commencement of a prosecution,[12] section 18, RIPA 2000 permits disclosure to a prosecutor and, if necessary, to a judge, for certain limited purposes (see **13.19** below). Section 18 (7), RIPA 2000 provides:

> 'Nothing in section 17(1) shall prohibit any such disclosure of any information that continues to be available for disclosure as is confined to –
>
> (a)   a disclosure to a person conducting a criminal prosecution for the purpose only of enabling that person to determine what is required of him by his duty to secure the fairness of the prosecution; ....'

13.12   The above exception to the prohibition against disclosure in section 17, RIPA 2000 does not mean that intercepted material should be retained against a remote possibility that it might be relevant to future proceedings, nor does it provide for any disclosure to the defence. The normal expectation is still for the intercepted material to be destroyed in accordance with the general safeguards provided by section 15, RIPA 2000[13] (see **13.10**).

---

6   i.e any prosecution material which might reasonably be considered capable of undermining the case for the prosecution against the accused or of assisting the case for the accused.

7   RIPA 2000, s 15(2).

8   RIPA 2000, s 15(3).

9   RIPA 2000, s 15(4)(d).

10   Pursuant to s 5(3)(b).

11   See RIPA 2000, s 5(3)(b); Interception of Communications Code of Practice, para 7, pursuant to RIPA 2000, s 71.

12   Interception of Communications Code of Practice, para 7.8 – such material will only be available for a prosecutor if a conscious decision has been made to retain it for an authorised purpose.

13   Interception of Communications Code of Practice, para 7.7.

13.13 If intercepted material is not in existence at the commencement of a prosecution, it cannot be revealed to the prosecutor and there is no duty on investigators to brief prosecutors where there has been an interception and no product remains. As a matter of good practice, the police should draw the attention of the prosecutor to the fact of the interception and provide an assurance that, to the best of their knowledge, the destroyed product contained nothing that would affect the fairness of the trial.[14]

13.14 The Attorney General has issued guidelines[15] on the approach to be taken in the application of section 18, RIPA 2000. If protected information is disclosed to a prosecutor under section 18, the prosecutor's first step should be to review any information from an interception that remains extant at the time he has conduct of the case. In reviewing it, the prosecutor should seek to identify any information whose existence, if the Crown took no action, might result in unfairness, e.g. the jury may draw an inference on the evidence which the intercepted material shows to be wrong and to leave uncorrected would disadvantage the accused.[16]

13.15 Where the prosecutor's view is that to take no action would render the proceedings unfair, the prosecutor should, after consulting with the relevant prosecution agency, take such steps as are available to secure the fairness of the proceedings provided these steps do not contravene the section 17 prohibition.[17]

13.16 The Attorney General's Section 18 RIPA Prosecutors Intercept Guidelines (RIPA Guidelines) state that steps which the prosecutor could take include:

'(i) putting the prosecution case in such a way that the misleading inference is not drawn by the jury; or

(ii) not relying upon the evidence which makes the information relevant; or

(iii) discontinuing that part of the prosecution case in relation to which the protected material is relevant, by amending a charge or count or offering no evidence on such a charge or count; or

---

14 CPS Disclosure Manual, para 27.20.
15 Attorney General's Section 18 RIPA Prosecutors Intercept Guidelines England and Wales are set out in **Appendix 17**.
16 RIPA Guidelines, para 5.
17 RIPA 2000, s 18(10); RIPA Guidelines, para 6.

(iv)   making an admission of fact [*provided that it does not contravene section 17, RIPA 2000, by revealing the existence of an interception warrant*].'[18]

13.17   There is no requirement for the prosecutor to notify the judge of the action he has taken or proposes to take.

13.18   Where the prosecutor considers that he cannot secure the fairness of the proceedings without assistance from the relevant judge, the prosecutor can invite the judge to order disclosure of the protected material to him alone.[19] A judge must not order disclosure to himself unless he is satisfied that the exceptional circumstances of the case make that disclosure essential in the interests of justice.[20] Any application must be made ex parte.[21]

13.19   Paragraph 8, RIPA Guidelines suggest that there are two situations which would justify any disclosure to a judge:

1   where the judge's assistance is necessary to ensure the fairness of the trial through summing up, giving appropriate directions or requiring the Crown to make an admission of fact; and[22]

2   where the judge requires knowledge of the protected material for some other purpose, such as to properly assess the significance of other public interest immunity material, or in order to ensure that section 17(1), RIPA 2000 is not contravened during cross-examination.

13.20   Where no action can be taken by the prosecutor and/or the judge to prevent the continuation of the proceedings being unfair, the prosecutor will have 'no option but to offer no evidence on the charge in question, or to discontinue the proceedings in their entirety'.[23]

13.21   Where the defence suspect interception has taken place (this information will not be volunteered or admitted by the prosecution),[24] they can do no more than remind the prosecutor of his duty to review any protected material which has been disclosed to him under section 18, RIPA 2000.

---

18   RIPA Guidelines, para 6. A breach of RIPA 2000, s 17 might occur not only from the factual content of the admission, but also from the circumstances in which it is made.
19   RIPA 2000, s 18(7)(b).
20   RIPA 2000, s 18(8).
21   RIPA Guidelines, para 11.
22   RIPA 2000, s 18(9).
23   RIPA Guidelines, para 9.
24   RIPA Guidelines, paras 10–11.

TYPES OF INTERCEPT NOT REQUIRING WARRANT

13.22 There is no prohibition on the evidential use of material obtained by lawful interception without the use of a warrant and therefore no prohibition on disclosure where it is sought to investigate the lawfulness of any interception. If the intercept is unlawful, it may be excluded from evidence.

13.23 Section 1(5), RIPA 2000 permits lawful interception without a warrant where:

- it is authorised by or under section 3 or 4 of the Act;

- it is in exercise, in relation to any stored communication, of some other statutory power exercised for the purpose of obtaining information or of taking possession of any document or other property.

13.24 Under sections 3 and 4, RIPA 2000 the intercept is lawful where, inter alia:

- there are reasonable grounds for believing that both the sender and the intended recipient of a communication have consented to its interception;

- either the sender or intended recipient of a communication has consented to its interception and directed surveillance by means of that interception has been authorised under Part II, RIPA 2000;[25] or

- the interception is listed in section 4, RIPA 2000 as a power that may be exercised without the need for a warrant. Under section 4(4), RIPA 2000 this includes 'conduct taking place in a prison … if it is conduct in exercise of any power conferred by or under any rules made under s 47 of the Prison Act 1952 …'.[26]

13.25 It is generally permissible to record all telephone calls of prison inmates with their family, friends and others.[27]

13.26 Under rule 35C, Prison Rules 1999[28] a governor may not disclose intercepted material to a third party unless he considers that such disclosure is necessary and proportionate to what is sought to be achieved by disclosure, or

---

25 Part II deals with surveillance and covert human intelligence sources.

26 Prison Act 1952, s 47 allows the Secretary of State to make rules for the regulation and management of prisons. In 1996 the Secretary of State directed that the PIN system, a system for recording calls, should be 'rolled out', pursuant to which it was rolled out to Category A and B prisons.

27 *R v Abiodun* [2005] EWCA Crim 9, para 55. In *Abiodun*, Clarke LJ gave detailed consideration to the system of recording prison calls.

28 Inserted Prison (Amendment) (No. 2) Rules 2000 (SI 2000/2641), r 5.

the parties consent. Under rule 35A(4) the grounds considered necessary and proportionate for disclosure are:

'(a)   the interests of national security;

(b)   the prevention, detection, investigation or prosecution of crime;

(c)   the interests of public safety;

(d)   securing or maintaining prison security or good order and discipline in prison;

(e)   the protection of health or morals; or

(f)   the protection of the rights and freedoms of any person.'

13.27   Once a judge has decided that the intercept is lawful, it is still open for the defence to argue its admissibility under the Police and Criminal Evidence Act 1984, ss 76 and 78.

13.28   Where one party to a telephone conversation tape records the call, that does not amount to an interception. Hughes LJ in *R v Hardy*[29] stated:

'It is exactly the same as the undercover officer secreting a tape recorder in his pocket or briefcase whilst meeting the suspect face-to-face ... it is surveillance and requires regulation. The Act provides for it, but it is not interception.' (para 30)

PRIVATE TELECOMMUNICATIONS

13.29   Under section 1(2), RIPA 2000 it is an offence for a person intentionally, and without lawful authority, to intercept any communication in the course of its communication by means of a private telecommunications system[30] unless the conduct is excluded from criminal liability under section 1(6). Such conduct is excluded from criminal liability under subsection (6) if the person intercepting:

•   is a person with a right to control the operation or the use of the system; or

•   has the express or implied consent of such a person to make the interception.

---

29   [2002] EWCA Crim 3012.

30   A private telecommunications system is any telecommunication system which is not a public telecommunications system but is attached to such a system.

13.30   A person has a right to control the operation or the use of the system if he has the right to 'authorise or forbid the operation or the use of the system'.[31] Merely having the right to access or operate the system without restriction will not suffice. This will include the private communications network of an employer or organisation that is linked to a public telecommunications system by a private exchange.

13.31   There is no prohibition on the evidential use of material obtained by lawful interception of a private telecommunications system and therefore no prohibition on disclosure where it is sought in order to investigate the lawfulness of any interception made. If the interception is unlawful, it may be excluded from evidence.

---

31   *R v Stanford* [2006] EWCA Crim 258, per Lord Phillips CJ.

Chapter 14

Disclosure in the magistrates' court

INTRODUCTION

14.01   This chapter will provide the practitioner with a working knowledge of disclosure in the magistrates' court. Reference is made to the magistrates' court protocol which, although not adopted, provides guidance for practitioners.[1]

14.02   This chapter deals with:

• the initial details of the prosecution case	**14.03–14.11**
• prosecution disclosure	**14.12–14.20**
• the consequences of prosecution non-disclosure	**14.21–14.22**
• defence disclosure	
– the preparation for trial form[2]	**14.23–14.24**
– defence statements	**14.25–14.30**
– privilege against self-incrimination	**14.31–14.35**
– putting the prosecution to proof	**14.36**
– sanctions for faults in the defence statement	**14.37–14.40**
– witness notices	**14.41–14.43**
– sanctions for faults in the witness notice	**14.44–14.46**
– time limits	**14.47**
• administrative sanctions	**14.48–14.50**

---

1   Protocol for the Provision of Advance Information, Prosecution Evidence and Disclosure of Unused Material in the Magistrates' Courts.
2   For a copy of the preparation for trial form (listed in the Consolidated Criminal Practice Direction, Annex E) see **Appendix 18**.

INITIAL DETAILS OF PROSECUTION CASE

14.03   The 'Criminal Justice: Simple, Speedy, Summary' (CJSSS) initiative[3] was rolled out across magistrates' courts during 2007/08 with the aim of, inter alia, reducing the number of hearings and the time taken before a case can be disposed of. This was supplemented by the 'Stop Delaying Justice' initiative introduced in January 2012. When introducing 'Stop delaying Justice',[4] Goldring LJ stated:

> '... Proper case management is an essential part of dealing effectively with ... cases. Proper case management requires no more than ensuring that the parties comply with the Criminal Procedure Rules. Compliance with the Rules is not an optional extra. They apply to the prosecution, they apply to the defence, they impose an obligation on the court ... Stop Delaying Justice is part of changing the culture of everyone who has a part to play in the magistrates' court.'

14.04   To implement the initiatives properly, the defence need to be armed with sufficient information at or before the first hearing where the offence is one that can be tried in a magistrates' court. The CPR 2010 initially gave effect to this requirement and now rule 21.2, CPR 2012[5] provides that:

'The prosecution must provide initial details of the prosecution case by –

(a)   serving those details on the court officer; and

(b)   making those details available to the defendant,

at, or before, the beginning of the day of the first hearing.'

14.05   Rule 21.3, CPR 2012 states that:

'Initial details of the prosecution case must include –

(a)   a summary of the evidence upon which the case will be based; or

(b)   any statement, document or extract setting out facts or other matters on which that case will be based; or

(c)   any combination of such summary, statement or extract; and

(d)   the defendant's previous convictions.'

---

3   This is a multi-agency initiative involving the CPS, HM Courts Service and the police.

4   Video prepared on behalf of the judicial college in February 2012. Goldring LJ is, at the time of writing, the Senior Presiding Judge.

5   CPR 2012, Part 21 is set out in **Appendix 19**.

14.06   There is no specific obligation to provide more than a case summary and details of the accused's previous convictions at the first hearing, although it is good practice and in the interests of the prosecution to provide more material.[6] The CPS Legal Guidance suggests that prosecutors should normally serve written statements (or parts thereof) when they are available and supply a copy of any other document that they intend to rely on. If a copy cannot be supplied the defence must be allowed to inspect the original or a copy.[7]

14.07   The prosecution are required to serve initial details of its case on the defence 'at, or before, the beginning of the day of the first hearing'.[8]

14.08   A record must be made on the file when initial details have been provided. The date of provision and the recipient should be noted.[9]

14.09   Where an offence can be tried only in the crown court, the details of the case are served on the accused after the case is sent for trial.[10]

14.10   There is no requirement at this stage for the prosecution to provide any unused material although the common law rules of disclosure still apply (see **14.12**).

14.11   The rules that formerly governed advance information[11] required that the court must adjourn proceedings where the prosecution have failed to provide advance information. This requirement is not present in the CPR 2012 but it is unlikely that the court would proceed with a case in the absence of the initial case details unless it were satisfied that the accused would not be prejudiced.[12]

---

6   'Stop Delaying Justice', p 14.

7   The CPS Legal Guidance on Advance Information suggests that decisions made under CPR 2005, Part 21 still apply: see *R v Calderdale Justices ex parte Donahue* [2001] Crim LR 141, paras 22–27 and *R (on the application of DPP) v Croydon Magistrates Court* [2001] EWHC Admin 552 on the need to supply CCTV or DNA profiling material as part of advance information.

8   CPR 2012, Part 21.

9   CPS Legal Guidance, Advance Information.

10   CPR 2012, Part 9. CPIA 1996, s 1 is amended by Criminal Justice Act 2003, s 41 which came into force on 18 June 2012 (see SI 2012/1320). This amendment only applies to certain local justice areas, other areas will follow. Where it applies, committal to the crown court is abolished and all relevant cases will be sent to the crown court under the Crime and Disorder Act 1998, as amended.

11   Advance Information Magistrates' Courts (Advance Information) Rules 1985; Criminal Procedure Rules 2005.

12   CPS Legal Guidance, Advance information, 'Non-compliance'.

PROSECUTION DISCLOSURE

14.12   Before statutory disclosure is triggered under the CPIA 1996, the common law principles of disclosure as set out by Kennedy LJ in *R v DPP ex parte Lee*[13] apply (see **Chapter 7**).

14.13   The initial duty of statutory disclosure under section 3, CPIA 1996 applies in the magistrates' court where –

'(a)   a person is charged with a summary offence in respect of which a court proceeds to summary trial and in respect of which he pleads not guilty,

(b)   a person who has attained the age of 18 is charged with an offence which is triable either way, in respect of which a court proceeds to summary trial and in respect of which he pleads not guilty, or

(c)   a person under the age of 18 is charged with an indictable offence in respect of which a court proceeds to summary trial and in respect of which he pleads not guilty.'[14]

14.14   Initial statutory disclosure should consist of[15] the endorsed non-sensitive schedule (MG6C) and copies of any documents that satisfy the prosecution disclosure test.[16] Once disclosure is triggered, it must be completed as soon as reasonably practicable.[17] Standard directions allow for 28 days following plea for initial statutory disclosure to be provided.[18] Where the case is sent to the crown court, initial statutory disclosure should be 'as soon as possible' after copies of the documents containing the evidence upon which the charge(s) are based are served on the accused.[19]

14.15   Where it is intended to serve a defence statement, a failure to serve the MG6C will not prevent time beginning to run for service of the defence statement as 'the schedule itself is not a necessary component of nor the mark of primary [*now called initial*] disclosure'.[20]

---

13   *R v DPP ex parte Lee* [1999] 2 All ER 737, per Kennedy LJ.

14   CPIA 1996, s 1(1).

15   CPS Disclosure Manual, paras 12.35–12.36. There is no statutory duty for the prosecutor to serve the MG6C unless he has it in his possession at that time (see CPIA 1996, s 4).

16   i.e. any prosecution material which might reasonably be considered capable of undermining the case for the prosecution against the accused or of assisting the case for the accused.

17   CPIA 1996, s 13.

18   Protocol for the Provision of Advance Information, Prosecution Evidence and Disclosure of Unused Material in the Magistrates' Courts, para 3.1.

19   CPS Disclosure Manual, para 12.36; CPIA 1996, s 13(1).

20   *DPP v Wood and McGillicuddy* [2006] EWCH 32 (Admin), per Ouseley J, para 24.

14.16 The magistrates' court protocol[21] provides examples of items that should regularly feature in an MG6C. These include:

- the custody record;

- records of emergency calls and/or crime reports;

- unused CCTV footage, if seized by the police during the course of the particular investigation;

- the record of examination of the accused by the police doctor;

- the notice given to the accused in relation to the provision of copies of audio tapes of the interview under caution at the police station;

- previous convictions of witnesses; and

- incident report books of officers not intended to give evidence at trial.

14.17 Paragraph 12, Attorney General's Guidelines on Disclosure (2005) provides examples of material that would satisfy the prosecution disclosure test,[22] namely:

'i.   Any material casting doubt upon the accuracy of any prosecution evidence.

ii.   Any material which may point to another person, whether charged or not (including a co-accused) having involvement in the commission of the offence.

iii.   Any material which may cast doubt upon the reliability of a confession.

iv.   Any material that might go to the credibility of a prosecution witness.

v.   Any material that might support a defence that is either raised by the defence or apparent from the prosecution papers.

vi.   Any material which may have a bearing on the admissibility of any prosecution evidence.'

14.18 In *R v Olu*[23] the court held that the defence should be provided with all notes, records and statements in relation to the evidence of eyewitnesses, irrespective of whether or not the prosecution deem them disclosable under the provisions of the CPIA 1996. The court said that the defence should be allowed to determine for themselves whether such material assists them.

---

21   Protocol for the Provision of Advance Information, Prosecution Evidence and Disclosure of Unused Material in the Magistrates' Court, Annex B.

22   i.e. any prosecution material which might reasonably be considered capable of undermining the case for the prosecution against the accused or of assisting the case for the accused.

23   [2010] EWCA Crim 2975, per Thomas LJ, para 45.

14.19   For the material that the prosecution should disclose to the defence, see **Chapter 7**. For third party material, see **Chapter 9**.

14.20   In summary trials, the defence need to apply to the court to review the question as to whether it is still not in the public interest to disclose material affected by its order;[24] whereas in the crown court, there is a duty on the court to keep this question under review without any application.[25] The practical effect of this distinction is unlikely to be significant, as in the majority of cases, the justices or district judge who rule on disclosure should proceed where possible to conduct the trial.[26] Where a different tribunal hears the trial, it should be made aware of the fact that there has been an application for public interest immunity.[27] Only exceptionally, where the material is so highly prejudicial as to create bias or the appearance of bias, should a differently constituted bench conduct the trial.[28] A case that raises complex and contentious public interest immunity issues should be committed to the crown court where possible.[29] For public interest immunity, see **Chapter 8**.

CONSEQUENCES OF PROSECUTION NON-DISCLOSURE

14.21   Potential consequences of prosecution non-disclosure are listed below (see **Chapter 11**):

* discontinuance;

* staying the proceedings;

* refusing to extend custody time limits;

* orders for costs;

* exclusion of evidence; and

* acquittal against the weight of the evidence.

14.22   In relation to sanctions against the prosecution, the 'Stop Delaying Justice' initiative states:[30]

---

24   CPIA 1996, s 14(2), (3).
25   CPIA 1996, s 15(3), (4).
26   *R v Acton Youth Court ex parte CPS* [2001] EWHC Admin 402, per Lord Woolf CJ, para 35.
27   *R v Acton Youth Court ex parte CPS* [2001] EWHC Admin 402, per Lord Woolf CJ, para 35.
28   *R v South Worcestershire Justices ex parte Lilley* [1995] 1 WLR 1595, per Rose LJ.
29   CPS Disclosure Manual, para 13.34.
30   At p 4.

'As for the sanctions, they are simple. If the defence has complied with all its responsibilities and is fully ready for trial, but the prosecution has failed to comply with all its responsibilities, then normally it would not be in the interests of justice for the Crown to be allowed an adjournment and the prosecution may fail.'

DEFENCE DISCLOSURE

Preparation for trial form[31]

14.23   An element of the overriding objective in the CPR 2012[32] requires that the magistrates' court deals with its cases efficiently and expeditiously. A duty is placed not only on the court to manage a case actively,[33] but also on each party to assist the court actively in the management of the case.[34] This requires the early identification of the real issues as trial by ambush is no longer permissible.[35] To enable the court to achieve this aim it is mandatory that parties complete a preparation for trial form[36] whenever a not guilty plea is entered. In *Malcolm v DPP*[37] Stanley Burnton J stated:

'Criminal trials are no longer to be treated as a game, in which each move is final and any omission by the prosecution leads to its failure. It is the duty of the defence to make its defence and the issues it raises clear to the prosecution and to the Court at an early stage. That duty is implicit in rule 3.3 of the Criminal Procedure Rules, which requires the parties actively to assist the exercise by the Court of its case management powers, the exercise of which requires early identification of the real issues.' (para 31)

14.24   Although pre-trial statements made in accordance with the spirit of the Criminal Procedure Rules will very rarely be admissible in evidence,[38] care must

---

31 For a copy of the preparation for trial form (listed in the Consolidated Criminal Practice Direction, Annex E) see **Appendix 18**.

32 CPR 2012, r 1.1(2)(e).

33 CPR 2012, r 3.2.

34 CPR 2012, r 3.3.

35 *R v Penner* [2010] EWCA Crim 1155; *DPP v Chorley Magistrates Court* [2006] EWHC 1795 (Admin).

36 Consolidated Criminal Practice Direction, para V.56.2 and Annex E.

37 [2007] EWHC 363 (Admin). Stanley Burton J also referred to the prosecution having to prove its case in its entirety before closing its case as having 'an anachronistic and obsolete ring'.

38 *R v Newell* [2012] EWCA Crim 650, per Thomas LJ, para 36; but see *Firth v Epping Magistrates' Court* [2011] EWHC 388 (Admin), per Toulson LJ.

still be taken to ensure that the preparation for trial form accurately reflects the lay client's instructions.

Defence statements[39]

14.25   The decision of whether to serve a defence statement in the magistrates' court is an entirely voluntary one for the accused.[40]

14.26   Where the defence have 'reasonable cause to believe' that there is prosecution material, which is required to be disclosed under the prosecution's continuing duty to disclose[41] and it has not been so disclosed, the defence would ordinarily make an application for disclosure under section 8, CPIA 1996. The service of a defence statement is a precondition to making an application under section 8, CPIA 1996. A section 8 application cannot be made where a defence statement has not been served. The obvious remedy for the defence would be to serve a defence statement forthwith and make a section 8 application.

14.27   In the absence of a defence statement, the court is arguably not powerless to intervene where it believes that there has been inadequate disclosure from the prosecution. The court is under a duty[42] to oversee and manage the disclosure process to ensure that the principle aim of the overriding objective in the CPR 2012 is achieved, namely that the case is dealt with justly.[43] Where it is clear that prosecution disclosure is incomplete, the court should be able to oversee the disclosure process and make directions outside the ambit of section 8, CPIA 1996.

14.28   The contents of a defence statement are provided under section 6A(1) (a)–(d), CPIA 1996[44] which states:

'.... a defence statement is a written statement –

   (a)   setting out the nature of the accused's defence, including any particular defences on which he intends to rely,

---

39   See **Chapter 4**.
40   CPIA 1996, s 6, unlike the crown court where under CPIA 1996, s 5 defence statements are compulsory.
41   CPIA 1996, s 7A.
42   Protocol for the Provision of Advance Information, Prosecution Evidence and Disclosure of Unused Material in the Magistrates' Court (2006), para 3.3.
43   CPR 2012, Part 1.
44   As amended.

(b)   indicating the matters of fact on which he takes issue with the prosecution,

(c)   setting out, in the case of each such matter, why he takes issue with the prosecution,

(ca)   setting out the particulars of the matters of fact on which he intends to rely for the purposes of his defence, and

(d)   indicating any point of law (including any point as to admissibility or an abuse of process) which he intends to take, and any authority on which he intends to rely for that purpose.'

14.29   A defence statement that discloses an alibi must under section 6A(2), CPIA 1996 give particulars of it, including:

'(a)   the name, address and date of birth of any witness the accused believes is able to give evidence in support of the alibi, or as many of those details as are known to the accused when the statement is given;

(b)   any information in the accused's possession which might be of material assistance in identifying or finding any such witness in whose case any of the details mentioned in paragraph (a) are not known to the accused when the statement is given.'

14.30   Under section 6A(3), CPIA 1996 evidence in support of an alibi is evidence tending to show that by reason of the presence of the accused at a particular place or in a particular area at a particular time he was not, or was unlikely to have been, at the place where the offence is alleged to have been committed at the time of its alleged commission.

Privilege against self-incrimination

14.31   The privilege against self-incrimination cannot be used to justify non-compliance with disclosure requirements under the Criminal Procedure Rules. In *R v Rochford*[45] Hughes LJ considered the disclosure that an accused is required to give in a defence statement. He stated:

'Do legal professional privilege and the defendant's privilege against self-incrimination survive section 6A?[46] The answer to that is "Yes". What the defendant is required to disclose by section 6A is what is going to happen at the trial. He is not required to disclose his confidential discussions with

---

45   [2010] EWCA Crim 1928, para 21.
46   See **14.28**.

his advocate, although of course they may bear on what is going to happen at the trial. Nor is he obliged to incriminate himself if he does not want to. Those are fundamental rights and they have certainly not been taken away by section 6A ...'

14.32   Rule 3.3, CPR 2012 requires all parties to assist the court in the early identification of the real issues: 'The use of a case progression form is part of this process'.[47] In *R (on the application of the CPS) v Norwich Magistrates' Court*[48] Richards LJ stated:

'... the case management process, especially following the introduction of the Criminal Procedure Rules, requires a greater level of cooperation between the parties than was once the case. The real issues are required to be identified at an early stage. The rules discourage a defendant from sitting on his hands in order to obtain a procedural advantage. If he does seek to gain advantage from earlier economies of participation ... the court should act to correct it, not condone it.'[49]

14.33   Any deficiency in the prosecution case that could give the accused an advantage must be identified in the case management form[50] even though it gives the prosecution the opportunity to rectify it.

14.34   Where there is a defence available but the accused refuses to allow his legal representative to disclose it, there is a positive duty under rule 1.2(1)(c), CPR 2012 to notify the court. It is then for the court to decide how to proceed. The legal representative must not make himself complicit in a manipulation of the court process.[51] The Law Society Practice Note states:[52]

'It is essential to appreciate that the purpose of Rule 1.2(1)(c) is to enable the court to control the preparation process and avoid ineffective and wasted hearings.

When something goes wrong because of a failure of a defendant to co-operate with you the court should be made aware of this and if you fail to keep the court informed, you risk breaching your duty to the court under the provisions of the Rules.'

---

47   *Firth v Epping Magistrates' Court* [2011] EWHC 388 (Admin), per Toulson LJ, paras 6–7.
48   [2011] EWHC 82 (Admin), para 11.
49   See also Leveson LJ, Senior Presiding Judge for England and Wales, 'Essential Case Management: Applying the Criminal Procedure Rules' (December 2009) on the use of the case management form to achieve effective management.
50   And in the defence statement if served.
51   See *R v SVS Solicitors* [2012] EWCA Crim 319.
52   Law Society Practice Note, Criminal Procedure Rules 2011, para 5.4.

14.35   Where issues are not raised at an early stage and unnecessary costs are incurred as a result, the court may impose a costs order[53] (see **Chapter 11**).

Putting the prosecution to proof

14.36   An accused who has no positive case to assert is entitled to require the prosecution to prove its case against him, but he must make his position clear to the court. It is no longer sufficient simply to record on the defence statement that the prosecution is put to 'strict proof'.[54] The court must be notified that he does not intend to assert a positive case (see **Chapter 4**).

Sanctions for faults in defence statement

14.37   Sections 11(2) and (3), CPIA 1996 identify eight triggers which will put the accused at risk of the sanctions.[55] These are:

- the accused is late in giving an initial defence statement;

- not applicable (section 6B updated defence statements not yet in force);

- not applicable (section 6B updated defence statements not yet in force);

- the accused sets out inconsistent defences in his defence statement; or

- at his trial the accused –

  (i)   puts forward a defence which was not mentioned in his defence statement or was different from any defence set out in that statement,

  (ii)   relies on a matter which, in breach of the requirements imposed by or under section 6A, was not mentioned in the defence statement,

  (iii) adduces evidence in support of an alibi without having given particulars of the alibi in his defence statement, or

  (iv)   calls a witness to give evidence in support of an alibi without having complied with section 6A(2)(a) or (b) as regards the witness in his defence statement.

---

53   Costs in Criminal Cases (General) Regulations 1986 and Prosecution of Offences Act 1985, ss 19, 19A.

54   In *Balogun v DPP* [2010] EWHC 799 (Admin), Leveson LJ, para 16, stated: 'For my part ... I do not accept that the spirit or letter of the Criminal Procedure Rules is complied with by asserting that the Crown is put to "strict proof"....'.

55   Only six triggers currently apply as CPIA 1996, s 6B is not yet in force.

14.38 The consequence of any of the above faults is that, unless the fault involves failing to mention a point of law, the court or any party (i.e. prosecution or co-accused) may make such comment as appears appropriate and the court or jury may draw such inferences as appear proper in deciding whether the accused is guilty of the offence concerned.[56]

14.39 If the fault involves reliance on a point of law (including any point on admissibility of evidence or abuse of process) which was not mentioned in the defence statement, leave of the court is required before another party can make comment.[57]

14.40 Where the accused puts forward a defence which is different from any defence set out in his defence statement, before deciding to do anything the court shall have regard to:

(a)   the extent of the differences in the defence; and

(b)   whether there is any justification for it.[58]

Witness notices[59]

14.41 Since 1 May 2010, the accused is required to provide a witness notice to the prosecutor and the court which must give the identity and particulars of any witness whom he intends to call. The notice applies to witnesses of fact and character. Section 6C, CPIA 1996[60] states:

'(1)   The accused must give to the court and the prosecutor a notice indicating whether he intends to call any persons (other than himself) as witnesses at his trial and, if so –

(a)   giving the name, address and date of birth of each such proposed witness, or as many of those details as are known to the accused when the notice is given;

(b)   providing any information in the accused's possession which might be of material assistance in identifying or finding any such proposed witness in whose case any of the details mentioned in paragraph (a) are not known to the accused when the notice is given.'

---

56   CPIA 1996, s 11(5).
57   CPIA 1996, s 11(6).
58   CPIA 1996, s11(8).
59   See **Chapter 5**.
60   Inserted by Criminal Justice Act 2003, s 34.

14.42   The requirement is only to provide the particulars of the witness. There is no requirement to disclose the substance of the evidence a witness is expected to give or identify the issue(s) to which his evidence relates.[61] This provision applies to witnesses of fact and character.

14.43   Irrespective of whether a defence statement is served in the magistrate's court, the accused must provide a witness notice stating whether he intends to call any defence witnesses and, if so, provide their details.[62]

Sanctions for faults in witness notice

14.44   Section 11(4), CPIA 1996 identifies two triggers which put the accused at risk of sanction. These are where the accused:

(a)   is late in giving the witness notice; and

(b)   at his trial calls a witness (other than himself) not included, or not adequately identified, in a witness notice.

14.45   The consequence of either of the above faults is that the court or any party (i.e. prosecution or co-accused) may make such comment as appears appropriate, but the prosecution or co-accused may only do so with leave of the court.[63] The court may draw such inferences as appear proper in deciding whether the accused is guilty of the offence concerned.[64]

14.46   Where the accused calls a witness whom he has failed to include or to identify adequately in a witness notice, the court must have regard as to whether there is any justification for the failure before it allows any comment to be made or adverse inference to be drawn.[65]

Time limits

14.47   The time limit for service of a defence statement and witness notice is 14 days[66] from when the prosecutor complies or purports to comply with his

---

61 Unless an expert witness. Advance disclosure of expert evidence is governed by CPR 2012, r 33.4.
62 CPIA 1996, s 6C.
63 CPIA 1996, s 11(7).
64 CPIA 1996, s 11(5).
65 CPIA 1996, s 11(9).
66 In the crown court the period is 28 days.

initial duty to disclose under section 3, CPIA 1996.[67] The court has power to extend the relevant period on application by the accused where it is satisfied that the accused could not reasonably provide a defence statement or witness notice within the relevant period. There is no limit to the period of extension or the number of extensions that can be made.[68]

ADMINISTRATIVE SANCTIONS

14.48   Rule 3.5(6), CPR 2012 provides that if a party fails to comply with a rule or a direction:

'… the court may –

(a)   fix, postpone, bring forward, extend, cancel or adjourn a hearing;

(b)   exercise its power to make a costs order; and

(c)   impose such other sanctions as may be appropriate.'

14.49   Where a party seeks to call a witness not previously identified in the witness notice, a refusal to allow that witness to be called is likely to be regarded as a step too far and one which would require primary legislative sanction.[69]

14.50   A party who does not call a witness indicated in a witness notice may be at risk of costs if there has been a clear wastage of police resources as a result of not amending the notice.

---

67   Criminal Procedure and Investigations Act 1996 (Defence Disclosure Time Limits) Regulations 2011, reg 2, which came into force on 28 February 2011.

68   Criminal Procedure and Investigations Act 1996 (Defence Disclosure Time Limits) Regulations 2011, regs 3–4.

69   *R (on the application of Tinnion) v Reading Crown Court* [2009] EWHC 2930 (Admin), per Mitting J, para 37; *R v Ullah* [2011] EWCA Crim 3275, per Moses LJ, para 13. Both cases were before the introduction of CPR 2012, r 3.5(6).

Appendix 1

Criminal Procedure and Investigations Act 1996, Parts I and II (as amended)

PART I   DISCLOSURE

Introduction

1.– Application of this Part.

(1)   This Part applies where –

    (a)   a person is charged with a summary offence in respect of which a court proceeds to summary trial and in respect of which he pleads not guilty,

    (b)   a person who has attained the age of 18 is charged with an offence which is triable either way, in respect of which a court proceeds to summary trial and in respect of which he pleads not guilty, or

    (c)   a person under the age of 18 is charged with an indictable offence in respect of which a court proceeds to summary trial and in respect of which he pleads not guilty.

(2)   This Part also applies where –

    [*(a)   a person is charged with an indictable offence and he is committed for trial for the offence concerned,*

    (b)   a person is charged with an indictable offence and proceedings for the trial of the person on the charge concerned are transferred to the Crown Court by virtue of a notice of transfer given under section 4 of the Criminal Justice Act 1987 (serious or complex fraud),

    (c)   a person is charged with an indictable offence and proceedings for the trial of the person on the charge concerned are transferred to the Crown Court by virtue of a notice of transfer served on a magistrates' court under section 53 of the Criminal Justice Act 1991 (certain cases involving children),][1]

[(cc)   a person is charged with an offence for which he is sent for trial [*under section 51 (no committal proceedings for indictable-only offences) of the Crime and Disorder Act 1998*][3,][2]

(d)   a count charging a person with a summary offence is included in an indictment under the authority of section 40 of the Criminal Justice Act 1988 (common assault etc.), or

(e)   a bill of indictment charging a person with an indictable offence is preferred under the authority of section 2(2)(b) of the Administration of Justice (Miscellaneous Provisions) Act 1933 (bill preferred by direction of Court of Appeal, or by direction or with consent of a judge) [,or][4]

[(f)   a bill of indictment charging a person with an indictable offence is preferred under section 22B(3)(a) of the Prosecution of Offences Act 1985.][4]

(3)   This Part applies in relation to alleged offences into which no criminal investigation has begun before the appointed day.

(4)   For the purposes of this section a criminal investigation is an investigation which police officers or other persons have a duty to conduct with a view to it being ascertained –

(a)   whether a person should be charged with an offence, or

(b)   whether a person charged with an offence is guilty of it.

(5)   The reference in subsection (3) to the appointed day is to such day as is appointed for the purposes of this Part by the Secretary of State by order.

[(6)   In this Part –

(a)   subsections (3) to (5) of section 3 (in their application for the purposes of section 3, 7, or 9), and

(b)   sections 17 and 18,

have effect subject to subsections (2) and (3) of section 9 of the Sexual Offences (Protected Material) Act 1997 (by virtue of which those provisions of this Act do not apply in relation to disclosures regulated by that Act).][5]

Notes

1   Repealed by Criminal Justice Act 2003, Sch 3, Pt 2, para 66(1), (2)(a), Sch 37, Pt 4, para 1 (18 June 2012: repeal has effect on 18 June 2012 in relation to the relevant local justice areas as specified in SI 2012/1320, art 4(1)(d) subject to savings as specified in SI 2012/1320, art 5; 18 June 2012 for purposes specified in SI 2012/1320, art 4(3) subject to savings as specified in SI 2012/1320, art 5; 5 November 2012 in relation to the relevant local justice areas as specified in SI 2012/2574, art 2(1)(c) subject to savings as specified in art 3; not yet in force otherwise).

2   Added by Crime and Disorder Act 1998, Sch 8, para 125(a) (4 January 1999 for purposes specified in SI 1998/2327, art 4(2) and Sch 2; 15 January 2001 subject to savings specified in SI 2000/3283, art 3 otherwise).

3   Words repealed by Criminal Justice Act 2003, Sch 37, Pt 4, para 1 (9 May 2005: repeal has effect on 9 May 2005 as SI 2005/1267 in relation to cases sent for trial under Crime and Disorder Act 1998, s 51 or 51A(3)(d); repeal has effect on 18 June 2012 in relation to the relevant local justice areas as specified in SI 2012/1320, art 4(1)(d) subject to savings as specified in SI 2012/1320, art 5; 18 June 2012 for purposes specified in SI 2012/1320, art 4(3) subject to savings as specified in SI 2012/1320, art 5; not yet in force otherwise).

4   Added by Crime and Disorder Act 1998, Sch 8, para 125(b) (1 June 1999).

5   Added by Sexual Offences (Protected Material) Act 1997, s 9(4) (date to be appointed).

Commencement

Pt I, s 1(1)–(5): 4 July 1996 (1 April 1997 in relation to England and Wales; 1 January 1998 otherwise).

Extent

Pt I, s. 1(1)–(6)(b): England, Wales, Northern Ireland.

2.– General interpretation.

(1)   References to the accused are to the person mentioned in section 1(1) or (2).

(2)   Where there is more than one accused in any proceedings this Part applies separately in relation to each of the accused.

(3)   References to the prosecutor are to any person acting as prosecutor, whether an individual or a body.

(4)   References to material are to material of all kinds, and in particular include references to –

> (a)   information, and

> (b)   objects of all descriptions.

(5)   References to recording information are to putting it in a durable or retrievable form (such as writing or tape).

(6)   This section applies for the purposes of this Part.

Commencement

Pt I, s 2(1)–(6): 4 July 1996 (1 April 1997 in relation to England and Wales; 1 January 1998 otherwise).

Extent

Pt I, s 2(1)–(6): England, Wales, Northern Ireland.

The main provisions

3.– [Initial duty of prosecutor to disclose].[1]

(1)   The prosecutor must –

(a)   disclose to the accused any prosecution material which has not previously been disclosed to the accused and which [might reasonably be considered capable of undermining][2] the case for the prosecution against the accused [or of assisting the case for the accused][2], or

(b)   give to the accused a written statement that there is no material of a description mentioned in paragraph (a).

(2)   For the purposes of this section prosecution material is material –

(a)   which is in the prosecutor's possession, and came into his possession in connection with the case for the prosecution against the accused, or

(b)   which, in pursuance of a code operative under Part II, he has inspected in connection with the case for the prosecution against the accused.

(3)   Where material consists of information which has been recorded in any form the prosecutor discloses it for the purposes of this section –

(a)   by securing that a copy is made of it and that the copy is given to the accused, or

(b)   if in the prosecutor's opinion that is not practicable or not desirable, by allowing the accused to inspect it at a reasonable time and a reasonable place or by taking steps to secure that he is allowed to do so;

and a copy may be in such form as the prosecutor thinks fit and need not be in the same form as that in which the information has already been recorded.

(4)   Where material consists of information which has not been recorded the prosecutor discloses it for the purposes of this section by securing that it is recorded in such form as he thinks fit and –

(a)   by securing that a copy is made of it and that the copy is given to the accused, or

(b)   if in the prosecutor's opinion that is not practicable or not desirable, by allowing the accused to inspect it at a reasonable time and a reasonable place or by taking steps to secure that he is allowed to do so.

(5)   Where material does not consist of information the prosecutor discloses it for the purposes of this section by allowing the accused to inspect it at a reasonable time and a reasonable place or by taking steps to secure that he is allowed to do so.

(6)   Material must not be disclosed under this section to the extent that the court, on an application by the prosecutor, concludes it is not in the public interest to disclose it and orders accordingly.

(7)   Material must not be disclosed under this section to the extent that [it is material the disclosure of which is prohibited by section 17 of the Regulation of Investigatory Powers Act 2000.][3]

(8)   The prosecutor must act under this section during the period which, by virtue of section 12, is the relevant period for this section.

Notes

1   Words substituted by Criminal Justice Act 2003, Sch 36, Pt 3, para 21 (15 July 2005 as SI 2005/1817).

2   Amended by Criminal Justice Act 2003, Pt 5, s 32 (15 July 2005 as SI 2005/1817).

3   Substituted by Regulation of Investigatory Powers Act 2000, Sch 4, para 7(1) (2 October 2000 subject to transitional provisions specified in SI 2000/2543, art 5).

Commencement

Pt I, s 3(1)–(8): 4 July 1996 (1 April 1997 in relation to England and Wales; 1 January 1998 otherwise).

Extent

Pt I, s 3(1)–(8): England, Wales, Northern Ireland.

4.– [Initial duty to disclose][1]: further provisions.

(1)   This section applies where –

    (a)   the prosecutor acts under section 3, and

    (b)   before so doing he was given a document in pursuance of provision included, by virtue of section 24(3), in a code operative under Part II.

(2)   In such a case the prosecutor must give the document to the accused at the same time as the prosecutor acts under section 3.

Appendix 1 *Criminal Procedure and Investigations Act 1996, Parts I and II*

Notes

1   Words substituted by Criminal Justice Act 2003, Sch 36(3), para 22 (15 July 2005 as SI 2005/1817).

Commencement

Pt I, s 4(1)–(2): 4 July 1996 (1 April 1997 in relation to England and Wales; 1 January 1998 otherwise).

Extent

Pt I, s 4(1)–(2): England, Wales, Northern Ireland.

5.– Compulsory disclosure by accused.

(1)   Subject to subsections [(3A) and]¹ (4) this section applies where –

    (a)   this Part applies by virtue of section 1(2), and

    (b)   the prosecutor complies with section 3 or purports to comply with it.

[(2)   *Where this Part applies by virtue of section 1(2)(b), this section does not apply unless –*

    (a)   a copy of the notice of transfer, and

    (b)   copies of the documents containing the evidence,

have been given to the accused under regulations made under section 5(9) of the Criminal Justice Act 1987.

(3)   Where this Part applies by virtue of section 1(2)(c), this section does not apply unless –

    (a)   a copy of the notice of transfer, and

    (b)   copies of the documents containing the evidence,

have been given to the accused under regulations made under paragraph 4 of Schedule 6 to the Criminal Justice Act 1991.]²

[(3A)   Where this Part applies by virtue of section 1(2)(cc), this section does not apply unless –

    (a)   copies of the documents containing the evidence have been served on the accused under regulations made under paragraph 1 of Schedule 3 to the Crime and Disorder Act 1998; and

    (b)   a copy of the notice under [subsection (1) of section 51D]⁴ of that Act has been served on him under that subsection.]³

(4)   Where this part applies by virtue of section 1(2)(e), this section does not apply unless the prosecutor has served on the accused a copy of the indictment

and a copy of the set of documents containing the evidence which is the basis of the charge.

(5)   Where this section applies, the accused must give a defence statement to the court and the prosecutor.

[(5A)   Where there are other accused in the proceedings and the court so orders, the accused must also give a defence statement to each other accused specified by the court.

(5B)   The court may make an order under subsection (5A) either of its own motion or on the application of any party.

(5C)   A defence statement that has to be given to the court and the prosecutor (under subsection (5)) must be given during the period which, by virtue of section 12, is the relevant period for this section.

(5D)   A defence statement that has to be given to a co-accused (under subsection (5A)) must be given within such period as the court may specify.][5]

[(6)   *For the purposes of this section a defence statement is a written statement –*

   (a)   setting out in general terms the nature of the accused's defence,

   (b)   indicating the matters on which he takes issue with the prosecution, and

   (c)   setting out, in the case of each such matter, the reason why he takes issue with the prosecution.

(7)   *If the defence statement discloses an alibi the accused must give particulars of the alibi in the statement, including –*

   (a)   the name and address of any witness the accused believes is able to give evidence in support of the alibi, if the name and address are known to the accused when the statement is given;

   (b)   any information in the accused's possession which might be of material assistance in finding any such witness, if his name or address is not known to the accused when the statement is given.

(8)   *For the purposes of this section evidence in support of an alibi is evidence tending to show that by reason of the presence of the accused at a particular place or in a particular area at a particular time he was not, or was unlikely to have been, at the place where the offence is alleged to have been committed at the time of its alleged commission.*

(9)   *The accused must give a defence statement under this section during the period which, by virtue of section 12, is the relevant period for this section.*][6]

Notes

1   Words substituted by Criminal Justice Act 2003, Sch 3, Pt 2, para 66(3)(a) (18 June 2012: substitution has effect on 18 June 2012 in relation to the relevant local justice areas subject to savings as specified in SI 2012/1320, art 5; 18 June 2012 for purposes specified in SI 2012/1320, art 4(3) subject to savings as specified in SI 2012/1320, art 5: not yet in force otherwise).

2   Repealed by Criminal Justice Act 2003, Sch 3, Pt 2, para 66(1), (3)(b), Sch 37, Pt 4, para 1 (18 June 2012: repeal has effect on 18 June 2012 in relation to the relevant local justice areas as specified in SI 2012/1320, art 4(1)(d) subject to savings as specified in SI 2012/1320, art 5; 18 June 2012 for purposes specified in SI 2012/1320, art 4(3) subject to savings as specified in SI 2012/1320, art 5; 5 November 2012 in relation to the relevant local justice areas as specified in SI 2012/2574, art 2(1)(c) subject to savings as specified in art 3; not yet in force otherwise).

3   Added by Crime and Disorder Act 1998, Sch 8, para 126 (4 January 1999 for purposes specified in SI 1998/2327, art 4(2) and Sch 2; 15 January 2001 subject to savings specified in SI 2000/3283, art 3 otherwise).

4   Words substituted by Criminal Justice Act 2003, Sch 3, Pt 2, para 66(3)(c) (9 May 2005 in relation to cases sent for trial under Crime and Disorder Act 1998, s 51A(3)(d); 18 June 2012 in relation to the relevant local justice areas subject to savings as specified in SI 2012/1320, art 5; 18 June 2012 for purposes specified in SI 2012/1320, art 4(3) subject to savings as specified in SI 2012/1320, art 5 not yet in force otherwise).

5   Added by Criminal Justice Act 2003, Pt 5, s 33(1) (24 July 2006 in relation to subs (5C) for purposes specified in SI 2006/1835, art 2(a) subject to transitional provisions specified in SI 2006/1835, art 3; not yet in force otherwise).

6   Repealed by Criminal Justice Act 2003, Sch 37, Pt 3, para 1 (15 July 2005 as SI 2007/1817).

Commencement

Pt I, s. 5(1)–(9): 4 July 1996 (1 April 1997 in relation to England and Wales; 1 January 1998 otherwise).

Extent

Pt I, s 5(1)–(9): England, Wales, Northern Ireland.

6.– Voluntary disclosure by accused.

(1)   This section applies where –

    (a)   this Part applies by virtue of section 1(1), and

    (b)   the prosecutor complies with section 3 or purports to comply with it.

(2)   The accused –

    (a)   may give a defence statement to the prosecutor, and

    (b)   if he does so, must also give such a statement to the court.

[*(3)   Subsections (6) to (8) of section 5 apply for the purposes of this section as they apply for the purposes of that.*][1]

(4)   If the accused gives a defence statement under this section he must give it during the period which, by virtue of section 12 is the relevant period for this section.

Notes

1   Repealed by Criminal Justice Act 2003, Sch 37, Pt 3, para 1 (15 July 2005 as SI 2007/1817).

Commencement

Pt I, s 6(1)–(4): 4 July 1996 (1 April 1997 in relation to England and Wales; 1 January 1998 otherwise).

Extent

Pt I, s 6(1)–(4): England, Wales, Northern Ireland.

[6A.– Contents of defence statement

(1)   For the purposes of this Part a defence statement is a written statement –

> (a)   setting out the nature of the accused's defence, including any particular defences on which he intends to rely,

> (b)   indicating the matters of fact on which he takes issue with the prosecution,

> (c)   setting out, in the case of each such matter, why he takes issue with the prosecution, [...]²

> [(ca)   setting out particulars of the matters of fact on which he intends to rely for the purposes of his defence, and]²

> (d)   indicating any point of law (including any point as to the admissibility of evidence or an abuse of process) which he wishes to take, and any authority on which he intends to rely for that purpose.

(2)   A defence statement that discloses an alibi must give particulars of it, including –

> (a)   the name, address and date of birth of any witness the accused believes is able to give evidence in support of the alibi, or as many of those details as are known to the accused when the statement is given;

> (b)   any information in the accused's possession which might be of material assistance in identifying or finding any such witness in whose case any of the details mentioned in paragraph (a) are not known to the accused when the statement is given.

(3)   For the purposes of this section evidence in support of an alibi is evidence tending to show that by reason of the presence of the accused at a particular place or in a particular area at a particular time he was not, or was unlikely to have been, at the place where the offence is alleged to have been committed at the time of its alleged commission.

(4)   The Secretary of State may by regulations make provision as to the details of the matters that, by virtue of subsection (1), are to be included in defence statements.][1]

Notes

1   Added by Criminal Justice Act 2003, Pt 5, s 33(2) (4 April 2005 as SI 2005/950).

2   Added by Criminal Justice and Immigration Act 2008, Pt 4, s 60(1) (3 November 2008: insertion has effect subject to savings and transitional provisions specified in SI 2008/2712, art.3).

Extent

Pt I, s 6A(1)–(4): England, Wales, Northern Ireland.

[6B.– Updated disclosure by accused

(1)   Where the accused has, before the beginning of the relevant period for this section, given a defence statement under section 5 or 6, he must during that period give to the court and the prosecutor either –

> (a)   a defence statement under this section (an 'updated defence statement'), or
>
> (b)   a statement of the kind mentioned in subsection (4).

(2)   The relevant period for this section is determined under section 12.

(3)   An updated defence statement must comply with the requirements imposed by or under section 6A by reference to the state of affairs at the time when the statement is given.

(4)   Instead of an updated defence statement the accused may give a written statement stating that he has no changes to make to the defence statement which was given under section 5 or 6.

(5)   Where there are other accused in the proceedings and the court so orders, the accused must also give either an updated defence statement or a statement of the kind mentioned in subsection (4), within such period as may be specified by the court, to each other accused so specified.

(6)   The court may make an order under subsection (5) either of its own motion or on the application of any party.][1]

Notes

1   Added by Criminal Justice Act 2003, Pt 5, s 33(3) (date to be appointed).

Extent

Pt I, s 68(1)–(6): England, Wales, Northern Ireland.

[6C.– Notification of intention to call defence witnesses

(1)   The accused must give to the court and the prosecutor a notice indicating whether he intends to call any persons (other than himself) as witnesses at his trial and, if so –

  (a)   giving the name, address and date of birth of each such proposed witness, or as many of those details as are known to the accused when the notice is given;

  (b)   providing any information in the accused's possession which might be of material assistance in identifying or finding any such proposed witness in whose case any of the details mentioned in paragraph (a) are not known to the accused when the notice is given.

(2)   Details do not have to be given under this section to the extent that they have already been given under section 6A(2).

(3)   The accused must give a notice under this section during the period which, by virtue of section 12, is the relevant period for this section.

(4)   If, following the giving of a notice under this section, the accused –

  (a)   decides to call a person (other than himself) who is not included in the notice as a proposed witness, or decides not to call a person who is so included, or

  (b)   discovers any information which, under subsection (1), he would have had to include in the notice if he had been aware of it when giving the notice,

he must give an appropriately amended notice to the court and the prosecutor.][1]

Notes

1   Added by Criminal Justice Act 2003, Pt 5, s 34 (1 May 2010 in relation to England and Wales subject to transitional provisions specified in SI 2010/1183, art 4(2); not yet in force otherwise).

Extent

Pt I, s 6C(1)–(4)(b): England, Wales, Northern Ireland.

[6D.– Notification of names of experts instructed by accused

(1)   If the accused instructs a person with a view to his providing any expert opinion for possible use as evidence at the trial of the accused, he must give to the court and the prosecutor a notice specifying the person's name and address.

(2)   A notice does not have to be given under this section specifying the name and address of a person whose name and address have already been given under section 6C.

(3)   A notice under this section must be given during the period which, by virtue of section 12, is the relevant period for this section.][1]

Notes

1   Added by Criminal Justice Act 2003, Pt 5, s 35 (date to be appointed).

Extent

Pt I, s 6D(1)–(3): England, Wales, Northern Ireland.

[6E.– Disclosure by accused: further provisions

(1)   Where an accused's solicitor purports to give on behalf of the accused –

   (a)   a defence statement under section 5, 6 or 6B, or

   (b)   a statement of the kind mentioned in section 6B(4),

the statement shall, unless the contrary is proved, be deemed to be given with the authority of the accused.

(2)   If it appears to the judge at a pre-trial hearing that an accused has failed to comply fully with section 5, 6B or 6C, so that there is a possibility of comment being made or inferences drawn under section 11(5), he shall warn the accused accordingly.

(3)   In subsection (2) 'pre-trial hearing' has the same meaning as in Part 4 (see section 39).

(4)   The judge in a trial before a judge and jury –

   (a)   may direct that the jury be given a copy of any defence statement, and

   (b)   if he does so, may direct that it be edited so as not to include references to matters evidence of which would be inadmissible.

(5)   A direction under subsection (4) –

   (a)   may be made either of the judge's own motion or on the application of any party;

(b)   may be made only if the judge is of the opinion that seeing a copy of the defence statement would help the jury to understand the case or to resolve any issue in the case.

(6)   The reference in subsection (4) to a defence statement is a reference –

(a)   where the accused has given only an initial defence statement (that is, a defence statement given under section 5 or 6), to that statement;

(b)   where he has given both an initial defence statement and an updated defence statement (that is, a defence statement given under section 6B), to the updated defence statement;

(c)   where he has given both an initial defence statement and a statement of the kind mentioned in section 6B(4), to the initial defence statement.]¹

Notes

1   Added by Criminal Justice Act 2003, Pt 5, s 36 (4 April 2005 as SI 2005/950).

Extent

Pt I, s 6E(1)–(6)(c): England, Wales, Northern Ireland.

[7.– Secondary disclosure by prosecutor

(1)   This section applies where the accused gives a defence statement under section 5 or 6.

(2)   The prosecutor must –

(a)   *disclose to the accused any prosecution material which has not previously been disclosed to the accused and which might be reasonably expected to assist the accused's defence as disclosed by the defence statement given under section 5 or 6, or*

(b)   *give to the accused a written statement that there is no material of a description mentioned in paragraph (a).*

(3)   For the purposes of this section prosecution material is material –

(a)   *which is in the prosecutor's possession and came into his possession in connection with the case for the prosecution against the accused, or*

(b)   *which, in pursuance of a code operative under Part II, he has inspected in connection with the case for the prosecution against the accused.*

(4)   Subsections (3) to (5) of section 3 (method by which prosecutor discloses) apply for the purposes of this section as they apply for the purposes of that.

(5)   Material must not be disclosed under this section to the extent that the court, on an application by the prosecutor, concludes it is not in the public interest to disclose it and orders accordingly.

(6)   Material must not be disclosed under this section to the extent that –

(a)   it has been intercepted in obedience to a warrant issued under section 2 of the Interception of Communications Act 1985, or

(b)   it indicates that such a warrant has been issued or that material has been intercepted in obedience to such a warrant.

(7)   The prosecutor must act under this section during the period which, by virtue of section 12, is the relevant period for this section.][1]

Notes

1   Repealed by Criminal Justice Act 2003, Sch 37, Pt 3, para 1 (England and Wales: 4 April 2005 as SI 2005/950; Northern Ireland:15 July 2005 as SI 2005/1817).

[7A.– Continuing duty of prosecutor to disclose

(1)   This section applies at all times –

(a)   after the prosecutor has complied with section 3 or purported to comply with it, and

(b)   before the accused is acquitted or convicted or the prosecutor decides not to proceed with the case concerned.

(2)   The prosecutor must keep under review the question whether at any given time (and, in particular, following the giving of a defence statement) there is prosecution material which –

(a)   might reasonably be considered capable of undermining the case for the prosecution against the accused or of assisting the case for the accused, and

(b)   has not been disclosed to the accused.

(3)   If at any time there is any such material as is mentioned in subsection (2) the prosecutor must disclose it to the accused as soon as is reasonably practicable (or within the period mentioned in subsection (5)(a) where that applies).

(4)   In applying subsection (2) by reference to any given time the state of affairs at that time (including the case for the prosecution as it stands at that time) must be taken into account.

(5)   Where the accused gives a defence statement under section 5, 6 or 6B –

    (a)   if as a result of that statement the prosecutor is required by this section to make any disclosure, or further disclosure, he must do so during the period which, by virtue of section 12, is the relevant period for this section;

    (b)   if the prosecutor considers that he is not so required, he must during that period give to the accused a written statement to that effect.

(6)   For the purposes of this section prosecution material is material –

    (a)   which is in the prosecutor's possession and came into his possession in connection with the case for the prosecution against the accused, or

    (b)   which, in pursuance of a code operative under Part 2, he has inspected in connection with the case for the prosecution against the accused.

(7)   Subsections (3) to (5) of section 3 (method by which prosecutor discloses) apply for the purposes of this section as they apply for the purposes of that.

(8)   Material must not be disclosed under this section to the extent that the court, on an application by the prosecutor, concludes it is not in the public interest to disclose it and orders accordingly.

(9)   Material must not be disclosed under this section to the extent that it is material the disclosure of which is prohibited by section 17 of the Regulation of Investigatory Powers Act 2000 (c. 23).][1]

Notes

1   Added by Criminal Justice Act 2003, Pt 5, s 37 (4 April 2005 as SI 2005/950).

Extent

Pt I, s 7A(1)–(9): England, Wales, Northern Ireland.

8.– Application by accused for disclosure.

[(1)   This section applies where the accused has given a defence statement under section 5, 6 or 6B and the prosecutor has complied with section 7A(5) or has purported to comply with it or has failed to comply with it.

(2)   If the accused has at any time reasonable cause to believe that there is prosecution material which is required by section 7A to be disclosed to him and has not been he may apply to the court for an order requiring the prosecutor to disclose it to him.][1]

(3)   For the purposes of this section prosecution material is material –

(a)   which is in the prosecutor's possession and came into his possession in connection with the case for the prosecution against the accused,

(b)   which, in pursuance of a code operative under Part II, he has inspected in connection with the case for the prosecution against the accused, or

(c)   which falls within subsection (4).

(4)   Material falls within this subsection if in pursuance of a code operative under Part II the prosecutor must, if he asks for the material, be given a copy of it or be allowed to inspect it in connection with the case for the prosecution against the accused.

(5)   Material must not be disclosed under this section to the extent that the court, on an application by the prosecutor, concludes it is not in the public interest to disclose it and orders accordingly.

(6)   Material must not be disclosed under this section to the extent that [it is material the disclosure of which is prohibited by section 17 of the Regulation of Investigatory Powers Act 2000.][2]

Notes

1   Substituted by Criminal Justice Act 2003, Pt 5, s 38 (15 July 2005 as SI 2005/1817).

2   Substituted by Regulation of Investigatory Powers Act 2000, Sch 4, para 7(1) (2 October 2000 subject to transitional provisions specified in SI 2000/2543, art 5).

Commencement

Pt I, s 8(1)–(6)(b): 4 July 1996 (1 April 1997 in relation to England and Wales; 1 January 1998 otherwise).

Extent

Pt I, s 8(1)–(6)(b): England, Wales, Northern Ireland.

[9.– *Continuing duty of prosecutor to disclose.*

(1)   Subsection (2) applies at all times –

(a)   after the prosecutor complies with section 3 or purports to comply with it, and

(b)   before the accused is acquitted or convicted or the prosecutor decides not to proceed with the case concerned.

(2)   The prosecutor must keep under review the question whether at any given time there is prosecution material which –

    (a)   *in his opinion might undermine the case for the prosecution against the accused, and*

    (b)   *has not been disclosed to the accused;*

and if there is such material at any time the prosecutor must disclose it to the accused as soon as is reasonably practicable.

(3)   *In applying subsection (2) by reference to any given time the state of affairs at that time (including the case for the prosecution as it stands at that time) must be taken into account.*

(4)   *Subsection (5) applies at all times –*

    (a)   *after the prosecutor complies with section 7 or purports to comply with it, and*

    (b)   *before the accused is acquitted or convicted or the prosecutor decides not to proceed with the case concerned.*

(5)   *The prosecutor must keep under review the question whether at any given time there is prosecution material which –*

    (a)   *might be reasonably expected to assist the accused's defence as disclosed by the defence statement given under section 5 or 6, and*

    (b)   *has not been disclosed to the accused;*

and if there is such material at any time the prosecutor must disclose it to the accused as soon as is reasonably practicable.

(6)   *For the purposes of this section prosecution material is material –*

    (a)   *which is in the prosecutor's possession and came into his possession in connection with the case for the prosecution against the accused, or*

    (b)   *which, in pursuance of a code operative under Part II, he has inspected in connection with the case for the prosecution against the accused.*

(7)   *Subsections (3) to (5) of section 3 (method by which prosecutor discloses) apply for the purposes of this section as they apply for the purposes of that.*

(8)   *Material must not be disclosed under this section to the extent that the court, on an application by the prosecutor, concludes it is not in the public interest to disclose it and orders accordingly.*

(9)   *Material must not be disclosed under this section to the extent that –*

    (a)   *it has been intercepted in obedience to a warrant issued under section 2 of the Interception of Communications Act 1985, or*

> (b)   it indicates that such a warrant has been issued or that material
> has been intercepted in obedience to such a warrant.]¹

Notes

1   Repealed by Criminal Justice Act 2003, Sch 37(3), para 1 (England and Wales: 4 April 2005 as
SI 2005/950; Northern Ireland: 15 July 2005 as SI 2005/1817).

10.– Prosecutor's failure to observe time limits.

(1)   This section applies if the prosecutor –

> (a)   purports to act under section 3 after the end of the period which, by
> virtue of section 12, is the relevant period for section 3, or

> [(b)   purports to act under section 7A(5) after the end of the period
> which, by virtue of section 12, is the relevant period for section
> 7A.]¹

(2)   Subject to subsection (3) the failure to act during the period concerned
does not on its own constitute grounds for staying the proceedings for abuse of
process.

(3)   Subsection (2) does not prevent the failure constituting such grounds if it
involves such delay by the prosecutor that the accused is denied a fair trial.

Notes

1   Substituted by Criminal Justice Act 2003, Sch 36, Pt 3, para 27 (15 July 2005 as SI 2005/1817).

Commencement

Pt I, s 10(1)–(3): 4 July 1996 (1 April 1997 in relation to England and Wales; 1 January 1998
otherwise).

Extent

Pt I, s 10(1)–(3): England, Wales, Northern Ireland.

11.– Faults in disclosure by accused.

The text of this provision varies depending on jurisdiction or other application.

Northern Ireland

[(1)   This section applies in the three cases set out in subsections (2), (3) and
(4).

(2)   The first case is where section 5 applies and the accused –

> (a)   fails to give an initial defence statement,

(b)   gives an initial defence statement but does so after the end of the period which, by virtue of section 12, is the relevant period for section 5,

(c)   is required by section 6B to give either an updated defence statement or a statement of the kind mentioned in subsection (4) of that section but fails to do so,

(d)   gives an updated defence statement or a statement of the kind mentioned in section 6B(4) but does so after the end of the period which, by virtue of section 12, is the relevant period for section 6B,

(e)   sets out inconsistent defences in his defence statement, or

(f)   at his trial –

   (i)   puts forward a defence which was not mentioned in his defence statement or is different from any defence set out in that statement,

   (ii)   relies on a matter [(or any particular of any matter of fact)]² which, in breach of the requirements imposed by or under section 6A, was not mentioned in his defence statement,

   (iii)   adduces evidence in support of an alibi without having given particulars of the alibi in his defence statement, or

   (iv)   calls a witness to give evidence in support of an alibi without having complied with section 6A(2)(a) or (b) as regards the witness in his defence statement.

(3)   The second case is where section 6 applies, the accused gives an initial defence statement, and the accused –

(a)   gives the initial defence statement after the end of the period which, by virtue of section 12, is the relevant period for section 6, or

(b)   does any of the things mentioned in paragraphs (c) to (f) of subsection (2).]¹

(4)   Where the accused puts forward a defence which is different from any defence set out in a defence statement given under section 5 or 6, in doing anything under subsection (3) or in deciding whether to do anything under it the court shall have regard –

(a)   to the extent of the difference in the defences, and

(b)   to whether there is any justification for it.

[(5)   Where this section applies –

    (a)   the court or any other party may make such comment as appears appropriate;

    (b)   the court or jury may draw such inferences as appear proper in deciding whether the accused is guilty of the offence concerned.

(6)   Where –

    (a)   this section applies by virtue of subsection (2)(f)(ii) (including that provision as it applies by virtue of subsection (3)(b)), and

    (b)   the matter which was not mentioned is a point of law (including any point as to the admissibility of evidence or an abuse of process) or an authority,

comment by another party under subsection (5)(a) may be made only with the leave of the court.]¹

[(8)   Where the accused puts forward a defence which is different from any defence set out in his defence statement, in doing anything under subsection (5) or in deciding whether to do anything under it the court shall have regard –

    (a)   to the extent of the differences in the defences, and

    (b)   to whether there is any justification for it.

(9)   Where the accused calls a witness whom he has failed to include, or to identify adequately, in a witness notice, in doing anything under subsection (5) or in deciding whether to do anything under it the court shall have regard to whether there is any justification for the failure.

(10)   A person shall not be convicted of an offence solely on an inference drawn under subsection (5).

(12)   In this section –

    (a)   'initial defence statement' means a defence statement given under section 5 or 6;

    (b)   'updated defence statement' means a defence statement given under section 6B;

    (c)   a reference simply to an accused's 'defence statement' is a reference –

        (i)   where he has given only an initial defence statement, to that statement;

        (ii)   where he has given both an initial and an updated defence statement, to the updated defence statement;

   (iii) where he has given both an initial defence statement and a statement of the kind mentioned in section 6B(4), to the initial defence statement;

 (d) a reference to evidence in support of an alibi shall be construed in accordance with section 6A(3);

 (e) 'witness notice' means a notice given under section 6C.]¹

Notes

1 Substituted by Criminal Justice Act 2003, Pt 5, s 39 (15 July 2005 as SI 2005/1817).

2 Words inserted by Criminal Justice and Immigration Act 2008, Pt 4, s 60(2) (3 November 2008: insertion has effect subject to savings and transitional provisions specified in SI 2008/2712, art 3).

England and Wales

[(1) This section applies in the three cases set out in subsections (2), (3) and (4).

(2) The first case is where section 5 applies and the accused –

 (a) fails to give an initial defence statement,

 (b) gives an initial defence statement but does so after the end of the period which, by virtue of section 12, is the relevant period for section 5,

 (c) is required by section 6B to give either an updated defence statement or a statement of the kind mentioned in subsection (4) of that section but fails to do so,

 (d) gives an updated defence statement or a statement of the kind mentioned in section 6B(4) but does so after the end of the period which, by virtue of section 12, is the relevant period for section 6B,

 (e) sets out inconsistent defences in his defence statement, or

 (f) at his trial –

  (i) puts forward a defence which was not mentioned in his defence statement or is different from any defence set out in that statement,

  (ii) relies on a matter (or any particular of any matter of fact) which, in breach of the requirements imposed by or under section 6A, was not mentioned in his defence statement,

(iii)   adduces evidence in support of an alibi without having given particulars of the alibi in his defence statement, or

(iv)   calls a witness to give evidence in support of an alibi without having complied with section 6A(2)(a) or (b) as regards the witness in his defence statement.

(3)   The second case is where section 6 applies, the accused gives an initial defence statement, and the accused –

(a)   gives the initial defence statement after the end of the period which, by virtue of section 12, is the relevant period for section 6, or

(b)   does any of the things mentioned in paragraphs (c) to (f) of subsection (2).

(4)   The third case is where the accused –

(a)   gives a witness notice but does so after the end of the period which, by virtue of section 12, is the relevant period for section 6C, or

(b)   at his trial calls a witness (other than himself) not included, or not adequately identified, in a witness notice.

(5)   Where this section applies –

(a)   the court or any other party may make such comment as appears appropriate;

(b)   the court or jury may draw such inferences as appear proper in deciding whether the accused is guilty of the offence concerned.

(6)   Where –

(a)   this section applies by virtue of subsection (2)(f)(ii) (including that provision as it applies by virtue of subsection (3)(b)), and

(b)   the matter which was not mentioned is a point of law (including any point as to the admissibility of evidence or an abuse of process) or an authority,

comment by another party under subsection (5)(a) may be made only with the leave of the court.

[(7)   Where this section applies by virtue of subsection (4), comment by another party under subsection (5)(a) may be made only with the leave of the court.][2]

(8)   Where the accused puts forward a defence which is different from any defence set out in his defence statement, in doing anything under subsection (5) or in deciding whether to do anything under it the court shall have regard –

(a)   to the extent of the differences in the defences, and

(b)   to whether there is any justification for it.

(9)   Where the accused calls a witness whom he has failed to include, or to identify adequately, in a witness notice, in doing anything under subsection (5) or in deciding whether to do anything under it the court shall have regard to whether there is any justification for the failure.

(10)   A person shall not be convicted of an offence solely on an inference drawn under subsection (5).

(12)   In this section –

(a)   'initial defence statement' means a defence statement given under section 5 or 6;

(b)   'updated defence statement' means a defence statement given under section 6B;

(c)   a reference simply to an accused's 'defence statement' is a reference –

(i)   where he has given only an initial defence statement, to that statement;

(ii)   where he has given both an initial and an updated defence statement, to the updated defence statement;

(iii)   where he has given both an initial defence statement and a statement of the kind mentioned in section 6B(4), to the initial defence statement;

(d)   a reference to evidence in support of an alibi shall be construed in accordance with section 6A(3);

(e)   'witness notice' means a notice given under section 6C.]¹

Notes

1   Amended by Criminal Justice Act 2003, Pt 5, s 39 (1 May 2010 as SI 2010/1183).

2   Substituted by Criminal Justice Act 2003, Pt 5, s 39 (1 May 2010 as SI 2010/1183).

Amendments pending

Pt I, s 11: substituted by Criminal Justice Act 2003, Pt 5, s 39 (date to be appointed).

Commencement

Pt I, s 11(1)–(6): 4 July 1996 (1 April 1997 in relation to England and Wales; 1 January 1998 otherwise).

Extent

Pt I, s. 11(1)–(12)(e): England. Wales, Northern Ireland.

Time limits

12.– Time limits.

(1)   This section has effect for the purpose of determining the relevant period for [sections 3, 5, 6, 6B, 6C and 7A(5)][1].

(2)   Subject to subsection (3), the relevant period is a period beginning and ending with such days as the Secretary of State prescribes by regulations for the purposes of the section concerned.

(3)   The regulations may do one or more of the following –

>   (a)   provide that the relevant period for any section shall if the court so orders be extended (or further extended) by so many days as the court specifies;

>   (b)   provide that the court may only make such an order if an application is made by a prescribed person and if any other prescribed conditions are fulfilled;

>   (c)   provide that an application may only be made if prescribed conditions are fulfilled;

>   (d)   provide that the number of days by which a period may be extended shall be entirely at the court's discretion;

>   (e)   provide that the number of days by which a period may be extended shall not exceed a prescribed number;

>   (f)   provide that there shall be no limit on the number of applications that may be made to extend a period;

>   (g)   provide that no more than a prescribed number of applications may be made to extend a period;

and references to the relevant period for a section shall be construed accordingly.

(4)   Conditions mentioned in subsection (3) may be framed by reference to such factors as the Secretary of State thinks fit.

(5)   Without prejudice to the generality of subsection (4), so far as the relevant period for [section 3 or 7A(5)][1] is concerned –

>   (a)   conditions may be framed by reference to the nature or volume of the material concerned;

> (b)   the nature of material may be defined by reference to the prosecutor's belief that the question of non-disclosure on grounds of public interest may arise.

(6)   In subsection (3) 'prescribed' means prescribed by regulations under this section.

Notes

1   Substituted by Criminal Justice Act 2003, Sch 36, Pt 3, para 28 (15 July 2005 as SI 2005/1817).

Commencement

Pt I, s 12(1)–(6): 4 July 1996 (1 April 1997 in relation to England and Wales; 1 January 1998 otherwise).

Extent

Pt I, s 12(1)–(6): England, Wales, Northern Ireland.

13.– Time limits: transitional.

(1)   As regards a case in relation to which no regulations under section 12 have come into force for the purposes of section 3, section 3(8) shall have effect as if it read –

'(8)   The prosecutor must act under this section as soon as is reasonably practicable after –

> [(a)   *the accused pleads not guilty (where this Part applies by virtue of section 1(1)),*
>
> (b)   *the accused is committed for trial (where this Part applies by virtue of section 1(2)(a)),*
>
> (c)   *the proceedings are transferred (where this Part applies by virtue of section 1(2)(b) or (c)),]*[1]
>
> [(ca)   copies of the documents containing the evidence on which the charge or charges are based are served on the accused (where this Part applies by virtue of section 1(2)(cc)),][2]
>
> (d)   the count is included in the indictment (where this Part applies by virtue of section 1(2)(d)), or
>
> (e)   the bill of indictment is preferred (where this Part applies by virtue of [section 1(2)(e) or (f)][3]).'

[(2)   As regards a case in relation to which no regulations under section 12 have come into force for the purposes of section 7A, section 7A(5) shall have effect as if –

(a)   in paragraph (a) for the words from 'during the period' to the end, and

(b)   in paragraph (b) for 'during that period',

there were substituted 'as soon as is reasonably practicable after the accused gives the statement in question'.][4]

Notes

1   Repealed by Criminal Justice Act 2003, Sch 3, Pt 2, para 66(1), (4), Sch 37, Pt 4, para 1 (18 June 2012: repeal has effect on 18 June 2012 in relation to the relevant local justice areas for purposes specified in SI 2012/1320, art 4(1)(d) subject to savings as specified in SI 2012/1320, art 5; 18 June 2012 for purposes specified in SI 2012/1320, art 4(3) subject to savings as specified in SI 2012/1320, art 5; 5 November 2012 in relation to the relevant local justice areas as specified in SI 2012/2574, art 2(1)(c) subject to savings as specified in art 3; not yet in force otherwise).

2   Added by Access to Justice Act 1999, Pt IV, s 67(2) (27 September 1999: 27 September 1997 in relation to petty sessions areas as specified in SI 1999/2657, Sch.1).

3   Words inserted by Crime and Disorder Act 1998, Sch 8, para 127(b) (1 June 1999).

4   Substituted by Criminal Justice Act 2003, Sch 36, Pt 3, para 29 (15 July 2005 as SI 2005/1817).

Commencement

Pt I, s 13(1)–(2): 4 July 1996 (1 April 1997 in relation to England and Wales; 1 January 1998 otherwise).

Extent

Pt I, s 13(1)–(2)(b): England, Wales, Northern Ireland.

Public interest

14.– Public interest: review for summary trials.

(1)   This section applies where this Part applies by virtue of section 1(1).

(2) At any time –

(a)   after a court makes an order under [section 3(6), 7A(8) or 8(5)][1] and

(b)   before the accused is acquitted or convicted or the prosecutor decides not to proceed with the case concerned,

the accused may apply to the court for a review of the question whether it is still not in the public interest to disclose material affected by its order.

(3)   In such a case the court must review that question, and if it concludes that it is in the public interest to disclose material to any extent –

(a)   it shall so order, and

(b)   it shall take such steps as are reasonable to inform the prosecutor of its order.

(4)   Where the prosecutor is informed of an order made under subsection (3) he must act accordingly having regard to the provisions of this Part (unless he decides not to proceed with the case concerned).

Notes

1   Words substituted by Criminal Justice Act 2003, Sch 36, Pt 3, para 30 (15 July 2005 as SI 2005/1817).

Commencement

Pt I, s 14(1)–(4): 4 July 1996 (1 April 1997 in relation to England and Wales; 1 January 1998 otherwise).

Extent

Pt I, s 14(1)–(4): England, Wales. Northern Ireland.

15.– Public interest: review in other cases.

(1)   This section applies where this Part applies by virtue of section 1(2).

(2)   This section applies at all times –

(a)   after a court makes an order under [section 3(6), 7A(8) or 8(5)]¹, and

(b)   before the accused is acquitted or convicted or the prosecutor decides not to proceed with the case concerned.

(3)   The court must keep under review the question whether at any given time it is still not in the public interest to disclose material affected by its order.

(4)   The court must keep the question mentioned in subsection (3) under review without the need for an application; but the accused may apply to the court for a review of that question.

(5)   If the court at any time concludes that it is in the public interest to disclose material to any extent –

(a)   it shall so order, and

(b)   it shall take such steps as are reasonable to inform the prosecutor of its order.

(6)   Where the prosecutor is informed of an order made under subsection (5) he must act accordingly having regard to the provisions of this Part (unless he decides not to proceed with the case concerned).

Notes

1   Words substituted by Criminal Justice Act 2003, Sch 36, Pt 3, para 31 (15 July 2005 as SI 2007/1817).

Commencement

Pt I, s 15(1)–(6): 4 July 1996 (1 April 1997 in relation to England and Wales; 1 January 1998 otherwise).

Extent

Pt I, s 15(1)–(6): England, Wales, Northern Ireland.

16.– Applications: opportunity to be heard.

Where –

   (a)   an application is made under [section 3(6), 7A(8), 8(5), 14(2) or 15(4)][1],

   (b)   a person claiming to have an interest in the material applies to be heard by the court, and

   (c)   he shows that he was involved (whether alone or with others and whether directly or indirectly) in the prosecutor's attention being brought to the material,

the court must not make an order under [section 3(6), 7A(8), 8(5), 14(3) or 15(5)][1] (as the case may be) unless the person applying under paragraph (b) has been given an opportunity to be heard.

Notes

1   Amended by Criminal Justice Act 2003, Sch 36, Pt 3, para 32 (15 July 2005 as SI 2005/1817).

Commencement

Pt I, s 16(a)–(c): 4 July 1996 (1 April 1997 in relation to England and Wales; 1 January 1998 otherwise).

Extent

Pt I, s 16(a)–(c): England, Wales, Northern Ireland.

Confidentiality

17.– Confidentiality of disclosed information.

(1)   If the accused is given or allowed to inspect a document or other object under –

(a)   [section 3, 4, 7A, 14 or 15]¹, or

(b)   an order under section 8,

then, subject to subsections (2) to (4), he must not use or disclose it or any information recorded in it.

(2)   The accused may use or disclose the object or information –

    (a)   in connection with the proceedings for whose purposes he was given the object or allowed to inspect it,

    (b)   with a view to the taking of further criminal proceedings (for instance, by way of appeal) with regard to the matter giving rise to the proceedings mentioned in paragraph (a), or

    (c)   in connection with the proceedings first mentioned in paragraph (b).

(3)   The accused may use or disclose –

    (a)   the object to the extent that it has been displayed to the public in open court, or

    (b)   the information to the extent that it has been communicated to the public in open court;

but the preceding provisions of this subsection do not apply if the object is displayed or the information is communicated in proceedings to deal with a contempt of court under section 18.

(4)   If –

    (a)   the accused applies to the court for an order granting permission to use or disclose the object or information, and

    (b)   the court makes such an order,

the accused may use or disclose the object or information for the purpose and to the extent specified by the court.

(5)   An application under subsection (4) may be made and dealt with at any time, and in particular after the accused has been acquitted or convicted or the prosecutor has decided not to proceed with the case concerned: but this is subject to rules made by virtue of section 19(2).

(6)   Where –

    (a)   an application is made under subsection (4), and

    (b)   the prosecutor or a person claiming to have an interest in the object or information applies to be heard by the court, the court must not make an order granting permission unless the person applying under paragraph (b) has been given an opportunity to be heard.

(7)   References in this section to the court are to –

   (a)   a magistrates' court, where this Part applies by virtue of section 1(1);

   (b)   the Crown Court, where this Part applies by virtue of section 1(2).

(8)   Nothing in this section affects any other restriction or prohibition on the use or disclosure of an object or information, whether the restriction or prohibition arises under an enactment (whenever passed) or otherwise.

Notes

1   Words substituted by Criminal Justice Act 2003, Sch 36, Pt 3, para 33 (15 July 2005 as SI 2005/1817).

Commencement

Pt I, s 17(1)–(8): 4 July 1996 (1 April 1997 in relation to England and Wales; 1 January 1998 otherwise).

Extent

Pt I, s 17(1)–(8): England, Wales, Northern Ireland.

18.– Confidentiality: contravention.

(1)   It is a contempt of court for a person knowingly to use or disclose an object or information recorded in it if the use or disclosure is in contravention of section 17.

(2)   The following courts have jurisdiction to deal with a person who is guilty of a contempt under this section –

   (a)   a magistrates' court, where this Part applies by virtue of section 1(1),

   (b)   the Crown Court, where this Part applies by virtue of section 1(2).

(3)   A person who is guilty of a contempt under this section may be dealt with as follows –

   (a)   a magistrates' court may commit him to custody for a specified period not exceeding six months or impose on him a fine not exceeding £5,000 or both;

   (b)   the Crown Court may commit him to custody for a specified period not exceeding two years or impose a fine on him or both.

(4)   If –

   (a)   a person is guilty of a contempt under this section, and

   (b)   the object concerned is in his possession,

the court finding him guilty may order that the object shall be forfeited and dealt with in such manner as the court may order.

(5)   The power of the court under subsection (4) includes power to order the object to be destroyed or to be given to the prosecutor or to be placed in his custody for such period as the court may specify.

(6)   If –

   (a)   the court proposes to make an order under subsection (4), and

   (b)   the person found guilty, or any other person claiming to have an interest in the object, applies to be heard by the court,

the court must not make the order unless the applicant has been given an opportunity to be heard.

(7)   If –

   (a)   a person is guilty of a contempt under this section and

   (b)   a copy of the object concerned is in his possession,

the court finding him guilty may order that the copy shall be forfeited and dealt with in such manner as the court may order.

(8)   Subsections (5) and (6) apply for the purposes of subsection (7) as they apply for the purposes of subsection (4), but as if references to the object were references to the copy.

(9)   An object or information shall be inadmissible as evidence in civil proceedings if to adduce it would in the opinion of the court be likely to constitute a contempt under this section and 'the court' here means the court before which the civil proceedings are being taken.

(10)   The powers of a magistrates' court under this section may be exercised either of the court's own motion or by order on complaint.

Commencement

Pt I, s 18(1)–(10): 4 July 1996 (1 April 1997 in relation to England and Wales; 1 January 1998 otherwise).

Extent

Pt I, s 18(1)–(10): England, Wales, Northern Ireland.

Other provisions

19.– Rules of court.

(1)   [The power to make Criminal Procedure Rules includes power to make provision mentioned in subsection (2).][1]

(2)   The provision is provision as to the practice and procedure to be followed in relation to –

    (a)   proceedings to deal with a contempt of court under section 18;

    (b)   an application under [section 3(6), 5(5B), 6B(6), 6E(5), 7A(8), 8(2) or (5), 14(2), 15(4), 16(b), 17(4), or (6)(b) or 18(6)][2];

    (c)   an application under regulations made under section 12;

    (d)   an order under [section 3(6), 5(5B), 6B(6), 6E(5), 7A(8), 8(2) or (5), 14(3), 17(4) or 18(4) or (7)][2];

    (e)   an order under section 15(5) (whether or not an application is made under section 15(4);

    (f)   an order under regulations made under section 12.

(3)   [Criminal Procedure Rules made][3] by virtue of subsection (2)(a) above may contain or include provision equivalent to Schedule 3 to the Contempt of Court Act 1981 (proceedings for disobeying magistrates' court order) [or such provision with modifications][4].

(4)   Rules made by virtue of subsection (2)(b) in relation to an application under section 17(4) may include provision –

    (a)   that an application to a magistrates' court must be made to a particular magistrates' court;

    (b)   that an application to the Crown Court must be made to the Crown Court sitting at a particular place;

    (c)   requiring persons to be notified of an application.

(5)   Rules made by virtue of this section may make different provision for different cases or classes of case.

Notes

1   Words substituted subject to saving specified in SI 2004/2066, art 3 by Courts Act 2003, Sch 8, para 377(2) (1 September 2004; substitution has effect subject to saving specified in SI 2004/2066, art 3).

2   Amended by Criminal Justice Act 2003, Sch 36, Pt 3, para 34 (15 July 2005 as SI 2005/1817).

3   Words substituted subject to saving specified in SI 2004/2066, art 3 by Courts Act 2003, Sch 8, para 377(3) (1 September 2004: substitution has effect subject to saving specified in SI 2004/2066, art 3).

4   Words substituted by Constitutional Reform Act 2005, Sch 4(1), para 251 (3 April 2006).

Commencement

Pt I, s 19(1)–(5): 4 July 1996 (1 April 1997 in relation to England and Wales; 1 January 1998 otherwise).

Extent

Pt I, s 19(1)–(5): England, Wales, Northern Ireland.

20.– Other statutory rules as to disclosure.

(1)   A duty under any of the disclosure provisions shall not affect or be affected by any duty arising under any other enactment with regard to material to be provided to or by the accused or a person representing him; but this is subject to subsection (2).

[(2)   *In making an order under section 9 of the Criminal Justice Act 1987 or section 31 of this Act (preparatory hearings) the judge may take account of anything which –*

    (a)   *has been done,*

    (b)   *has been required to be done, or*

    (c)   *will be required to be done,*

in pursuance of any of the disclosure provisions.][1]

(3)   [The power to make Criminal Procedure Rules][2] includes power to make, with regard to any proceedings before a magistrates' court which relate to an alleged offence, provision for –

    (a)   requiring any party to the proceedings to disclose to the other party or parties any expert evidence which he proposes to adduce in the proceedings;

    (b)   prohibiting a party who fails to comply in respect of any evidence with any requirement imposed by virtue of paragraph (a) from adducing that evidence without the leave of the court.

(4)   Rules made by virtue of subsection (3) –

    (a)   may specify the kinds of expert evidence to which they apply;

    (b)   may exempt facts or matters of any description specified in the rules.

(5)   For the purposes of this section –

    (a)   the disclosure provisions are [sections 3 to 8][3];

    (b)   'enactment" includes an enactment comprised in subordinate legislation (which here has the same meaning as in the Interpretation Act 1978).

Notes

1   Repealed by Criminal Justice Act 2003, Sch 37, Pt 3, para 1 (15 July 2005 as SI 2005/1817).

2   Words substituted subject to saving specified in SI 2004/2066, art 3 by Courts Act 2003, Sch 8, para 378 (1 September 2004: substitution has effect subject to saving specified in SI 2004/2066, art 3).

3   Words substituted by Criminal Justice Act 2003, Sch 36, Pt 3, para 35(b) (15 July 2005 as SI 2005/1817).

Commencement

Pt I, s 20(1)–(5)(b): 4 July 1996 (1 April 1997 in relation to England and Wales; 1 January 1998 otherwise).

Extent

Pt I, s 20(1)–(5)(b): England, Wales, Northern Ireland.

21.– Common law rules as to disclosure.

(1)   Where this Part applies as regards things falling to be done after the relevant time in relation to an alleged offence, the rules of common law which –

    (a)   were effective immediately before the appointed day, and

    (b)   relate to the disclosure of material by the prosecutor,

do not apply as regards things falling to be done after that time in relation to the alleged offence.

(2)   Subsection (1) does not affect the rules of common law as to whether disclosure is in the public interest.

(3)   References in subsection (1) to the relevant time are to the time when –

    (a)   the accused pleads not guilty (where this Part applies by virtue of section 1(1)),

    [(b)   the accused is sent for trial (where this Part applies by virtue of section 1(2)(cc)),][1]

    (d)   the count is included in the indictment (where this Part applies by virtue of section 1(2)(d), or (e)　　the bill of indictment is preferred (where this Part applies by virtue of section 1(2)(e)).

(4)　The reference in subsection (1) to the appointed day is to the day appointed under section 1(5).

Notes

1　　Section 21(3)(b) substituted for s 21(3)(b) and (c) by Criminal Justice Act 2003, Sch 3, Pt 2, para 66(5) (18 June 2012: repeal has effect on 18 June 2012 in relation to the relevant local justice areas subject to savings as specified in SI 2012/1320, art 5; 18 June 2012 for purposes specified in SI 2012/1320, art 4(3) subject to savings as specified in SI 2012/1320, art 5; 5 November 2012 in relation to the relevant local justice areas as specified in SI 2012/2574, art 2(1)(c) subject to savings as specified in art 3; not yet in force otherwise).

Commencement

Pt I, s 21(1)–(4): 4 July 1996 (1 April 1997 in relation to England and Wales; 1 January 1998 otherwise).

Extent

Pt I, s 21(1)–(4): England, Wales, Northern Ireland.

[21A.– Code of practice for police interviews of witnesses notified by accused.

(1)　The Secretary of State shall prepare a code of practice which gives guidance to police officers, and other persons charged with the duty of investigating offences, in relation to the arranging and conducting of interviews of persons –

(a)　　particulars of whom are given in a defence statement in accordance with section 6A(2), or

(b)　　who are included as proposed witnesses in a notice given under section 6C.

(2)　The code must include (in particular) guidance in relation to –

(a)　　information that should be provided to the interviewee and the accused in relation to such an interview;

(b)　　the notification of the accused's solicitor of such an interview;

(c)　　the attendance of the interviewee's solicitor at such an interview;

(d)　　the attendance of the accused's solicitor at such an interview;

(e)　　the attendance of any other appropriate person at such an interview taking into account the interviewee's age or any disability of the interviewee.

(3)   Any police officer or other person charged with the duty of investigating offences who arranges or conducts such an interview shall have regard to the code.

(4)   In preparing the code, the Secretary of State shall consult –

[(za)   the Association of Chief Police Officers of England, Wales and Northern Ireland;]²

(a)   to the extent the code applies to England and Wales –

(i)   [...]³

(ii)   the General Council of the Bar;

(iii)   the Law Society of England and Wales;

(iv)   the Institute of Legal Executives;

(b)   to the extent the code applies to Northern Ireland –

(i)   the Chief Constable of the Police Service of Northern Ireland;

(ii)   the General Council of the Bar of Northern Ireland;

(iii)   the Law Society of Northern Ireland;

(c)   such other persons as he thinks fit.

(5)   The code shall not come into operation until the Secretary of State by order so provides.

(6)   The Secretary of State may from time to time revise the code and subsections (4) and (5) shall apply to a revised code as they apply to the code as first prepared.

(7)   An order bringing the code into operation may not be made unless a draft of the order has been laid before each House of Parliament and approved by a resolution of each House.

(8)   An order bringing a revised code into operation shall be laid before each House of Parliament if the order has been made without a draft having been so laid and approved by a resolution of each House.

(9)   When an order or a draft of an order is laid in accordance with subsection (7) or (8), the code to which it relates shall also be laid.

(10)   No order or draft of an order may be laid until the consultation required by subsection (4) has taken place.

(11)   A failure by a person mentioned in subsection (3) to have regard to any provision of a code for the time being in operation by virtue of an order under this section shall not in itself render him liable to any criminal or civil proceedings.

(12)   In all criminal and civil proceedings a code in operation at any time by virtue of an order under this section shall be admissible in evidence.

(13)   If it appears to a court or tribunal conducting criminal or civil proceedings that –

> (a)   any provision of a code in operation at any time by virtue of an order under this section, or
>
> (b)   any failure mentioned in subsection (11),

is relevant to any question arising in the proceedings, the provision or failure shall be taken into account in deciding the question.]¹

Notes

1   Added by Criminal Justice Act 2003, Pt 5, s 40 (5 April 2004 in relation to England and Wales).

2   Added by Police and Justice Act 2006, Sch 4, para 9(a) (1 April 2007).

3   Repealed subject to savings and transitional provisions specified in 2007/709, art 6(2)–(5) by Police and Justice Act 2006, Sch 15(1)(B), para 1 (1 April 2007 as SI 2007/709 subject to savings and transitional provisions specified in 2007/709, art 6(2)–(5)).

Extent

Pt I, s 21A(1)–(13)(b): England, Wales, Northern Ireland.

PART II   CRIMINAL INVESTIGATIONS

22.– Introduction.

(1)   For the purposes of this Part a criminal investigation is an investigation conducted by police officers with a view to it being ascertained –

> (a)   whether a person should be charged with an offence, or
>
> (b)   whether a person charged with an offence is guilty of it.

(2)   In this Part references to material are to material of all kinds, and in particular include references to –

> (a)   information, and
>
> (b)   objects of all descriptions.

(3)   In this Part references to recording information are to putting it in a durable or retrievable form (such as writing or tape).

Commencement

Pt II, s 22(1)–(3): 4 July 1996.

Extent

Pt II, s 22(1)–(3); England, Wales, Northern Ireland.

23.– Code of practice.

(1)   The Secretary of State shall prepare a code of practice containing provisions designed to secure –

(a)   that where a criminal investigation is conducted all reasonable steps are taken for the purposes of the investigation and, in particular, all reasonable lines of inquiry are pursued;

(b)   that information which is obtained in the course of a criminal investigation and may be relevant to the investigation is recorded;

(c)   that any record of such information is retained;

(d)   that any other material which is obtained in the course of a criminal investigation and may be relevant to the investigation is retained;

(e)   that information falling within paragraph (b) and material falling within paragraph (d) is revealed to a person who is involved in the prosecution of criminal proceedings arising out of or relating to the investigation and who is identified in accordance with prescribed provisions;

(f)   that where such a person inspects information or other material in pursuance of a requirement that it be revealed to him, and he requests that it be disclosed to the accused, the accused is allowed to inspect it or is given a copy of it;

(g)   that where such a person is given a document indicating the nature of information or other material in pursuance of a requirement that it be revealed to him, and he requests that it be disclosed to the accused, the accused is allowed to inspect it or is given a copy of it;

(h)   that the person who is to allow the accused to inspect information or other material or to give him a copy of it shall decide which of those (inspecting or giving a copy) is appropriate;

(i)   that where the accused is allowed to inspect material as mentioned in paragraph (f) or (g) and he requests a copy, he is given one unless the person allowing the inspection is of opinion that it is not practicable or not desirable to give him one;

(j)   that a person mentioned in paragraph (e) is given a written statement that prescribed activities which the code requires have been carried out.

(2)   The code may include provision –

    (a)   that a police officer identified in accordance with prescribed provisions must carry out a prescribed activity which the code requires;

    (b)   that a police officer so identified must take steps to secure the carrying out by a person (whether or not a police officer) of a prescribed activity which the code requires;

    (c)   that a duty must be discharged by different people in succession in prescribed circumstances (as where a person dies or retires).

(3)   The code may include provision about the form in which information is to be recorded.

(4)   The code may include provision about the manner in which and the period for which –

    (a)   a record of information is to be retained, and

    (b)   any other material is to be retained;

and if a person is charged with an offence the period may extend beyond a conviction or an acquittal.

(5)   The code may include provision about the time when, the form in which, the way in which, and the extent to which, information or any other material is to be revealed to the person mentioned in subsection (1)(c).

(6)   The code must be so framed that it does not apply to material intercepted in obedience to a warrant issued under section 2 of the Interception of Communications Act 1985 [or under the authority of an interception warrant under section 5 of the Regulation of Investigatory Powers Act 2000.][1]

(7)   The code may –

    (a)   make different provision in relation to different cases or descriptions of case;

    (b)   contain exceptions as regards prescribed cases or descriptions of case.

(8)   In this section 'prescribed' means prescribed by the code.

Notes

1   Words added by Regulation of Investigatory Powers Act 2000, Sch 4, para 7(2) (2 October 2000 subject to transitional provisions specified in SI 2000/2543, art 5).

Commencement

Pt II, s 23(1)–(8): 4 July 1996.

Extent

Pt II, s 23(1)–(8); England, Wales, Northern Ireland.

24.– Examples of disclosure provisions.

(1)   This section gives examples of the kinds of provision that may be included in the code by virtue of section 23(5).

(2)   The code may provide that if the person required to reveal material has possession of material which he believes is sensitive he must give a document which –

> (a)   indicates the nature of that material, and
>
> (b)   states that he so believes.

(3)   The code may provide that if the person required to reveal material has possession of material which is of a description prescribed under this subsection and which he does not believe is sensitive he must give a document which –

> (a)   indicates the nature of that material, and
>
> (b)   states that he does not so believe.

(4)   The code may provide that if –

> (a)   a document is given in pursuance of provision contained in the code by virtue of subsection (2), and
>
> (b)   a person identified in accordance with prescribed provisions asks for any of the material,

the person giving the document must give a copy of the material asked for to the person asking for it or (depending on the circumstances) must allow him to inspect it.

(5)   The code may provide that if –

> (a)   a document is given in pursuance of provision contained in the code by virtue of subsection (3),
>
> (b)   all or any of the material is of a description prescribed under this subsection, and
>
> (c)   a person is identified in accordance with prescribed provisions as entitled to material of that description,

the person giving the document must give a copy of the material of that description to the person so identified or (depending on the circumstances) must allow him to inspect it.

(6)   The code may provide that if –

(a)   a document is given in pursuance of provision contained in the code by virtue of subsection (3),

(b)   all or any of the material is not of a description prescribed under subsection (5), and

(c)   a person identified in accordance with prescribed provisions asks for any of the material not of that description,

the person giving the document must give a copy of the material asked for to the person asking for it or (depending on the circumstances) must allow him to inspect it.

(7)   The code may provide that if the person required to reveal material has possession of material which he believes is sensitive and of such a nature that provision contained in the code by virtue of subsection (2) should not apply with regard to it –

(a)   that provision shall not apply with regard to the material,

(b)   he must notify a person identified in accordance with prescribed provisions of the existence of the material, and

(c)   he must allow the person so notified to inspect the material.

(8)   For the purposes of this section material is sensitive to the extent that its disclosure under Part I would be contrary to the public interest.

(9)   In this section 'prescribed' means prescribed by the code.

Commencement

Pt II, s 24(1)–(9): 4 July 1996.

Extent

Pt II, s 24(1)–(9): England, Wales, Northern Ireland.

25.– Operation and revision of code.

(1)   When the Secretary of State has prepared a code under section 23 –

(a)   he shall publish it in the form of a draft,

(b)   he shall consider any representations made to him about the draft, and

(c)   he may modify the draft accordingly.

(2)   When the Secretary of State has acted under subsection (1) he shall lay the code before each House of Parliament, and when he has done so he may bring it into operation on such day as he may appoint by order.

(3)   A code brought into operation under this section shall apply in relation to suspected or alleged offences into which no criminal investigation has begun before the day so appointed.

(4)   The Secretary of State may from time to time revise a code previously brought into operation under this section; and the preceding provisions of this section shall apply to a revised code as they apply to the code as first prepared.

Commencement

Pt II, s 25(1)–(4): 4 July 1996.

Extent

Pt II, s 25(1)–(4): England, Wales, Northern Ireland.

26.– Effect of code.

(1)   A person other than a police officer who is charged with the duty of conducting an investigation with a view to it being ascertained –

    (a)   whether a person should be charged with an offence, or

    (b)   whether a person charged with an offence is guilty of it,

shall in discharging that duty have regard to any relevant provision of a code which would apply if the investigation were conducted by police officers.

(2)   A failure –

    (a)   by a police officer to comply with any provision of a code for the time being in operation by virtue of an order under section 25, or

    (b)   by a person to comply with subsection (1),

shall not in itself render him liable to any criminal or civil proceedings.

(3)   In all criminal and civil proceedings a code in operation at any time by virtue of an order under section 25 shall be admissible in evidence.

(4)   If it appears to a court or tribunal conducting criminal or civil proceedings that –

    (a)   any provision of a code in operation at any time by virtue of an order under section 25, or

    (b)   any failure mentioned in subsection (2)(a) or (b),

is relevant to any question arising in the proceedings, the provision or failure shall be taken into account in deciding the question.

Commencement

Pt II, s 26(1)–(4)(b): 4 July 1996.

Extent

Pt II, s 26(1)–(4)(b): England, Wales, Northern Ireland.

27.– Common law rules as to criminal investigations.

(1)   Where a code prepared under section 23 and brought into operation under section 25 applies in relation to a suspected or alleged offence, the rules of common law which –

    (a)   were effective immediately before the appointed day, and

    (b)   relate to the matter mentioned in subsection (2),

shall not apply in relation to the suspected or alleged offence.

(2)   The matter is the revealing of material –

    (a)   by a police officer or other person charged with the duty of conducting an investigation with a view to it being ascertained whether a person should be charged with an offence or whether a person charged with an offence is guilty of it;

    (b)   to a person involved in the prosecution of criminal proceedings.

(3)   In subsection (1) 'the appointed day' means the day appointed under section 25 with regard to the code as first prepared.

Commencement

Pt II, s 27(1)–(3): 4 July 1996.

Extent

Pt II, s 27(1)–(3): England, Wales, Northern Ireland.

Appendix 2

Criminal Procedure and Investigations Act 1996: Code of Practice

CONTENTS   PAGE

Preamble

This code of practice is issued under Part II of the Criminal Procedure and Investigations Act 1996 ('the Act'). It sets out the manner in which police officers are to record, retain and reveal to the prosecutor material obtained in a criminal investigation and which may be relevant to the investigation, and related matters.

Introduction

1.1   This code of practice applies in respect of criminal investigations conducted by police officers which begin on or after the day on which this code comes into effect. Persons other than police officers who are charged with the duty of conducting an investigation as defined in the Act are to have regard to the relevant provisions of the code, and should take these into account in applying their own operating procedures.

1.2   This code does not apply to persons who are not charged with the duty of conducting an investigation as defined in the Act.

1.3   Nothing in this code applies to material intercepted in obedience to a warrant issued under section 2 of the Interception of Communications Act 1985 or section 5 of the Regulation of Investigatory Powers Act 2000, or to any copy of that material as defined in section 10 of the 1985 Act or section 15 of the 2000 Act.

1.4   This code extends only to England and Wales.

Definitions

2.1   In this code:

–   *a criminal investigation* is an investigation conducted by police officers with a view to it being ascertained whether a person should be charged with an offence, or whether a person charged with an offence is guilty of it. This will include:

   –   investigations into crimes that have been committed;

   –   investigations whose purpose is to ascertain whether a crime has been committed, with a view to the possible institution of criminal proceedings; and

   –   investigations which begin in the belief that a crime may be committed, for example when the police keep premises or individuals under observation for a period of time, with a view to the possible institution of criminal proceedings;

–   charging a person with an offence includes prosecution by way of summons;

–   *an investigator* is any police officer involved in the conduct of a criminal investigation. All investigators have a responsibility for carrying out the duties imposed on them under this code, including in particular recording information, and retaining records of information and other material;

–   *the officer in charge of an investigation* is the police officer responsible for directing a criminal investigation. He is also responsible for ensuring that proper procedures are in place for recording information, and retaining records of information and other material, in the investigation;

–   *the disclosure officer* is the person responsible for examining material retained by the police during the investigation; revealing material to the prosecutor during the investigation and any criminal proceedings resulting from it, and certifying that he has done this; and disclosing material to the accused at the request of the prosecutor;

–   *the prosecutor* is the authority responsible for the conduct, on behalf of the Crown, of criminal proceedings resulting from a specific criminal investigation;

–   *material* is material of any kind, including information and objects, which is obtained in the course of a criminal investigation and which may be relevant to the investigation. This includes not only material coming into the possession of the investigator (such as documents seized in the course of searching premises) but also material generated by him (such as interview records);

–   material may be *relevant to an investigation* if it appears to an investigator, or to the officer in charge of an investigation, or to the disclosure officer, that it has some bearing on any offence under investigation or any person being investigated, or on the surrounding circumstances of the case, unless it is incapable of having any impact on the case;

–   *sensitive material* is material, the disclosure of which, the disclosure officer believes, would give rise to a real risk of serious prejudice to an important public interest;

–   references to *prosecution disclosure* are to the duty of the prosecutor under sections 3 and 7A of the Act to disclose material which is in his possession or which he has inspected in pursuance of this code, and which might reasonably be considered capable of undermining the case against the accused, or of assisting the case for the accused;

–   references to the disclosure of material to a person accused of an offence include references to the disclosure of material to his legal representative;

–   references to police officers and to the chief officer of police include those employed in a police force as defined in section 3(3) of the Prosecution of Offences Act 1985.

General responsibilities

3.1   The functions of the investigator, the officer in charge of an investigation and the disclosure officer are separate. Whether they are undertaken by one, two or more persons will depend on the complexity of the case and the administrative arrangements within each police force. Where they are undertaken by more than one person, close consultation between them is essential to the effective performance of the duties imposed by this code.

3.2   In any criminal investigation, one or more deputy disclosure officers may be appointed to assist the disclosure officer, and a deputy disclosure officer may perform any function of a disclosure officer as defined in paragraph 2.1.

3.3   The chief officer of police for each police force is responsible for putting in place arrangements to ensure that in every investigation the identity of the officer in charge of an investigation and the disclosure officer is recorded. The chief officer of police for each police force shall ensure that disclosure officers and deputy disclosure officers have sufficient skills and authority, commensurate with the complexity of the investigation, to discharge their functions effectively. An individual must not be appointed as disclosure officer, or continue in that role, if that is likely to result in a conflict of interest, for instance, if the disclosure officer is the victim of the alleged crime which is the subject of the investigation. The advice of a more senior officer must always be sought if there is doubt as to whether a conflict of interest precludes an individual acting as disclosure officer. If thereafter the doubt remains, the advice of a prosecutor should be sought.

3.4   The officer in charge of an investigation may delegate tasks to another investigator, to civilians employed by the police force, or to other persons participating in the investigation under arrangements for joint investigations, but he remains responsible for ensuring that these have been carried out and for accounting for any general policies followed in the investigation. In particular, it is an essential part of his duties to ensure that all material which may be relevant to an investigation is retained, and either made available to the disclosure officer or (in exceptional circumstances) revealed directly to the prosecutor.

3.5   In conducting an investigation, the investigator should pursue all reasonable lines of inquiry, whether these point towards or away from the suspect. What is reasonable in each case will depend on the particular circumstances. For example, where material is held on computer, it is a matter for the investigator to decide which material on the computer it is reasonable to inquire into, and in what manner.

3.6   If the officer in charge of an investigation believes that other persons may be in possession of material that may be relevant to the investigation, and if this has not been obtained under paragraph 3.5 above, he should ask the disclosure officer to inform them of the existence of the investigation and to invite them to retain the material in case they receive a request for its disclosure. The disclosure officer should inform the prosecutor that they may have such material. However, the officer in charge of an investigation is not required to make speculative enquiries of other persons; there must be some reason to believe that they may have relevant material. That reason may come from information provided to the police by the accused or from other inquiries made or from some other source.

3.7   If, during a criminal investigation, the officer in charge of an investigation or disclosure officer for any reason no longer has responsibility for the functions falling to him, either his supervisor or the police officer in charge of criminal investigations for the police force concerned must assign someone else to assume that responsibility. That person's identity must be recorded, as with those initially responsible for these functions in each investigation.

Recording of information

4.1   If material which may be relevant to the investigation consists of information which is not recorded in any form, the officer in charge of an investigation must ensure that it is recorded in a durable or retrievable form (whether in writing, on video or audio tape, or on computer disk).

4.2   Where it is not practicable to retain the initial record of information because it forms part of a larger record which is to be destroyed, its contents should be transferred as a true record to a durable and more easily-stored form before that happens.

4.3   Negative information is often relevant to an investigation. If it may be relevant it must be recorded. An example might be a number of people present in a particular place at a particular time who state that they saw nothing unusual.

4.4   Where information which may be relevant is obtained, it must be recorded at the time it is obtained or as soon as practicable after that time. This includes, for example, information obtained in house-to-house enquiries, although the requirement to record information promptly does not require an investigator to take a statement from a potential witness where it would not otherwise be taken.

Retention of material

(a) Duty to retain material

5.1   The investigator must retain material obtained in a criminal investigation which may be relevant to the investigation. Material may be photographed, video-recorded, captured digitally or otherwise retained in the form of a copy rather than the original at any time, if the original is perishable; the original was supplied to the investigator rather than generated by him and is to be returned to its owner; or the retention of a copy rather than the original is reasonable in all the circumstances.

5.2   Where material has been seized in the exercise of the powers of seizure conferred by the Police and Criminal Evidence Act 1984, the duty to retain it under this code is subject to the provisions on the retention of seized material in section 22 of that Act.

5.3   If the officer in charge of an investigation becomes aware as a result of developments in the case that material previously examined but not retained (because it was not thought to be relevant) may now be relevant to the investigation, he should, wherever practicable, take steps to obtain it or ensure that it is retained for further inspection or for production in court if required.

5.4   The duty to retain material includes in particular the duty to retain material falling into the following categories, where it may be relevant to the investigation:

–   crime reports (including crime report forms, relevant parts of incident report books or police officer's notebooks);

–   custody records;

–   records which are derived from tapes of telephone messages (for example, 999 calls) containing descriptions of an alleged offence or offender;

–   final versions of witness statements (and draft versions where their content differs from the final version), including any exhibits mentioned (unless these have been returned to their owner on the understanding that they will be produced in court if required);

–   interview records (written records, or audio or video tapes, of interviews with actual or potential witnesses or suspects);

–   communications between the police and experts such as forensic scientists, reports of work carried out by experts, and schedules of scientific material prepared by the expert for the investigator, for the purposes of criminal proceedings;

– records of the first description of a suspect by each potential witness who purports to identify or describe the suspect, whether or not the description differs from that of subsequent descriptions by that or other witnesses;

– any material casting doubt on the reliability of a witness.

5.5 The duty to retain material, where it may be relevant to the investigation, also includes in particular the duty to retain material which may satisfy the test for prosecution disclosure in the Act, such as:

– information provided by an accused person which indicates an explanation for the offence with which he has been charged;

– any material casting doubt on the reliability of a confession;

– any material casting doubt on the reliability of a prosecution witness.

5.6 The duty to retain material falling into these categories does not extend to items which are purely ancillary to such material and possess no independent significance (for example, duplicate copies of records or reports).

(b) Length of time for which material is to be retained

5.7 All material which may be relevant to the investigation must be retained until a decision is taken whether to institute proceedings against a person for an offence.

5.8 If a criminal investigation results in proceedings being instituted, all material which may be relevant must be retained at least until the accused is acquitted or convicted or the prosecutor decides not to proceed with the case.

5.9 Where the accused is convicted, all material which may be relevant must be retained at least until:

– the convicted person is released from custody, or discharged from hospital, in cases where the court imposes a custodial sentence or a hospital order;

– six months from the date of conviction, in all other cases.

If the court imposes a custodial sentence or hospital order and the convicted person is released from custody or discharged from hospital earlier than six months from the date of conviction, all material which may be relevant must be retained at least until six months from the date of conviction.

5.10 If an appeal against conviction is in progress when the release or discharge occurs, or at the end of the period of six months specified in paragraph 5.9, all material which may be relevant must be retained until the appeal is determined. Similarly, if the Criminal Cases Review Commission is considering an application at that point in time, all material which may be relevant must be retained at least until the Commission decides not to refer the case to the Court.

Preparation of material for prosecutor

(a)   Introduction

6.1   The officer in charge of the investigation, the disclosure officer or an investigator may seek advice from the prosecutor about whether any particular item of material may be relevant to the investigation.

6.2   Material which may be relevant to an investigation, which has been retained in accordance with this code, and which the disclosure officer believes will not form part of the prosecution case, must be listed on a schedule.

6.3   Material which the disclosure officer does not believe is sensitive must be listed on a schedule of non-sensitive material. The schedule must include a statement that the disclosure officer does not believe the material is sensitive.

6.4   Any material which is believed to be sensitive must be either listed on a schedule of sensitive material or, in exceptional circumstances, revealed to the prosecutor separately. If there is no sensitive material, the disclosure officer must record this fact on a schedule of sensitive material.

6.5   Paragraphs 6.6 to 6.11 below apply to both sensitive and non-sensitive material. Paragraphs 6.12 to 6.14 apply to sensitive material only.

(b)   Circumstances in which a schedule is to be prepared

6.6   The disclosure officer must ensure that a schedule is prepared in the following circumstances:

–   the accused is charged with an offence which is triable only on indictment;

–   the accused is charged with an offence which is triable either way, and it is considered either that the case is likely to be tried on indictment or that the accused is likely to plead not guilty at a summary trial;

–   the accused is charged with a summary offence, and it is considered that he is likely to plead not guilty.

6.7   In respect of either way and summary offences, a schedule may not be needed if a person has admitted the offence, or if a police officer witnessed the offence and that person has not denied it.

6.8   If it is believed that the accused is likely to plead guilty at a summary trial, it is not necessary to prepare a schedule in advance. If, contrary to this belief, the accused pleads not guilty at a summary trial, or the offence is to be tried on indictment, the disclosure officer must ensure that a schedule is prepared as soon as is reasonably practicable after that happens.

(c) Way in which material is to be listed on schedule

6.9   The disclosure officer should ensure that each item of material is listed separately on the schedule, and is numbered consecutively. The description of each item should make clear the nature of the item and should contain sufficient detail to enable the prosecutor to decide whether he needs to inspect the material before deciding whether or not it should be disclosed.

6.10   In some enquiries it may not be practicable to list each item of material separately. For example, there may be many items of a similar or repetitive nature. These may be listed in a block and described by quantity and generic title.

6.11   Even if some material is listed in a block, the disclosure officer must ensure that any items among that material which might satisfy the test for prosecution disclosure are listed and described individually.

(d) Treatment of sensitive material

6.12   Subject to paragraph 6.13 below, the disclosure officer must list on a sensitive schedule any material, the disclosure of which he believes would give rise to a real risk of serious prejudice to an important public interest, and the reason for that belief. The schedule must include a statement that the disclosure officer believes the material is sensitive. Depending on the circumstances, examples of such material may include the following among others:

–   material relating to national security;

–   material received from the intelligence and security agencies;

–   material relating to intelligence from foreign sources which reveals sensitive intelligence gathering methods;

–   material given in confidence;

–   material relating to the identity or activities of informants, or undercover police officers, or witnesses, or other persons supplying information to the police who may be in danger if their identities are revealed;

–   material revealing the location of any premises or other place used for police surveillance, or the identity of any person allowing a police officer to use them for surveillance;

–   material revealing, either directly or indirectly, techniques and methods relied upon by a police officer in the course of a criminal investigation, for example covert surveillance techniques, or other methods of detecting crime;

–   material whose disclosure might facilitate the commission of other offences or hinder the prevention and detection of crime;

–   material upon the strength of which search warrants were obtained;

–   material containing details of persons taking part in identification parades;

–   material supplied to an investigator during a criminal investigation which has been generated by an official of a body concerned with the regulation or supervision of bodies corporate or of persons engaged in financial activities, or which has been generated by a person retained by such a body;

–   material supplied to an investigator during a criminal investigation which relates to a child or young person and which has been generated by a local authority social services department, an Area Child Protection Committee or other party contacted by an investigator during the investigation;

–   material relating to the private life of a witness.

6.13   In exceptional circumstances, where an investigator considers that material is so sensitive that its revelation to the prosecutor by means of an entry on the sensitive schedule is inappropriate, the existence of the material must be revealed to the prosecutor separately. This will apply only where compromising the material would be likely to lead directly to the loss of life, or directly threaten national security.

6.14   In such circumstances, the responsibility for informing the prosecutor lies with the investigator who knows the detail of the sensitive material. The investigator should act as soon as is reasonably practicable after the file containing the prosecution case is sent to the prosecutor. The investigator must also ensure that the prosecutor is able to inspect the material so that he can assess whether it is disclosable and, if so, whether it needs to be brought before a court for a ruling on disclosure.

Revelation of material to prosecutor

7.1   The disclosure officer must give the schedules to the prosecutor. Wherever practicable this should be at the same time as he gives him the file containing the material for the prosecution case (or as soon as is reasonably practicable after the decision on mode of trial or the plea, in cases to which paragraph 6.8 applies).

7.2   The disclosure officer should draw the attention of the prosecutor to any material an investigator has retained (including material to which paragraph 6.13 applies) which may satisfy the test for prosecution disclosure in the Act, and should explain why he has come to that view.

7.3   At the same time as complying with the duties in paragraphs 7.1 and 7.2, the disclosure officer must give the prosecutor a copy of any material which falls into the following categories (unless such material has already been given to the prosecutor as part of the file containing the material for the prosecution case):

–   information provided by an accused person which indicates an explanation for the offence with which he has been charged;

–   any material casting doubt on the reliability of a confession;

–   any material casting doubt on the reliability of a prosecution witness;

–   any other material which the investigator believes may satisfy the test for prosecution disclosure in the Act.

7.4   If the prosecutor asks to inspect material which has not already been copied to him, the disclosure officer must allow him to inspect it. If the prosecutor asks for a copy of material which has not already been copied to him, the disclosure officer must give him a copy. However, this does not apply where the disclosure officer believes, having consulted the officer in charge of the investigation, that the material is too sensitive to be copied and can only be inspected.

7.5   If material consists of information which is recorded other than in writing, whether it should be given to the prosecutor in its original form as a whole, or by way of relevant extracts recorded in the same form, or in the form of a transcript, is a matter for agreement between the disclosure officer and the prosecutor.

Subsequent action by disclosure officer

8.1   At the time a schedule of non-sensitive material is prepared, the disclosure officer may not know exactly what material will form the case against the accused, and the prosecutor may not have given advice about the likely relevance of particular items of material. Once these matters have been determined, the disclosure officer must give the prosecutor, where necessary, an amended schedule listing any additional material:

–   which may be relevant to the investigation,

–   which does not form part of the case against the accused,

–   which is not already listed on the schedule, and

–   which he believes is not sensitive,

unless he is informed in writing by the prosecutor that the prosecutor intends to disclose the material to the defence.

8.2   Section 7A of the Act imposes a continuing duty on the prosecutor, for the duration of criminal proceedings against the accused, to disclose material which satisfies the test for disclosure (subject to public interest considerations). To enable him to do this, any new material coming to light should be treated in the same way as the earlier material.

8.3   In particular, after a defence statement has been given, the disclosure officer must look again at the material which has been retained and must draw the attention of the prosecutor to any material which might reasonably be considered capable of undermining the case for the prosecution against the accused or of assisting the case for the accused; and he must reveal it to him in accordance with paragraphs 7.4 and 7.5 above.

Certification by disclosure officer

9.1   The disclosure officer must certify to the prosecutor that to the best of his knowledge and belief, all relevant material which has been retained and made available to him has been revealed to the prosecutor in accordance with this code. He must sign and date the certificate. It will be necessary to certify not only at the time when the schedule and accompanying material is submitted to the prosecutor, and when relevant material which has been retained is reconsidered after the accused has given a defence statement, but also whenever a schedule is otherwise given or material is otherwise revealed to the prosecutor.

Disclosure of material to accused

10.1   If material has not already been copied to the prosecutor, and he requests its disclosure to the accused on the ground that:

–   it satisfies the test for prosecution disclosure, or

–   the court has ordered its disclosure after considering an application from the accused,

the disclosure officer must disclose it to the accused.

10.2   If material has been copied to the prosecutor, and it is to be disclosed, whether it is disclosed by the prosecutor or the disclosure officer is a matter of agreement between the two of them.

10.3   The disclosure officer must disclose material to the accused either by giving him a copy or by allowing him to inspect it. If the accused person asks for a copy of any material which he has been allowed to inspect, the disclosure officer must give it to him, unless in the opinion of the disclosure officer that is either not practicable (for example because the material consists of an object which cannot be copied, or because the volume of material is so great), or not desirable (for example because the material is a statement by a child witness in relation to a sexual offence).

10.4   If material which the accused has been allowed to inspect consists of information which is recorded other than in writing, whether it should be given to the accused in its original form or in the form of a transcript is matter for the discretion of the disclosure officer. If the material is transcribed, the disclosure officer must ensure that the transcript is certified to the accused as a true record of the material which has been transcribed.

10.5   If a court concludes that an item of sensitive material satisfies the prosecution disclosure test and that the interests of the defence outweigh the public interest in withholding disclosure, it will be necessary to disclose the material if the case is to proceed. This does not mean that sensitive documents must always be disclosed in their original form: for example, the court may agree that sensitive details still requiring protection should be blocked out, or that documents may be summarised, or that the prosecutor may make an admission about the substance of the material under section 10 of the Criminal Justice Act 1967.

Appendix 3

Criminal Procedure Rules 2012 (SI 2012/1726), Parts 1 to 3

Part 1
The Overriding Objective

Contents of this Part

The overriding objective

1.1.–(1) The overriding objective of this new code is that criminal cases be dealt with justly.

(2) Dealing with a criminal case justly includes –

    (a)   acquitting the innocent and convicting the guilty;

    (b)   dealing with the prosecution and the defence fairly;

    (c)   recognising the rights of a defendant, particularly those under Article 6 of the European Convention on Human Rights;

    (d)   respecting the interests of witnesses, victims and jurors and keeping them informed of the progress of the case;

    (e)   dealing with the case efficiently and expeditiously;

    (f)   ensuring that appropriate information is available to the court when bail and sentence are considered; and

    (g)   dealing with the case in ways that take into account –

        (i)   the gravity of the offence alleged,

        (ii)   the complexity of what is in issue,

    (iii)   the severity of the consequences for the defendant and others affected, and

    (iv)   the needs of other cases.

The duty of the participants in a criminal case

1.2.–(1)   Each participant, in the conduct of each case, must –

    (a)   prepare and conduct the case in accordance with the overriding objective;

    (b)   comply with these Rules, practice directions and directions made by the court; and

    (c)   at once inform the court and all parties of any significant failure (whether or not that participant is responsible for that failure) to take any procedural step required by these Rules, any practice direction or any direction of the court. A failure is significant if it might hinder the court in furthering the overriding objective.

(2)   Anyone involved in any way with a criminal case is a participant in its conduct for the purposes of this rule.

The application by the court of the overriding objective

1.3.–   The court must further the overriding objective in particular when –

    (a)   exercising any power given to it by legislation (including these Rules);

    (b)   applying any practice direction; or

    (c)   interpreting any rule or practice direction.

Part 2

Understanding and Applying the Rules

Contents of this Part

When the Rules apply

2.1.–(1)   In general, the Criminal Procedure Rules apply –

(a)   in all criminal cases in magistrates' courts and in the Crown Court; and

(b)   in all cases in the criminal division of the Court of Appeal.

(2)   If a rule applies only in one or two of those courts, the rule makes that clear.

(3)   The Rules apply on and after 1st October, 2012, but unless the court otherwise directs they do not affect a right or duty existing under The Criminal Procedure Rules 2011.

(4)   Rule 9.6, and the rules in Section 3 of Part 9 (Allocation and sending for trial), apply only where there have come into force the amendments made by Schedule 3 to the Criminal Justice Act 2003 (Allocation of cases triable either way, and sending cases to the Crown Court, etc.) which confer the powers to which those rules apply.

[Note. The rules replaced by the first Criminal Procedure Rules (The Criminal Procedure Rules 2005) were revoked when those Rules came into force by provisions of the Courts Act 2003, The Courts Act 2003 (Consequential Amendments) Order 2004 and The Courts Act 2003 (Commencement No. 6 and Savings) Order 2004. The first Criminal Procedure Rules reproduced the substance of all the rules they replaced]

Definitions

2.2.–(1)   In these Rules, unless the context makes it clear that something different is meant:

'business day' means any day except Saturday, Sunday, Christmas Day, Boxing Day, Good Friday, Easter Monday or a bank holiday;

'court' means a tribunal with jurisdiction over criminal cases. It includes a judge, recorder, District Judge (Magistrates' Court), lay justice and, when exercising their judicial powers, the Registrar of Criminal Appeals, a justices' clerk or assistant clerk;

'court officer' means the appropriate member of the staff of a court;

'justices' legal adviser' means a justices' clerk or an assistant to a justices' clerk;

'live link' means an arrangement by which a person can see and hear, and be seen and heard by, the court when that person is not in court;

'Practice Direction' means the Lord Chief Justice's Consolidated Criminal Practice Direction, as amended and 'Criminal Costs Practice

Direction' means the Lord Chief Justice's Practice Direction (Costs in Criminal Proceedings), as amended;

'public interest ruling' means a ruling about whether it is in the public interest to disclose prosecution material under sections 3(6), 7A(8) or 8(5) of the Criminal Procedure and Investigations Act 1996; and

'Registrar' means the Registrar of Criminal Appeals or a court officer acting with the Registrar's authority.

(2)   Definitions of some other expressions are in the rules in which they apply.

[Note. The glossary at the end of the Rules is a guide to the meaning of certain legal expressions used in them.]

References to Acts of Parliament and to Statutory Instruments

2.3.–   In these Rules, where a rule refers to an Act of Parliament or to subordinate legislation by title and year, subsequent references to that Act or to that legislation in the rule are shortened: so, for example, after a reference to the Criminal Procedure and Investigations Act 1996 that Act is called 'the 1996 Act'; and after a reference to The Criminal Procedure and Investigations Act 1996 (Defence Disclosure Time Limits) Regulations 2011 those Regulations are called 'the 2011 Regulations'.

Representatives

2.4.–(1)   Under these Rules, unless the context makes it clear that something different is meant, anything that a party may or must do may be done –

(a)   by a legal representative on that party's behalf;

(b)   by a person with the corporation's written authority, where that party is a corporation;

(c)   with the help of a parent, guardian or other suitable supporting adult where that party is a defendant –

(i)   who is under 18, or

(ii)   whose understanding of what the case involves is limited.

(2)   Anyone with a prosecutor's authority to do so may, on that prosecutor's behalf –

(a)   serve on the magistrates' court officer, or present to a magistrates' court, an information under section 1 of the Magistrates' Courts Act 1980; or

(b)   issue a written charge and requisition under section 29 of the Criminal Justice Act 2003.

[Note.   See also section 122 of the Magistrates' Courts Act 1980. A party's legal representative must be entitled to act as such under section 13 of the Legal Services Act 2007.

Section 33(6) of the Criminal Justice Act 1925, section 46 of the Magistrates' Courts Act 1980 and Schedule 3 to that Act provide for the representation of a corporation.

Section 223 of the Local Government Act 1972 allows a member or officer of a local authority on that authority's behalf to prosecute or defend a case before a magistrates' court, and to appear in and to conduct any proceedings before a magistrates' court.

Part 7 contains rules about starting a prosecution.]

Part 3
Case Management

Contents of this Part

The scope of this Part

3.1.–   This Part applies to the management of each case in a magistrates' court and in the Crown Court (including an appeal to the Crown Court) until the conclusion of that case.

[Note.   Rules that apply to procedure in the Court of Appeal are in Parts 65 to 73 of these Rules.]

The duty of the court

3.2.–(1)   The court must further the overriding objective by actively managing the case.

(2)   Active case management includes –

(a)   the early identification of the real issues;

(b)   the early identification of the needs of witnesses;

(c)   achieving certainty as to what must be done, by whom, and when, in particular by the early setting of a timetable for the progress of the case;

(d)   monitoring the progress of the case and compliance with directions;

(e)   ensuring that evidence, whether disputed or not, is presented in the shortest and clearest way;

(f)   discouraging delay dealing with as many aspects of the case as possible on the same occasion, and avoiding unnecessary hearings;

(g)   encouraging the participants to co-operate in the progression of the case; and

(h)   making use of technology.

(3)   The court must actively manage the case by giving any direction appropriate to the needs of that case as early as possible.

The duty of the parties

3.3.–   Each party must –

(a)   actively assist the court in fulfilling its duty under rule 3.2, without or if necessary with a direction; and

(b)   apply for a direction if needed to further the overriding objective.

Case progression officers and their duties

3.4.–(1)   At the beginning of the case each party must, unless the court otherwise directs –

(a)   nominate an individual responsible for progressing that case; and

(b)   tell other parties and the court who he is and how to contact him.

(2)   In fulfilling its duty under rule 3.2, the court must where appropriate –

    (a)   nominate a court officer responsible for progressing the case; and

    (b)   make sure the parties know who he is and how to contact him.

(3)   In this Part a person nominated under this rule is called a case progression officer.

(4)   A case progression officer must –

    (a)   monitor compliance with directions;

    (b)   make sure that the court is kept informed of events that may affect the progress of that case;

    (c)   make sure that he can be contacted promptly about the case during ordinary business hours;

    (d)   act promptly and reasonably in response to communications about the case; and

    (e)   if he will be unavailable, appoint a substitute to fulfil his duties and inform the other case progression officers.

The court's case management powers

3.5.–(1)   In fulfilling its duty under rule 3.2 the court may give any direction and take any step actively to manage a case unless that direction or step would be inconsistent with legislation, including these Rules.

(2)   In particular, the court may –

    (a)   nominate a judge, magistrate or justices' legal adviser to manage the case;

    (b)   give a direction on its own initiative or on application by a party;

    (c)   ask or allow a party to propose a direction;

    (d)   for the purpose of giving directions, receive applications and representations by letter, by telephone or by any other means of electronic communication, and conduct a hearing by such means;

    (e)   give a direction –

        (i)   at a hearing, in public or in private, or

        (ii)   without a hearing;

    (f)   fix, postpone, bring forward, extend, cancel or adjourn a hearing;

    (g)   shorten or extend (even after it has expired) a time limit fixed by a direction;

(h)   require that issues in the case should be –

    (i)   identified in writing,

    (ii)   determined separately, and decide in what order they will be determined; and

(i)   specify the consequences of failing to comply with a direction.

(3)   A magistrates' court may give a direction that will apply in the Crown Court if the case is to continue there.

(4)   The Crown Court may give a direction that will apply in a magistrates' court if the case is to continue there.

(5)   Any power to give a direction under this Part includes a power to vary or revoke that direction.

(6)   If a party fails to comply with a rule or a direction, the court may –

(a)   fix, postpone, bring forward, extend, cancel or adjourn a hearing;

(b)   exercise its powers to make a costs order; and

(c)   impose such other sanction as may be appropriate.

[Note.   Depending upon the nature of a case and the stage that it has reached, its progress may be affected by other Criminal Procedure Rules and by other legislation. The note at the end of this Part lists other rules and legislation that may apply.

See also rule 3.10.

The court may make a costs order under –

    (a)   section 19 of the Prosecution of Offences Act 1985, where the court decides that one party to criminal proceedings has incurred costs as a result of an unnecessary or improper act or omission by, or on behalf of, another party;

    (b)   section 19A of that Act, where the court decides that a party has incurred costs as a result of an improper, unreasonable or negligent act or omission on the part of a legal representative;

    (c)   section 19B of that Act, where the court decides that there has been serious misconduct by a person who is not a party.

Under some other legislation, including Parts 33, 34 and 35 of these Rules, if a party fails to comply with a rule or a direction then in some circumstances –

    (a)   the court may refuse to allow that party to introduce evidence;

    (b)   evidence that that party wants to introduce may not be admissible;

    (c)   the court may draw adverse inferences from the late introduction of an issue or evidence.

See also –

    (a)   section 81(1) of the Police and Criminal Evidence Act 1984 and section 20(3) of the Criminal Procedure and Investigations Act 1996 (advance disclosure of expert evidence);

(b)   *section 11(5) of the Criminal Procedure and Investigations Act 1996 (faults in disclosure by accused);*

(c)   *section 132(5) of the Criminal Justice Act 2003 (failure to give notice of hearsay evidence).]*

Application to vary a direction

3.6.–(1)   A party may apply to vary a direction if –

(a)   the court gave it without a hearing;

(b)   the court gave it at a hearing in his absence; or

(c)   circumstances have changed.

(2)   A party who applies to vary a direction must –

(a)   apply as soon as practicable after he becomes aware of the grounds for doing so; and

(b)   give as much notice to the other parties as the nature and urgency of his application permits.

Agreement to vary a time limit fixed by a direction

3.7.–(1)   The parties may agree to vary a time limit fixed by a direction, but only if –

(a)   the variation will not –

(i)   affect the date of any hearing that has been fixed, or

(ii)   significantly affect the progress of the case in any other way;

(b)   the court has not prohibited variation by agreement; and

(c)   the court's case progression officer is promptly informed.

(2)   The court's case progression officer must refer the agreement to the court if he doubts the condition in paragraph (1)(a) is satisfied.

Case preparation and progression

3.8.–(1)   At every hearing, if a case cannot be concluded there and then the court must give directions so that it can be concluded at the next hearing or as soon as possible after that.

(2)   At every hearing the court must, where relevant –

(a)   if the defendant is absent, decide whether to proceed nonetheless;

(b)   take the defendant's plea (unless already done) or if no plea can be taken then find out whether the defendant is likely to plead guilty or not guilty;

(c)   set, follow or revise a timetable for the progress of the case, which may include a timetable for any hearing including the trial or (in the Crown Court) the appeal;

(d)   in giving directions, ensure continuity in relation to the court and to the parties' representatives where that is appropriate and practicable; and

(e)   where a direction has not been complied with, find out why, identify who was responsible, and take appropriate action.

(3)   In order to prepare for a trial in the Crown Court, the court must conduct a plea and case management hearing unless the circumstances make that unnecessary.

(4)   In order to prepare for the trial, the court must take every reasonable step to encourage and to facilitate the attendance of witnesses when they are needed.

Readiness for trial or appeal

3.9.–(1)   This rule applies to a party's preparation for trial or appeal, and in this rule and rule 3.10 trial includes any hearing at which evidence will be introduced.

(2)   In fulfilling his duty under rule 3.3, each party must –

(a)   comply with directions given by the court;

(b)   take every reasonable step to make sure his witnesses will attend when they are needed;

(c)   make appropriate arrangements to present any written or other material; and

(d)   promptly inform the court and the other parties of anything that may –

(i)   affect the date or duration of the trial or appeal, or

(ii)   significantly affect the progress of the case in any other way.

(3)   The court may require a party to give a certificate of readiness.

Conduct of a trial or an appeal

3.10–   In order to manage a trial or an appeal, the court –

    (a)   must establish, with the active assistance of the parties, what are the disputed issues;

    (b)   must consider setting a timetable that –

        (i)   takes account of those issues and of any timetable proposed by a party, and

        (ii)   may limit the duration of any stage of the hearing;

    (c)   may require a party to identify –

        (i)   which witnesses that party wants to give evidence in person,

        (ii)   the order in which that party wants those witnesses to give their evidence,

        (iii)   whether that party requires an order compelling the attendance of a witness,

        (iv)   what arrangements are desirable to facilitate the giving of evidence by a witness,

        (v)   what arrangements are desirable to facilitate the participation of any other person, including the defendant,

        (vi)   what written evidence that party intends to introduce,

        (vii)   what other material, if any, that person intends to make available to the court in the presentation of the case, and

        (viii)   whether that party intends to raise any point of law that could affect the conduct of the trial or appeal; and

    (d)   may limit –

        (i)   the examination, cross-examination or re-examination of a witness, and

        (ii)   the duration of any stage of the hearing.

[Note. See also rules 3.5 and 3.8.]

Case management forms and records

3.11.–(1)   The case management forms set out in the Practice Direction must be used, and where there is no form then no specific formality is required.

(2)   The court must make available to the parties a record of directions given.

(3)   Where a person is entitled or required to attend a hearing, the court officer must give as much notice as reasonably practicable to –

    (a)   that person; and

    (b)   that person's custodian (if any).

[Note. Case management may be affected by the following other rules and legislation:

Criminal Procedure Rules

Rules 10.4 and 27.4: reminders of right to object to written evidence being read at trial

Part 13: dismissal of charges transferred or sent to the Crown Court

Part 14: the indictment

Part 15: preparatory hearings in the Crown Court

Part 21: initial details of the prosecution case

Part 22: disclosure

Parts 27–36: the rules that deal with evidence

Part 37: trial and sentence in a magistrates' court

Part 39: trial on indictment

Regulations

The Prosecution of Offences (Custody Time Limits) Regulations 1987

The Criminal Justice Act 1987 (Notice of Transfer) Regulations 1988

The Criminal Justice Act 1991 (Notice of Transfer) Regulations 1992

The Criminal Procedure and Investigations Act 1996 (Defence Disclosure Time Limits) Regulations 2011

The Crime and Disorder Act 1998 (Service of Prosecution Evidence) Regulations 2005

Provisions of Acts of Parliament

Sections 5, 10 and 18, Magistrates ' Courts Act 1980: powers to adjourn hearings

Sections 128 and 129, Magistrates' Courts Act 1980: remand in custody by magistrates' courts

Part 1, Criminal Procedure and Investigations Act 1996: disclosure

Schedule 2, Criminal Procedure and Investigations Act 1996: use of witness statements at trial

Section 2, Administration of Justice (Miscellaneous Provisions) Act 1933: procedural conditions for trial in the Crown Court

Section 6, Magistrates' Courts Act 1980: committal for trial

Section 4, Criminal Justice Act 1987; section 53, Criminal Justice Act 1991; sections 51 and 51A, Crime and Disorder Act 1998: other procedures by which a case reaches the Crown Court

Section 7 Criminal Justice Act 1987; Parts III and IV, Criminal Procedure and Investigations Act 1996: pre-trial and preparatory hearings in the Crown Court

Section 8A. Magistrates' Courts Act 1980

Section 9. Criminal Justice Act 1967: proof by written witness statement.]

Appendix 4

Criminal Procedure Rules 2012 (SI 2012/1726), Part 22

Part 22
Disclosure

Contents of this Part

When this Part applies

22.1– This Part applies –

(a) in a magistrates' court and in the Crown Court;

(b) where Parts I and II of the Criminal Procedure and Investigations Act 1996 apply.

[Note. A summary of the disclosure requirements of the Criminal Procedure and Investigations Act 1996 is at the end of this Part.]

Prosecution disclosure

22.2.–(1)   This rule applies in the Crown Court where, under section 3 of the Criminal Procedure and Investigations Act 1996, the prosecutor –

    (a)   discloses prosecution material to the defendant; or

    (b)   serves on the defendant a written statement that there is no such material to disclose.

(2)   The prosecutor must at the same time so inform the court officer.

Prosecutor's application for public interest ruling

22.3.–(1)   This rule applies where –

    (a)   without a court order, the prosecutor would have to disclose material; and

    (b)   the prosecutor wants the court to decide whether it would be in the public interest to disclose it.

(2)   The prosecutor must –

    (a)   apply in writing for such a decision; and

    (b)   serve the application on –

        (i)   the court officer,

        (ii)   any person who the prosecutor thinks would be directly affected by disclosure of the material, and

        (iii)   the defendant, but only to the extent that serving it on the defendant would not disclose what the prosecutor thinks ought not be disclosed.

(3)   The application must –

    (a)   describe the material, and explain why the prosecutor thinks that –

        (i)   it is material that the prosecutor would have to disclose,

        (ii)   it would not be in the public interest to disclose that material, and

        (iii)   no measure such as the prosecutor's admission of any fact, or disclosure by summary, extract or edited copy, adequately would protect both the public interest and the defendant's right to a fair trial;

(b)   omit from any part of the application that is served on the defendant anything that would disclose what the prosecutor thinks ought not be disclosed (in which case, paragraph (4) of this rule applies); and

(c)   explain why, if no part of the application is served on the defendant.

(4)   Where the prosecutor serves only part of the application on the defendant, the prosecutor must –

(a)   mark the other part, to show that it is only for the court; and

(b)   in that other part, explain why the prosecutor has withheld it from the defendant.

(5)   Unless already done, the court may direct the prosecutor to serve an application on –

(a)   the defendant;

(b)   any other person who the court considers would be directly affected by the disclosure of the material.

(6)   The court must determine the application at a hearing which –

(a)   will be in private, unless the court otherwise directs; and

(b)   if the court so directs, may take place, wholly or in part, in the defendant's absence.

(7)   At a hearing at which the defendant is present –

(a)   the general rule is that the court will receive, in the following sequence –

(i)   representations first by the prosecutor and any other person served with the application, and then by the defendant, in the presence of them all, and then

(ii)   further representations by the prosecutor and any such other person in the defendant's absence; but

(b)   the court may direct other arrangements for the hearing.

(8)   The court may only determine the application if satisfied that it has been able to take adequate account of –

(a)   such rights of confidentiality as apply to the material; and

(b)   the defendant's right to a fair trial.

(9)   Unless the court otherwise directs, the court officer –

    (a)   must not give notice to anyone other than the prosecutor –

        (i)   of the hearing of an application under this rule, unless the prosecutor served the application on that person, or

        (ii)   of the court's decision on the application;

    (b)   may –

        (i)   keep a written application or representations, or

        (ii)   arrange for the whole or any part to be kept by some other appropriate person, subject to any conditions that the court may impose.

[Note. The court's power to order that it is not in the public interest to disclose material is provided for by sections 3(6), 7(6) (where the investigation began between 1st April, 1997 and 3rd April, 2005) and 7A(8) (where the investigation began on or after 4th April, 2005) of the Criminal Procedure and Investigations Act 1996.

See also sections 16 and 19 of the 1996 Act.]

Defence disclosure

22.4.–(1)   This rule applies where –

    (a)   under section 5 or 6 of the Criminal Procedure and Investigations Act 1996, the defendant gives a defence statement;

    (b)   under section 6C of the 1996 Act, the defendant gives a defence witness notice.

(2)   The defendant must serve such a statement or notice on –

    (a)   the court officer; and

    (b)   the prosecutor.

[Note. The Practice Direction sets out forms of –

    (a)   defence statement; and

    (b)   defence witness notice.

Under section 5 of the 1996 Act, in the Crown Court the defendant must give a defence statement. Under section 6 of the Act, in a magistrates' court the defendant may give such a statement but need not do so.

Under section 6C of the 1996 Act, in the Crown Court and in magistrates' courts the defendant must give a defence witness notice indicating whether he or she intends to call any witnesses (other than him or herself) and, if so, identifying them.]

Defendant's application for prosecution disclosure

22.5.–(1)   This rule applies where the defendant –

    (a)   has served a defence statement given under the Criminal Procedure and Investigations Act 1996; and

    (b)   wants the court to require the prosecutor to disclose material.

(2)   The defendant must serve an application on –

    (a)   the court officer; and

    (b)   the prosecutor.

(3)   The application must –

    (a)   describe the material that the defendant wants the prosecutor to disclose;

    (b)   explain why the defendant thinks there is reasonable cause to believe that –

        (i)   the prosecutor has that material, and

        (ii)   it is material that the Criminal Procedure and Investigations Act 1996 requires the prosecutor to disclose; and

    (c)   ask for a hearing, if the defendant wants one, and explain why it is needed.

(4)   The court may determine an application under this rule –

    (a)   at a hearing, in public or in private; or

    (b)   without a hearing.

(5)   The court must not require the prosecutor to disclose material unless the prosecutor –

    (a)   is present; or

    (b)   has had at least 14 days in which to make representations.

[Note. The Practice Direction sets out a form of application for use in connection with this rule.

Under section 8 of the Criminal Procedure and Investigations Act 1996, a defendant may apply for prosecution disclosure only if the defendant has given a defence statement.]

Review of public interest ruling

22.6.–(1)   This rule applies where the court has ordered that it is not in the public interest to disclose material that the prosecutor otherwise would have to disclose, and –

(a)   the defendant wants the court to review that decision; or

(b)   the Crown Court reviews that decision on its own initiative.

(2)   Where the defendant wants the court to review that decision, the defendant must –

(a)   serve an application on –

(i)   the court officer, and

(ii)   the prosecutor; and

(b)   in the application –

(i)   describe the material that the defendant wants the prosecutor to disclose, and

(ii)   explain why the defendant thinks it is no longer in the public interest for the prosecutor not to disclose it.

(3)   The prosecutor must serve any such application on any person who the prosecutor thinks would be directly affected if that material were disclosed.

(4)   The prosecutor, and any such person, must serve any representations on –

(a)   the court officer; and

(b)   the defendant, unless to do so would in effect reveal something that either thinks ought not be disclosed.

(5)   The court may direct –

(a)   the prosecutor to serve any such application on any person who the court considers would be directly affected if that material were disclosed;

(b)   the prosecutor and any such person to serve any representations on the defendant.

(6)   The court must review a decision to which this rule applies at a hearing which –

(a)   will be in private, unless the court otherwise directs; and

(b)   if the court so directs, may take place, wholly or in part, in the defendant's absence.

(7)   At a hearing at which the defendant is present –

(a)   the general rule is that the court will receive, in the following sequence –

        (i)   representations first by the defendant, and then by the prosecutor and any other person served with the application. in the presence of them all, and then

        (ii)   further representations by the prosecutor and any such other person in the defendant's absence; but

   (b)   the court may direct other arrangements for the hearing.

(8)   The court may only conclude a review if satisfied that it has been able to take adequate account of –

   (a)   such rights of confidentiality as apply to the material; and

   (b)   the defendant's right to a fair trial.

[Note. The court's power to review a public interest ruling is provided for by sections 14 and 15 of the Criminal Procedure and Investigations Act 1996. Under section 14 of the Act, a magistrates' court may reconsider an order for non-disclosure only if a defendant applies. Under section 15, the Crown Court may do so on an application, or on its own initiative.

See also sections 16 and 19 of the 1996 Act.]

Defendant's application to use disclosed material

22.7.–(1)   This rule applies where a defendant wants the court's permission to use disclosed prosecution material –

   (a)   otherwise than in connection with the case in which it was disclosed; or

   (b)   beyond the extent to which it was displayed or communicated publicly at a hearing.

(2)   The defendant must serve an application on –

   (a)   the court officer; and

   (b)   the prosecutor.

(3)   The application must –

   (a)   specify what the defendant wants to use or disclose; and

   (b)   explain why.

(4)   The court may determine an application under this rule –

   (a)   at a hearing, in public or in private; or

   (b)   without a hearing.

(5)   The court must not permit the use of such material unless –

(a)   the prosecutor has had at least 28 days in which to make representations; and

(b)   the court is satisfied that it has been able to take adequate account of any rights of confidentiality that may apply to the material.

[Note. The court's power to allow a defendant to use disclosed material is provided for by section 17 of the Criminal Procedure and Investigations Act 1996.

See also section 19 of the 1996 Act.]

Unauthorised use of disclosed material

22.8.–(1)   This rule applies where a person is accused of using disclosed prosecution material in contravention of section 17 of the Criminal Procedure and Investigations Act 1996.

(2)   A party who wants the court to exercise its power to punish that person for contempt of court must comply with the rules in Part 62 (Contempt of court).

(3)   The court must not exercise its power to forfeit material used in contempt of court unless –

(a)   the prosecutor; and

(b)   any other person directly affected by the disclosure of the material,

is present, or has had at least 14 days in which to make representations.

[Note. Under section 17 of the Criminal Procedure and Investigations Act 1996, a defendant may use disclosed prosecution material –

(a)   in connection with the case in which it was disclosed, including on an appeal;

(b)   to the extent to which it was displayed or communicated publicly at a hearing in public; or

(c)   with the court's permission.

Under section 18 of the 1996 Act, the court can punish for contempt of court any other use of disclosed prosecution material. See also section 19 of the 1996 Act.]

Court's power to vary requirements under this Part

22.9–   The court may –

(a)   shorten or extend (even after it has expired) a time limit under this Part;

(b)   allow a defence statement, or a defence witness notice, to be in a different written form to one set out in the Practice Direction, as long as it contains what the Criminal Procedure and Investigations Act 1996 requires;

(c)   allow an application under this Part to be in a different form to one set out in the Practice Direction, or to be presented orally; and

(d)   specify the period within which –

   (i)   any application under this Part must be made, or

   (ii)   any material must be disclosed, on an application to which rule 22.5 applies (defendant's application for prosecution disclosure).

Summary of disclosure requirements of Criminal Procedure and Investigations Act 1996

The Criminal Procedure and Investigations Act 1996 came into force on 1st April, 1997. It does not apply where the investigation began before that date. With effect from 4th April, 2005, the Criminal Justice Act 2003 made changes to the 1996 Act that do not apply where the investigation began before that date.

In some circumstances, the prosecutor may be required to disclose material to which the 1996 Act does not apply: see sections 1 and 21.

Part I of the 1996 Act contains sections 1 to 21A. Part II, which contains sections 22 to 27, requires an investigator to record information relevant to an investigation that is obtained during its course. See also The Criminal Procedure and Investigations Act 1996 (Code of Practice) (No. 2) Order 1997 and The Criminal Procedure and Investigations Act 1996 (Code of Practice) Order 2005.

Prosecution disclosure

Where the investigation began between 1st April, 1997, and 3rd April, 2005, sections 3 and 7 of the 1996 Act require the prosecutor –

   (a)   to disclose material not previously disclosed that in the prosecutor's opinion might undermine the case for the prosecution against the defendant –

      (i)   in a magistrates' court, as soon as is reasonably practicable after the defendant pleads not guilty, and

      (ii)   in the Crown Court, as soon as is reasonably practicable after the case is committed or transferred for trial, or after the evidence is served where the case is sent for trial; and

   (b)   as soon as is reasonably practicable after service of the defence statement, to disclose material not previously disclosed that might be reasonably expected to assist the defendant's case as disclosed by that defence statement; or in either event

   (c)   if there is no such material, then to give the defendant a written statement to that effect.

Where the investigation began on or after 4th April, 2005, sections 3 and 7A of the 1996 Act require the prosecutor –

   (a)   to disclose prosecution material not previously disclosed that might reasonably be considered capable of undermining the case for the prosecution against the defendant or of assisting the case for the defendant –

      (i)   in a magistrates ' court, as soon as is reasonably practicable after the defendant pleads not guilty, or

      (ii)   in the Crown Court, as soon as is reasonably practicable after the case is committed or transferred for trial, or after the evidence is served where the case is sent for trial, or after a count is added to the indictment; and in either case

(b)   *if there is no such material, then to give the defendant a written statement to that effect; and after that*

(c)   *in either court, to disclose such material –*

         (i)   *whenever there is any, until the court reaches its verdict or the prosecutor decides not to proceed with the case, and*

         (ii)   *in particular, after the service of the defence statement.*

Sections 2 and 3 of the 1996 Act define material, and prescribe how it must be disclosed.

In some circumstances, disclosure is prohibited by section 17 of the Regulation of Investigatory Powers Act 2000.

The prosecutor must not disclose material that the court orders it would not be in the public interest to disclose: see sections 3(6), 7(6) and 7A(8) of the 1996 Act.

Sections 12 and 13 of the 1996 Act prescribe the time for prosecution disclosure. See also sections 1, 4 and 10 of the 1996 Act.

Defence disclosure

Under section 5 of the 1996 Act, in the Crown Court the defendant must give a defence statement. Under section 6 of the Act, in a magistrates' court the defendant may give such a statement but need not do so.

Under section 6C of the 1996 Act, in the Crown Court and in magistrates' courts the defendant must give a defence witness notice indicating whether he or she intends to call any witnesses (other than him or herself) and, if so, identifying them.

The time for service of a defence statement is prescribed by section 12 of the 1996 Act and by The Criminal Procedure and Investigations Act 1996 (Defence Disclosure Time Limits) Regulations 2011. It is –

(a)   *in a magistrates' court, not more than 14 days after the prosecutor –*

         (i)   *discloses material under section 3 of the 1996 Act, or*

         (ii)   *serves notice that there is no such material to disclose;*

(b)   *in the Crown Court, not more than 28 days after either of those events, if the prosecution evidence has been served on the defendant.*

The requirements for the content of a defence statement are set out in –

(a)   *section 5 of the 1996 Act, where the investigation began between 1st April, 1997 and 3rd April, 2005;*

(b)   *section 6A of the 1996 Act, where the investigation began on or after 4th April, 2005. See also section 6E of the Act.*

Where the investigation began between 1st April, 1997 and 3rd April, 2005, the defence statement must –

(a)   *set out in general terms the nature of the defence;*

(b)   *indicate the matters on which the defendant takes issue with the prosecutor, and, in respect of each, explain why;*

(c)   *if the defence statement discloses an alibi, give particulars, including –*

         (i)   *the name and address of any witness whom the defendant believes can give evidence in support (that is, evidence that the defendant was in a place, at a time, inconsistent with having committed the offence),*

         (ii)   *where the defendant does not know the name or address, any information that might help identify or find that witness.*

Appendix 4 *Criminal Procedure Rules 2012, Part 22*

Where the investigation began on or after 4th April, 2005, the defence statement must –

    (a)   *set out the nature of the defence, including any particular defences on which the defendant intends to rely;*

    (b)   *indicate the matters of fact on which the defendant takes issue with the prosecutor, and in respect of each, explain why;*

    (c)   *set out particulars of the matters of fact on which the defendant intends to rely for the purposes of the defence;*

    (d)   *indicate any point of law that the defendant wants to raise, including any point about the admissibility of evidence or about abuse of process, and any authority relied on; and*

    (e)   *if the defence statement discloses an alibi, give particulars, including –*

        (i)   *the name, address and date of birth of any witness whom the defendant believes can give evidence in support (that is, evidence that the defendant was in a place, at a time, inconsistent with having committed the offence),*

        (ii)   *where the defendant does not know any of those details, any information that might help identify or find that witness.*

The time for service of a defence witness notice is prescribed by section 12 of the 1996 Act and by The Criminal Procedure and Investigations Act 1996 (Defence Disclosure Time Limits) Regulations 2011. The time limits are the same as those for a defence statement.

A defence witness notice that identifies any proposed defence witness (other than the defendant) must –

    (a)   *give the name, address and date of birth of each such witness, or as many of those details as are known to the defendant when the notice is given;*

    (b)   *provide any information in the defendant's possession which might be of material assistance in identifying or finding any such witness in whose case any of the details mentioned in paragraph (a) are not known to the defendant when the notice is given; and*

    (c)   *amend any earlier such notice, if the defendant –*

        (i)   *decides to call a person not included in an earlier notice as a proposed witness,*

        (ii)   *decides not to call a person so included, or*

        (iii)   *discovers any information which the defendant would have had to include in an earlier notice, if then aware of it.*

Under section 11 of the 1996 Act, if a defendant –

    (a)   *fails to disclose what the Act requires;*

    (b)   *fails to do so within the time prescribed;*

    (c)   *at trial, relies on a defence, or facts, not mentioned in the defence statement;*

    (d)   *at trial, introduces alibi evidence without having given in the defence statement –*

        (i)   *particulars of the alibi, or*

        (ii)   *the details of the alibi witness, or witnesses, required by the Act; or*

    (e)   *at trial, calls a witness not identified in a defence witness notice,*

then the court or another party at trial may comment on that, and the court may draw such inferences as appear proper in deciding whether the defendant is guilty.

Under section 6E(2) of the 1996 Act, if before trial in the Crown Court it seems to the court that section 11 may apply, then the court must warn the defendant.

Attorney General's Guidelines on Disclosure (2005)

FOREWORD

Disclosure is one of the most important issues in the criminal justice system and the application of proper and fair disclosure is a vital component of a fair criminal justice system. The 'golden rule' is that fairness requires full disclosure should be made of all material held by the prosecution that weakens its case or strengthens that of the defence.

This amounts to no more and no less than a proper application of the Criminal Procedure and Investigations Act 1996 (CPIA) recently amended by the Criminal Justice Act 2003. The amendments in the Criminal Justice Act 2003 abolished the concept of 'primacy' and 'secondary' disclosure, and introduced an amalgamated test for disclosure of material that 'might reasonably be considered capable of undermining the prosecution case or assisting the case for accused'. It also introduced a new Code of Practice. In the light of these, other new provisions and case law I conducted a review of the Attorney General's Guidelines issued in November 2000.

Concerns had previously been expressed about the operation of the then existing provisions by judges, prosecutors, and defence practitioners. It seems to me that we must all make a concerted effort to comply with the CPIA disclosure regime robustly in a consistent way in order to regain the trust and confidence of all those involved in the criminal justice system. The House of Lords in *R v H & C* made it clear that so long as the current disclosure system was operated with scrupulous attention, in accordance with the law and with proper regard to the interests of the defendant, it was entirely compatible with Article 6 of the European Convention on Human Rights.

It is vital that everybody in the criminal justice system operates these procedures properly and fairly to ensure we protect the integrity of the criminal justice system whilst at the same time ensuring that a just and fair disclosure process is not abused so that it becomes unwieldy, bureaucratic and effectively unworkable. This means that all those involved must play their role.

Investigators must provide detailed and proper schedules. Prosecutors must not abrogate their duties under the CPIA by making wholesale disclosure in order to avoid carrying out the disclosure exercise themselves. Likewise, defence practitioners should avoid fishing expeditions and where disclosure is not provided using this as an excuse for an abuse of process application. I hope also that the courts will apply the legal regime set out under the CPIA rather than ordering disclosure because either it is easier or it would not 'do any harm'.

This disclosure regime must be made to work and it can only work if there is trust and confidence in the system and everyone plays their role in it. If this is achieved applications for a stay of proceedings on the grounds of non disclosure will only be made exceedingly sparingly and never on a speculative basis. Likewise such applications are only likely to succeed in extreme cases and certainly not where the alleged disclosure is in relation to speculative requests for material.

I have therefore revised the Guidelines to take account of developments and to start the process of ensuring that everyone works to achieve consistency of approach to CPIA disclosure. The amalgamated test should introduce a more streamlined process which is more objective and should therefore deal with some of the concerns about inconsistency in the application of the disclosure regime by prosecutors.

A draft set of these revised Guidelines went out for consultation, and resulted in many thoughtful and detailed responses from practitioners, including members of the judiciary, who have to work with the scheme on a daily basis. The Group that was established to advise me on the revision of the Guidelines has taken account of the results of the consultation exercise. I give my warm thanks to all who have offered responses on the consultation and assisted in the revision of these Guidelines.

I am publishing today the revised Guidelines that, if properly, applied will contribute to ensuring that the disclosure regime operates effectively, fairly and justly – which is vitally important to the integrity of the criminal justice system and the way in which it is perceived by the general public.

DISCLOSURE OF UNUSED MATERIAL IN CRIMINAL PROCEEDINGS

INTRODUCTION

1.   Every accused person has a right to a fair trial, a right long embodied in our law and guaranteed under Article 6 of the European Convention on Human Rights (ECHR). A fair trial is the proper object and expectation of all participants in the trial process. Fair disclosure to an accused is an inseparable part of a fair trial.

2. What must be clear is that a fair trial consists of an examination not just of all the evidence the parties wish to rely on but also all other relevant subject matter. A fair trial should not require consideration of irrelevant material and should not involve spurious applications or arguments which serve to divert the trial process from examining the real issues before the court.

3. The scheme set out in the Criminal Procedure and Investigations Act 1996 (as amended by the Criminal Justice Act 2003) (the Act) is designed to ensure that there is fair disclosure of material which may be relevant to an investigation and which does not form part of the prosecution case. Disclosure under the Act should assist the accused in the timely preparation and presentation of their case and assist the court to focus on all the relevant issues in the trial. Disclosure which does not meet these objectives risks preventing a fair trial taking place.

4. This means that the disclosure regime set out in the Act must be scrupulously followed. These Guidelines build upon the existing law to help to ensure that the legislation is operated more effectively, consistently and fairly.

5. Disclosure must not be an open ended trawl of unused material. A critical element to fair and proper disclosure is that the defence play their role to ensure that the prosecution are directed to material which might reasonably be considered capable of undermining the prosecution case or assisting the case for the accused. This process is key to ensuring prosecutors make informed determinations about disclosure of unused material.

6. Fairness does recognise that there are other interests that need to be protected, including those of victims and witnesses who might otherwise be exposed to harm. The scheme of the Act protects those interests. It should also ensure that material is not disclosed which overburdens the participants in the trial process, diverts attention from the relevant issues, leads to unjustifiable delay, and is wasteful of resources.

7. Whilst it is acknowledged that these Guidelines have been drafted with a focus on Crown Court proceedings the spirit of the Guidelines must be followed where they apply to proceedings in the magistrates' court.

GENERAL PRINCIPLES

8. Disclosure refers to providing the defence with copies of, or access to, any material which might reasonably be considered capable of undermining the case for the prosecution against the accused, or of assisting the case for the accused, and which has not previously been disclosed.

9.   Prosecutors will only be expected to anticipate what material might weaken their case or strengthen the defence in the light of information available at the time of the disclosure decision, and this may include information revealed during questioning.

10.   Generally, material which can reasonably be considered capable of undermining the prosecution case against the accused or assisting the defence case will include anything that tends to show a fact inconsistent with the elements of the case that must be proved by the prosecution. Material can fulfil the disclosure test:

   (a)   by the use to be made of it in cross-examination; or

   (b)   by its capacity to support submissions that could lead to:

      (i)   the exclusion of evidence; or

      (ii)   a stay of proceedings; or

      (iii)   a court or tribunal finding that any public authority had acted incompatibly with the accused's rights under the ECHR, or

   (c)   by its capacity to suggest an explanation or partial explanation of the accused's actions.

11.   In deciding whether material may fall to be disclosed under paragraph 10, especially (b)(ii), prosecutors must consider whether disclosure is required in order for a proper application to be made. The purpose of this paragraph is not to allow enquiries to support speculative arguments or for the manufacture of defences.

12.   Examples of material that might reasonably be considered capable of undermining the prosecution case or of assisting the case for the accused are:

   i.   Any material casting doubt upon the accuracy of any prosecution evidence.

   ii.   Any material which may point to another person, whether charged or not (including a co-accused) having involvement in the commission of the offence.

   iii.   Any material which may cast doubt upon the reliability of a confession.

   iv.   Any material that might go to the credibility of a prosecution witness.

   v.   Any material that might support a defence that is either raised by the defence or apparent from the prosecution papers.

vi.   Any material which may have a bearing on the admissibility of any prosecution evidence.

13.   It should also be borne in mind that while items of material viewed in isolation may not be reasonably considered to be capable of undermining the prosecution case or assisting the accused, several items together can have that effect.

14.   Material relating to the accused's mental or physical health, intellectual capacity, or to any ill treatment which the accused may have suffered when in the investigator's custody is likely to fall within the test for disclosure set out in paragraph 8 above.

DEFENCE STATEMENTS

15.   A defence statement must comply with the requirements of section 6A of the Act. A comprehensive defence statement assists the participants in the trial to ensure that it is fair. The trial process is not well served if the defence make general and unspecified allegations and then seek far-reaching disclosure in the hope that material may turn up to make them good. The more detail a defence statement contains the more likely it is that the prosecutor will make an informed decision about whether any remaining undisclosed material might reasonably be considered capable of undermining the prosecution case or of assisting the case for the accused, or whether to advise the investigator to undertake further enquiries. It also helps in the management of the trial by narrowing down and focussing on the issues in dispute. It may result in the prosecution discontinuing the case. Defence practitioners should be aware of these considerations when advising their clients.

16.   Whenever a defence solicitor provides a defence statement on behalf of the accused it will be deemed to be given with the authority of the solicitor's client.

CONTINUING DUTY OF PROSECUTOR TO DISCLOSE

17.   Section 7A of the Act imposes a continuing duty upon the prosecutor to keep under review at all times the question of whether there is any unused material which might reasonably be considered capable of undermining the prosecution case against the accused or assisting the case for the accused and which has not previously been disclosed. This duty arises after the prosecutor has complied with the duty of initial disclosure or purported to comply with it and before the accused is acquitted or convicted or the prosecutor decides not to proceed with the case. If such

material is identified, then the prosecutor must disclose it to the accused as soon as is reasonably practicable.

18.   As part of their continuing duty of disclosure, prosecutors should be open, alert and promptly responsive to requests for disclosure of material supported by a comprehensive defence statement. Conversely, if no defence statement has been served or if the prosecutor considers that the defence statement is lacking specificity or otherwise does not meet the requirements of section 6A of the Act, a letter should be sent to the defence indicating this. If the position is not resolved satisfactorily, the prosecutor should consider raising the issue at a hearing for directions to enable the court to give a warning or appropriate directions.

19.   When defence practitioners are dissatisfied with disclosure decisions by the prosecution and consider that they are entitled to further disclosure, applications to the court should be made pursuant to section 8 of the Act and in accordance with the procedures set out in the Criminal Procedure Rules. Applications for further disclosure should not be made as ad hoc applications but dealt with under the proper procedures.

APPLICATIONS FOR NON-DISCLOSURE IN THE PUBLIC INTEREST

20.   Before making an application to the court to withhold material which would otherwise fall to be disclosed, on the basis that to disclose would give rise to a real risk of serious prejudice to an important public interest, prosecutors should aim to disclose as much of the material as they properly can (for example, by giving the defence redacted or edited copies or summaries). Neutral material or material damaging to the defendant need not be disclosed and must *not* be brought to the attention of the court. It is only in truly borderline cases that the prosecution should seek a judicial ruling on the disclosability of material in its possession.

21.   Prior to or at the hearing, the court must be provided with full and accurate information. Prior to the hearing the prosecutor and the prosecution advocate must examine all material, which is the subject matter of the application and make any necessary enquiries of the investigator. The prosecutor (or representative) and/or investigator should attend such applications.

22.   The principles set out at paragraph 36 of *R v H & C* should be rigorously applied firstly by the prosecutor and then by the court considering the material. It is essential that these principles are scrupulously attended to to ensure that the procedure for examination of material in the absence of the accused is compliant with Article 6 of ECHR.

RESPONSIBILITIES

Investigators and disclosure officers

23. Investigators and disclosure officers must be fair and objective and must work together with prosecutors to ensure that disclosure obligations are met. A failure to take action leading to inadequate disclosure may result in a wrongful conviction. It may alternatively lead to a successful abuse of process argument, an acquittal against the weight of the evidence or the appellate courts may find that a conviction is unsafe and quash it.

24. Officers appointed as disclosure officers must have the requisite experience, skills, competence and resources to undertake their vital role. In discharging their obligations under the Act, code, common law and any operational instructions, investigators should always err on the side of recording and retaining material where they have any doubt as to whether it may be relevant.

25. An individual must not be appointed as disclosure officer, or continue in that role, if that is likely to result in a conflict of interest, for instance, if the disclosure officer is the victim of the alleged crime which is the subject of investigation. The advice of a more senior investigator must always be sought if there is doubt as to whether a conflict of interest precludes an individual acting as the disclosure officer. If thereafter a doubt remains, the advice of a prosecutor should be sought.

26. There may be a number of disclosure officers, especially in large and complex cases. However, there must be a lead disclosure officer who is the focus for enquiries and whose responsibility it is to ensure that the investigator's disclosure obligations are complied with. Disclosure officers, or their deputies, must inspect, view or listen to all relevant material that has been retained by the investigator, and the disclosure officer must provide a personal declaration to the effect that this task has been undertaken.

27. Generally this will mean that such material must be examined in detail by the disclosure officer or the deputy, but exceptionally the extent and manner of inspecting, viewing or listening will depend on the nature of material and its form. For example, it might be reasonable to examine digital material by using software search tools, or to establish the contents of large volumes of material by dip sampling. If such material is not examined in detail, it must nonetheless be described on the disclosure schedules accurately and as clearly as possible. The extent and manner of its examination must also be described together with justification for such action.

28.   Investigators must retain material that may be relevant to the investigation. However, it may become apparent to the investigator that some material obtained in the course of an investigation because it was considered potentially relevant, is in fact incapable of impact. It need not then be retained or dealt with in accordance with these Guidelines, although the investigator should err on the side of caution in coming to this conclusion and seek the advice of the prosecutor as appropriate.

29.   In meeting the obligations in paragraph 6.9 and 8.1 of the Code, it is crucial that descriptions by disclosure officers in non-sensitive schedules are detailed, clear and accurate. The descriptions may require a summary of the contents of the retained material to assist the prosecutor to make an informed decision on disclosure. Sensitive schedules must contain sufficient information to enable the prosecutor to make an informed decision as to whether or not the material itself should be viewed, to the extent possible without compromising the confidentiality of the information.

30.   Disclosure officers must specifically draw material to the attention of the prosecutor for consideration where they have any doubt as to whether it might reasonably be considered capable of undermining the prosecution case or of assisting the case for the accused.

31.   Disclosure officers must seek the advice and assistance of prosecutors when in doubt as to their responsibility as early as possible. They must deal expeditiously with requests by the prosecutor for further information on material, which may lead to disclosure.

Prosecutors

32.   Prosecutors must do all that they can to facilitate proper disclosure, as part of their general and personal professional responsibility to act fairly and impartially, in the interests of justice and in accordance with the law. Prosecutors must also be alert to the need to provide advice to, and where necessary probe actions taken by, disclosure officers to ensure that disclosure obligations are met.

33.   Prosecutors must review schedules prepared by disclosure officers thoroughly and must be alert to the possibility that relevant material may exist which has not been revealed to them or material included which should not have been. If no schedules have been provided, or there are apparent omissions from the schedules, or documents or other items are inadequately described or are unclear, the prosecutor must at once take action to obtain properly completed schedules. Likewise schedules should be returned for amendment if irrelevant items are included. If prosecutors

remain dissatisfied with the quality or content of the schedules they must raise the matter with a senior investigator, and if necessary, persist, with a view to resolving the matter satisfactorily.

34. Where prosecutors have reason to believe that the disclosure officer has not discharged the obligation in paragraph 26 to inspect, view or listen to relevant material, they must at once raise the matter with the disclosure officer and, if it is believed that the officer has not inspected, viewed or listened to the material, request that it be done.

35. When prosecutors or disclosure officers believe that material might reasonably be considered capable of undermining the prosecution case or assisting the case for the accused, prosecutors must always inspect, view or listen to the material and satisfy themselves that the prosecution can properly be continued having regard to the disclosability of the material reviewed. Their judgement as to what other material to inspect, view or listen to will depend on the circumstances of each case.

36. Prosecutors should copy the defence statement to the disclosure officer and investigator as soon as reasonably practicable and prosecutors should advise the investigator if, in their view, reasonable and relevant lines of further enquiry should be pursued.

37. Prosecutors cannot comment upon, or invite inferences to be drawn from, failures in defence disclosure otherwise than in accordance with section 11 of the Act. Prosecutors may cross-examine the accused on differences between the defence case put at trial and that set out in his or her defence statement. In doing so, it may be appropriate to apply to the judge under section 6E of the Act for copies of the statement to be given to a jury, edited if necessary to remove inadmissible material. Prosecutors should examine the defence statement to see whether it points to other lines of enquiry. If the defence statement does point to other reasonable lines of inquiry further investigation is required and evidence obtained as a result of these enquiries may be used as part of the prosecution case or to rebut the defence.

38. Once initial disclosure is completed and a defence statement has been served requests for disclosure should ordinarily only be answered if the request is in accordance with and relevant to the defence statement. If it is not, then a further or amended defence statement should be sought and obtained before considering the request for further disclosure.

39. Prosecutors must ensure that they record in writing all actions and decisions they make in discharging their disclosure responsibilities, and this information is to be made available to the prosecution advocate if requested or if relevant to an issue.

40.   If the material does not fulfil the disclosure test there is no requirement to disclose it. For this purpose, the parties' respective cases should not be restrictively analysed but must be carefully analysed to ascertain the specific facts the prosecution seek to establish and the specific grounds on which the charges are resisted. Neutral material or material damaging to the defendant need not be disclosed and must not be brought to the attention of the court. Only in truly borderline cases should the prosecution seek a judicial ruling on the disclosability of material in its hands.

41.   If prosecutors are satisfied that a fair trial cannot take place where material which satisfies the disclosure test cannot be disclosed, and that this cannot or will not be remedied including by, for example, making formal admissions, amending the charges or presenting the case in a different way so as to ensure fairness or in other ways, they must not continue with the case.

Prosecution advocates

42.   Prosecution advocates should ensure that all material that ought to be disclosed under the Act is disclosed to the defence. However, prosecution advocates cannot be expected to disclose material if they are not aware of its existence. As far as is possible, prosecution advocates must place themselves in a fully informed position to enable them to make decisions on disclosure.

43.   Upon receipt of instructions, prosecution advocates should consider as a priority all the information provided regarding disclosure of material. Prosecution advocates should consider, in every case, whether they can be satisfied that they are in possession of all relevant documentation and that they have been instructed fully regarding disclosure matters. Decisions already made regarding disclosure should be reviewed. If as a result, the advocate considers that further information or action is required, written advice should be promptly provided setting out the aspects that need clarification or action. Prosecution advocates must advise on disclosure in accordance with the Act. If necessary and where appropriate a conference should be held to determine what is required.

44.   The prosecution advocate must keep decisions regarding disclosure under review until the conclusion of the trial. The prosecution advocate must in every case specifically consider whether he or she can satisfactorily discharge the duty of continuing review on the basis of the material supplied already, or whether it is necessary to inspect further material or to reconsider material already inspected. Prosecution advocates must not abrogate their responsibility under the Act by disclosing material which

could not be considered capable of undermining the prosecution case or of assisting the case for the accused.

45.   Prior to the commencement of a trial, the prosecuting advocate should always make decisions on disclosure in consultation with those instructing him or her and the disclosure officer. After a trial has started, it is recognised that in practice consultation on disclosure issues may not be practicable; it continues to be desirable, however, whenever this can be achieved without affecting unduly the conduct of the trial.

46.   There is no basis in law or practice for disclosure on a 'counsel to counsel' basis.

INVOLVEMENT OF OTHER AGENCIES

Material held by Government departments or other Crown bodies

47.   Where it appears to an investigator, disclosure officer or prosecutor that a Government department or other Crown body has material that may be relevant to an issue in the case, reasonable steps should be taken to identify and consider such material. Although what is reasonable will vary from case to case, the prosecution should inform the department or other body of the nature of its case and of relevant issues in the case in respect of which the department or body might possess material, and ask whether it has any such material.

48.   It should be remembered that investigators, disclosure officers and prosecutors cannot be regarded to be in constructive possession of material held by Government departments or Crown bodies simply by virtue of their status as Government departments or Crown bodies.

49.   Departments in England and Wales should have identified personnel as established Enquiry Points to deal with issues concerning the disclosure of information in criminal proceedings.

50.   Where, after reasonable steps have been taken to secure access to such material, access is denied the investigator, disclosure officer or prosecutor should consider what if any further steps might be taken to obtain the material or inform the defence.

Material held by other agencies

51.   There may be cases where the investigator, disclosure officer or prosecutor believes that a third party (for example, a local authority, a social services department, a hospital, a doctor, a school, a provider of forensic services) has material or information which might be relevant to the prosecution case. In such cases, if the material or information might reasonably be considered capable of undermining the prosecution case or of assisting the case for the accused prosecutors should take what steps they regard as appropriate in the particular case to obtain it.

52.   If the investigator, disclosure officer or prosecutor seeks access to the material or information but the third party declines or refuses to allow access to it, the matter should not be left. If despite any reasons offered by the third party it is still believed that it is reasonable to seek production of the material or information, and the requirements of section 2 of the Criminal Procedure (Attendance of Witnesses) Act 1965 or as appropriate section 97 of the Magistrates Courts Act 1980[1] are satisfied, then the prosecutor or investigator should apply for a witness summons causing a representative of the third party to produce the material to the Court.

53.   Relevant information which comes to the knowledge of investigators or prosecutors as a result of liaison with third parties should be recorded by the investigator or prosecutor in a durable or retrievable form (for example potentially relevant information revealed in discussions at a child protection conference attended by police officers).

54.   Where information comes into the possession of the prosecution in the circumstances set out in paragraphs 51–53 above, consultation with the other agency should take place before disclosure is made: there may be public interest reasons which justify withholding disclosure and which would require the issue of disclosure of the information to be placed before the court.

OTHER DISCLOSURE

Disclosure prior to initial disclosure

55.   Investigators must always be alive to the potential need to reveal and prosecutors to the potential need to disclose material, in the interests of justice and fairness in the particular circumstances of any case, after the

---

1   The equivalent legislation in Northern Ireland is section 51A of the Judicature (Northern Ireland) Act 1978 and Article 118 of the Magistrates' Courts (Northern Ireland) Order 1981.

commencement of proceedings but before their duty arises under the Act. For instance, disclosure ought to be made of significant information that might affect a bail decision or that might enable the defence to contest the committal proceedings.

56. Where the need for such disclosure is not apparent to the prosecutor, any disclosure will depend on what the accused chooses to reveal about the defence. Clearly, such disclosure will not exceed that which is obtainable after the statutory duties of disclosure arise.

Summary trial

57. The prosecutor should, in addition to complying with the obligations under the Act, provide to the defence all evidence upon which the Crown proposes to rely in a summary trial. Such provision should allow the accused and their legal advisers sufficient time properly to consider the evidence before it is called.

Material relevant to sentence

58. In all cases the prosecutor must consider disclosing in the interests of justice any material, which is relevant to sentence (e.g. information which might mitigate the seriousness of the offence or assist the accused to lay blame in part upon a co-accused or another person).

Post-conviction

59. The interests of justice will also mean that where material comes to light after the conclusion of the proceedings, which might cast doubt upon the safety of the conviction, there is a duty to consider disclosure. Any such material should be brought immediately to the attention of line management.

60. Disclosure of any material that is made outside the ambit of Act will attract confidentiality by virtue of *Taylor v SFO* [1998].

APPLICABILITY OF THESE GUIDELINES

61. Although the relevant obligations in relation to unused material and disclosure imposed on the prosecutor and the accused are determined by the date on which the investigation began, these Guidelines should be adopted with immediate effect in relation to all cases submitted to

the prosecuting authorities in receipt of these Guidelines save where they specifically refer to the statutory or Code provisions of the Criminal Justice Act 2003 that do not yet apply to the particular case.

Appendix 6

Supplementary Attorney General's Guidelines on Disclosure – Digitally Stored Material (2011)

1.   The Guidelines are intended to supplement the Attorney General's Guidelines on Disclosure (reissued in April 2005) and specifically paragraph 27. Paragraph 27 explains that the disclosure officer's obligation to inspect retained material may be fulfilled in relation to digitally stored material by using search terms or dip sampling methods, so long as the material is described on the schedules as clearly as possible and the manner and extent of the inspection is recorded along with the justification for adopting that approach.

2.   As a result of the number of cases now involving digitally stored material and the scale of the digital material that may be involved, more detailed guidance is considered to be needed. The objective of these Guidelines is to set out how material satisfying the tests for disclosure can best be identified and disclosed to the defence without imposing unrealistic or disproportionate demands on the investigator and prosecutor.

3.   The approach set out in these Guidelines is in line with existing best practice, in that:

    (i)   Investigating and prosecuting agencies, especially in large and complex cases, will apply their respective case management and disclosure strategies and policies and be transparent with the defence and the courts about how the prosecution has approached complying with its disclosure obligations in the context of the individual case.

    (ii)   The defence will be expected to play their part in defining the real issues in the case. In this context, the defence will be invited to participate in defining the scope of the reasonable searches that may be made of digitally stored material by the investigator to identify material that might reasonably be expected to undermine the prosecution case or assist the defence.

4.   If this approach is followed the courts will be in a good position to use their case management powers effectively and to determine applications for disclosure fairly.

5.   The Attorney General's Guidelines are not detailed operational guidelines. They are intended to set out a common approach to be adopted in the context of digitally stored material.

Types of digital material

6.   Digital material falls into two categories: the first category is material which is created natively within an electronic environment (e.g. email, office files, system files, digital photographs, audio etc.); the second category is material which has been digitised from an analogue form (e.g. scanned copy of a document, scanned photograph, a faxed document). Irrespective of the way in which technology changes, the categorisation of digital material will remain the same.

7.   Digital material is usually held on one of the three types of media. Optical media (e.g. CD, DVD, Blu-ray) and Solid-State media (e.g. removable memory cards, solid state music players or mobile devices etc.) cater for usually lower volume storage. Magnetic media (e.g. disk drives and back up tapes) usually cater for the high volume storage.

General principles for investigators

8.   The general principles[1] to be followed by investigators in handling and examining digital material are:

(i)   No action taken by investigators or their agents should change data held on a computer or storage media which may subsequently be relied upon in court;

(ii)   In circumstances where a person finds it necessary to access original data held on computer or storage media, that person must be competent to do so and be able to give evidence explaining the relevance and implications of their actions;

(iii)   An audit trail or other record of all processes applied to computer-based electronic evidence should be created and preserved. An independent third party should be able to examine those processes

---

1   Based on: Association of Chief Police Officers: Good Practice Guide for Computer Based Electronic Evidence version 4

(see further the section headed Record keeping and scheduling below); and

(iv)   The person in charge of the investigation has overall responsibility for ensuring that the law and these principles are followed.

9.   Where an investigator has reasonable grounds for believing that digital material may contain material subject to legal professional privilege, very strong legal constraints apply. No digital material may be seized which an investigator has reasonable grounds for believing to be subject to legal privilege, other than where the provisions of the Criminal Justice and Police Act 2001 apply. Strict controls need to be applied where privileged material is seized. See the more detailed section on Legal Professional Privilege starting at paragraph 27 below.

Seizure, relevance and retention

10.   The legal obligations are to be found in a combination of the Police and Criminal Evidence Act 1984 (PACE), the Criminal Justice and Police Act 2001 (CJPA 2001) and the Criminal Procedure and Investigations Act 1996 (the CPIA 1996).

11.   These Guidelines also apply to digital material seized or imaged under other statutory provisions. For example, the Serious Fraud Office has distinct powers of seizure under warrant obtained under section 2(4) of the Criminal Justice Act 1987. And in cases concerning obscene material special provisions apply to the handling, storage and copying of such material. Practitioners should refer to specific guidance on the application of those provisions.

Seizure

12.   Before searching a suspect's premises where digital evidence is likely to be found, consideration must be given to what sort of evidence is likely to be found and in what volume, whether it is likely to be possible to view and copy, if relevant, the material at the location – it is not uncommon with the advent of cloud computing for digital material to be hosted by a third party – and to what should be seized. Business and commercial premises will often have very substantial amounts of digital material stored on computers and other media. Investigators will need to consider the practicalities of seizing computer hard drives and other media, the effect this may have on the business and, where it is not feasible to obtain an image of digital material, the likely timescale for returning seized items.

13.   In deciding whether to seize and retain digital material it is important that the investigator either complies with the procedure under the relevant statutory authority, relying either on statutory powers or a search warrant, or obtains the owner's consent. In particular, investigators need to be aware of the strong constraints applying to legally privileged material.

14.   A computer hard drive or single item of media, such as a back up tape, is a single storage entity. This means that if any digital material found on the hard drive or other media can lawfully be seized the computer hard drive or single item of media may, if appropriate, be seized or imaged. In some circumstances investigators may wish to image specific folders, files or categories of data where it is feasible to do so without seizing the hard drive or other media, or instead of taking an image of all data on the hard drive or other media. In practice, the configuration of most systems means that data may be contained across a number of hard drives and more than one hard drive or item of media may be required in order to access the information sought.

15.   Digital material must not be seized if an investigator has reasonable grounds for believing it is subject to legal professional privilege, other than where sections 50 or 51 of the Criminal Justice and Police Act 2001 apply. If such material is seized it must be isolated from other seized material and any other investigation material in the possession of the investigating authority.

The Police and Criminal Evidence Act 1984

16.   PACE 1984 provides powers to seize and retain anything for which the search has been authorised or after arrest, other than items attracting legal professional privilege.[2] In addition, there is a general power to seize anything which is on the premises if there are reasonable grounds to believe that it has been obtained in the commission of an offence, or that it is evidence and that it is necessary to seize it to prevent it being concealed, lost, altered or destroyed.[3] There is another related power to require information which is stored in any electronic form and is accessible from the premises to be produced in a form in which it can be taken away and in which it is visible and legible or from which it can readily be produced in a visible and legible form.[4]

---

2   By warrant under section 8 and Schedule 1 and section 18 of the 1984 Act
3   Section 19 of the 1984 Act
4   Section 20 of the 1984 Act

17.   An image (a forensically sound copy) of the digital material may be taken at the location of the search. Where the investigator makes an image of the digital material at the location, the original need not be seized. Alternatively, when originals are taken, investigators must be prepared to copy or image the material for the owners when reasonably practicable in accordance with PACE 1984 Code B 7.17.

18.   Where it is not possible or reasonably practicable to image the computer or hard drive, it will need to be removed from the location or premises for examination elsewhere. This allows the investigator to seize and sift material for the purpose of identifying that which meets the tests for retention in accordance with the 1984 Act.[5]

The Criminal Justice and Police Act 2001

19.   The additional powers of seizure in sections 50 and 51 of the CJPA 2001 Act only extend the scope of existing powers of search and seizure under the 1984 Act and other specified statutory authority[6] where the relevant conditions and circumstances apply.

20.   Investigators must be careful only to exercise powers under the CJPA when it is necessary and not to remove any more material than is justified. The removal of large volumes of material, much of which may not ultimately be retainable, may have serious consequences for the owner of the material, particularly when they are involved in business or other commercial activities.

21.   A written notice must be given to the occupier of the premises where items are seized under sections 50 and 51.[7]

22.   Until material seized under the CJPA 2001 has been examined, it must be kept securely and separately from any material seized under other powers. Any such material must be examined as soon as reasonably practicable to determine which elements may be retained and which should be returned. Regard must be had to the desirability of allowing the person from whom the property was seized, or a person with an interest in the property, an opportunity of being present or represented at the examination.

---

5   Special provisions exist for the investigations conducted by Her Majesty's Revenue and Customs in the application of their powers under the 1984 Act – see section 114(2)(b) – and the 2001 Act

6   Schedule 1 of the 2001 Act

7   Section 52 of the 2001 Act

Retention

23. Where material is seized under the powers conferred by PACE 1984 the duty to retain it under the Code of Practice issued under the CPIA 1996 is subject to the provisions on retention under section 22 of the 1984 Act. Material seized under sections 50 and 51 of the CJPA 2001 may be retained or returned in accordance with sections 53–58 of that Act.

24. Retention is limited to evidence and relevant material (as defined in the Code of Practice issued under the CPIA 1996). Where either evidence or relevant material is inextricably linked to non-relevant material which is not reasonably practicable to separate, that material can also be retained. Inextricably linked material is material that is not reasonably practicable to separate from other linked material without prejudicing the use of that other material in any investigation or proceedings.

25. However, inextricably linked material must not be examined, imaged, copied or used for any purpose other than for providing the source of or the integrity of the linked material.

26. There are four categories of material that may be retained:

    (i) Material that is evidence or potential evidence in the case. Where material is retained for evidential purposes there will be a strong argument that the whole thing (or an authenticated image or copy) should be retained for the purpose of proving provenance and continuity.

    (ii) Where evidential material has been retained, inextricably linked non relevant material which is not reasonably practicable to separate can also be retained (PACE Code B paragraph 7).

    (iii) An investigator should retain material that is relevant to the investigation and required to be scheduled as unused material. This is broader than but includes the duty to retain material which may satisfy the test for prosecution disclosure. The general duty to retain relevant material is set out in the CPIA Code at paragraph 5.

    (iv) Material which is inextricably linked to relevant unused material which of itself may not be relevant material. Such material should be retained (PACE Code B paragraph 7).

27. The balance of any digital material should be returned in accordance with sections 53–55 of the 2001 Act and also note paragraph 28 of the Attorney General's Guidelines on Disclosure.

Legal Professional Privilege (LPP)

28.   No digital material may be seized which an investigator has reasonable grounds for believing to be subject to legal privilege, other than under the additional powers of seizure in the CJPA 2001.

29.   The CJPA 2001 enables an investigator to seize relevant items which contain LPP material where it is not reasonably practicable on the search premises to separate LPP material from non-LPP material.

30.   Where LPP material or material suspected of containing LPP is seized it must be isolated from the other material which has been seized in the investigation. The mechanics of securing property vary according to the circumstances; 'bagging up', i.e. placing materials in sealed bags or containers, and strict subsequent control of access, is the appropriate procedure in many cases.

31.   Examination of material may be undertaken by a person independent of the investigation, who may be employed within an investigative body so long as he or she is not one of the investigators or anyone connected with the investigation, to determine whether material may attract LPP.

32.   Where material has been identified as potentially containing LPP it must be reviewed by an independent lawyer. No member of the investigative or prosecution team involved in either the current investigation or, if the LPP material relates to other criminal proceedings, in those proceedings should have sight of or access to the LPP material.

33.   If the material is voluminous, search terms or other filters may have to be used to identify the LPP material. If so this will also have to be done by someone independent and not connected with the investigation.

34.   It is essential that anyone dealing with LPP material maintains proper records showing the way in which the material has been handled and those who have had access to it as well as decisions taken in relation to that material.

35.   LPP material can only be retained in specific circumstances in accordance with section 54 of the CJPA 2001 i.e. where the property which comprises the LPP material has been lawfully seized and it is not reasonably practicable for the item to be separated from the rest of the property without prejudicing the use of the rest of the property. LPP material which cannot be retained must be returned as soon as practicable after the seizure without waiting for the whole examination of the seized material.

Excluded and special procedure material

36.   Similar principles to those that apply to LPP material apply to excluded or special procedure material, as set out in section 55 of the CJPA 2001.[8]

Encryption

37.   Part III of the Regulation of Investigatory Powers Act 2000 (RIPA) and the Investigation of Protected Electronic Information Code of Practice govern encryption. See the CPS's Guidance RIPA Part III

38.   RIPA enables specified law enforcement agencies to compel individuals or companies to provide passwords or encryption keys for the purpose of rendering protected material readable. Failure to comply with RIPA Part III orders is a criminal offence. The Code of Practice provides guidance when exercising powers under RIPA, to require disclosure of protected electronic data in an intelligible form or to acquire the means by which protected electronic data may be accessed or put in an intelligible form.

Sifting/examination

39.   In complying with its duty of disclosure, the prosecution should follow the procedure as outlined below.

40.   Where digital material is examined, the extent and manner of inspecting, viewing or listening will depend on the nature of the material and its form.

41.   It is important for investigators and prosecutors to remember that the duty under the 1996 Act Code of Practice is to 'pursue all reasonable lines of enquiry including those that point away from the suspect'. Lines of enquiry, of whatever kind, should be pursued only if they are reasonable in the context of the individual case. It is not the duty of the prosecution to comb through all the material in its possession – e.g. every word or byte of computer material – on the look out for anything which might conceivably or speculatively assist the defence. The duty of the prosecution is to disclose material which might reasonably be considered capable of undermining its case or assisting the case for the accused which they become aware of, or to which their attention is drawn.

---

8   Special provisions exist for investigations conducted by Her Majesty's Revenue and Customs in the application of the powers under the 1984 Act – see section 114(2)(b) – and the 2001 Act

42. In some cases the sift may be conducted by an investigator/disclosure officer manually assessing the content of the computer or other digital material from its directory and determining which files are relevant and should be retained for evidence or unused material.

43. In other cases such an approach may not be feasible. Where there is an enormous volume of material it is perfectly proper for the investigator/disclosure officer to search it by sample, key words, or other appropriate search tools or analytical techniques to locate relevant passages, phrases and identifiers.

44. In cases involving very large quantities of data, the person in charge of the investigation will develop a strategy setting out how the material should be analysed or searched to identify categories of data. Where search tools are used to examine digital material it will usually be appropriate to provide the accused and his or her legal representative with a copy of reasonable search terms used, or to be used, and invite them to suggest any further reasonable search terms. If search terms are suggested which the investigator or prosecutor believes will not be productive – for example because of the use of common words that are likely to identify a mass of irrelevant material, the investigator or prosecutor is entitled to open a dialogue with the defence representative with a view to agreeing sensible refinements. The purpose of this dialogue is to ensure that reasonable and proportionate searches can be carried out.

45. It may be necessary to carry out sampling and searches on more than one occasion, especially as there is a duty on the prosecutor to keep duties of disclosure under review. To comply with this duty it may be appropriate (and should be considered) where further evidence or unused material is obtained in the course of the investigation; the defence statement is served on the prosecutor; the defendant makes an application under section 8 of the CPIA for disclosure; or the defendant requests that further sampling or searches be carried out (provided it is a reasonable line of enquiry).

Record keeping

46. A record or log must be made of all digital material seized or imaged and subsequently retained as relevant to the investigation.

47. In cases involving very large quantities of data where the person in charge of the investigation has developed a strategy setting out how the material should be analysed or searched to identify categories of data, a record should be made of the strategy and the analytical techniques used to search the data. The record should include details of the person who has carried out the process and the date and time it was carried out. In such

cases the strategy should record the reasons why certain categories have been searched for (such as names, companies, dates etc).

48. In any case it is important that any searching or analytical processing of digital material, as well as the data identified by that process, is properly recorded. So far as practicable, what is required is a record of the terms of the searches or processing that has been carried out. This means that in principle the following details may be recorded:

(i) A record of all searches carried out, including the date of each search and the person(s) who conducted it;

(ii) A record of all search words or terms used on each search. However where it is impracticable to record each word or terms (such as where Boolean searches or search strings or conceptual searches are used) it will usually be sufficient to record each broad category of search;

(iii) A log of the key judgements made while refining the search strategy in the light of what is found, or deciding not to carry out further searches;

(iv) Where material relating to a 'hit' is not examined, the decision not to examine should be explained in the record of examination or in a statement. For instance, a large number of 'hits' may be obtained in relation to a particular search word or term, but material relating to the 'hits' is not examined because they do not appear to be relevant to the investigation. Any subsequent refinement of the search terms and further hits should also be noted and explained as above.

49. Just as it is not necessary for the investigator or prosecutor to produce records of every search made of hard copy material, it is not necessary to produce records of what may be many hundreds of searches or analyses that have been carried out on digitally stored material, simply to demonstrate that these have been done. It should be sufficient for the prosecution to explain how the disclosure exercise has been approached and to give the accused or suspect's legal representative an opportunity to participate in defining the reasonable searches to be made, as described in the section on sifting/examination.

Scheduling

50. The disclosure officer should ensure that scheduling of relevant material is carried out in accordance with the 1996 Act Code of Practice. This requires each item of unused material to be listed separately on the

unused material schedule and numbered consecutively. The description of each item should make clear the nature of the item and should contain sufficient detail to enable the prosecutor to decide whether he needs to inspect the material before deciding whether or not it should be disclosed (see paragraph 24).

51.   In some enquiries it may not be practicable to list each item of material separately. If so, these may be listed in a block and described by quantity and generic title. Even if the material is listed in a block, the search terms used and any items of material which might satisfy the disclosure test are listed and described separately. In practical terms this will mean, where appropriate, cross referencing the schedules to your disclosure management document.

52.   The remainder of any computer hard drive/media containing material which is not responsive to search terms or other analytical technique or not identified by any 'hits', and material identified by 'hits' but not examined, is unused material and should be recorded (if appropriate by a generic description) and retained.

53.   Where continuation sheets of the unused material schedule are used, or additional schedules are sent subsequently, the item numbering must be sequential to all other items on earlier schedules.

Third party material

54.   Third party material is material held by a person, organisation, or government department other than the investigator and prosecutor within the UK or outside the UK.

Within the UK

55.   The CPIA Code and the AG's Guidelines makes clear the obligation on the prosecution to pursue all reasonable lines of enquiry in relation to material held by third parties within the UK.

56.   If as a result of the duty to pursue all reasonable lines of enquiry, the investigator or prosecutor obtains or receives the material from the third party, then it must be dealt with in accordance with the CPIA 1996 i.e. the prosecutor must disclose material if it meets the disclosure tests, subject to any public interest immunity claim. The person who has an interest in the material (the third party) may make representations to the court concerning public interest immunity (see section 16 of the CPIA 1996).

57.   Material not in the possession of an investigator or prosecutor falls
        outside the CPIA 1996. In such cases the Attorney General Guidelines
        on Disclosure prescribe the approach to be taken to disclosure of material
        held by third parties (paragraphs 51–54) as does the judicial disclosure
        protocol (paragraphs 52–62).

Outside the UK

58.   The obligation on the investigator and prosecutor under the CPIA Code
        and the AG's Guidelines to pursue all reasonable lines of enquiry also
        applies to material held overseas.

59.   Where it appears that there is relevant material, the prosecution must
        take reasonable steps to obtain it, either informally or making use of the
        powers contained in the Crime (International Co-operation) Act 2003
        and any EU and international conventions. See CPS Guidance Obtaining
        Evidence and Information from Abroad

60.   There may be cases where a foreign state or a foreign court refuses to
        make the material available to the investigator or prosecutor. There may
        be other cases where the foreign state, though willing to show the material
        to investigators will not allow the material to be copied or otherwise made
        available and the courts of the foreign state will not order its provision.

61.   It is for these reasons that there is no absolute duty on the prosecutor
        to disclose relevant material held overseas by entities not subject to the
        jurisdiction of the courts in England and Wales.

62.   The obligation on the investigator and prosecutor under the CPIA 1996
        is to take reasonable steps. Where investigators are allowed to examine
        files of a foreign state but are not allowed to take copies or notes or list
        the documents held, there is no breach by the prosecution in its duty
        of disclosure by reason of its failure to obtain such material, provided
        reasonable steps have been taken to try and obtain the material. Whether
        the prosecution has complied with its duty is for the court to judge in each
        case.

63.   In these circumstances it is important that the position is clearly set out
        in writing so that the court and the defence know what the position is.
        Investigators and prosecutors must record and explain the situation and
        set out, insofar as they are permitted by the foreign state, such information
        as they can and the steps they have taken.

Attorney General's Guidelines Issued on the
14th day of July 2011

Disclosure: A Protocol for the Control and Management of Unused Material in the Crown Court

Introduction

1. Disclosure is one of the most important – as well as one of the most abused – of the procedures relating to criminal trials. There needs to be a sea-change in the approach of both judges and the parties to all aspects of the handling of the material which the prosecution do not intend to use in support of their case. For too long, a wide range of serious misunderstandings has existed, both as to the exact ambit of the unused material to which the defence is entitled, and the role to be played by the judge in ensuring that the law is properly applied. All too frequently applications by the parties and decisions by the judges in this area have been made based either on misconceptions as to the true nature of the law or a general laxity of approach (however well intentioned). This failure properly to apply the binding provisions as regards disclosure has proved extremely and unnecessarily costly and has obstructed justice. It is, therefore, essential that disclosure obligations are properly discharged – by both the prosecution and the defence – in all criminal proceedings, and the court's careful oversight of this process is an important safeguard against the possibility of miscarriages of justice.

2. The House of Lords stated in *R v H and C [2004] 2 AC 134*, at 147:

    Fairness ordinarily requires that any material held by the prosecution which weakens its case or strengthens that of the defendant, if not relied on as part of its formal case against the defendant, should be disclosed to the defence. Bitter experience has shown that miscarriages of justice may occur where such material is withheld from disclosure. The golden rule is that full disclosure of such material should be made.

3. However, it is also essential that the trial process is not overburdened or diverted by erroneous and inappropriate disclosure of unused prosecution material, or by misconceived applications in relation to such material.

4. The overarching principle is therefore that unused prosecution material will fall to be disclosed if, and only if, it satisfies the test for disclosure applicable to the proceedings in question, subject to any overriding public interest considerations. The relevant test for disclosure will depend on the date the criminal investigation in question commenced (see the section on Sources below), as this will determine whether the common law disclosure regime applies, or either of the two disclosure regimes under the Criminal Procedure and Investigations Act 1996 (CPIA).

5. There is very clear evidence that, without active judicial oversight and management, the handling of disclosure issues in general, and the disclosure of unused prosecution material in particular, can cause delays and adjournments.

6. The failure to comply fully with disclosure obligations, whether by the prosecution or the defence, may disrupt and in some cases even frustrate the course of justice.

7. Consideration of irrelevant unused material may consume wholly unjustifiable and disproportionate amounts of time and public resources, undermining the overall performance and efficiency of the criminal justice system. The aim of this Protocol is therefore to assist and encourage judges when dealing with all disclosure issues, in the light of the overarching principle set out in paragraph 4 above. This guidance is intended to cover all Crown Court cases (including cases where relevant case management diredions are made at the Magistrates' Court). It is not, therefore, confined to a very few high profile and high cost cases.

8. Unused material which has been gathered during the course of a criminal investigation and disclosed by the prosecution pursuant to their duties (as set out elsewhere in this Protocol) is received by the defence subject to a prohibition not to use or disclose the material for any purpose which is not connected with the proceedings for whose purposes they were given it (s. 17 CPIA). The common law, which applies to all disclosure not made under the CPIA, achieves the same result by the creation of an implied undertaking not to use the material for any purposes other than the proper conduct of the particular case (see *Taylor v Director of the Serious Fraud Office HL [1999] 2 A.C. 177*). A breach of that undertaking would constitute a contempt of court. These provisions are designed to ensure that the privacy and confidentiality of those who provided the material to the investigation (as well as those who are mentioned in the material) is protected and is not invaded any more than is absolutely necessary.

However, neither statute nor the common law prevents any one from using or disclosing such material if it has been displayed or communicated to the public in open court (unless the evidence is subject to continuing reporting restriction), and moreover, an application can be made to the court for permission to use or disclose the object or information.

Sources

9. It is not the purpose of this Protocol to rehearse the law in detail; however, some of the principal sources are set out here.

10. The correct test for disclosure will depend upon the date the relevant criminal investigation commenced:

   a. In relation to offences in respect of which the criminal investigation began prior to 1 April 1997, the common law will apply, and the test for disclosure is that set out in *R v Keane [1994] 1 W.L.R. 746; (1994) 99 Cr. App. R. 1.*

   b. If the criminal investigation commenced on or after 1 April 1997, but before 4 April 2005, then the CPIA in its original form will apply, with separate tests for disclosure of unused prosecution material at the primary and secondary disclosure stages (the latter following service of a defence statement by the accused). The disclosure provisions of the Act are supported by the 1997 edition of the Code of Practice issued under section 23(1) of the CPIA (Statutory Instrument 1997 No. 1033)

   c. Where the criminal investigation has commenced on or after 4 April 2005, the law is set out in the CPIA as amended by Part V of the Criminal Justice Act 2003. There is then a single test for disclosure of unused prosecution material and the April 2005 edition of the Code of Practice under section 23(1) of the CPIA will apply (see SI 2005 No. 985).

   The CPIA also identifies the stage(s) at which the prosecution is required to disclose material, and the formalities relating to defence statements. The default time limit for prosecution disclosure is set out in section 13 of the Act (see further at paragraph 13 below). The time limits applicable to defence disclosure are set out in the Criminal Procedure and Investigations Act 1996 (Defence Disclosure Regulations) 1997 (S.I. 1997 No. 684).

10. Regard must be had to the Attorney General's Guidelines on Disclosure (April 2005). Although these do not have the force of law (*R v Winston Brown [1995] 1 Cr. App. R. 191: [1994] 1 WLR 1599*) they should be given due weight.

11.   Part 25 of the Criminal Procedure Rules 2005 (see SI 2005 No. 384) sets out the procedures to be followed for applications to the court concerning both sensitive and non-sensitive unused material. Part 3 of the Rules is also relevant in respect of the court's general case management powers, and parties should also have regard to the Consolidated Criminal Practice Direction.

12.   Parts 22 and 23 of the Criminal Procedure Rules are set aside to make provision for other rules concerning disclosure by the prosecution and the defence, although at the date of this Protocol there are no rules under those Parts.

The duty to gather and record unused material

13.   For the statutory scheme to work properly, investigators and disclosure officers responsible for the gathering, inspection, retention and recording of relevant unused prosecution material must perform their tasks thoroughly, scrupulously and fairly. In this, they must adhere to the appropriate provisions of the CPIA Code of Practice.

14.   It is crucial that the police (and indeed all investigative bodies) implement appropriate training regimes and appoint competent disclosure officers, who have sufficient knowledge of the issues in the case. This will enable them to make a proper assessment of the unused prosecution material in the light of the test for relevance under paragraph 2.1 of the CPIA Code of Practice, with a view to preparing full and accurate schedules of the retained material. In any criminal investigation, the disclosure officer must retain material that may be relevant to an investigation. This material must be listed on a schedule. Each item listed on the schedule should contain sufficient detail to enable the prosecutor to decide whether or not the material falls to be disclosed. The schedules must be sent to the prosecutor. Wherever possible this should be at the same time as the file containing the material for the prosecution case but the duty to disclose does not end at this point and must continue while relevant material is received even after conviction.

15.   Furthermore, the scheduling of the relevant material must be completed expeditiously, so as to enable the prosecution to comply promptly with the duty to provide primary (or, when the amended CPIA regime applies) initial disclosure as soon as practicable after:

    •   the case has been committed for trial under section 6(1) or 6(2) of the Magistrates' Courts Act 1980; or

- • the case has been transferred to the Crown Court under section 4 of the Criminal Justice Act 1987, or section 53 of the Criminal Justice Act 1991; or

- • copies of documents containing the evidence are served on the accused in accordance with the Crime and Disorder Act 1998 (Service of Prosecution Evidence) Regulations 2005 (S.I. 2005 No. 902), where the matter has been sent to the Crown Court pursuant to section 51 or 51A of the Crime and Disorder Act 1998; or

- • a matter has been added to an indictment in accordance with section 40 of the Criminal Justice Act 1988; or

- • a bill of indictment has been preferred under section 2(2)(b) of the Administration of Justice (Miscellaneous Provisions) Act 1933 or section 22B(3)(a) of the Prosecution of Offences Act 1985.

16. Investigators, disclosure officers and prosecutors must promptly and properly discharge their responsibilities under the Act and statutory Code, in order to ensure that justice is not delayed, denied or frustrated. In this context, under paragraph 3.5 of the Code of Practice, it is provided 'an investigator should pursue all reasonable lines of inquiry, whether these point towards or away from the suspect'.

17. CPS lawyers advising the police pre-charge at police stations should consider conducting a preliminary review of the unused material generated by the investigation, where this is practicable, so as to give early advice on disclosure issues. Otherwise, prosecutors should conduct a preliminary review of disclosure at the same time as the initial review of the evidence. It is critical that the important distinction between the evidence in the case, on the one hand, and any unused material, on the other, is not blurred. Items such as exhibits should be treated as such and the obligation to serve them is not affected by the disclosure regime.

18. Where the single test for disclosure applies under the amended CPIA disclosure regime, the prosecutor is under a duty to consider, at an early stage of proceedings, whether there is any unused prosecution material which is reasonably capable of assisting the case for the accused. What a defendant has said by way of defence or explanation either in interview or by way of a prepared statement can be a useful guide to making an objective assessment of the material which would satisfy this test.

19. There may be some occasions when the prosecution, pursuant to surviving common law rules of disclosure, ought to disclose an item or items of unused prosecution material, even in advance of primary or initial disclosure under section 3 of the CPIA. This may apply, for instance,

where there is information which might affect a decision as to bail; where an abuse of process is alleged; where there is material which might assist the defence to make submissions as to the particular charge or charges, if any, the defendant should face at the Crown Court; and when it is necessary to enable particular preparation to be undertaken at an early stage by the defence. Guidance as to occasions where such disclosure may be appropriate is provided in *R v DPP ex parte Lee (1999) 2 Cr App R 304*. However, once the CPIA is triggered (for instance, by committal, or service of case papers following a section 51 sending) it is the CPIA which determines what material should be disclosed.

The judge's duty to enforce the statutory scheme

20.   When cases are sent to the Crown Court under section 51 of the Crime and Disorder Act 1998, the Crime and Disorder Act 1998 (Service of Prosecution Evidence) Regulations 2005 allow the prosecution 70 days from the date the matter was sent (50 days, where the accused is in custody) within which to serve on the defence and the court copies of the documents containing the evidence upon which the charge or charges are based (in effect, sufficient evidence to amount to a prima facie case). These time limits may be extended and varied at the court's direction. Directions for service of these case papers may be given at the Magistrates' Court.

21.   While it is important to note that this time limit applies to the service of evidence, rather than unused prosecution material, the court will need to consider at the Magistrates' Court or preliminary hearing whether it is practicable for the prosecution to comply with primary or initial disclosure at the same time as service of such papers, or whether disclosure ought to take place after a certain interval, but before the matter is listed for a PCMH.

22.   If the nature of the case does not allow service of the evidence and initial or primary disclosure within the 70, or if applicable 50, days (or such other period as directed by the Magistrates' Court), the investigator should ensure that the prosecution advocate at the Magistrates' Court, preliminary Crown Court hearing, or further hearing prior to the PCMH, is aware of the problems, knows why and how the position has arisen and can assist the court as to what revised time limits are realistic.

23.   It would be helpful if the prosecution advocate could make any foreseeable difficulties clear as soon as possible, whether this is at the Magistrates' Court or in the Crown Court at the preliminary hearing (where there is one).

24. Failing this, where such difficulties arise or have come to light after directions for service of case papers and disclosure have been made, the prosecution should notify the court and the defence promptly. This should be done in advance of the PCMH date, and prior to the date set by the court for the service of this material.

25. It is important that this is done in order that the listing for the PCMH is an effective one, as the defence must have a proper opportunity to read the case papers and to consider the initial or primary disclosure, with a view to timely drafting of a defence case statement (where the matter is to be contested), prior to the PCMH.

26. In order to ensure that the listing of the PCMH is appropriate, Judges should not impose time limits for service of case papers or initial/primary disclosure unless and until they are confident that the prosecution advocate has taken the requisite instructions from those who are actually going to do the work specified. It is better to impose a realistic timetable from the outset than to set unachievable limits. Reference should be made to Part 3 of the Criminal Procedure Rules and the Consolidated Practice Direction in this respect.

27. This is likewise appropriate where directions, or further directions, are made in relation to prosecution or defence disclosure at the PCMH. Failure to consider whether the timetable is practicable may dislocate the court timetable and can even imperil trial dates. At the PCMH, therefore, all the advocates – prosecution and defence – must be fully instructed about any difficulties the parties may have in complying with their respective disclosure obligations, and must be in a position to put forward a reasonable timetable for resolution of them.

28. Where directions are given by the court in the light of such inquiry, extensions of time should not be given lightly or as a matter of course. If extensions are sought, then an appropriately detailed explanation must be given. For the avoidance of doubt, it is not sufficient merely for the CPS (or other prosecutor) to say that the papers have been delivered late by the police (or other investigator): the court will need to know why they have been delivered late. Likewise, where the accused has been dilatory in serving a defence statement (where the prosecution has complied with the duty to make primary or initial disclosure of unused material, or has purported to do so), it is not sufficient for the defence to say that insufficient instructions have been taken for service of this within the 14-day time limit: the court will need to know why sufficient instructions have not been taken, and what arrangements have been made for the taking of such instructions.

29.   Delays and failures by the defence are as damaging to the timely, fair and efficient hearing of the case as delays and failures by the prosecution, and judges should identify and deal with all such failures firmly and fairly.

30.   Judges should not allow the prosecution to abdicate their statutory responsibility for reviewing the unused material by the expedient of allowing the defence to inspect (or providing the defence with copies of) everything on the schedules of non-sensitive unused prosecution material, irrespective of whether that material, or all of that material, satisfies the relevant test for disclosure. Where that test is satisfied it is for the prosecutor to decide the form in which disclosure is made. Disclosure need not be in the same form as that in which the information was recorded. Guidance on case management issues relating to this point was given by Rose LJ in *R v CPS (Interlocutory Application under sections 35/36 CPIA) [2005] EWCA Crim 2342.*

31.   Indeed, the larger and more complex the case, the more important it is for the prosecution to adhere to the overarching principle in paragraph 4 and ensure that sufficient prosecution resources are allocated to the task. Handing the defence the 'keys to the warehouse' has been the cause of many gross abuses in the past, resulting in huge sums being run up by the defence without any proportionate benefit to the course of justice. These abuses must end.

The defence case statement

32.   Reference has been made above to defence disclosure obligations. After the provision of primary or initial disclosure by the prosecution, the next really critical step in the preparation for trial is the service of the defence statement. It is a mandatory requirement for a defence statement to be served, where section 5(5) of the CPIA applies to the proceedings. This is due within 14 days of the date upon which the prosecution has complied with, or purported to comply with, the duty of primary or initial disclosure. Service of the defence statement is a critical stage in the disclosure process, and timely service of the statement will allow for the proper consideration of disclosure issues well in advance of the trial date.

33.   There may be some cases where it is simply not possible to serve a proper defence case statement within the 14-day time limit; well founded defence applications for an extension of time under paragraph (2) of regulation 3 of the Criminal Procedure and Investigations Act 1996 (Defence Disclosure Time Limits) Regulations 1997 may therefore be granted. In a proper case, it may be appropriate to put the PCMH back by a week or so,

to enable a sufficient defence case statement to be filed and considered by the prosecution.

34. In the past, the prosecution and the court have too often been faced with a defence case statement that is little more than an assertion that the Defendant is not guilty. As was stated by the Court of Appeal in *R v Patrick Bryant [2005] EWCA Crim 2079* (per Judge LJ, paragraph 12), such a reiteration of the defendant's plea is not the purpose of a defence statement. Defence statements must comply with the requisite formalities set out in section 5(6) and (7), or section 6A, of the CPIA, as applicable.

35. Where the enhanced requirements for defence disclosure apply under section 6A of the CPIA (namely, where the case involves a criminal investigation commencing on or after 4 April 2005) the defence statement must spell out, in detail, the nature of the defence, and particular defences relied upon; it must identify the matters of fact upon which the accused takes issue with the prosecution, and the reason why, in relation to each disputed matter of fact. It must further identify any point of law (including points as to the admissibility of evidence, or abuse of process) which the accused proposes to take, and identify authorities relied on in relation to each point of law. Where an alibi defence is relied upon, the particulars given must comply with section 6(2)(a) and (b) of the CPIA. Judges will expect to see defence case statements that contain a clear and detailed exposition of the issues of fact and law in the case.

36. Where the pre-4 April 2005 CPIA disclosure regime applies, the accused must, in the defence statement, set out the nature of the defence in general terms, indicate the matters upon which the defendant takes issue with the prosecution and set out (in relation to each such matter) why issue is taken. Any alibi defence relied upon should comply with the formalities in section 5(7)(a) and (b) of the Act.

37. There must be a complete change in the culture. The defence must serve the defence case statement by the due date. Judges should then examine the defence case statement with care to ensure that it complies with the formalities required by the CPIA. As was stated in paragraph 35 of *R v H and C [2004]*:

> If material does not weaken the prosecution case or strengthen that of the defendant, there is no requirement to disclose it. For this purpose the parties' respective cases should not be restrictively analysed. But they must be carefully analysed, to ascertain the specific facts the prosecution seek to establish and the specific grounds on which the charges are resisted. The trial process is not well served if the defence are permitted to make general and unspecified allegations and then seek far-reaching disclosure in the hope that material may

turn up to make them good. Neutral material or material damaging to the defendant need not be disclosed and should not be brought to the attention of the court.

38.   If no defence case statement – or no sufficient case statement – has been served by the PCMH, the judge should make a full investigation of the reasons for this failure to comply with the mandatory obligation of the accused, under section 5(5) of the CPIA.

39.   If there is no – or no sufficient – defence statement by the date of PCMH, or any pre-trial hearing where the matter falls to be considered, the judge must consider whether the defence should be warned, pursuant to section 6E(2) of the CPIA, that an adverse inference may be drawn at the trial. In the usual case, where section 6E(2) applies and there is no justification for the deficiency, such a warning should be given.

40.   Judges must, of course, be alert to ensure that defendants do not suffer because of the faults and failings of their lawyers, but there must be a clear indication to the professions that if justice is to be done, and if disclosure to be dealt with fairly in accordance with the law, a full and careful defence case statement is essential.

41.   Where there are failings by either the defence or the prosecution, judges should, in exercising appropriate oversight of disclosure, pose searching questions to the parties and, having done this and explored the reasons for default, give clear directions to ensure that such failings are addressed and remedied well in advance of the trial date.

42.   The ultimate sanction for a failure in disclosure by the accused is the drawing of an inference under section 11 of the CPIA. Where the amended CPIA regime applies, the strict legal position allows the prosecution to comment upon any failure of defence disclosure, with a view to seeking such an inference (except where the failure relates to identifying a point of law), without leave of the court, but often it will be helpful to canvass the matter with the judge beforehand. In suitable cases, the prosecution should consider commenting upon failures in defence disclosure, with a view to such an inference, more readily than has been the practice under the old CPIA regime, subject to any views expressed by the judge.

43.   It is vital to a fair trial that the prosecution are mindful of their continuing duty of disclosure, and they must particularly review disclosure in the light of the issues identified in the defence case statement. As part of the timetabling exercise, the judge should set a date by which any application under section 8 (if there is to be one) should be made. While the defence may indicate, in advance of the cut-off date, what items of unused material they are interested in and why, such requests must relate to matters raised in the accused's defence statement. The prosecution should only disclose

material in response to such requests if the material meets the appropriate test for disclosure, and the matter must proceed to a formal section 8 hearing in the event that the prosecution declines to make disclosure of the items in question. Paragraphs 4(iv)–(vi)(a) of the Lord Chief Justice's March 2005 Protocol for the Control and Management of Heavy Fraud and Other Complex Criminal Cases should be construed accordingly.

44.   If, after the prosecution have complied with, or purported to comply with, primary or initial disclosure, and after the service of the defence case statement and any further prosecution disclosure flowing there from, the defence have a reasonable basis to claim disclosure has been inadequate, they must make an application to the court under section 8 of the CPIA. The procedure for the making of such an application is set out in the Criminal Procedure Rules, Part 25, r 25.6. This requires written notice to the prosecution in the form prescribed by r 25.6(2). The prosecution is then entitled (r 25.6(5)) to 14 days within which to agree to provide the specific disclosure requested or to request a hearing in order to make representations in relation to the defence application. As part of the timetabling exercise, the judge should set a date by which any applications under section 8 are to be made and should require the defence to indicate in advance of the cut-off date for specific disclosure applications what documents they are interested in and from what source; in appropriate cases, the judge should require justification of such requests.

45.   The consideration of detailed defence requests for specific disclosure (so-called 'shopping lists') otherwise than in accordance with r 25.6, is wholly improper. Likewise, defence requests for specific disclosure of unused prosecution material in purported pursuance of section 8 of the CPIA and r 25.6, which are not referable to any issue in the case identified by the defence case statement, should be rejected. Judges should require an application to be made under section 8 and in compliance with r 25.6 before considering any order for further disclosure.

46.   It follows that the practice of making blanket orders for disclosure in all cases should cease, since such orders are inconsistent with the statutory framework of disclosure laid down by the CPIA, and which was endorsed by the House of Lords in *R v H and C (supra)*.

Listing

47.   It will be clear that the conscientious discharge of a judge's duty at the PCMH requires a good deal more time than under the old PDH regime; furthermore a good deal more work is required of the advocate. The listing of PCMHs must take this into account. Unless the court can sit at

10am and finish the PCMH by 10.30am, it will not therefore usually be desirable for a judge who is part-heard on a trial to do a PCMH.

48.   It follows that any case which raises difficult issues of disclosure should be referred to the Resident Judge for directions. Cases of real complexity should, if possible, be allocated to a specific trial judge at a very early stage, and usually before the PCMH.

49.   Although this Protocol is addressed to the issues of disclosure, it cannot be seen in isolation; it must be seen in the context of general case management.

Public Interest Immunity

50.   Recent authoritative guidance as to the proper approach to PII is provided by the House of Lords in *R v H and C (supra)*. It is clearly appropriate for PII applications to be considered by the trial judge. No judge should embark upon a PII application without considering that case and addressing the questions set out in paragraph 36, which for ease of reference we reproduce here:

'36. When any issue of derogation from the golden rule of full disclosure comes before it, the court must address a series of questions:

(1)   What is the material which the prosecution seek to withhold? This must be considered by the court in detail.

(2)   Is the material such as may weaken the prosecution case or strengthen that of the defence? If No, disclosure should not be ordered. If Yes, full disclosure should (subject to (3), (4) and (5) below) be ordered.

(3)   Is there a real risk of serious prejudice to an important public interest (and, if so, what) if full disclosure of the material is ordered? If No, full disclosure should be ordered.

(4)   If the answer to (2) and (3) is Yes, can the defendant's interest be protected without disclosure or disclosure be ordered to an extent or in a way which will give adequate protection to the public interest in question and also afford adequate protection to the interests of the defence?

This question requires the court to consider, with specific reference to the material which the prosecution seek to withhold and the facts of the case and the defence as disclosed, whether the prosecution should formally admit what the defence seek to establish or whether disclosure short of full disclosure may be ordered. This may be done in appropriate cases by the preparation of summaries or extracts of evidence, or the provision of documents in an edited or anonymised form, provided the documents supplied are in each instance approved by the judge. In appropriate cases the appointment of special counsel may be a necessary step to ensure that the contentions of the prosecution are tested and the interests of the defendant protected (see paragraph 22 above). In cases of exceptional difficulty the court may require the appointment of special counsel to ensure a correct answer to questions (2) and (3) as well as (4).

(5)   Do the measures proposed in answer to (4) represent the minimum derogation necessary to protect the public interest in question? If No, the court should order such greater disclosure as will represent the minimum derogation from the golden rule of full disclosure.

(6)   If limited disclosure is ordered pursuant to (4) or (5), may the effect be to render the trial process, viewed as a whole, unfair to the defendant? If Yes, then fuller disclosure should be ordered even if this leads or may lead the prosecution to discontinue the proceedings so as to avoid having to make disclosure.

(7)   If the answer to (6) when first given is No, does that remain the correct answer as the trial unfolds, evidence is adduced and the defence advanced?

It is important that the answer to (6) should not be treated as a final, once-and-for-all, answer but as a provisional answer which the court must keep under review.'

51.   In this context, the following matter are emphasised:

a.   The procedure for making applications to the Court is as set out in the Criminal Procedure Rules 2005, Part 25 (r 25.1–r 25.5);

b.   Where the PII application is a Type 1 or Type 2 application, proper notice to the defence is necessary to allow them to make focused submissions to the court before hearing an application to withhold material; the notice should be as specific as the nature of the material allows. It is appreciated that in some cases only the generic nature of the material can properly be identified. In some wholly exceptional cases (Type 3 cases) it may even be justified to give no notice at all. The judge should always ask the prosecution to justify the form of notice given (or the decision to give no notice at all).

c.   The prosecution should be alert to the possibility of disclosing a statement in redacted form by, for example simply removing personal details. This may obviate the need for a PII application, unless the redacted material in itself would also satisfy the test for disclosure.

d.   Except where the material is very short (say a few sheets only), or where the material is of such sensitivity that [to] do so would be inappropriate, the prosecution should have supplied securely sealed copies to the judge beforehand, together with a short statement of the reasons why each document is said to be relevant and fulfils the disclosure test and why it is said that its disclosure would cause a real risk of serious prejudice to an important public interest; in undertaking this task, the use of merely formulaic expressions is to be discouraged. In any case of complexity a schedule of the material should be provided showing the specific objection to disclosure in relation to each item, leaving a space for the decision.

e.   The application, even if held in private or in secret, should be recorded. The judge should give some short statement of reasons; this is often best done document by document as the hearing proceeds.

f.   The tape, copies of the judge's orders (and any copies of the material retained by the court) should be clearly identified, securely sealed and kept in the court building in a safe or stout lockable cabinet consistent with its security classification, and there should be a proper register of all such material kept. Some arrangement should be made between the court and the prosecution authority for the periodic removal of such material once the case is concluded and the time for an appeal has passed.

Third party disclosure

52.   The disclosure of unused material that has been gathered or generated by a third party is an area of the law that has caused some difficulties: indeed, a Home Office Working Party has been asked to report on it. This is because there is no specific procedure for the disclosure of material held by third parties in criminal proceedings, although the procedure under section 2 of the Criminal Procedure (Attendance of Witnesses) Act 1965 or section 97 of the Magistrates' Courts Act 1980 is often used in order to effect such disclosure. It should, however, be noted that the test applied under both Acts is not the text to be applied under the CPIA, whether in the amended or unamended form. These two provision require that the

material in question is material evidence, ie, immediately admissible in evidence in the proceedings (see in this respect *R v Reading Justices ex parte Berkshire County Council [1996] 1 Cr. App. R. 239, R v Derby Magistrates' Court ex parte B [1996] AC 487; [1996] 1 Cr App R 385 and R v Alibhai and others [2004] EWCA Crim 681*).

53. Material held by other government departments or other Crown agencies will not be prosecution material for the purposes of section 3(2) or section 8(4) of the CPIA, if it has not been inspected, recorded and retained during the course of the relevant criminal investigation. The Attorney General's Guidelines on Disclosure, however, impose a duty upon the investigators and the prosecution to consider whether such departments or bodies have material which may satisfy the test for disclosure under the Act. Where this is the case, they must seek appropriate disclosure from such bodies, who should themselves have an identified point for such enquiries (see paragraphs 47 to 51, Attorney General's Guidelines on Disclosure).

54. Where material is held by a third party such as a local authority, a social services department, hospital or business, the investigators and the prosecution may seek to make arrangements to inspect the material with a view to applying the relevant test for disclosure to it and determining whether any or all of the material should be retained, recorded and, in due course, disclosed to the accused. In considering the latter, the investigators and the prosecution will establish whether the holder of the material wishes to raise PII issues, as a result of which the material may have to be placed before the court. Section 16 of the CPIA gives such a party a right to make representations to the court.

55. Where the third party in question declines to allow inspection of the material, or requires the prosecution to obtain an order before handing over copies of the material, the prosecutor will need to consider whether it is appropriate to obtain a witness summons under either section 2 of the Criminal Procedure (Attendance of Witnesses) Act 1965 or section 97 of the Magistrates' Court Act 1980. However, as stated above, this is only appropriate where the statutory requirements are satisfied, and where the prosecutor considers that the material may satisfy the test for disclosure. *R v Alibhai and others (supra)* makes it clear that the prosecutor has a 'margin of consideration' in this regard.

56. It should be understood that the third party may have a duty to assert confidentiality, or the right to privacy under article 8 of the ECHR, where requests for disclosure are made by the prosecution, or anyone else. Where issues are raised in relation to allegedly relevant third party material, the judge must ascertain whether inquiries with the third party are likely to be appropriate, and, if so, identify who is going to make the request, what

material is to be sought, from whom is the material to be sought and within what time scale must the matter be resolved.

57.   The judge should consider what action would be appropriate in the light of the third party failing or refusing to comply with a request, including inviting the defence to make the request on its own behalf and, if necessary, to make an application for a witness summons. Any directions made (for instance, the date by which an application for a witness summons with supporting affidavit under section 2 of the 1965 [Act] should be served) should be put into writing at the time. Any failure to comply with the timetable must immediately be referred back to the court for further directions, although a hearing will not always be necessary.

58.   Where the prosecution do not consider it appropriate to seek such a summons, the defence should consider doing so, where they are of the view (notwithstanding the prosecution assessment) that the third party may hold material which might undermine the prosecution case or assist that for the defendant, and the material would be likely to be 'material evidence' for the purposes of the 1965 Act. The defence must not sit back and expect the prosecution to make the running. The judge at the PCMH should specifically enquire whether any such application is to be made by the defence and set out a clear timetable. The objectionable practice of defence applications being made in the few days before trial must end.

59.   It should be made clear, though, that 'fishing' expeditions in relation to third party material – whether by the prosecution or the defence – must be discouraged, and that, in appropriate cases, the court will consider making an order for wasted costs where the application is clearly unmeritorious and ill-conceived.

60.   Judges should recognise that a summons can only be issued where the document(s) sought would be admissible in evidence. While it may be that the material in question may be admissible in evidence as a result of the hearsay provisions of the CJA (sections 114 to 120), it is this that determines whether an order for production of the material is appropriate, rather than the wider considerations applicable to disclosure in criminal proceedings: see *R v Reading Justices* (supra), upheld by the House of Lords in *R v Derby Magistrates' Court* (supra).

61.   A number of Crown Court centres have developed local protocols, usually in respect of sexual offences and material held by social services and health and education authorities. Where these protocols exist they often provide an excellent and sensible way to identify relevant material that might assist the defence or undermine the prosecution.

62.   Any application for third party disclosure must identify what documents are sought and why they are said to be material evidence. This is

particularly relevant where attempts are made to access the medical reports of those who allege that they are victims of crime. Victims do not waive the confidentiality of their medical records, or their right to privacy under article 8 of the ECHR, by the mere fact of making a complaint against the accused. Judges should be alert to balance the rights of victims against the real and proven needs of the defence. The court, as a public authority, must ensure that any interference with the article 8 rights of those entitled to privacy is in accordance with the law and necessary in pursuit of a legitimate public interest. General and unspecified requests to trawl through such records should be refused. If material is held by any person in relation to family proceedings (eg, where there have been care proceedings in relation to a child, who has also complained to the police of sexual or other abuse) then an application has to be made by that person to the family court for leave to disclose that material to a third party, unless the third party, and the purpose for which disclosure is made, is approved by Rule 10.20A(3) of the Family Proceedings Rules 1991 (SI 1991 No. 1247). This would permit, for instance, a local authority, in receipt of such material, to disclose it to the police for the purpose of a criminal investigation, or to the CPS, in order for the latter to discharge any obligations under the CPIA.

Conclusion

63.   The public rightly expects that the delays and failures which have been present in some cases in the past where there has been scant adherence to sound disclosure principles will be eradicated by observation of this Protocol. The new regime under the Criminal Justice Act and the Criminal Procedure Rules gives judges the power to change the culture in which such cases are tried. It is now the duty of every judge actively to manage disclosure issues in every case. The judge must seize the initiative and drive the case along towards an efficient, effective and timely resolution, having regard to the overriding objective of the Criminal Procedure Rules (Part 1). In this way the interests of justice will be better served and public confidence in the criminal justice system will be increased.

Appendix 8

Manual of Guidance Forms

(Those forms reproduced in the following pages are marked with an asterisk.)

MG1	File Front Sheet
MG2	Initial Witness Assessment
MG3	Report to Crown Prosecutor for Charging Decision
MG3A	Further Report to Crown Prosecutor for Charging Decision
MG4	Charge Sheet
MG4A	Conditional Bail – Grant/Variation
MG4B	Request to Vary Conditional Bail
MG4C	Surety/Security
MG5	Case Summary
MG6	Case File Information
MG6B	Police Officer's Disciplinary Record
MG6C*	Police Schedule of Non-sensitive Unused Material
MG6D*	Police Schedule of Sensitive Material
MG6E*	Disclosure Officer's Report
MG7	Remand Application
MG8	Breach of Bail Conditions
MG9	Witness List
MG10	Witness Non-availability
MG11	Witness Statement
MG12	Exhibit List
MG13	Application for Order on Conviction
MG15	Record of Interview
MG18	Other Offences (TIC)
MG19	Compensation Claim
MG20*	Further Evidence/Information Report
MG(c)	Continuation Sheet
MGFSP	Submission of Case for Scientific Examination
MGNFA	No Further Action Letter Template

MG 6C

Page No .... of ....

RESTRICTED (when complete)

POLICE SCHEDULE OF NON-SENSITIVE UNUSED MATERIAL

R v ....

URN [ ] [ ] [ ] [ ]

Is there any material in this case which has not been examined by either the investigating or disclosure officer? Yes [ ] No [ ]

If 'Yes' please attach MG11 (refer to the Manual of Guidance)

The Disclosure Officer believes that the following material, which does not form part of the prosecution case, is NOT SENSITIVE.

FOR CPS USE:
* Enter: D = Disclose to defence
I = Defence may inspect
CND = Clearly not disclosable

Item No.	DESCRIPTION AND RELEVANCE (Give sufficient detail for CPS to decide if material should be disclosed or requires more detailed examination)	LOCATION	*	COMMENT

Signature:

Name:

Date:

Reviewing lawyer signature:

Print name:

Date:

2004/05 (1)

281

MG 6D

RESTRICTED/CONFIDENTIAL * –
FOR POLICE AND PROSECUTION ONLY (when complete)

*delete as applicable

POLICE SCHEDULE OF SENSITIVE MATERIAL

R v ....

URN

Page No .... of ....

The Disclosure Officer believes that the following material, which does not form part of the prosecution case, is SENSITIVE.

*Tick if copy supplied to CPS

Item No.	Description	Reason for sensitivity	*

FOR CPS USE		
Agree sensitive Yes/No	Court application Yes/No	CPS views

Signature:

Name:

Date:

Reviewing lawyer signature:

Print name:

Date:

MG 6E

RESTRICTED/CONFIDENTIAL* – FOR POLICE AND PROSECUTION ONLY (when complete)

DISCLOSURE OFFICER'S REPORT

Page No .... of ....

R v ....

URN

The following items are listed on the schedule(s) for this case and might:

*undermine the prosecution case (primary disclosure) / *reasonably assist the defence (secondary disclosure) /
*are required to be supplied under paragraph 7.3 of the Code (see overleaf)   *(*delete as applicable)*.

*Enter C or D to denote schedule MG6C or 6D and enter item no. from schedule

* Schedule	Item no.	Reason	Tick if attached

Certification in all cases:
I certify that, to the best of my knowledge and belief, all material which has been retained and made available to me has been inspected, viewed, or listened to (other than unexamined irrelevant material) and revealed to the prosecutor in accordance with the Criminal Procedure and Investigations Act 1996 Code of Practice, and the Attorney General's Guidelines 2000* and

*(Primary Disclosure only) – those items that might undermine the prosecution are listed above *OR* to the best of my knowledge and belief there are no items that might undermine the prosecution case.

*(Secondary Disclosure only) – items that might assist the defence in the light of the defence statement are listed above *OR* to the best of my knowledge and belief there are no items that might assist the defence in light of the defence statement.
(*Delete as appropriate)

Signature of Disclosure Officer: .... Date:.............................

Name of Disclosure Officer: ....

2004/05 (1)

MG 20

RESTRICTED (when complete)

FURTHER EVIDENCE / INFORMATION REPORT

To: Crown Prosecution Service   URN

Office:..

R v ....

Next Court date:.. at:................................. Magistrates' / Youth / Crown Court

Offence(s):..

Submitted as indicated

Compensation form(s)	☐	Proceedings outstanding further information (as below)	☐
Case file information form	☐	Receipts/estimates re compensation claim	☐
Conviction memorandum (certified copy)	☐	Record(s) of interview	☐
Custody record (copy)	☐	Statement (copy) – witness	☐
Custody record – updated (copy)	☐	Statement (original) – witness	☐
Drink drive forms roadside/hospital/station procedure	☐	Recorded evidence of interview of defendant(s)	☐
DVLA printout	☐	TIC schedule(s)	☐
Exhibit list	☐	Witness availability list updated	☐
Exhibit (copy documents)	☐	Witness – list of convictions/cautions	☐
Medical report/Surgeon's statement (copy)	☐	Witness list	☐
Previous convictions/cautions (defendant's)	☐	Other – specify	☐
Prisoner production copy Home Office order attached	☐		

Further information/remarks (continued on separate sheets if necessary)

All documents indicated above are attached

Officer in case: ....   Rank/Job title: ....   No. ....   Date: ....

Supervisor's name: ....   Rank/Job title:: ....   No. ....   Date: ....

2004/05 (1)

Appendix 9

Defence Statement
Form for use with CPR 2012, Part 22

[Form reproduced overleaf.]

Appendix 9   *Defence Statement*

DEFENCE STATEMENT

(Criminal Procedure and Investigations Act 1996, section 5 & 6; Criminal Procedure and Investigations Act 1996 (Defence Disclosure Time Limits) Regulations 2011; Criminal Procedure Rules, rule 22.4)

Case details

Name of defendant:

Court:

Case reference number:

Charge(s):

When to use this form

If you are a defendant pleading not guilty:

> (a) in a Crown Court case, you **must** give the information listed in Part 2 of this form;

> (b) in a magistrates' court case, you **may** give that information but you do not have to do so.

The time limit for giving the information is:

> **14 days** (in a magistrates' court case)

> **28 days** (in a Crown Court case)

after initial prosecution disclosure (or notice from the prosecutor that there is no material to disclose).

How to use this form

1. Complete the case details box above, and Part 1 below.

2. Attach as many sheets as you need to give the information listed in Part 2.

3. Sign and date the completed form.

4. Send a copy of the completed form to:

> **(a) the court, and**
> **(b) the prosecutor**

> **before the time limit expires.**

If you need more time, you **must** apply to the court **before** the time limit expires. You should apply in writing, but no special form is needed.

Part 1: Plea

I confirm that I intend to plead not guilty to [all the charges] [the following charges] against me:

Part 2: Nature of the defence

Attach as many sheets as you need to give the information required.

Under section 6A of the Criminal Procedure and Investigations Act 1996, you must:

(a) set out the nature of your defence, including any particular defences on which you intend to rely;

(b) indicate the matters of fact on which you take issue with the prosecutor, and in respect of each explain why;

(c) set out particulars of the matters of fact on which you intend to rely for the purposes of your defence;

(d) indicate any point of law that you wish to take, including any point about the admissibility of evidence or about abuse of process, and any authority relied on; and

(e) if your defence statement includes an alibi (i.e. an assertion that you were in a place, at a time, inconsistent with you having committed the offence), give particulars, including –

(i) the name, address and date of birth of any witness who you believe can give evidence in support of that alibi,

(ii) if you do not know all of those details, any information that might help identify or find that witness.

Signed: .... defendant / defendant's solicitor

Date: ....

WARNING: Under section 11 of the Criminal Procedure and Investigations Act 1996, **if you (a) do not disclose what the Act requires; (b) do not give a defence statement before the time limit expires; (c) at trial, rely on a defence, or facts, that you have not disclosed; or (d) at trial, call an alibi witness whom you have not identified in advance, then the court, the prosecutor or another defendant may comment on that, and the court may draw such inferences as it thinks proper in deciding whether you are guilty.**

Defence Witness Notice
Form for use with CPR 2012, Part 22

[Form reproduced on opposite page.]

DEFENCE WITNESS NOTICE

(Criminal Procedure and Investigations Act 1996, section 6C; Criminal Procedure and Investigations Act 1996 (Defence Disclosure Time Limits) Regulations 2011; Criminal Procedure Rules, rule 22.4)

Case details

Name of defendant:

Court:

Case reference number:

Charge(s):

When to use this form

Under section 6C of the Criminal Procedure and Investigations Act 1996, if you are a defendant pleading not guilty you must:

(a) let the court and the prosecutor know **whether you intend to call anyone other than yourself as a witness at your trial;**

(b) do so **not more than -**

14 days (in a magistrates' court case)

28 days (in a Crown Court case)

after initial prosecution disclosure (or notice from the prosecutor that there is no material to disclose);

(c) give as many details of each witness as you can (see the list below);

(d) let the court and the prosecutor know if you later -

(i) decide to call a witness, other than yourself, whom you have not already identified in a defence witness notice,

(ii) decide not to call a witness you have listed in a notice, or

(iii) discover information which you should have included in a notice if you had known it then.

How to use this form

1. Complete the case details box above and give the details required below.

2. Sign and date the completed form.

3. Send a copy of the completed form to:

(a) **the court, and**

(b) **the prosecutor**

before the time limit expires.

If you need more time, you **must** apply to the court **before** the time limit expires. You should apply in writing, but no special form is needed.

List of intended defence witness(es)

1. Do you intend to call anyone other than yourself as a witness at your trial? ☐ **No** **Yes** ☐ If yes, give details below. If you use an electronic version of this form, the boxes will expand. If you use a paper version and need more space, you may attach extra sheets.

Name	Date of birth (if known)	Address, or any other contact or identifying details

2. Have you given a defence witness notice in this case before?
No ☐ Yes ☐ If yes, give the date(s).

Signed: .... [defendant / defendant's solicitor]
Date: ....

WARNING: Under section 11 of the Criminal Procedure and Investigations Act 1996, **if you (a) do not give a defence witness notice before the time limit expires, or (b) at trial, call a witness whom you have not identified in a witness notice then the court, the prosecutor or another defendant may comment on that, and the court may draw such inferences as it thinks proper in deciding whether you are guilty.**

Appendix 11

Pre-trial Witness Interviews: Code of Practice

Introduction

In December 2004 the Attorney General published a report which concluded that prosecutors should be able to speak to witnesses for the purpose of clarifying or assessing the reliability of the evidence they could give. The report also concluded that the interview process should be supported by a Code of Practice. This Code of Practice, issued by the Director of Public Prosecutions, provides guidance to prosecutors conducting pre-trial interviews with witnesses.

Interviews to which this Code of Practice applies

This Code of Practice applies to interviews for the purpose of assisting a prosecutor to assess the reliability of a witness's evidence or to understand complex evidence (referred to throughout this document as a pre-trial interview). It does not apply to other meetings with witnesses such as special measures meetings, court familiarisation visits or meetings to explain a decision to discontinue a case or to significantly alter a charge.

A prosecutor may conduct a pre-trial interview with a witness when they consider that it will enable them to reach a better informed decision about any aspect of the case. Pretrial interviews must not be held for the purpose of improving a witness's evidence or performance although a prosecutor conducting a pre-trial interview may answer a witness's questions about court procedure.

Where a prosecutor conducts a pre-trial interview to assess the reliability of a witness's evidence, the witness may be asked about the content of their statement or other issues that relate to reliability. This may include taking the witness through their statement, asking questions to clarify and expand evidence, asking questions relating to character, exploring new evidence or probing the witness's account.

A pre-trial interview may take place at any stage of the proceedings (including precharge) until the witness starts to give evidence at trial. However, no interview should be conducted until the witness has provided to the police a signed witness statement or has taken part in a visually recorded evidential interview. Once a prosecutor has decided that a pre-trial interview is appropriate it should be conducted as soon as reasonably practicable.

Before a pre-trial interview takes place the prosecutor should consult the Senior Investigating Officer (SIO) (or the officer in the case if there is no SIO). The prosecutor will require confirmation that the person to be interviewed is not, and is not likely to become, a suspect in the case. If there is any possibility that the witness may come under suspicion the interview must not take place until that possibility ceases to exist.

If, during an interview, the witness comes under suspicion, whether in relation to the offence then under investigation or another offence the prosecutor must terminate the interview immediately. The prosecutor can also terminate the interview for other reasons (such as hostility) at any time.

Persons who may conduct an interview

A pre-trial interview may be conducted by a Crown Prosecutor designated by the Chief Crown Prosecutor for their Area or Head of Division to conduct such interviews, or by an independent advocate on the authority of a designated Crown Prosecutor.

Persons present at interview

The presence of a police officer will not normally be necessary but exceptionally the prosecutor or other designated person conducting the interview may request the presence of a police officer if they deem this necessary. The officer attending the interview must be familiar with the case but if possible they should not be the officer who obtained the witness's original statement. An officer attending an interview under these circumstances should play no part in the questioning of the witness. If, as a result of something said in interview, the officer and prosecutor need to confer about an evidential point, the interview should be suspended and the discussion take place in the absence of the witness.

An interview may be conducted by more than one prosecutor or by a prosecutor and an independent advocate. However, where this is done, the interview process should be led by one person.

Other CPS staff may also be present to provide administrative support to the prosecutor.

In any case where the prosecutor considers it necessary for the witness to have the assistance of an interpreter or intermediary, (whether or not the original statement was taken in such manner), the prosecutor shall arrange for the attendance of a suitably qualified person to attend the pre-trial interview. Persons who may themselves be potential witnesses must not act in the role of interpreter or intermediary but a person who assisted in the taking of a witness statement may assist at a pre-trial interview. Prosecutors should refer to existing guidance on the selection of interpreters.

Witness support

The witness may be accompanied by a supporter. The prosecutor must satisfy themself that the supporter has no actual or potential involvement in the case and has no personal knowledge of the matters likely to be discussed. The prosecutor conducting the interview has discretion as to whether the supporter should be permitted to be present at, or remain in, the interview. If the proposed supporter is, in the view of the prosecutor, unsuitable to act as a supporter then the witness should be given an opportunity to arrange for an alternative suitable supporter and the interview should be rearranged for this purpose.

The prosecutor must outline the supporter's role and ensure that they do not prompt, influence or inhibit the witness in any way.

The interview

The attendance of a witness at a pre-trial interview is voluntary and cannot be compelled. If a witness declines to attend a pre-trial interview, this fact and any reasons advanced by the witness should normally be disclosed to the defence in accordance with the prosecutor's disclosure obligations.

The prosecutor must remain objective and dispassionate at all times during the interview. They shall explain to the witness their statutory role, having regard to the duties of the prosecutor set out in the Code for Crown Prosecutors and this Code of Practice. They should also explain in advance to the witness in clear terms the purpose of the interview and deal with any questions that the witness may have in relation to the process.

A witness must not be interviewed in the presence of any other witness in the case (except the officer in the case where they are present at the invitation of the person conducting the interview).

The witness should see copies of their witness statement(s) before or during the interview. Where the witness has participated in a visually recorded interview, they should be given an opportunity of viewing it again. Where the prosecutor considers it to be necessary the witness should be given an opportunity of commenting on the contents of his/her statement or visually recorded interview.

If the witness has seen a copy of their written statement, or has viewed their visually recorded statement in advance of the interview then this fact should be confirmed at the start of the interview.

Where the prosecutor considers it to be necessary, the witness may be shown items or documents exhibited by him/her.

Questioning

Training or coaching for witnesses is not permitted (see R v Momodou and Limani (2005) EWCA Crim 177). Prosecutors must not under any circumstances train, practise or coach the witness or ask questions that may taint the witness's evidence. Leading questions should be avoided.

Where there is significant conflict between witnesses that cannot be resolved by careful questioning, alternative accounts may be put to the witness for comment so long as any source of the alternative account is not attributed. If this is done, it should never be suggested to the witness that they adopt the alternative account.

Prosecutors should remain dispassionate about the responses that a witness gives. In particular they must never suggest to the witness that he/she might be wrong, indicate approval or disapproval in any way to any answer given by the witness. To depart from this standard carries with it the risk of allegations that the witness has been led or coached in their evidence.

Recording and disclosure

A comprehensive audio recording of the interview must be made. If a witness has previously given a visually recorded evidential interview the pre-trial interview may also be video recorded.

Where, in the course of an interview, the witness provides further evidence which is material to the case, a further witness statement should be taken (or visual interview conducted) by a police officer and served upon the defence.

The disclosure officer will be notified of any unused material generated through this process and will record it on the appropriate disclosure schedule.

The record of a pre-trial interview will generally be unused material and disclosure should be determined by the application of the appropriate statutory test(s). A record of a pre-trial interview will normally meet these tests and, subject to the application of Public Interest Immunity, the recording of the interview will be supplied automatically to the defence as unused material. When a recording is supplied to the defence a transcript will not be prepared.

Children and other vulnerable witnesses

Special care will be taken in making a decision to hold a pre-trial interview with a child. The purpose of video recording the evidence in chief of children and other vulnerable witnesses is to preserve their evidence at an early stage and to protect them from the necessity to continually repeat their account during the course of the criminal prosecution process. Further, in cases where children and other vulnerable witnesses are victims of abuse, therapy may have commenced following the video recording of their testimony.

It will only be in exceptional cases, therefore, that pre-trial interviews are considered for children and vulnerable witnesses. Prosecutors will have the benefit of the video recording in order to assess the witness and if there are areas that require further clarification, consideration will be given to asking the original interviewer to explore these by way of an additional video recorded interview. The investigative interviewers will have already built a rapport with the witness and have the special skills required to gently probe the issue in a simple and non-suggestive way.

In reaching a decision to hold a pre-trial interview consideration will be given to the age, degree of vulnerability and status of the witness. Where the original statement was video recorded the pre-trial interview will also be video recorded. The venue must be appropriate for the witness and in most cases the police video interview suite will be used. The witness must have appropriate support and the prosecutor will take advice from the trained police interviewer as to the type and level of questions to be put. The prosecutor must also be conversant with the practice guidance 'Achieving Best Evidence in Criminal Proceedings'.

Witness expenses

A witness will be reimbursed for any expense reasonably incurred in attending the place at which the pre-trial interview is held. This may include the expenses of a supporter. Payment will be in accordance with standard witness allowances.

Remote interviewing

In order to provide the greatest opportunity to assess the reliability or credibility of a witness's evidence, a pre-trial interview should, wherever practicable, involve face to face contact between the prosecutor and the witness. Face-to-face contact affords greater opportunities to the witness to raise issues of concern and to be put at their ease about the process of giving evidence.

However, a prosecutor may at their discretion conduct a pre-trial interview by indirect means including (but not limited to) telephone or video-link. In such cases the prosecutor must make arrangements for a record of the interview to be made in compliance with the requirements set out above.

February 2008

The Crown Prosecution Service

Defendant's Application for Prosecution Disclosure
Form for use with CPR 2012, Part 22 (section 8 application)

[Form reproduced overleaf.]

DEFENDANT'S APPLICATION FOR PROSECUTION DISCLOSURE

(Criminal Procedure and Investigations Act 1996, section 8;
Criminal Procedure Rules, rule 22.5)

Case details

Name of defendant:

Court:

Case reference number:

Charge(s):

Note: You <u>must</u> give a defence statement, and allow the prosecutor time to respond, <u>before</u> you can make an application for prosecution disclosure.

<u>**How to use this form**</u>

1. Complete the Case details box above and answer the questions set out in the boxes below. If you use an electronic version of this form, the boxes will expand. If you use a paper version and need more space, you may attach extra sheets.

2. Attach to this form:

    (a) a copy of your defence statement, and

    (b) copies of any correspondence with the prosecutor about disclosure.

3. Sign and date the completed form.

4. Send a copy of the completed form and everything attached to:

    (a) the court, and

    (b) the prosecutor.

1) What material do you want the prosecutor to disclose?

2) Why do you think the prosecutor has that material?

3) Why might that material:
      (a) undermine the prosecutor's case against you, or
      (b) assist your case?

4) Do you want the court to arrange a hearing of this application? YES / NO

If YES, explain why you think a hearing is needed. (If you do not ask for a hearing, the court may arrange one anyway.)

Signed: .... **defendant / defendant's solicitor**

Date: ....

A Protocol between the Crown Prosecution Service, Police and Local Authorities in the Exchange of Information in the Investigation and Prosecution of Child Abuse Cases

1. PARTIES

The parties to this protocol are the [name of the Local Authority], [name of Police Force] and the Crown Prosecution Service.

2. AIM

The aim of this protocol is to provide an agreed framework between the parties for the sharing and exchange of relevant information in child protection investigations for the purposes of criminal prosecutions in [specify Area].

3. OBJECTIVES

The objectives of this protocol are:

> To provide guidance in obtaining and sharing information between the Parties in order to protect the welfare of children by investigating and prosecuting offenders through the criminal justice system;

> To provide guidance that enables the Parties to apply a consistent approach to information sharing locally; and

> To foster a greater understanding between the Parties of their respective roles within the criminal justice system.

4. INTRODUCTION

4.1   Good practice calls for effective co-operation between the parties; working in the best interests of the child; and careful exercise of professional judgment based on thorough assessment and analysis of relevant information.

This protocol is addressed to those who work in the investigation and prosecution of offenders in relation to child abuse cases.

4.2   The Parties recognise the fundamental importance of inter-agency working in combating child abuse. The Parties are committed to share information and intelligence between them where this is necessary to protect children as set out in The Government's Guidance entitled Working Together to Safeguard Children (1999).

4.3   This protocol recognises:

Social Services and Education departments of Local Authorities will always seek to act in the best interests of the children with whom they are involved; and

The Police and the Crown Prosecution Service are bound by a duty to protect the confidentiality of material held by Local Authorities (dealing with the appropriate Social Services or Education department) and will not disclose to third parties, except with the leave of the court, or with the consent of the Local Authority, any material obtained directly or indirectly as a result of having access to material held by Local Authorities.

5. THE LEGAL FRAMEWORK

5.1   The duties of the Parties are set out in the legal framework at Annex A. This also sets out the legal obligations, on which this protocol is based, of the Parties in relation to exchanging and sharing of information.

6. PROCEDURE

6.1   As soon as the Police investigating a suspected crime believe material exists within the Social Services and Education files which may be relevant to the investigation, they will notify the Local Authority by means of a written notice.

6.2   The Police will appoint, as appropriate, a suitably trained disclosure officer who will carry out the examination of relevant material on Social Services and Education files held by the Local Authority and whose task it will be to liaise with the Local Authority.

6.3   The written notice used by the police disclosure officer will include: (see attached draft letter at Annex B)

The identity and contact details of the police disclosure officer;

The identity and contact details of the officer in the case;

A summary of the case and the details of the offences being investigated;

A statement of the relevant information which is sought from the records in order to pursue all reasonable lines of enquiry, and why that information is thought likely to be relevant to the investigation;

A statement of how failure to disclose relevant information would prejudice or delay the investigation.

6.4   Upon receipt of a request from the Police under 6.3, the Local Authority will appoint a suitably trained disclosure officer from the legal department who will liaise with the Police disclosure officer throughout the enquiry. The Local Authority disclosure officer will identify and collate relevant material from the Social Services/Education files which it is necessary to disclose for the purposes of the police investigation, in the light of the information provided by the Police in 6.3 above.[1] The review by the police will usually take place on Local Authority premises but may be elsewhere by agreement between the disclosure officers.

6.5   The Local Authority will ensure that documents filed in family court proceedings are not included in the files to be seen by the police and/or Crown Prosecution Service. Where there are documents filed in family court proceedings, the Local Authority will provide a list of that material without describing what it is, in order for the police, if appropriate, to apply to the Family Court for disclosure.

6.6   The Local Authority will not reveal to the police relevant medical reports or other medical information without the consent of the author of that material. Where there is such material, the Local Authority will seek consent from the author to reveal it to the police. Where consent is refused, the Local Authority will inform the police that the material exists. The police and the Crown Prosecution Service may seek consent from the author of the material and/or apply for a witness summons to obtain the material.

6.7   When the Local Authority voluntarily discloses material to the defence they will reveal it to the police and/or Crown Prosecution Service. In addition, when the defence request material from the Local Authority under the Data Protection Act 1998, the Local Authority will notify the police and/or Crown Prosecution Service of the fact of that request.

6.8   The Police disclosure officer will be given priority to review the material within a specified period oftime.[2] If there are difficulties in complying with the agreed timescale or if the material is ready for review more quickly, the Local Authority disclosure officer will notify the Police disclosure officer immediately.

---

1   At this stage, the local authority will disclose to the police information that is relevant for the purposes of the police investigation. This does not mean that the local authority, by so doing, is agreeing that the information disclosed to the police should in due course be disclosed to the defence. Such disclosure will be decided either by agreement between the local authority and The CPS or in default of such an agreement, an order of the court made under the CIPA.

2   To be agreed between local signatories.

6.9   Where the Police review the material, the Local Authority will accept that the Police may take notes or copies of the material as appropriate, as they require for the purposes of their investigation. The Police will accept that any material they read and any notes or copies they take are to be regarded as sensitive material which is subject to public interest immunity.

6.10   Any material identified by the Police disclosure officer during the review as being relevant to the issues in any criminal proceedings which may undermine the prosecution case or may reasonably assist any apparent defence case, must be brought to the attention of the Local Authority disclosure officer with a view to the Police disclosure officer obtaining a copy of the relevant documents. Any copy documents provided by the Local Authority to the Police will be treated as sensitive material which is subject to public interest immunity.

6.11   When the Police submit a full file to the Crown Prosecution Service, including all correspondence between the Police and the Local Authority, the Police disclosure officer will identify all unused material on the appropriate (MG) forms and in particular material that is viewed and obtained from the Local Authority. It will be the duty of the Police disclosure officer to identify any material which might undermine the prosecution case or might reasonably assist the defence case.

6.12   In the event of further relevant material coming into the possession of the Social Services and Education departments, the Local Authority disclosure officer will disclose to the Police disclosure officer that material and will provide a continuous opportunity to review and take copies of that material. Further, it is accepted by the Local Authority that as an enquiry develops, the material may have to be re-visited.

6.13   On receipt of the full file the Crown Prosecution Service will review the unused material in accordance with its statutory duties under the Criminal Procedure and Investigations Act 1996 (CPIA).

6.14   The Crown Prosecution Service shall treat all material disclosed by the Local Authority as sensitive material.

6.15   Where any Local Authority material reviewed by the Crown Prosecution Service falls within the statutory disclosure tests under the CPIA, the Crown Prosecution Service shall write to the Local Authority disclosure officer, within a number of days[3] of review, setting out the reasons why the material falls to be disclosed and informing them of that decision. Within a number of days[4] of receipt of that notification, the Local Authority disclosure officer shall be given an opportunity to make any representations in writing to the Crown Prosecution Service on the issues of disclosure.

---

3   To be agreed between local signatories.
4   To be agreed between local signatories.

6.16   The Crown Prosecution Service will not disclose any material to the defence unless by agreement with the Local Authority or by order of the court following a public interest immunity application.

6.17   If the Local Authority agrees with the Crown Prosecution Service to disclose material identified by the Crown Prosecution Service which falls within the statutory disclosure tests under the CPIA, the Crown Prosecution Service will disclose the material to the defence.

6.18   If the Local Authority asserts public interest immunity and objects to disclosure, to the defence, of any material identified by the Crown Prosecution Service which falls within the statutory disclosure tests under the CPIA, the Crown Prosecution Service will make a public interest immunity application to the court as soon as reasonably practical. The Crown Prosecution Service will notify the Local Authority of the date and venue of the public interest immunity application and inform the Local Authority of their rights to make representations to the court under the Crown Court (Criminal Procedure and Investigations Act 1996) (Disclosure) Rules 1997 and the Magistrates' Court (Criminal Procedure and Investigations Act 1996) (Disclosure) Rules 1997.

6.19   Following receipt of a defence statement, the Police disclosure officer will send a copy of the defence statement to the Local Authority disclosure officer.

6.20   The Local Authority disclosure officer will reconsider the relevance of the material held by the Local Authority in the light of the defence statement. Where the Local Authority identify further material to be revealed, the Local Authority disclosure officer will notify the Police disclosure officer of that material.

6.21   The Police disclosure officer will review that material held by the Local Authority and any material previously revealed to the Police for the purposes of carrying out secondary disclosure. The Local Authority disclosure officer will arrange for the material to be available for further review by the Police disclosure officer within a number of[5] working days of receiving a written request. The Local Authority disclosure officer will retain a copy of the defence statement.

6.22   In the event of the Defence making an application under section 8 of the CPIA for further disclosure of material held by the Local Authority and already considered by the Police and/or the Crown Prosecution Service in the criminal proceedings, the Crown Prosecution Service will liaise with the Police and Local Authority disclosure officers prior to the hearing of the application.

6.23   Where the defence apply for a witness summons against the Local Authority for disclosure of material not in the possession of the Police or the Crown Prosecution Service, the Local Authority will inform the Police disclosure

---

5   To be agreed between local signatories.

officer and the Crown Prosecution Service of the time and place of the hearing of the witness summons and the nature and grounds of such an application.

6.24   The Prosecutor has a duty to keep under continuing review the question of whether there is any unused material, which might undermine the prosecution case or might reasonably assist the defence case. The Parties recognise that they may need to review the material again if other issues become relevant during the course of the criminal proceedings.

6.25   In the event that there are no criminal proceedings, or the proceedings are discharged, or the accused is acquitted, the police and/or Crown Prosecution Service will return all material in their possession belonging to the Local Authority.

7. SCHOOLS AND OTHER ORGANISATIONS INVOLVED IN THE CARE OF CHILDREN

7.1   Where the Police investigating a suspected crime believe material exists with Schools the Police should contact the Local Authority to identify the status of the school. Where the Local Authority identifies the school as an Independent School, it should inform the police, so that the police may approach the school directly to obtain the material.

7.2   The Parties to this protocol would encourage other organisations that are involved in the care of children, to follow the provisions laid down in this protocol in the sharing of information with the Police and Crown Prosecution Service in criminal proceedings.

8. MISCELLANEOUS PROVISIONS

8.1   In some cases to which this protocol applies a child concerned may be (or have been) the subject of court proceedings in the family jurisdiction. Nothing in this protocol authorises the disclosure of any document filed with the court in such proceedings or any information relating to them. This applies whether the proceedings are concluded or still pending. If material is identified that falls into this category then leave must be obtained from the court in which the family proceedings are being (or were) conducted.

8.2   This protocol does not diminish the existing legal rights of the Parties. Specifically, it will not operate to restrict the right of any Party to claim public interest immunity in connection with any material which has come within the ambit of the police investigation.

8.3   All signatories to this protocol accept that the protocol is entered into in good faith and on that basis all signatories will use their best endeavours to comply with their terms and the spirit of the protocol.

8.4 Effect should be given to this protocol locally by a suitable service level agreement between the Parties, and any other organisation that the Parties think appropriate.

8.5   Any disagreement over the workings of this protocol or local arrangements will be referred to the agreed level of management for early and informal resolution, wherever possible.

8.6   The Parties will at an agreed interval, monitor the workings of this protocol and any local agreement with a view to improving the efficiency and the well being of local professional working arrangements.

ANNEX A

Legal Framework

INTRODUCTION

1.   Professionals can only work together effectively to protect children if there is an exchange of relevant information between them. This has been recognised by the courts. In Re G (a minor) [1996] 2 AER 65 Butler Sloss LJ said: 'The consequences of interagency co-operation is that there has to be a free exchange of information between social workers and police officers together engaged in an investigation ... The information obtained by social workers in the course of their duties is however confidential and covered by the umbrella of public interest immunity ... It can however be disclosed to fellow members of the child protection team engaged in the investigation of possible abuse of the child concerned'.

2.   Any disclosure of personal information to others must always have regard to both common law and statute law. This framework sets out the legal position of the local authority, police and the Crown Prosecution Service in relation to exchanging and sharing of information.

THE COMMON LAW OF CONFIDENTIALITY

3.   Personal information about children and families held by the agencies is subject to the legal duty of confidence, and should not normally be disclosed without the consent of the subject. The law permits the disclosure of confidential information where a countervailing public interest can be identified. Such a public interest might relate to the proper administration of justice and to the prevention of wrongdoing. The court in R v Chief Constable of North Wales

Police, ex parte Thorpe [1996] QB 396 Lord Bingham CJ considered that where a public body acquires information relating to a member of the public which is not generally available and is potentially damaging, the body ought not to disclose such information save for the purpose of and to the extent necessary for performance of its public duty or enabling some other public body to perform its public duty.

4.   There is a public interest in the prevention and detection of crime and in the apprehension or prosecution of offenders. Both domestic case law and the Data Protection Act 1998 recognise that it may be necessary for a local social services authority or education authority to disclose confidential material in its possession to the police for the purposes of a police investigation or criminal proceedings. The material to be disclosed must be both relevant and necessary for the purposes of the police investigation.

5.   The information the Parties to this protocol possess will have usually come to the local authority from the individual him/herself and a range of other sources. There is no publication to any member of the public. The purpose of disclosure is to facilitate the more effective administration of justice, either by providing further evidence of criminal conduct or by revealing the hopelessness of cases that might otherwise have reached the trial stage. Therefore, disclosure of material between the Parties to this protocol is permitted both by the general law on confidentiality and in particular by the law governing such disclosures by public bodies.

6.   It is acknowledged that the law in the disclosure of confidential information is complex. There are restrictions on the sharing of information between the parties under the Data Protection Act and the Human Rights Act. However, the sharing of information is not necessarily contrary to these Acts.

DATA PROTECTION ACT 1998

7.   The Data Protection Act 1998 (the 1998 Act) requires that personal information is obtained and processed fairly and lawfully; only disclosed in appropriate circumstances; is accurate, relevant and not held longer than necessary; and is kept securely. The Act allows for disclosure without the consent of the subject in certain conditions, including for the purposes of the prevention or detection of crime, or the apprehension or prosecution of offenders, and where failure to disclose would be likely to prejudice those objectives in a particular case.

8.   When disclosing personal information, many of the data protection issues surrounding disclosure can be avoided if the consent of the individual has been sought and obtained. Where consent of the individual is not sought, or is sought but withheld, there can be an exchange of information between the Parties

where there is an overriding public interest or justification for doing so. The Act contains general nondisclosure provisions, but sections 27–31 provide a number of specific exemptions. Section 29 covers crime. In the context of social services and education material, personal data processed for the purposes of prevention or detection of crime and the apprehension or prosecution of offenders is exempt from the first data principle (except to the extent to which it complies with the requirements of the second and third schedules of the 1998 Act).

9.   Section 35 of the 1998 Act allows for disclosure by exempting data from the nondisclosure provisions (except to the extent to which it complies with the requirements of the second and third schedules of the 1998 Act), where disclosure is required by any enactment, rule of law, or an order of the court and, where disclosure is necessary for the purpose of, or in connection with, any legal proceedings (including prospective legal proceedings), or for the purpose of obtaining legal advice or is necessary for the purposes of establishing, exercising or defending legal rights.

10.   This means that the exchange of relevant information between the Parties in this protocol is not restricted under the Act because it will nearly always be the case that the exemptions constitute an overriding public interest in favour of sharing the information.

CRIMINAL PROCEDURE AND INVESTIGATIONS ACT 1996

11.   The Criminal Procedure and Investigations Act 1996 (the 1996 Act), the Code of Practice made under section 23 of the 1996 Act, and the Attorney General's Guidelines on the disclosure of information in criminal proceedings, published November 2000, govern the disclosure of unused prosecution material to the defence. Guidance to the police and the Crown Prosecution Service is contained in the Joint Operational Instructions. The 1996 Act applies to all criminal investigations begun on or after 1 April 1997 and applies to a two-stage disclosure process. As soon as reasonably practicable after a not guilty plea in the Magistrates' Court, or service of the prosecution case, committal or transfer to the Crown Court, the prosecution must disclose to the defence any prosecution material that has not been previously disclosed and which might undermine the prosecution case (primary disclosure).

12.   In Crown Court cases, the defence is required to provide, within 14 days of primary disclosure by the prosecution, a statement setting out in general terms their defence and particulars of any alibi witnesses. On receipt of the defence statement, the prosecution must as soon as reasonably practicable disclose any further material which may reasonably be expected to assist the accused's defence, as disclosed by the defence statement (secondary disclosure).

13.   In magistrates' court cases, the defence may give a defence statement to the prosecutor. The requirements of a defence statement voluntarily given in Magistrates' Court cases are the same as those in Crown Court cases.

14.   Throughout the proceedings, the prosecution is under a continuing duty to keep under review whether material should be disclosed to the defence. After the defence has provided a defence statement, the 1996 Act enables them to apply to the court for an order requiring the prosecution to disclose material if the defence considers that the prosecution has failed to comply with secondary disclosure.

15.   Where the prosecution holds relevant sensitive material that meets the criteria for disclosure under the 1996 Act, then a public interest immunity application should be made to the court to withhold this material from the defence. Any decision to withhold such material is a matter for the court to determine.

16.   Public interest immunity (PII) enables the courts to reconcile two conflicting public interests – the public interest in the fair administration of justice and the need to maintain the confidentiality of information the disclosure of which would be damaging to the public interest. PII is an exception to the general rule that all material which falls within the tests for disclosure must be disclosed. Special care needs to be taken in deciding where the balance lies between the two competing public interests.

17.   Local authority social services files are no longer a 'class' of material to which PII automatically applies. Each case, and each document should be considered individually. Where PII can, or may apply, the local authority may itself conduct the balancing exercise and agree that, in an individual case, the conflicting public interest in the investigation and prosecution of crime overrides the PII interests in confidentiality R v Chief Constable of West Midlands Police ex parte Wiley [1995] 1 AC 274.

18.   The position of PII with respect to social services files has recently been summarised in Re R (Care: Disclosure: Nature of Proceedings) [2002] 1 FLR 755. Any person advancing a claim to PII in respect of material held by a local authority should set out with particularity the harm that it is alleged will be caused to the public interest. Before embarking on a claim for PII, consideration should be given to the question whether the material passes the threshold test for disclosure under the Criminal Procedure and Investigations Act 1996, and if so why.

THE EUROPEAN CONVENTION ON HUMAN RIGHTS

19.   The Human Rights Act 1998 gives effect to the rights and freedoms guaranteed under the European Convention on Human Rights. Article 6 ensures that every accused has the right to fair trial. It states that in the determination of his civil rights and obligations or of any criminal charge against him, everyone is

entitled to a fair and public hearing within a reasonable time by an independent and impartial tribunal established by law. Article 8 protects the right to respect for private and family life, home and correspondence.

20.   Article 6 is a 'special' right which means that it cannot be balanced against other public interests. On the other hand, Article 8 is a 'qualified' right which means that it can be interfered with where it is in the interests of national security, public safety or the economic well-being of the country, for the prevention of disorder or crime, for the protection of health or morals, or for the protection of the rights and freedoms of others.

21.   The court will order disclosure of information regarding sexual and physical abuse of children (social service and education records) where it is necessary for an accused to have a fair trial (Article 6). The court will also order disclosure of the information where it is necessary for the protection of health or morals, for the protection of the rights and freedoms of others and for the prevention of disorder or crime (Article 8(2)). Disclosure should be appropriate for the purpose and only to the extent necessary to achieve that purpose.

JOINT INVESTIGATIONS

22.   Section 26 of the 1996 Act provides that a person other than a police officer, who is charged with a duty of conducting an investigation with a view to it being ascertained, whether a person should be charged with an offence, or whether a person charged with an offence is guilty, shall have regard to any of the provisions in the Code of Practice made under the 1996 Act. Material obtained by social services in the course of an investigation under section 47 of the Children Act 1989, which may be obtained jointly with the police, but not in the possession of the police, is not subject to section 26. However, it is acknowledged that where such material is obtained jointly with the police, the local authority should as a matter of good practice, have regard to the Code of Practice.

23.   Relevant material acquired during the course of a joint investigation should be given to the police disclosure officer and listed on a sensitive or non-sensitive MG form. If there is any disagreement between the police and the local authority on the material, then this will be resolved by the Court by way of a public interest immunity application (see section 16 of the 1996 Act). Where material which has been jointly obtained is in the possession of the police, then that material is subject to the provisions of the Criminal Procedure and Investigations Act 1996.

24.   In most cases social workers will be involved where the police are investigating allegations of sexual or physical abuse of children. In addition to complying with the 1996 Act, they should also adopt the Attorney General's

guidelines and have regard [to] Article 6 of the European Convention on Human Rights.

NON-JOINT INVESTIGATIONS

25.   Where a person subject to a criminal investigation has not been charged, it is often the case that the investigating police officer will require to know about the background of the complainant, family and associates. Such information may be helpful in assessing the veracity of any complaint and the likelihood of conviction. Occasionally, if the local authority had disclosed material to the police at an earlier stage the person under investigation would not have been charged.

26.   In these circumstances, the only mechanism to enable the investigators to make application to the court for the disclosure of such material is to consider whether it is appropriate to make an application for Special Procedure Material, under Schedule 1 of the Police and Criminal Evidence Act 1984. However, this is not a satisfactory approach because it goes against the ethos and spirit of the Parties exchanging and sharing information where it is necessary to protect children.

27.   Therefore, where full details of the nature of the investigation and the reasons for requiring such material are given to the local authority and that the material is treated as confidential, then it is in the interests of justice for there to be disclosure of relevant material before charge. This would be considered 'necessary' in accordance with Schedule 3 of the 1998 Act.

28.   Where a person has been charged with an offence and the social services and/or education departments of a local authority have not been involved in the investigation, but holds or is believed to hold material that could be relevant, then the local authority fall within the category of a third party. The procedure for the police in obtaining such information should be in accordance with this protocol.

29.   Schedule 2 of the 1998 Act allows disclosure of non-sensitive material. Such material should be listed on a nonsensitive material form which will be sent, together with the material, to the police disclosure officer who will forward it to the Crown Prosecution Service.

30.   The majority of the material held by a local authority will be of a confidential nature. Where the conditions are met in Schedule 3 of the 1998 Act, material should be revealed to the police disclosure officer and the Crown Prosecution Service. The material should be listed on a sensitive material schedule and this together with the documents should be given to the police disclosure officer and the Crown Prosecution Service. Where the local authority assert public interest immunity then section 16 of the 1996 Act provides that the

court must not make a disclosure order unless a person claiming an interest in the material is given the opportunity to be heard.

31.   Paragraphs 30–33 of the Attorney General's Guidelines refer to material held by other agencies, which includes a local authority. If it is believed by the investigator, the police disclosure officer or the prosecutor that it is reasonable to seek production of material held by the local authority and the request is refused then application should be made for a witness summons requiring production of the material to the court. The prosecution should be pro-active in such circumstances.

CONCLUSION

32.   The aim of the protocol is to provide an agreed framework between the Parties for the sharing and exchange of relevant material in child protection investigations. While there is a difficult balance between the local authority complying with their duty of confidentiality, and the police and the Crown Prosecution Service obtaining relevant material from the local authority at the earliest stage possible in any criminal investigation, there are no legal reasons why the Parties should not exchange the material expeditiously, as outlined in this protocol. This would benefit everyone involved in any criminal child protection investigation and promote the efficiency of the criminal justice system.

ANNEX B

Draft Notice from the Police Disclosure Officer to the Local Authority Legal Department

IN CONFIDENCE

Date:

Heading

Dear Sir/Madam

PROTECTION OF CHILDREN: REQUEST FOR DISCLOSURE OF MATERIAL HELD BY

_____ [INSERT NAME OF COUNCIL]

_____ Police are conducting a criminal investigation into allegations made against _____ [name of the alleged offender] of _____ [address of alleged offender], _____ [date of birth].

The allegations being investigated are, in general terms, that _____
[set out the circumstances of the offence(s) being investigated and the charges if any.]

The following child is the alleged victim of the offences:

Name of the child: _____

Address: _____

Date of Birth: _____

Social worker/office previously involved: _____

Relationship to the alleged offender (if any): _____

Name and dates of the school attended (if appropriate): _____

Other children in the family:_____

In addition, we have obtained evidence from the following child/children:

Name of child: _____

Address: _____

Date of Birth: _____

Social worker/office previously involved: _____

Relationship to the alleged offender (if any): _____

Name and dates of the school attended (if appropriate): _____

I believe that your Authority may hold material relating to the alleged offender or the above-mentioned child/children, which may be relevant to our investigation.

[Set out the nature of the material sought and the reasons why it may be relevant to the criminal investigation]

I should be grateful if you would ascertain whether or not your Authority holds any such material.

[Set out any prejudice or delay to the investigation, which may be caused by the material not being disclosed.]

Any material obtained by us in the course of our investigation will be treated as sensitive and dealt with in accordance with the Criminal Procedure and Investigations Act 1996.

I should be grateful if you were able to reply by _____ [date].

I should be grateful if you would reply to me at the above address. If you wish to discuss this request, or any further information, please do not hesitate to contact either myself or _____ [name of officer] on _____ [telephone number].

Thank you in advance for your assistance.

Yours faithfully,

Officer in charge of the Investigation/Disclosure Officer

Plea and Case Management Hearing Form: Advocates' Questionnaire For use with CPR 2012, Part 3

[Form reproduced overleaf.]

Appendix 14 *PCMH Form: Advocates' Questionnaire*

The Crown Court	Plea and Case Managemen Hearing
CC Case Number D1 [＿＿＿＿＿＿]	**Advocates' Questionnaire**
Date of trial [＿＿＿＿＿＿]	⬚Parties must complete this form.
Fixed ☐ Warned ☐	⬚This form is to be used at all Crown Court Centres, without local variation. There is an electronic version of the form on the Ministry of Justice website, at: http://www.justice.gov.uk/guidance/courts-and-tribunals/courts/procedure-rules/criminal/formspage.htm

---

PART ONE
(Questions 1 to 15 are to be completed in all cases, together with question 37 'Witness Lis

1   Date of trial and custody time limits

1.1   Date of PCMH   PTI URN

[＿＿＿＿＿＿＿＿＿]   [＿＿＿＿＿＿＿＿＿]

Judge   Estimated length of trial

[＿＿＿＿＿＿＿＿＿]   [＿＿＿＿＿＿＿＿＿]

1.2   What are the custody time limit expiry dates as agreed between the parties? *(If different custody time limits attach to different offences or defendants, please give details.)*

[＿＿＿＿＿＿＿＿＿＿＿＿＿＿＿＿＿＿]

1.3   Can an application to extend any custody time limit be made today?   ☐ No ☐ Yes

2   Parties

Parties' names	Age	Remand status	Instructed Advocate	PCMH Advocate (if not the Instructed Advocate)
P				
D1		C ☐ B ☐		

316

Contact details

Parties

P   Office

Name	Phone
Email	

Advocate

Name	Phone
Email	

D1   Solicitor

Name	Phone
Email	

Advocate

Name	Phone
Email	

Case progression officers

Name	Phone
Email	

1

Name	Phone
Email	

urt

Name	Phone
Email	

Which, if any, of the orders made at the magistrates' court have not been complied with?

D1   Has the defendant been advised that he or she will receive credit for a guilty plea?   ☐ No ☐ Yes

D1   Has the defendant been warned that the case may proceed in his or her absence?   ☐ No ☐ Yes

What plea(s) is / are the defendant(s) offering?

D1

Should the case be referred to the Resident Judge for a trial judge to be allocated?   ☐ No ☐ Yes

9   Give details of any issues relating to the fitness to plead or to stand trial.

D1

10   **Disclosure, the defence statement and notification of defence witnesses**

10.1   Has the prosecution made statutory disclosure?

P

D1

10.2   Has a defence statement been served?

D1

10.3   Does it comply with the statutory requirements?

P

10.4   If not clear from the defence statement, what are the real issues?

D1

10.5
D1   Has / will the defence made / make an application in writing under section 8 of the Criminal Procedure and Investigations Act 1996?   ☐ No   ☐ Yes

10.6
D1   Has the time limit for the notification of defence witnesses expired?   ☐ No   ☐ Yes

If yes, give particulars (preferably on the relevant from of Notice).

If no, can any orders be made even at this stage?   ☐ No   ☐ Yes

Details of any proposed order(s)

11   **Further evidence**

What further evidence is to be served by the prosecution? By when is it reasonably practicable to serve this?

P

2 Expert evidence

2.1 Give details of any expert evidence likely to be relied upon, including why it is required and by when it is reasonably practicable to serve this.

P

D1

2.2 Is a note of agreement / disagreement required?

3 Witnesses

3.1 Have the parties completed the Witness List (see 37)? ☐ No ☐ Yes

3.2 Are the parties satisfied that all the listed witnesses are needed (see 37)? ☐ No ☐ Yes
If 'no', give details.

3.3 Are the parties satisfied that the time estimates for questioning witnesses are realistic (see 37)? ☐ No ☐ Yes
If 'no', give details.

3.4 Is any witness summons necessary? ☐ No ☐ Yes
If 'yes', give particulars:

3.5 Can a timetable be fixed now for the calling of witnesses? ☐ No ☐ Yes
If 'no', why not?

4 Timetabling of the trial

4.1 Are there matters which need to be determined at the start of the trial, which may affect the timetable? ☐ No ☐ Yes

> If so, when will (1) the jury and (2) the witnesses be required?

14.2   What timetable can now be set for the conduct of the trial (see rule 3.10)?

15   The indictment

15.1   Has the indictment been signed and dated as required by Part 14 of the CrimPR?   ☐ No ☐ Ye

15.2   Is any amendment of the indictment required?   ☐ No ☐ Ye

---

PART TWO question 37 (Witness list) is to be completed in every case

Answer the remaining questions only where relevant

---

16   Admissions and agreed facts

What matters can usefully be admitted or put into schedules, diagrams, visual aids etc.?

17   Case summary

P   Is it proposed to serve a case summary or note of opening?   ☐ No ☐ Ye

18   Measures to assist witnesses and defendants in giving evidence

18A   **Measures to assist a witness in giving evidence.**

> *Each of these issues must be addressed separately in respect of each young vulnerable or intimidated witness who is may be required to give evidence in person. (If completed electronically, the form will expand to deal with each separai witness separately. If completed manually, attach separate sheets if necessary.)*
>
> Name and age of witness:
>
> name: age:

What arrangements have been made for a pre-trial visit?

What arrangements have been made to ensure that the witness sees the video of their evidence BEFORE the trial (i.e. not immediately before giving their evidence over the live link)?

Has the witness been offered a 'supporter'?　　　　　　　　　　　　　☐ No　　☐ Yes
If 'yes', give particulars:

Does the witness need an intermediary?　　　　　　　　　　　　　　☐ No　　☐ Yes
If 'yes', give particulars:

What arrangements have been made for the witness to access the court building other than by the main public entrance?

What are the arrangements to ensure that this witness can give evidence without waiting or at least by reducing waiting to a minimum *(e.g. by ensuring that the opening and any preliminary points will be finished before the time appointed for the witness to attend or by agreeing and fixing a timed witness order in advance)*?

Have the views of the witness been sought and, if so, has s/he expressed any particular view or concerns?　　　　　　　　　　　　　　　　　　　　　　　☐ No　　☐ Yes

If 'yes', give particulars:

If views not sought, why not?

What material (if any) needs to be available to the witness in the video suite?

Defendant's evidence direction

Is any defendant's evidence direction to be sought?	☐ No	☐ Yes
If so, has the necessary application been made, complying with Section 4 of CrimPR Part 29?	☐ No	☐ Yes

If so, give details

18C **Witness anonymity order**

Is any witness anonymity order sought / to be made?	☐ No ☐ Ye
If so, has an application been made, complying with Section 5 of CrimPR Part 29?	☐ No ☐ Ye
If so give details (subject to the restrictions in Section 5 of CrimPR Part 29).	

19 Young or vulnerable defendants

Are any other arrangements needed for any young or vulnerable defendants?

D1

20 Reporting restrictions

State type and grounds of any reporting restriction sought.

P

D1

21 Third party material

21. Is any application to be made for the production of third party material?   ☐ No   ☐ Yes

22 Defendant's interview(s)

22.1 Specify any issue relating to the admissibility of all or any part of the defendant's interview(s). Can the issue be resolv now ? If not, when ? Are skeleton arguments needed and, if so, when ?

22.2 By how much can the interview(s) be shortened by editing / summary for trial ? Give a timetable for the service of any proposed summary by the prosecution and agreement / counter-proposal by the defence.

Hearsay

Are any directions necessary in relation to hearsay applications? Are there to be any further applications?

P

1

Admissibility and legal issues

What points on admissibility / other legal issues are to be taken? Is it necessary for any to be resolved before trial?

P

1

Public interest immunity

Is any 'on notice' public interest immunity application to be made?

P

Jury bundle

What proposals do the prosecution make for a jury bundle?

P

Concurrent family proceedings

Give details of any concurrent family proceedings.

34 Other special arrangements

Give details of any special arrangements (e.g., interpreter, intermediary, wheelchair access, hearing loop system, breaks) needed for anyone attending the trial.

35 Linked criminal proceedings

Are there other criminal proceedings against the defendant or otherwise linked?

36 Additional orders

Are any additional orders required?

37 Witness List (see table for completion, over page)

Witness List

The parties should indicate here which prosecution witnesses are required to give evidence at trial. The attendance of any witness is subject to the judge's direction.

Name of witness	Page No.	Required by	What is the relevant, disputed issue?	Estimated time for questioning	
				Chief	X - exam

Appendix 15

Criminal Procedure Rules 2012 (SI 2012/1726), Part 28

Part 28
Witness Summonses, Warrants and Orders

Contents of this Part

[Note. A magistrates' court may require the attendance of a witness to give evidence or to produce in evidence a document or thing by a summons, or in some circumstances a warrant for the witness' arrest, under section 97 of the Magistrates' Courts Act 1980. The Crown Court may do so under sections 2, 2D, 3 and 4 of the Criminal Procedure (Attendance of Witnesses) Act 1965. Either court may order the production in evidence of a copy of an entry in a banker's book without the attendance of an officer of the bank, under sections 6 and 7 of the Bankers' Books Evidence Act 1879.

See Part 3 for the court's general powers to consider an application and to give directions.]

When this Part applies

28.1.–(1)   This Part applies in magistrates' courts and in the Crown Court where –

       (a)   a party wants the court to issue a witness summons, warrant or order under –

(i)   section 97 of the Magistrates' Courts Act 1980,

(ii)   section 2 of the Criminal Procedure (Attendance of Witnesses) Act 1965, or

(iii)   section 7 of the Bankers' Books Evidence Act 1879;

(b)   the court considers the issue of such a summons, warrant or order on its own initiative as if a party had applied; or

(c)   one of those listed in rule 28.7 wants the court to withdraw such a summons, warrant or order.

(2)   A reference to a 'witness' in this Part is a reference to a person to whom such a summons, warrant or order is directed.

[Note. See section 2D of the Criminal Procedure (Attendance of Witnesses) Act 1965 for the Crown Court's power to issue a witness summons on the court's own initiative.]

Issue etc. of summons, warrant or order with or without a hearing

28.2.– (1)   The court may issue or withdraw a witness summons, warrant or order with or without a hearing.

(2)   A hearing under this Part must be in private unless the court otherwise directs.

[Note. If rule 28.5 applies, a person served with an application for a witness summons will have an opportunity to make representations about whether there should be a hearing of that application before the witness summons is issued.]

Application for summons, warrant or order: general rules

28.3.–(1)   A party who wants the court to issue a witness summons, warrant or order must apply as soon as practicable after becoming aware of the grounds for doing so.

(2)   The party applying must –

(a)   identify the proposed witness;

(b)   explain –

(i)   what evidence the proposed witness can give or produce,

(ii)   why it is likely to be material evidence, and

(iii)   why it would be in the interests of justice to issue a summons, order or warrant as appropriate.

(3)   The application may be made orally unless –

(a)   rule 28.5 applies; or

(b)   the court otherwise directs.

[Note. The court may issue a warrant for a witness' arrest if that witness fails to obey a witness summons directed to him: see section 97(3) of the Magistrates' Courts Act 1980 and section 4 of the Criminal Procedure (Attendance of Witnesses) Act 1965. Before a magistrates' court may issue a warrant under section 97(3) of the 1980 Act, the witness must first be paid or offered a reasonable amount for costs and expenses.]

Written application: form and service

28.4.–(1)   An application in writing under rule 28.3 must be in the form set out in the Practice Direction, containing the same declaration of truth as a witness statement.

(2)   The party applying must serve the application –

(a)   in every case, on the court officer and as directed by the court; and

(b)   as required by rule 28.5, if that rule applies.

[Note. Declarations of truth in witness statements are required by section 9 of the Criminal Justice Act 1967 and section 5B of the Magistrates' Courts Act 1980. Section 89 of the 1967 Act makes it an offence to make a written statement under section 9 of that Act which the person making it knows to be false or does not believe to be true.]

Application for summons to produce a document, etc.: special rules

28.5.–(1)   This rule applies to an application under rule 28.3 for a witness summons requiring the proposed witness –

(a)   to produce in evidence a document or thing; or

(b)   to give evidence about information apparently held in confidence, that relates to another person.

(2)   The application must be in writing in the form required by rule 28.4.

(3)   The party applying must serve the application –

(a)   on the proposed witness, unless the court otherwise directs; and

(b)   on one or more of the following, if the court so directs –

(i)   a person to whom the proposed evidence relates,

(ii)   another party.

(4)   The court must not issue a witness summons where this rule applies unless –

(a)   everyone served with the application has had at least 14 days in which to make representations, including representations about whether there should be a hearing of the application before the summons is issued; and

(b) the court is satisfied that it has been able to take adequate account of the duties and rights, including rights of confidentiality, of the proposed witness and of any person to whom the proposed evidence relates.

(5) This rule does not apply to an application for an order to produce in evidence a copy of an entry in a banker's book.

[Note. Under section 2A of the Criminal Procedure (Attendance of Witnesses) Act 1965, a witness summons to produce a document or thing issued by the Crown Court may require the witness to produce it for inspection by the applicant before producing it in evidence.]

Application for summons to produce a document, etc.: court's assessment of relevance and confidentiality

28.6.–(1) This rule applies where a person served with an application for a witness summons requiring the proposed witness to produce in evidence a document or thing objects to its production on the ground that –

(a) it is not likely to be material evidence; or

(b) even if it is likely to be material evidence, the duties or rights, including rights of confidentiality, of the proposed witness or of any person to whom the document or thing relates, outweigh the reasons for issuing a summons.

(2) The court may require the proposed witness to make the document or thing available for the objection to be assessed.

(3) The court may invite –

(a) the proposed witness or any representative of the proposed witness; or

(b) a person to whom the document or thing relates or any representative of such a person, to help the court assess the objection.

Application to withdraw a summons, warrant or order

28.7.–(1) The court may withdraw a witness summons, warrant or order if one of the following applies for it to be withdrawn –

(a) the party who applied for it, on the ground that it no longer is needed;

(b) the witness on the grounds that –

(i) he was not aware of any application for it, and

(ii) he cannot give or produce evidence likely to be material evidence, or

        (iii)   even if he can, his duties or rights, including rights of confidentiality, or those of any person to whom the evidence relates, outweigh the reasons for the issue of the summons, warrant or order, or

    (c)   any person to whom the proposed evidence relates, on the grounds that –

        (i)   he was not aware of any application for it, and

        (ii)   that evidence is not likely to be material evidence, or

        (iii)   even if it is, his duties or rights, including rights of confidentiality, or those of the witness, outweigh the reasons for the issue of the summons, warrant or order.

(2)   A person applying under the rule must –

    (a)   apply in writing as soon as practicable after becoming aware of the grounds for doing so, explaining why he wants the summons, warrant or order to be withdrawn; and

    (b)   serve the application on the court officer and as appropriate on –

        (i)   the witness,

        (ii)   the party who applied for the summons, warrant or order, and

        (iii)   any other person who he knows was served with the application for the summons, warrant or order.

(3)   Rule 28.6 applies to an application under this rule that concerns a document or thing to be produced in evidence.

[Note. See sections 2B, 2C and 2E of the Criminal Procedure (Attendance of Witnesses) Act 1965 for the Crown Court's powers to withdraw a witness summons, including the power to order costs.]

Court's power to vary requirements under this Part

28.8.–(1)   The court may –

    (a)   shorten or extend (even after it has expired) a time limit under this Part; and

    (b)   where a rule or direction requires an application under this Part to be in writing, allow that application to be made orally instead.

(2) Someone who wants the court to allow an application to be made orally under paragraph (1)(b) of this rule must –

(a) give as much notice as the urgency of his application permits to those on whom he would otherwise have served an application in writing; and

(b) in doing so explain the reasons for the application and for wanting the court to consider it orally.

Appendix 16

Application for a Witness Summons Form for use with CPR 2012, Part 28

[Form reproduced on opposite page.]

APPLICATION FOR A WITNESS SUMMONS:
CONFIDENTIAL INFORMATION RELATING TO ANOTHER PERSON
(Criminal Procedure Rules, rr: 28.3, 28.4 and 28.5)

Case details

Name of defendant:

Court:

Court office address:

Court phone number:

Case reference number:

Charge(s):

THIS IS AN APPLICATION FOR AN ORDER THAT

.... **(name of proposed witness)**

must [produce in evidence] [give evidence about information contained in]

(tick as applicable)	**social services records** ☐	
	health records	☐
	education records	☐
	other documents	☐ *(describe them)*

that relate to *(name the person concerned)*

How to use this form

This form is for use where the applicant wants the witness to give in evidence **confidential information about another person** (sometimes called 'third party material').

The form includes notes to help you complete it. There are notes for guidance for the applicant **and for the witness** at the end of the form.

1. Complete the boxes above and Parts A, B, C and D below. If you use an electronic version of this form, the boxes will expand. If you use a paper version and need more space, you may attach extra sheets.

2. Sign and date the completed form.

3. Send a copy of the completed form to:

    (a) the court, and

    (b) the proposed witness, unless the court allows you not to do so.

A witness who wants to make representations to the court about this application must do so **not more than 14 days after receiving it.** See the notes for guidance.

Appendix 16   *Application for a Witness Summons*

PART A: information about the applicant *(tick and delete as applicable)*

[I am] [I represent]

the prosecutor ☐

the defendant ☐

Name: ....

Address: ....

Phone: ....

Fax: ....

Email: ....

PART B: information about the application

Describe as fully as you can the documents that you want the witness to produce, or the information that you want the witness to give evidence about:

I think the witness has the documents or information I have described above because:

The documents, or the information contained in them, are likely to be material to what is in issue in the case because:
(Explain why you think the evidence would be material. The court CANNOT order the witness to produce documents, or give evidence about information contained in them, unless you can show that it is likely to be material evidence.)

I have taken the following steps to obtain the documents or information, but the witness will not provide them without a summons:
(Explain why it is in the interests of justice to issue a summons.)

I have made this application as soon as reasonably practicable because:
(Explain any delay.)

PART C: supporting material

Have you included with this application any other information?
　　　　No □　　　　Yes □ If yes, list it here (e.g. charge sheet, indictment, defence statement).

PART D: declaration

The statements contained in this application are true to the best of my knowledge and belief. I make them knowing that if I have wilfully stated anything which I know to be false or do not believe to be true I may be liable to prosecution.

Signed: ....

[[for] prosecutor]
[defendant / defendant's solicitor]

Date: ....

Notes for Guidance

A. If you are the applicant

1. When to use this form

Unless the court otherwise allows, you **MUST** use this form if you want the court to issue a witness summons for the proposed witness to produce in evidence, or to give evidence about information contained in, a document that records confidential information relating to another person - for example, information recorded in notes kept by a social services authority, in a patient's health records, or in a pupil's school records. See Criminal Procedure Rule 28.5.

Other appropriate steps to obtain the relevant information should be taken first. In particular, the prospective witness usually should be asked to supply the information voluntarily. Some prosecuting authorities, and some courts, have arrangements with other authorities under which there can be obtained material that otherwise would have to be the subject of an application for a witness summons. Where such arrangements apply, there may be no need to make an application using this form.

2. Letting the witness know about the application

Unless, exceptionally, the court otherwise allows, you **MUST** serve a copy of the **application** on the witness. Before the court decides the application, it may require you to serve a copy on someone else (e.g. the person to whom the information relates): Criminal Procedure Rule 28.5(3).

The court cannot usually issue a summons for a witness to produce documents in evidence, or give evidence about information that that witness holds in confidence, unless that witness has had **at least 14 days** in which to respond: Criminal Procedure Rule 28.5(4).

B. If you are the witness

This is an application for the court to order you to produce in evidence, or to give evidence about information contained in, documents that relate to another person. The applicant thinks you have the documents or information described in the application, and thinks you can give material evidence in the case described at the beginning of the form. **Unless you are willing to do so voluntarily, you do not have to give any documents or information unless the court issues a summons. You are encouraged to take legal advice.**

If a witness summons is issued, you can be arrested, and fined, imprisoned or both, for failure to obey.

1. Objecting to an application

You can ask the court not to issue a witness summons if

- you do not have the documents or information the applicant thinks you have
- you do not think the documents or information would be material evidence
- you think your duties or rights, or those of the person to whom the documents or information relate (including that person's rights of confidentiality), outweigh the reasons for the application.

If any of these apply to you, you must contact the court office **as soon as possible.** You should explain your objection in writing and send copies to the court office and to the person who applied for the witness summons.

2. Applying to the court to withdraw a summons

Usually, you will have 14 days from receiving this application to decide how to respond.

If the court has already issued a witness summons and you did not know about the application, in time or at all, you can ask the court to withdraw the summons if

- you do not have the documents or information required of you
- you do not think the documents or information would be material evidence
- you think your duties or rights, or those of the person to whom the documents or information relate (including that person's rights of confidentiality), outweigh the reasons for the issue of the summons.

If any of these apply to you, you must apply to the court at once. Contact the court office **urgently**. See Criminal Procedure Rule 28.7.

In a Crown Court case, if the court withdraws the summons it may order the person who applied for it to pay your legal costs. See Criminal Procedure Rule 76.7.

Attorney General's Section 18 RIPA Prosecutors Intercept Guidelines

England and Wales

Section 18 RIPA: Prosecutors Guidelines

1. These guidelines concern the approach to be taken by prosecutors in applying section 18 of the Regulation of Investigatory Powers Act (RIPA) in England and Wales.

Background

2. It has been long-standing Government policy that the fact that interception of communications has taken place in any particular case should remain secret and not be disclosed to the subject. This is because of the need to protect the continuing value of interception as a vital means of gathering intelligence about serious crime and activities which threaten national security. The Government judges that if the use of the technique in particular cases were to be confirmed, the value of the technique would be diminished because targets would either know, or could deduce, when their communications might be intercepted and so could take avoiding action by using other, more secure means of communication.

3. In the context of legal proceedings, the policy that the fact of interception should remain secret is implemented by section 17 of RIPA. Section 17 provides that no evidence shall be adduced, question asked, assertion or disclosure made or other thing done in, for the purposes of, or in connection with, any legal proceedings which discloses the contents of a communication which has been obtained following the issue of an interception warrant or a warrant under the Interception of Communications Act 1985, or any related communications data ('protected information'), or tends to suggest that certain events have occurred.

4. The effect of section 17 is that the fact of interception of the subject's communications and the product of that interception cannot be relied

upon or referred to by either party to the proceedings. This is given further effect by sections 3(7), 7(6), 7A(9) and 9(9) of the Criminal Procedure and Investigations Act 1996 (as amended). This protects the continuing value of interception whilst also creating a 'level playing-field', in that neither side can gain any advantage from the interception. In the context of criminal proceedings, this means that the defendant cannot be prejudiced by the existence in the hands of the prosecution of intercept material which is adverse to his interests.

Detailed Analysis

First Stage: action to be taken by the prosecutor

5.   Section 18(7)(a) of RIPA provides:-

'Nothing in section 17(1) shall prohibit any such disclosure of any information that continues to be available for disclosure as is confined to ... a disclosure to a person conducting a criminal prosecution for the purpose only of enabling that person to determine what is required of him by his duty to secure the fairness of the prosecution;'

If protected information is disclosed to a prosecutor, as permitted by section 18(7)(a), the first step that should be taken by the prosecutor is to review any information regarding an interception that remains extant at the time that he or she has conduct of the case[1]. In reviewing it, the prosecutor should seek to identify any information whose existence, if no action was taken by the Crown, might result in unfairness. Experience suggests that the most likely example of such potential unfairness is where the evidence in the case is such that the jury may draw an inference which intercept shows to be wrong, and to leave this uncorrected will result in the defence being disadvantaged.

6.   If in the view of the prosecutor to take no action would render the proceedings unfair, the prosecutor should, first consulting with the relevant prosecution agency, take such steps as are available to him or her to secure the fairness of the proceedings provided these steps do not contravene section 18(10). In the example given above, such steps could include:

---

1   Section 15(1) of RIPA provides that it is the duty of the Secretary of State to ensure that arrangements are in place to ensure that (amongst other matters) intercept material is retained by the intercepting agencies only for as long as is necessary for any of the authorised purposes. The authorised purposes include retention which:-

'is necessary to ensure that a person conducting a criminal prosecution has the information he needs to determine what is required of him by his duty to secure the fairness of the prosecution.' (section 15(4)(d))

(i)   putting the prosecution case in such a way that the misleading inference is not drawn by the jury; or

(ii)   not relying upon the evidence which makes the information relevant; or

(iii)   discontinuing that part of the prosecution case in relation to which the protected information is relevant, by amending a charge or count on the indictment or offering no evidence on such a charge or count; or

(iv)   making an admission of fact[2].

There is no requirement for the prosecutor to notify the judge of the action that he or she has taken or proposes to take. Such a course should only be taken by the prosecutor if he considers it essential in the interests of justice to do so (see below).

Second Stage: disclosure to the judge

7.   There may be some cases (although these are likely to be rare) where the prosecutor considers that he cannot secure the fairness of the proceedings without assistance from the relevant judge. In recognition of this, section 18(7)(b) of RIPA provides that in certain limited circumstances, the prosecutor may invite the judge to order a disclosure of the protected information to him.

8.   If the prosecutor considers that he requires the assistance of the trial judge to ensure the fairness of the proceedings, or he is in doubt as to whether the result of taking the steps outlined at para 6 above would ensure fairness, he must apply to see the judge *ex parte*. Under section 18(8), a judge shall not order a disclosure to him except where he is satisfied that the exceptional circumstances of the case make that disclosure essential in the interests of justice. Before the judge is in a position to order such disclosure the prosecutor will need to impart to the judge such information, but only such information, as is necessary to demonstrate that exceptional circumstances mean that the prosecutor acting alone cannot secure the fairness of the proceedings. Experience suggests that exceptional circumstances in the course of a trial justifying disclosure to a judge arise only in the following two situations:

---

2   This is acceptable as long as to do so would not contravene section 17 i.e. reveal the existence of an interception warrant. Prosecutors must bear in mind that such a breach might conceivably occur not only from the factual content of the admission, but also from the circumstances in which it is made.

(1) **where the judge's assistance is necessary to ensure the fairness of the trial**

This situation may arise in the example given at paragraph 5 above, where there is a risk that the jury might draw an inference from certain facts, which protected information shows would be the wrong inference, and the prosecutor is unable to ensure that the jury will not draw this inference by his actions alone. The purpose in informing the judge is so that the judge will then be in a position to ensure fairness by:-

(i)   summing up in a way which will ensure that the wrong inference is not drawn; or

(ii)   giving appropriate directions to the jury; or

(iii)   requiring the Crown to make an admission of fact which the judge thinks *essential in the interests of justice* if he is of the opinion that *exceptional circumstances* require him to make such a direction (section 18(9)). However, such a direction **must not** authorise or require anything to be done which discloses any of the contents of an intercepted communication or related data or tends to suggest that anything falling within section 17(2) has or may have occurred or be going to occur (section 18(10)). Situations where an admission of fact is required are likely to be rare. The judge must be of the view that proceedings could not be continued unless an admission of fact is made (and the conditions in section 18(9) are satisfied). There may be other ways in which it is possible for a judge to ensure fairness, such as those outlined at (i) and (ii) above.

In practice, no question of taking the action at (i)–(iii) arises if the protected information is already contained in a separate document in another form that has been or can be disclosed without contravening section 17(1), and this disclosure will secure the fairness of the proceedings.

(2) **where the judge requires knowledge of the protected material for some other purpose**

This situation may arise where, usually in the context of a PII application, the true significance of, or duty of disclosure in relation to, other material being considered for disclosure by a judge, cannot be appraised by the judge without reference to protected information. Disclosure to the judge of the protected information without more may be sufficient to enable him to appraise the material, but once he has seen the protected information the judge may also conclude that the conditions in section 18(9) are satisfied so that an admission of fact by the Crown is required in addition to or instead of disclosure of the non-protected material.

Another example is a case where protected information underlies operational decisions which are likely to be the subject of cross-examination and it is necessary to inform the judge of the existence of the protected information to enable him to deal with the issue when the questions are first posed in a way which ensures section 17(1) is not contravened.

What if the actions of the prosecutor and/or the judge cannot ensure the fairness of the proceedings?

9. There may be very rare cases in which no action taken by the prosecutor and/or judge can prevent the continuation of the proceedings being unfair, e.g. where the requirements of fairness could only be met if the Crown were to make an admission, but it cannot do so without contravening section 18(10). In that situation the prosecutor will have no option but to offer no evidence on the charge in question, or to discontinue the proceedings in their entirety.

Responding to questions about interception

10. Prosecutors are sometimes placed in a situation in which they are asked by the court or by the defence whether interception has taken place or whether protected information exists. Whether or not interception has taken place or protected information exists, an answer in the following terms, or similar should be given:

> 'I am not in a position to answer that, but I am aware of sections 17 and 18 of the Regulation of Investigatory Powers Act 2000 and the Attorney General's Guidelines on the Disclosure of Information in Exceptional Circumstances under section 18.'

In a case where interception has taken place or protected information exists, an answer in these terms will avoid a breach of the prohibition in section 17 while providing assurance that the prosecutor is aware of his obligations.

11. For the avoidance of doubt, any notification or disclosure of information to the judge in accordance with paragraphs 7–10 must be *ex parte*. It will never be appropriate for prosecutors to volunteer, either *inter partes* or

to the Court *ex parte*, that interception has taken place or that protected information exists, save in accordance with section 18 as elaborated in these Guidelines.

Further Assistance

12.   Should a prosecutor be unsure as to the application of these guidelines in any particular case, further guidance should be sought from those instructing him or her. In those cases where a prosecutor has been instructed by the Crown Prosecution Service, the relevant CPS prosecutor must seek appropriate guidance from Casework Directorate, CPS Headquarters, Ludgate Hill.

Preparation for Trial Form: Magistrates' Court
For use with CPR 2012, Part 3

[Form reproduced overleaf.]

.... Magistrates' Court   # Preparation for trial

◨ This form:
- collects information about the case that the court will need to arrange for trial: Criminal Procedure Rules 3.2 and 3.3
- records the court's directions: Criminal Procedure Rules 3.5.

See the separate notes for guidance on the use of this form.

◨ After the court gives directions for trial, if:
- information about the case changes, or
- you think another direction is needed

you must tell the court at once.

◨ If the defendant pleads not guilty, and the court requires:
- the prosecutor must complete Parts 1 and 3
- the defendant must complete Parts 2 and 3
- the court will record directions in Parts 3 and 4.

The prosecutor may start filling in the form earlier.

Attach extra sheets if required. The electronic version of this form will expand.

There is a list of case preparation time limits on page 6.

Part 1: to be completed by the prosecutor

Defendant

☐ Summons ☐ Bail
☐ Requisition ☐ Custody   Time limit expires:

Offence(s)

Police / CPS URN _____   **Date of first hearing** _____

1   Prosecution contact details

Prosecuting authority		Phone Fax
	Email	

2   Case management information

2.1   Is the investigation complete ?
If no, give brief details: ☐ Yes ☐ No

2.2   Does the prosecutor intend to serve more evidence ?
If yes, give brief details: ☐ Yes ☐ No

2.3   The prosecution will rely on:
Tick / delete as appropriate

- defendant's admissions in interview   ☐
- defendant's failure to mention facts in interview   ☐
- [a summary] [a record] of the defendant's interview   ☐
- [expert] [hearsay] [bad character] evidence   ☐
- [CCTV] [electronically recorded] evidence   ☐

What equipment (tape / DVD player, etc.) will be needed in the trial courtroom ?

3   Application for directions

3.1   Does the prosecutor want the court to vary a case preparation time limit ?
If yes, give details: ☐ Yes ☐ No

3.2   Does the prosecutor want the court to make any other direction ?
If yes, give details: ☐ Yes ☐ No

Part 2: to be completed by defendant or defendant's legal representative

Defendant's contact details

Defendant	Address		Phone Mobile	
	Email			

Defendant's representative *(if applicable)*

Solicitor		Phone Fax Ref	
	Address		
	Email		

Representation is:	granted	☐
Defendant's representative to complete	applied for	☐
	privately funded	☐

Advice on plea and absence

Does the defendant understand that:

(a) he or she will receive credit for a guilty plea ?   ☐ Yes ☐ No
   A guilty plea may affect the sentence and any order for costs

(b) the trial can go ahead even if he or she does not attend ?   ☐ Yes ☐ No
   CrimPR rule 37.11

Partial or different guilty plea

If more than one offence is alleged, does the defendant want to plead guilty to any of them ?   ☐ Yes ☐ No ☐ N/A
If yes, which offence(s) ?

Does the defendant want to plead guilty, but not on the facts alleged ?   ☐ Yes ☐ No
If yes, attach a written basis of plea.

Does the defendant want to plead guilty, but to a different offence ?   ☐ Yes ☐ No
If yes, what offence ?

Case management information

Which of the following (if applicable) is **AGREED** ? *Tick / delete as appropriate*

The defendant [carried out] [took part in] the conduct alleged (i.e. identification)   ☐ Yes ☐ No ☐ N/A

The defendant was present at the scene of the offence alleged   ☐ Yes ☐ No ☐ N/A

The defendant was arrested lawfully   ☐ Yes ☐ No ☐ N/A

[Nature of injury] [extent of loss or damage]   ☐ Yes ☐ No ☐ N/A
If not agreed, explain what is in dispute:

[Fingerprint] [DNA] evidence   ☐ Yes ☐ No ☐ N/A
If not agreed, explain what is in dispute:

[Medical] [identification of drug] [other scientific] evidence   ☐ Yes ☐ No ☐ N/A
If not agreed, explain what is in dispute:

The [alcohol] [drug] testing procedure was carried out correctly   ☐ Yes ☐ No ☐ N/A
If not agreed, explain what is in dispute:

Exhibits and samples were collected and delivered as stated (i.e. continuity)   ☐ Yes ☐ No
If not agreed, explain what is in dispute:

Defendant's interview [summary] [record] is accurate   ☐ Yes ☐ No
If not agreed, explain what is in dispute:

The defendant was [disqualified from driving] [subject to the alleged court order] at the time of   ☐ Yes ☐ No
the offence alleged

The list of the defendant's previous convictions is accurate   ☐ Yes ☐ No
If not agreed, explain what is in dispute:

8.2   Other **AGREED** facts or issues are:
Give details

8.3   Can **AGREED** facts be recorded in a written admission ?   ☐ Yes ☐ No
If yes, a written admission [is set out here] [is attached] [will be served later].
If no, explain why:

8.4   What are the **DISPUTED** issues of fact or law for trial, in addition to any identified in   *CrimPR rules 3.2(2)(a)*
paragraph 8.1 ?

8.5   Will the defendant give a defence statement ?   ☐ Yes ☐ No
A defence statement must include particulars of facts relied on for the defence: Criminal
Procedure and Investigations Act 1996, s.6A; Criminal Procedure Rules, r.22.4. There is a
form of defence statement for use in connection with the rule.

Whether or not the defendant gives a defence statement, the defendant must give a notice
indicating whether he or she intends to call any person (other than him or herself) as witnesses
at trial and, if so, identifying them: Criminal Procedure and Investigations Act 1996, s.6C.

9   **Application for directions**
9.1   Does the defendant want the court to vary a case preparation time limit ?   ☐ Yes ☐ No
If yes, give details:

9.2   Does the defendant want the court to make any other direction ?   ☐ Yes ☐ No
If yes, give details:

Defendant's name:

Part 3: to be completed by prosecutor, defendant (or representative) and court

Prosecution witnesses

Name of witness	Prosecutor to complete		Defendant to complete		For the court
	Tick if under 18	Attendance proposed	Can the evidence be read to the court ?	If no, what disputed issue in the case makes it necessary for the witness to give evidence in person ?	Attendance justified
	☐	☐	☐ Yes ☐ No		☐
	☐	☐	☐ Yes ☐ No		☐
	☐	☐	☐ Yes ☐ No		☐
	☐	☐	☐ Yes ☐ No		☐
	☐	☐	☐ Yes ☐ No		☐
	☐	☐	☐ Yes ☐ No		☐
	☐	☐	☐ Yes ☐ No		☐
	☐	☐	☐ Yes ☐ No		☐
	☐	☐	☐ Yes ☐ No		☐
	☐	☐	☐ Yes ☐ No		☐

Prosecutor to complete

Does the prosecutor want special measures for a witness ?   ☐ Yes ☐ No
If yes, give details:

If the defendant is not represented, does the prosecutor want the court to prohibit cross-examination of a witness ?   ☐ Yes ☐ No
If yes, give details:

Does any witness need an interpreter ?   ☐ Yes ☐ No
If yes, in what language ?

Defence witnesses

Defendant to complete

Is the defendant likely to give evidence ?   ☐ Yes ☐ No

How many other defence witnesses are likely to give evidence in person ?
The defendant must give details separately of intended defence witnesses: see paragraph 8.5.

Does the defendant want measures to assist him/herself, or for a defence witness ?   ☐ Yes ☐ No
If yes, give details:

Will the defendant or any defence witness need an interpreter ?   ☐ Yes ☐ No
If yes, in what language ?

Signatures

Signed: .... for prosecution
Date: ....

Signed: .... [defendant] [defendant's solicitor]
Date: ....

Defendant's name:

Part 4: court's directions for trial

12   Directions for trial

12.1   ☐ The prosecutor must serve any further evidence by: *(date)*

12.2   ☐ The prosecutor must complete initial disclosure by: *(date)*

12.3   The court expects those prosecution witnesses to give evidence in person whose names it has ticked in paragraph 10.1.

12.4   The court expects the evidence of other prosecution witness listed in paragraph 10.1 to be read.

12.5   ☐ Witness [summons] [warrant] for witness(es): *insert name(s)*   *CrimPR Part 28*

12.6   ☐ Interpreter in language(s):   for: arranged by: *specify court, prosecution or defence*

                           prosecution witness(es)   _____

                           defendant   _____

                           defence witness(es)   _____

12.7   ☐ Special measures of: *tick as appropriate*   for witness(es): *insert name(s)*   *CrimPR Part 29*

           screening witness from defendant ☐ _____

                evidence by live link ☐ _____

                 evidence in private ☐ _____

       video recorded interview as evidence in chief ☐ _____

                      intermediary ☐

12.8   ☐ Defendant may not cross-examine witness(es): *insert name(s)*   *CrimPR Part 31*

       and the court directs representation by: *name representative*

12.9   ☐ Other arrangements for defendant or witnesses (specify):   *CrimPR rule 3.8(4)*

                                                  CrimPR Part 29

12.10   Standard case preparation time limits apply [except] [with these variations]:   *CrimPR Part 3 etc*

12.11   ☐ Other directions:

12.12   Arrangements for hearing

         Date: _____

         Time: _____

         Court: _____

         Time estimate: .... hours

                         A detailed trial timetable may be needed: CrimPR rules 3.8 & 3.10

Signed: ....

Name: .... *(block capitals)* [on the direction of] [court]

Date: ....

Standard case preparation time limits

The court can vary any of these time limits. Time limits marked * are not prescribed by rules.

The total time needed to comply with all these time limits is 6 weeks (9 weeks if paragraph m applies).

ritten admissions (Criminal Procedure Rules, r.37.6; Criminal Justice Act 1967, s.10)
he parties must serve any written admissions of agreed facts within **14 days.***

fence statement (Criminal Procedure Rules, r.22.4; Criminal Procedure and Investigations Act 1996, s.6)
ny defence statement must be served within **14 days** of the prosecutor completing or purporting to complete initial disclosure.

fence witnesses (Criminal Procedure and Investigations Act 1996, s.6C)
efence witness names, etc. must be notified within **14 days** of the prosecutor completing or purporting to complete initial disclosure.

plication for disclosure (Criminal Procedure Rules, rr.22.2 & 22.5; Criminal Procedure and Investigations Act 1996, s.8)
he defendant must serve any application for prosecution disclosure when serving any defence statement.*
he prosecutor must serve any representations in response within **14 days** after that.

tness statements (Criminal Procedure Rules, r.27.4; Criminal Justice Act 1967, s.9)
he defendant must serve any defence witness statement to be read at trial at least **14 days before the trial.***
ny objection to a witness statement being read at trial must be made within **7 days of service of the statement.** *This does not apply to the statements listed in paragraph 10.1.*

asures to assist a witness or defendant to give evidence (Criminal Procedure Rules, rr.29.3, 29.13, 29.17, 29.22, 29.26)
ny [further] application for special or other measures must be served within **28 days.**
ny representations in response must be served within **14 days after that.**

oss-examination where defendant not represented (Criminal Procedure Rules, rr.31.1, 31.4)
he defendant must serve notice of any representative appointed to cross-examine within **7 days.**
he prosecutor must serve any application to prohibit cross-examination by the defendant in person as soon as reasonably racticable.
ny representations in response must be served within **14 days after that.**

pert evidence (Criminal Procedure Rules, rr.33.4, 33.6)
either party relies on expert evidence, the directions below apply.
(i)   The expert's report must be served within **28 days.***
(ii)   A party who wants that expert to attend the trial must give notice within **7 days after (i).***
(iii)   A party who relies on expert evidence in response must serve it within **14 days after (ii).***
(iv)   There must be a meeting of experts under rule 33.6 within **14 days after (iii).***
(v)   The parties must notify the court **immediately after (iv)** if the length of the trial is affected by the outcome of the meeting.*

arsay evidence (Criminal Procedure Rules, rr.34.2, 34.3)
he prosecutor must serve any notice to introduce hearsay evidence within **28 days.**
he defendant must serve any notice to introduce hearsay evidence as soon as reasonably practicable.
ny application to determine an objection to hearsay evidence must be served within **14 days of service** of the notice or evidence.

d character evidence (Criminal Procedure Rules, rr.35.2, 35.3, 35.4)
he prosecutor must serve any notice to introduce evidence of the defendant's bad character within **28 days.**
ny application to determine an objection to that notice must be served within **14 days after that.**
ny application to introduce evidence of a non-defendant's bad character must be served within **14 days** of prosecution disclosure.
ny notice of objection to that evidence must be served within **14 days after that.**

evious sexual behaviour evidence (Criminal Procedure Rules, rr.36.2, 36.3, 36.4, 36.5)
he defendant must serve any application for permission to introduce evidence of a complainant's previous sexual behaviour within
8 days of prosecution disclosure.
he prosecutor must serve any representations in response within **14 days after that.**

int of law (Criminal Procedure Rules, rr.3.3, 3.9)
ny skeleton argument must be served at least **14 days before the trial.***
ny skeleton argument in reply must be served within **7 days after that.***

al readiness (Criminal Procedure Rules, rr.3.3, 3.9)
he parties must certify readiness for trial at least **14 days before the trial,** confirming which witnesses will give evidence in person
nd the trial time estimate.*

Criminal Procedure Rules 2012 (SI 2012/1726), Part 21

Part 21
Initial Details of the Prosecution Case

Contents of this Part

When this Part applies

21.1.–(1)   This Part applies in a magistrates' court, where the offence is one that can be tried in a magistrates' court.

(2)   The court may direct that, for a specified period, this Part will not apply –

>   (a)   to any case in that court; or

>   (b)   to any specified category of case.

[Note. An offence may be classified as –

>   *(a)   one that can be tried only in a magistrates' court (in other legislation, described as triable only summarily);*

>   *(b)   one that can be tried either in a magistrates' court or in the Crown Court (in other legislation described as triable either way); or*

>   *(c)   one that can be tried only in the Crown Court (in other legislation, described as triable only on indictment).*

See the definitions contained in Schedule 1 to the Interpretation Act 1978. In some circumstances, the Crown Court can try an offence that usually can be tried only in a magistrates' court.

This Part does not apply where an offence can be tried only in the Crown Court. In such a case, details are served on the defendant after the case is sent for trial. Part 9 contains relevant rules.]

Providing initial details of the prosecution case

21.2.–   The prosecutor must provide initial details of the prosecution case by –

    (a)   serving those details on the court officer; and

    (b)   making those details available to the defendant,

at, or before, the beginning of the day of the first hearing.

Content of initial details

21.3.–   Initial details of the prosecution case must include –

    (a)   a summary of the evidence on which that case will be based; or

    (b)   any statement, document or extract setting out facts or other matters on which that case will be based; or

    (c)   any combination of such a summary, statement, document or extract; and

    (d)   the defendant's previous convictions.

Index

All references are to paragraph number.

R

S